Lecture Notes in Computer Science

Commenced Publication in 1973
Founding and Former Series Editors:
Gerhard Goos, Juris Hartmanis, and Jan van Leeuwen

Shmuel Katz   Harold Ossher
Robert France   Jean-Marc Jézéquel (Eds.)

Transactions on Aspect-Oriented Software Development VI

Special Issue on Aspects
and Model-Driven Engineering

 Springer

Editors-in-Chief

Shmuel Katz
The Technion
Department of Computer Science
Haifa 32000, Israel
E-mail: katz@cs.technion.ac.il

Harold Ossher
IBM Thomas J. Watson Research Center
P.O. Box 704
Yorktown Heights, NY 10598, USA
E-mail: ossher@us.ibm.com

Guest Editors

Robert France
Colorado State University
Computer Science Department
Fort Collins, CO 80523-1873, USA
E-mail: france@cs.colostate.edu

Jean-Marc Jézéquel
Université de Rennes 1, IRISA
Campus de Beaulieu
35042 Rennes Cedex, France
E-mail: Jean-Marc.Jezequel@irisa.fr

Library of Congress Control Number: 2009935702

CR Subject Classification (1998): D.2, D.1, D.3, F.3.2, I.2.2, I.2.5, I.2.8

ISSN   0302-9743 (Lecture Notes in Computer Science)
ISSN   1864-3027 (Transactions on Aspect-Oriented Software Development)
ISBN-10 3-642-03763-1 Springer Berlin Heidelberg New York
ISBN-13 978-3-642-03763-4 Springer Berlin Heidelberg New York

springer.com

© Springer-Verlag Berlin Heidelberg 2009
Printed in Germany

Typesetting: Camera-ready by author, data conversion by Scientific Publishing Services, Chennai, India
Printed on acid-free paper   SPIN: 12732333   06/3180   5 4 3 2 1 0

Editorial

Welcome to Volume VI of Transactions on Aspect-Oriented Software Development. This volume is a special issue on "Aspects and Model-Driven Engineering," with guest editors Robert France and Jean-Marc Jézéquel, under the management of one of the co-editors-in-chief, Harold Ossher. Robert and Jean-Marc are both well-known experts in the field of model-driven engineering, and they have attracted an excellent set of papers on the role AOSD can play in this important area of software engineering. We thank them for their effort and commitment in producing such a high-quality special issue.

We also thank the Editorial Board for their continued guidance, commitment and input on the policies of the journal, the choice of special issues, and associate-editorship of regular submissions. Thanks are also due to the reviewers, who volunteered significant time, despite their busy schedules, to ensure the quality of articles published in the journal. Most importantly, we wish to thank the authors who have submitted papers to the journal so far.

There are two exciting special issues on the horizon. The first, with guest editor Jörg Kienzle, is titled "A Common Case Study for Aspect-Oriented Modeling Approaches." A variety of notations and abstraction techniques for modeling aspect systems will be demonstrated and evaluated for the same case study, a fairly complex crisis management system. This will allow readers to understand the relative strengths of each approach, and encourage cross-fertilization among the techniques. The second will be on "Industrial Applications of Aspect Technology," with guest editors Wouter Joosen and Christa Schwanninger. One of the major impediments to broader industry adoption of AOSD is the lack of accessible success stories and experience reports on the application of AOSD in commercial software projects. This special issue will offer a collection such examples, experience reports and success stories, and report on insights gained that should be of value to (potential) industrial users.

Linda Northrop has left the Editorial Board after serving since the inception of the journal. Many thanks to Linda for her years of devoted service to TAOSD, and much valuable guidance she gave during that time. In the next issue we will announce some new members of the Board, who will give us the opportunity to benefit from the insights of additional members of the software engineering community expert in areas related to AOSD.

June 2009

Shmuel Katz
Harold Ossher
Co-Editors-in-Chief

Aspects and Model-Driven Engineering
Guest Editors' Foreword

Model-Driven Engineering (MDE) is an approach to software development in which models are used to drive the development of all software artifacts, from code to documentation to tests. MDE is gaining acceptance in several software domains with demonstrated benefits such as cost reduction and quality improvement.

Modeling is not just about expressing a solution at a higher abstraction level than code. This limited view on modeling has been useful in the past (e.g., assembly languages abstracting away from machine code, 3GL abstracting over assembly languages) and it is still useful today, but much more can be accomplished using modeling techniques.

A model can be an abstraction of an aspect of a system (existing or under development) that handles a given concern. Complex systems typically give rise to more than one model because many aspects must be considered when addressing all relevant software development concerns. These models may be expressed with a general purpose modeling language such as the UML, or with Domain Specific Languages when they are deemed more appropriate.

From a modeling point of view, the terms aspect and model can be considered synonymous. This notion of aspect goes beyond the usual meaning found in the Aspect Oriented Programming community where an aspect is often narrowly defined as the modularization of a cross-cutting concern. Given a "main" decomposition paradigm (such as object orientation), there are many classes of concerns (e.g., security, mobility, availability, distribution) for which clear allocation into modules is not possible (i.e., they are "cross-cutting" concerns).

However, the growing uptake of the term aspect outside of the programming world, has resulted in a growing acceptance of a broader definition in which an aspect is a concern that can be modularized. Work on aspect-oriented techniques above the code level is concerned with the systematic identification, modularization, representation, and composition of concerns. The goal of work in this area is to improve our ability to reason about the problem domain and the corresponding solution, thereby reducing the size of software models and application code, development costs, and maintenance time.

From the above, an important software development activity is the separation of concerns in problem domains. This activity is called *analysis*. If solutions to these concerns can be described as aspects, the design process can then be characterized as a weaving of these aspects into a base design model. This is not new: designers have been doing this for some time. However, the various aspects are often not *explicitly* defined, and when they are, it is done informally. Currently, designers do the weaving mentally (i.e., in their heads), and then produce the resulting detailed design as a tangled structure of design elements. This may work for small problems, but it introduces significant accidental complexities when tackling larger problems.

Note that the real challenge here is not how to design the system to take a particular aspect into account: there is significant design know-how in industry on this and it is often captured in the form of design patterns. Taking into account more than one aspect can be a little harder, but many large scale successful projects in industry provide some evidence that engineers know how different concerns should be handled. The real challenge is reducing the effort that the engineer has to expend when grappling with many inter-dependent concerns. For example, in a product-line context, when an engineer wants to replace a variant of an aspect used in a system, she should be able to do this cheaply, quickly and safely. Manually weaving every aspect is not an option.

Unlike many models used in the sciences, models in software and in linguistics have the same nature as the things they model. In software, this provides an opportunity to automatically derive software from its model, that is, to automate the weaving process. This requires models to be formal, and the weaving process be described as a program (i.e., an executable meta-model) manipulating models to produce a detailed design. The detailed design produced by the weaving process can ultimately be transformed to code or at least test suites.

In the above, we make the case that aspects are at the core of Model Driven Engineering. From this perspective, work on aspect-oriented approaches to modeling is important because it can yield significant insights into how the MDE vision of software development can be realized. There is thus a growing community interested in the convergence of Aspect-Oriented Software Development (AOSD) and MDE ideas. In this issue, we present papers that provide good examples of how AOSD and MDE ideas can be integrated to produce techniques that manage software complexity.

The papers in this issue cover a number of issues including the following:

- Methods and techniques supporting separation, composition, and evolution of aspects identified in different development phases (e.g., requirements, architecture, detailed design, deployment).
- Simulating runtime weaving of aspects using aspect-oriented models.
- Techniques for verifying and validating aspect-oriented models.
- AOM case studies that provide significant insights into how aspect-oriented modeling techniques can be applied across the development life-cycle.
- Providing tool support for use of integrated AOSD and MDE techniques.
- Providing language support for aspect-oriented modeling.

Submissions

Dynamic Weaving of Aspect-Oriented Executable UML Models. In this paper, the authors, *Lidia Fuentes and Pablo Sanchez*, present a model weaver that can be used to simulate runtime weaving of aspects at design time. This allows designers to identify and correct errors that can arise as a result of dynamic weaving before expending significant effort and cost on implementing the design. The ideas are illustrated using a location-aware intelligent transportation system.

On Language-Independent Model Modularisation. In this paper, the authors, *Florian Heidenreich, Jakob Henriksson, Jendrik Johannes, and Steffen Zschaler*, present a generic approach to modularizing and composing models. The approach can be adapted to construct language- and purpose-specific composition techniques for specific modelling languages. The authors claim that the approach can be used as (1) a tool for developing specific model modularisation and composition techniques, and (2) a research instrument for studying properties and concepts of model modularisation.

Aspects across Software Life Cycle: A Goal-Driven Approach. In this paper, the authors, *Nan Niu, Yijun Yu, Bruno Gonzalez-Baixauli, Neil Ernst, Julio Cesar Sampaio do Prado Leite, and John Mylopoulos*, propose a model-driven framework for tracing aspects from requirements to testing and implementation. In the framework, goal models are engineering assets and model-to-code transformations are used to bridge the gap between domain concepts and implementation technologies. The frameworks applicability and usefulness is evaluated using an open-source e-commerce platform case study.

Aspect-Oriented Model-Driven Software Product Line Engineering. In this paper, the authors, *Iris Groher and Markus Voelter*, present an integrated AOSD and MDE approach to variability implementation, management, and tracing in product-line development of software. Features are modeled separately and the models are composed using aspect-oriented composition techniques. Model transformations are used to transform problem models to solution models. The ideas presented in the paper are illustrated using a home automation system case study.

Constraint-Based Model Weaving. In this paper, the authors, *Jules White, Jeff Gray, and Douglas C. Schmidt*, present a constraint-based weaving technique that reduces model weaving to a constraint satisfaction problem (CSP). A constraint solver is used to deduce an appropriate weaving strategy. The paper also presents the results of a case study in which the constraint-based weaving technique is applied to an enterprise Java application. The evaluation showed that use of the technique resulted in a reduction of manual effort.

MATA: A Unified Approach for Composing UML Aspect Models Based on Graph Transformation. In this paper, the authors, *Jon Whittle, Praveen Jayaraman, Ahmed Elkhodary, Ana Moreira and Joo Arajo*, describe an aspect-oriented modeling technique called MATA (Modeling Aspects Using a Transformation Approach). MATA uses graph transformations to specify and compose aspects. In MATA, any model element can be a join point and composition is a special case of model transformation. MATA has been applied to a number of realistic case studies and is supported by a tool built on top of IBM Rational Software Modeler.

Model Driven Theme/UML. In this paper, the authors, *Andrew Carton, Cormac Driver, Andrew Jackson and Siobhan Clarke*, describe how the Theme/UML approach to modularizing and composing concerns can be integrated with

MDE techniques. The resulting method includes a tool-supported technique for transforming platform-independent models to platform-specific models. The transformation tool utilizes standards defined in the Object Management Group's Model Driven Architecture. The paper also describes a process that guides the use of the MDE/AOSD techniques. The utility of the approach is demonstrated through a case study.

Biographies

Robert France: Professor Robert France is a full professor in the Department of Computer Science at Colorado State University. He is actively engaged in research on object-oriented (OO) modeling, aspect-oriented modeling, model transformations, and formal description techniques. He is an editor-in-chief for the journal on Software and System Modeling (SoSyM) and is an Software Area Editor for the IEEE Computer. He was organizing chair for the Second Conference on the UML, past chair of the UML Conference steering committee and member of the MoDELS Conference steering committee.

Jean-Marc Jézéquel: Prof. Jean-Marc Jézéquel received an engineering degree in Telecommunications from the ENSTB in 1986, and a Ph.D. degree in Computer Science from the University of Rennes, France, in 1989. He first worked in Telecom industry (at Transpac) before joining the CNRS (Centre National de la Recherche Scientifique) in 1991. Since October 2000, he is a Professor at the University of Rennes, leading an INRIA research team called Triskell. His interests include model driven software engineering based on object oriented technologies for telecommunications and distributed systems. He is the author of the books "Object-Oriented Software Engineering with Eiffel" and "Design Patterns and Contracts" (Addison-Wesley 1996 and 1999), and of more than 100 publications in international journals and conferences. He is a member of the steering committees of the AOSD and the MODELS/UML conference series. He also served on the editorial boards of IEEE Transactions on Software Engineering and on the Journal on Software and System Modeling: SoSyM and the Journal of Object Technology: JOT.

For more information please visit http://www.irisa.fr/prive/jezequel

June 2009   Robert France
Jean-Marc Jézéquel

Table of Contents

Special Issue: Aspects and Model-Driven Engineering

Dynamic Weaving of Aspect-Oriented Executable UML Models*

Lidia Fuentes and Pablo Sánchez

Dpto. de Lenguajes y Ciencias de la Computación
University of Málaga, Málaga, Spain
{lff,pablo}@lcc.uma.es

Abstract. Several efforts have been made to incorporate aspect-oriented abstractions into the modelling level. Several modelling languages have appeared, which are mainly UML extensions that incorporate aspect-oriented constructions (e.g. advices or pointcuts). Although these extensions help to improve the modularisation of software designs, their incorporation makes it more complex to understand how the model works after being composed (e.g. woven). In order to overcome this problem, different aspect-oriented model weavers, such as Motorola WEAVR, AOEM and KerTheme, were proposed. These weavers provide the infrastructure for testing and debugging the models before moving into an implementation. However, these model weavers are static in the sense that aspects cannot be woven and unwoven at run time (i.e. during model execution). Hence, software systems that require dynamic weaving (e.g. adaptive applications) are not properly supported. Reasoning about this kind of application can be more complex due to the intrinsic dynamic nature. The novel contribution of this work is an aspect-oriented dynamic model weaver that can be used for running aspect-oriented models where aspects are woven and unwoven during model execution. These ideas are illustrated using a location-aware intelligent transportation system.

1 Introduction

Aspect-Oriented technologies improve the modularisation of software systems by defining: (1) new constructions (e.g. aspects and advices) for the suitable encapsulation of crosscutting concerns into single modules; and (2) mechanisms (e.g. pointcuts and weavers) for composing crosscutting concerns with base modules. Due to the separate definitions of crosscutting concerns and weaving information, it is often difficult to understand how the system works once it is woven. This increase in reasoning complexity is mainly due to: (1) developers not being familiar with the new aspect-oriented constructions; (2) developer being forced to compose (or weave) the aspect-oriented programs or models

---

* This work has been supported by Spanish Ministerio de Ciencia y Tecnología (MCYT) Project TIN2005-09405-C02-01 and European Commission Grant IST-2-004349-NOE AOSD-Europe and the European Commission STREP Project AMPLE IST-033710.

S. Katz et al. (Eds.): Transactions on AOSD VI, LNCS 5560, pp. 1–38, 2009.

mentally; and/or (3) aspect-orientation causing new problems, such as undesirable execution scenarios caused by unexpected aspect interactions. It should be observed that to help developers envision and reason about a woven program, some aspect-oriented languages provide extra facilities, such as crosscutting maps of AJDT[1] [1] (AspectJ Development Tools) in the AspectJ [2] case.

Aspect-Oriented modelling approaches focused initially on providing the set of constructions that enable separation of concerns at the modelling level. As a result, several UML Profiles [3,4,5] and design languages [6,7,8] appeared. Nevertheless, these notations do not provide any extra facilities or tool-support to aid designers to visualise and understand how the models behave after they are composed. As a consequence, software designers are forced to weave their aspect-oriented models "manually" and/or "mentally", which is a cumbersome and error-prone task. Further discussions about reasoning on the behaviour of a system in the presence of aspects can be found in Clifton and Leavens [9] and Kiczales and Mezini [10].

In order to overcome this problem, different aspect-oriented model weavers, such as Kompose [11], KerTheme [12], Motorola WEAVR [13], AOEM [14] and MATA [15] have been proposed.

The common idea behind all of them is to verify that the composed system works as desired. Some of them, specifically KerTheme [12], Motorola WEAVR [13] and AOEM [14], focus on providing the infrastructure for executing aspect-oriented models as a stepping stone towards model simulation, model testing and/or model debugging.

Using model simulation, inaccuracies inherent in an aspect-oriented design can be detected during the model execution, before moving on to implementation. Arguments about the benefits of simulation in software development can be found in the Saturn experience [16], in Doldi [17], the Motorola experience [18] and the Motorla WEAVR report [19].

Nevertheless, these model weavers are static, which means that aspects cannot be woven or unwoven during model execution. There are several situations where dynamic aspect weaving is preferred to a static one [20,21,22]. For instance, in a mobile pervasive system running in a specific context, some aspects (e.g. authentication, specific encryption mechanisms or specific error handling strategies) must be applied in order to interact accordingly with the environment. When the context changes, these aspects may no longer be required, and so they can be simply unwoven. This kind of dynamic evolution by weaving/unweaving aspects cannot be properly simulated using the currently available model weavers.

This paper presents as a novel contribution an aspect-oriented dynamic model weaver for aspect-oriented models expressed in the Aspect-Oriented Executable Modelling (AOEM) UML 2.0 Profile developed by the authors [14].

This dynamic model weaver is able to compose at model execution time crosscutting concerns separated following a pointcut plus advice scheme based on method interception.

---

[1] http://www.eclipse.org/ajdt/

Using this dynamic model weaver and the AOEM Profile, software designers can construct aspect-oriented Platform Independent Models (PIM) and can execute these aspect-oriented models in the same way as if they were running aspect-oriented programs built on top of implementation platforms with run time weaving. Thus, designers can visualise the behaviour of a model, reason more easily about it, analyse different alternative solutions and/or fix errors before moving on to implementation.

In order to illustrate these concepts, a location-aware intelligent transportation system, taken from the literature [23], consisting of a set of cooperating sentient vehicles, is used as a motivating example.

In the following, the paper is structured as follows: Sect. 2 explains the reasons aspect-oriented dynamic weaving is required, using a motivating example, and provides a general overview of our approach. Section 3 describes how an aspect-oriented model with dynamic reconfiguration by means of dynamic aspect-weaving can be specified using the AOEM Profile [14] and the solution proposed in this paper. Section 4 explains how aspects can be woven and unwoven during model execution following a dynamic weaving strategy. Section 5 focuses on the tool-support for our approach. Section 6 provides some reflections on the benefits of the presented solution. Finally, Sect. 7 comments on related work and Sect. 8 outlines conclusions and future work.

2 Dynamic Weaving of AO UML Models

2.1 Motivating Example

A cooperating sentient vehicle application

Intelligent transportation systems exploit intervehicle cooperation without human assistance to provide autonomous vehicle navigation from a given origin to a pre-determined destination[2] [23].

The goal is for a set of autonomous vehicles to be able to drive with only minimum driver assistance. Each vehicle travels along a 'virtual' circuit [23], which has to be previously calculated with the aid of a GPS for a given target point. Vehicle sensors are used to ensure safe driving. These sensors measure the distance with respect to the obstacles, such as other vehicles, pedestrians or crash barriers. The vehicles can also use information received from surrounding vehicles, such as their speed or distance, for safety purposes. Thus, vehicles must be able to communicate with each other in order to coordinate the interaction. Finally, and not less important, vehicles must obey traffic signals and rules, such as stop signal or speed limits. These signals send information to the vehicles to inform them about traffic constraints and regulations.

The system reliability is considered critical as a small error could cause a vehicle crash with potentially dramatic consequences. For this reason, it should

---

[2] The cooperating sentient vehicle application is a key demonstrator of the technology developed by the EU funded project CORTEX [24].

be carefully designed and tested, and in addition, the designer should pay special attention to error handling, and all the possible conflicting situations considered. Moreover, the strategy to be applied in the presence of an error should be selected according to the context, as this would dictate which specific strategy would be more suitable.

For instance, as previously commented, vehicles drive using a GPS on a virtual circuit. The vehicle receives the information from the GPS periodically, the time interval being dependent on the vehicle speed. An error-handling module (an aspect) should monitor that the response time of the GPS is never exceeded, and react when this constraint is violated. If this constraint is violated, one specific error-handling strategy would be more suitable than the others. One possible solution, for instance, could be to temporarily use the GPS data from a nearby vehicle. This is only feasible, however, if the vehicle is circulating on a highway where the neighbouring vehicles are going in the same direction, with an almost constant speed. If the vehicle were in the city, where vehicle behaviour is less predictable, information on the other vehicles is of no use and the human driver would be forced to control the vehicle manually, until the GPS recovers.

Why we need dynamic aspect weaving

As commented before, the error-handling strategy depends on the context. There are large number of existing contexts, since the context depends upon a wide range of variables. For instance, the vehicle may be on a highway, circulating fast and there may be good weather or the vehicle can be on a narrow city street, circulating slowly and it could also be raining. Depending on these contextual variable values, one specific error-handling strategy will be more suitable than another. For instance, if the GPS signal is lost whenever it is snowing, the human driver is forced to manage the vehicle manually. If the GPS signal is lost and the vehicle is on a highway, circulating fast or at normal speed, and there is another vehicle near, the vehicle is driven automatically using the GPS information of the other vehicle until the next highway exit (which is signposted by the corresponding traffic signal). In general, for each different combination of contextual variable values, a different error-handling strategy might be designed to achieve a compromise between automation and safety.

Let us descend to the implementation level for a while. Using a static aspect-oriented language, such as AspectJ [2], all these strategies would be hard-coded in a large or heavyweight error-handler aspect that is always woven into the application. Depending on the context, this aspect executes a different strategy. Using a dynamic aspect-oriented language, such as JAsCo [25] or DAOP-ADL [26], the different error-handling strategies can be coded in separate aspects, which will be smaller, more lightweight and manageable than the AspectJ counterpart. These lightweight aspects can be woven and unwoven at run time depending on the context. Hence, the application is able to reconfigure itself at run time as the context changes. Further motivations for this kind of run time adaptation can be found in Kon et al. [20] and Grace et al. [21].

These dynamic adaptations require ensuring that the run time weaving and unweaving of aspects works properly, and that an erroneous situation does not arise as a result of this reconfiguration process. This kind of scenario cannot be easily simulated or tested at the modelling level using the currently available static aspect-oriented model weavers, as they are not able to weave/unweave aspects at run time, which is precisely what designers want to simulate.

In order to overcome this limitation, we present in this paper a dynamic model weaver able to simulate dynamic aspect weaving independent of any dynamic aspect-oriented execution platform. Designers can use this platform to test that their models behave as desired even in the presence of dynamic aspect weaving.

Our dynamic weaver promotes the definition of an aspect-oriented design where the pointcuts contemplate the weaving and unweaving of aspects at run time. Consequently, the designer can observe, by simulation, the advantages of dynamic weaving that can be extended to an aspect-oriented implementation platform offering similar facilities [25,26,27]. In the case where the developer chooses an aspect-oriented dynamic platform for embedded systems such as proposed by Fuentes and Jiménez [28], he/she will start to work from a design which is very close to that required by these kinds of platforms.

2.2   Our Approach

This section provides a brief overview of our proposed solution. Our goal is to execute aspect-oriented models where aspects are woven at model execution time, facilitating the modelling of self-reconfigurable aspect-oriented applications.

Figure 1 illustrates the different elements that comprise our proposed solution:

First, the non-crosscutting concerns of the application are modelled using the common UML 2.0 language. These concerns are modelled without taking aspects into consideration. Then, a dynamic weaving platform (modelled as a UML class), named *Cencibel*, is added to the model as q reusable external module or *model library*. This platform provides an interface for weaving and unweaving aspects during model execution.

The aspect-oriented part of the application model is then constructed using the AOEM UML 2.0 Profile [14], developed previously by the authors of this paper and one of the few AOEM approaches, based on method interception, together with Motorola WEAVR [13]. According to this Profile, an aspect is a class that contains common methods and advices. Advices are methods that use special aspect-oriented behaviours, such as *proceed*.

Pointcuts are composition rules defined outside the aspects specifying that when certain conditions are satisfied during the execution of an application, a certain crosscutting behaviour must be executed.

The Cencibel platform is responsible for composing aspects with the design modules they crosscut according to the pointcuts specification. Hence, to achieve dynamic weaving, the Cencibel platform provides operations for loading and unloading composition rules, i.e. pointcuts, at model execution time.

These composition rules or pointcuts bind aspects with specific events that occur during model execution. Either aspects or base classes of the application

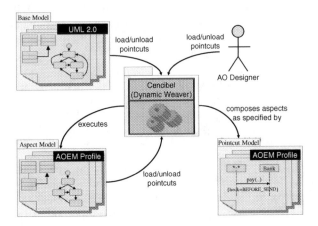

Fig. 1. Dynamic Weaving of AO Executable models

model can perform calls to Cencibel requesting the loading and unloading of pointcuts. The addition of a new composition rule results in the weaving of the aspect it binds. Similarly, the removal of a new composition rule results in the unweaving of the aspect it binds. Therefore, the application is able to reconfigure itself at run time.

For instance, in our example the context-awareness aspect will cause the unweaving and weaving of different versions of the error-handler aspect as the context changes.

Cencibel is modelled using UML 2.0 and its action language, so it is an executable model (with some extensions that will be explained later). Hence, following our approach, both the models constructed and the Cencibel platform are executable models, and so they can be run for simulation or testing purposes. The Cencibel platform, as already commented, performs the composition between aspects and the modules they crosscut dynamically during model execution. This composition (weaving) process is specified in pure UML 2.0 (with slight extensions), avoiding UML and aspect-oriented expert designers having to learn a new language to update or customize this weaving process.

During model execution, the designer can also interact with the dynamic model weaver, loading and unloading pointcuts that activate and/or deactivate aspects, which results in a more interactive model simulation.

The general idea behind constructing this platform is to provide an infrastructure that enables software engineers to test and debug their models before moving into an implementation. Once they have checked if the models are correct, code for an implementation platform would be created. This code can be created either manually or, more in accordance with a model-driven vision, generated automatically from them. In the latter case, since the models are correct and the implementation code is generated automatically from the models, the implementation code would be "correct by construction". However, here we focus on providing the mechanisms for model simulation, the code generation being outside the scope of this paper.

3   Modelling the Sentient Vehicles in AOEM

This section describes how our motivating example can be modelled in UML 2.0 as an aspect-oriented self-reconfigurable application using the AOEM Profile and the Cencibel model library. Before explaining this, a brief introduction to executable modelling in UML 2.0 is provided.

3.1   Executable UML in a Nutshell

This section describes briefly how executable models in UML 2.0 can be constructed. Two main elements are required for making a modelling language executable: (1) an *action language*, which contains those elements that abstract the atomic actions the models can carry out; and (2) an *operational semantics*, which specifies where and how the actions can be placed in a model and how a model must be interpreted. Both elements in the UML 2.0 standard are described below.

Operational semantics for UML models

The operational semantics of UML is still in the process of standardisation [29]. Nevertheless, several tools implementing non-standard operational semantics for UML models already exist (e.g. Rational RT, Rhapsody or Tau G2).

The ideas behind them are quite similar, and so the process of constructing a UML executable model using these tools can be generalised and summarised as follows: First, the global system structure is established as a set of components. Then, the structure of each component is detailed by means of class diagrams. The behaviour of each class is specified using a state machine, where each state represents a stage in the typical class instance life cycle. A transition rule specifies the behaviour and the new state reached when an object in a given state receives a particular event. Each event represents something that occurs during object execution, such as a method invocation, a signal or the expiration of a timer. States can have associated procedures (sets of actions) that model the behaviour executed when a class instance enters, stays in or exits a state. Procedures are specified using an action language, described in the next subsection.

Action language

As previously commented, procedures are specified by means of an action language. UML defines its own action language [30], which aims to provide modelers with the basis for a complete and precise specification of UML models. Using this action language, the full behaviour of UML models can be specified using

Table 1. UML actions used throughout this paper

ReadSelf	Returns a reference to the object where it is executed
AddStructuralFeature	Adds a value to an attribute of an object
ReadStructuralFeature	Reads the value of an attribute of an object
CallBehavior	Invokes a procedure (an activity diagram with actions)
CallOperation	Invokes an object method
CreateLink	Creates a link between two objects

a set of platform-independent atomic actions. These atomic actions can be used for either the execution of UML models or even the generation of 100% of the code if desired [31].

The UML standard [32] defines an *action* as "the fundamental unit of behaviour specification, which takes a set of inputs and converts them into a set of outputs". The UML action language defines operations that support the manipulation of objects and the logical constructors for the specification of algorithms. Examples of these actions are object creation, calls to methods or writing an attribute value, among others. The specific set of actions used in this paper are explained in Table 1.

Intentionally, the UML action language does not enforce any notation for drawing actions. Thus, each tool defines its own notation. However, procedures are commonly represented by means of UML activity diagrams. Actions are nodes of activity diagrams. For each action, a general action symbol (a round cornered rectangle) is used. Inputs and outputs are depicted as pins. To distinguish each specific action (object creation, attribute reading/writing, etc.), they are stereotyped with their name (e.g. ≪ReadSelf≫).

3.2   The Cooperating Sentient Vehicle Application

We show in this section the executable design model for the core logic (or primary model) of the cooperating sentient vehicle application.

First, the system is decomposed into a set of interacting components. Figure 2 shows such a decomposition. Each vehicle has a VehicleController component, which receives requests from a GUI component and receives information about traffic regulations from the TrafficSignal components. VehicleController components can communicate with each other through the ICarInfo interface.

Second, the internal part of each component is modelled as a set of connected classes. We focus on the VehicleController. This component is responsible for driving the vehicle with as little human assistance as possible. To achieve this goal, it contains (see Fig. 3): (1) a GPS module for location sensing; (2) an electronic Compass for orientation; (3) four UltrasonicSensors to detect the presence of neighboring physical objects; (4) a SpeedController which acts as a sensor and actuator for the velocity of the vehicle; (5) a Context object that stores information about the vehicle current context; and (6) a Coordinator object, which ensures that the

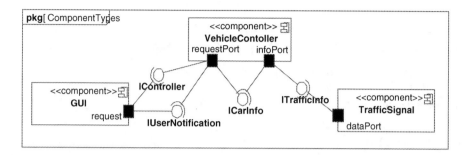

Fig. 2. Cooperating Sentient Vehicles System Architecture

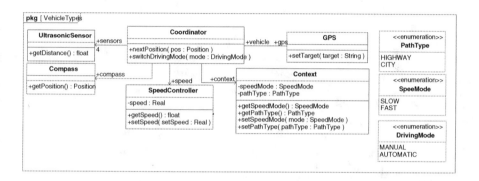

Fig. 3. VehicleController internal classes

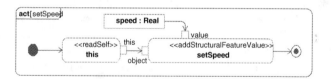

Fig. 4. setSpeed activity

previous elements cooperate adequately to achieve the global task of driving the car safely.

Finally, as commented in the previous section, the behaviour of each class is described by means of state machines and activities containing actions.

As an example, Fig. 4 shows the activity that specifies the setSpeed method of the SpeedController. This activity has an input parameter, which is the new speed value to be set. The activity initially gets a reference to the object where it is being executed (readSelf action), and using this reference, it sets (addStructuralFeatureValue action) the speed attribute of the referenced object to the value specified by the parameter.

Table 2. Aspect-oriented actions

GetMessName	Returns the name of the intercepted message
GetMessArg(n)	Returns the n-argument of the intercepted message
GetTarget	Returns a reference to the target of the intercepted message
GetSource	Returns a reference to the source of the intercepted message
Proceed	Executes the intercepted behaviour

This initial model is fully executable, but it does not contain crosscutting concerns, such as context-awareness or error handling, which are added in the next section as aspects.

3.3 Aspect Modelling

This subsection explains how error-handling and context-awareness crosscutting concerns are added to the application by means of aspects using the AOEM UML 2.0 Profile [14] and the Cencibel model library.

An aspect, according to the AOEM Profile, is modelled as a class, stereotyped as ≪aspect≫. This class contains the logic of a crosscutting concern. An aspect can contain, in addition to basic operations, special operations called *advices*[3]. An advice, in AOEM, differs from common operations in that: (1) they can contain special aspect-oriented actions such as *proceed*. This set of special aspect-oriented actions is provided by the AOEM Profile [14] as a lightweight extension to the UML standard (Table 2 shows a subset of such aspect-oriented actions that are relevant in the context of this paper); and (2) they are never explicitly invoked by common classes. Instead, they are invoked by the aspect-oriented weaver as specified by the pointcuts. The reason for distinguishing between common operations and advices is that the set of aspect-oriented actions provided by the AOEM Profile, such as *proceed*, would make sense only in the context of non implicit method invocation as a result of method interception.

As already commented in Sect. 2.2, pointcuts are composition rules defined outside the aspects, which specify that when certain conditions are satisfied during the execution of an application, a certain behaviour must be executed. Pointcuts can invoke both advices and common operations. This allows operations that do not require using any of the aspect-oriented special actions to be also used by common classes, thereby increasing reusability and symmetry.

Each ≪aspect≫ class, like common classes, can also contain a state machine that specifies the behaviour of the aspect instances. Advices are also specified by means of activities that contain actions. Such actions could be normal ones or those special aspect-oriented actions previously mentioned.

---

[3] Although, in proper English, *advice* is non-countable and therefore its plural would be pieces of advice, in the context of aspect-oriented software development, since a piece of advice is similar to a method and method is considered countable, we will also consider advice countable by extension and we use *advices* as the plural of advice instead of pieces of advices, which improves readability, in our humble opinion.

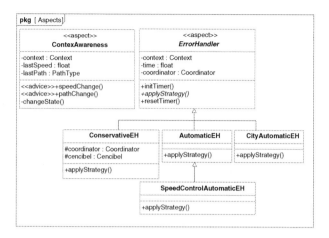

Fig. 5. Aspect classes

Figure 5 shows the structure of the classes that model error-handling and context awareness. The different error-handling strategies are defined as subclasses of an abstract ErrorHandler aspect, which encapsulates the common part of all the error-handling strategies. Each specific ErrorHandler aspect redefines the applyStrategy operation, which contains the specific logic to be applied in case of an error situation. These aspects are described in the following subsections.

The ContextAwareness aspect

The ContextAwareness aspect must detect all the events or messages that might result in changes of the contextual information, requiring an appropriate update of the context object. This aspect can be considered as a "big" observer, using the terminology of the subject-observer pattern [33], which monitors multiple subjects, e.g. vehicle speed or current path type.

In our example, the system simply observes changes in the route type and speed. The speedChange and the pathChange advices are the update methods, according to the subject-observer terminology, which are notified when an observed entity changes its state. Both operations are specified by means of activities.

Figure 6 shows part of the speedChange advice. This advice is executed whenever a call to the setSpeed operation of the SpeedController object (see Fig. 3) is performed (this is enforced by the corresponding composition rule that will be explained in the next subsection).

When the speed value exceeds a certain constant value (which we call SPEED), it is considered that the vehicle is in the FAST mode; otherwise, it is in the SLOW mode. This advice, first, gets a reference (≪readSelf≫ action) to the object where it is being executed, and using this reference, it reads the lastSpeed attribute (≪readStructuralFeature≫ action). Using the aspect-oriented action ≪GetArgNamed≫, the advice recovers the value of the new speed set in the

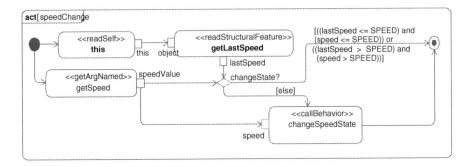

Fig. 6. ContextAwareness.speedChange advice (I)

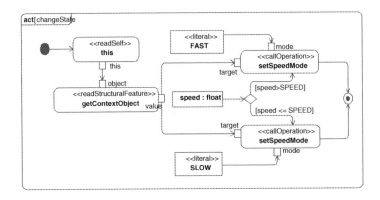

Fig. 7. ContextAwareness.speedChange advice (II)

SpeedController object: then, it checks when this new speed value and the old speed value (lastSpeed) are within the same speed mode interval. If both values are greater than the SPEED constant value, the vehicle remains in the FAST mode (no extra action needs to be carried out). If both values are lower than the SPEED constant value, the vehicle remains in the SLOW mode (no extra action needs to be carried out). Otherwise, the system moves to a new speed mode and the subactivity changeState (≪callBehavior≫ action) is invoked with the current speed value as a parameter. This subactivity is depicted in Fig. 7. It is not described as it is considered self-explanatory[4].

The ErrorHandler aspect

The ErrorHandler aspect is responsible, in the scope of this paper, for checking that the GPS data are received on time. If it were not so, a specific error-handling strategy, depending on the context, must be executed.

---

[4] In our experience, readers are able to interpret it easily even if they are not familiar with activity diagrams.

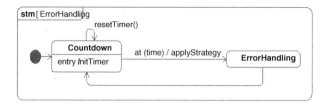

Fig. 8. ErrorHandler state-based behaviour

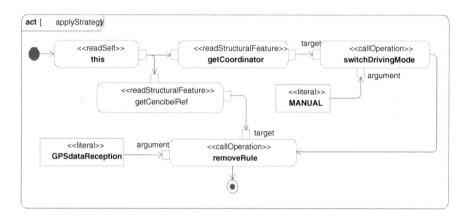

Fig. 9. Conservative Error Handling Strategy

The behaviour of the ErrorHandler aspect is modelled using the state machine depicted in Fig. 8. When the ErrorHandler aspect is created (i.e. when the automatic driving mode is switched on), it initially enters the countdown state, where the timer is initialised. When a message from the GPS with the nextPosition data (see Fig. 5) is received by the Coordinator object, the aspect-oriented weaver sends a message resetTimer to the ErrorHandler and the countdown is restarted (this is enforced by the corresponding composition rule), just in case this countdown has not finished. If the countdown ends, the ErrorHandler moves to the ErrorHandling state, where a specific error-handling strategy is applied. This strategy will be different depending on the specific subclass of the ErrorHandler aspect that is woven at the current point in the application.

Figure 9 shows the strategy applied by the conservative error-handler aspect. First, it switches the system to the manual driving mode (the sequence of actions this, getCoordinator plus swicthDrivingMode in the upper part of the figure). Then, it makes a call to the Cencibel platform requesting the removal of the GPSDataReception composition rule (the sequence of actions this, getCencibelRef plus removeRule in the lower part of the figure). The GPSDataReception composition rule, or pointcut, is what binds the ErrorHandler aspect with the application. Therefore, by removing the GPSDataReception pointcut, the ErrorHandler aspect is removed from the application and it is not applied while the system is in the manual driving mode. The GPSDataReception composition rule is described with more detail in the next subsection. Other error-handling strategies are not shown here as they are not relevant for the purpose of the paper.

Thus, it is the responsibility of the cooperating sentient vehicle application itself to weave and unweave the concrete subclass of the ErrorHandler aspect that corresponds to the current status of the Context object. This reconfiguration process is carried out by a Reconfigurator aspect that will be described in a later subsection. Before describing this aspect, however, we need to explain how the composition relationships between the ContextAwareness and the ErrorHandler aspects can be specified, since the Reconfigurator needs to handle these relationships in order to trigger the weaving/unweaving of the different versions of the ErrorHandler aspect.

3.4   Pointcut Modelling

This section describes how the aspects modelled in the previous sections are composed, by means of pointcut specifications, with the classes of the VehicleController component they crosscut.

A pointcut, according to the AOEM Profile [14], is expressed by means of a sequence diagram, stereotyped as ≪pointcut≫. This stereotype has a tagged value called advice, which specifies the method to be invoked when the pattern specified by the sequence diagram is matched. The specific message that must be intercepted in order to execute the advice is stereotyped as ≪joinpoint≫. This stereotype has two tagged values: (1) point, indicating whether the interception point is either the sending (SEND) or the reception (RECEIVE) of the message; and (2) time, specifying when the advice is executed in relation to the joinpoint (BEFORE, AFTER or AROUND). Similar to aspect-oriented languages (e.g. AspectJ [2] or JAsCo [25]), wildcards are available in lifelines and method names: "*" represents any sequence of characters and ".." any sequence of arguments.

The ContextAwareness aspect has to be applied when any subject observed by this aspect changes. For instance, Fig. 10 shows the SpeedChanges pointcut that specifies when SpeedController receives a message (setSpeed()) for setting a new speed; after the reception of such a message (AFTER RECEIVE), the speedChange() advice of the ContextAwareness aspect has to be executed. In the same way, when a message, informing about a change in the type of road where the vehicle is

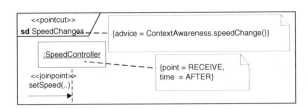

Fig. 10. SpeedChanges pointcut

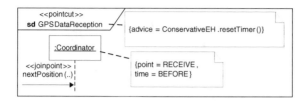

Fig. 11. GPSdataReception pointcut

circulating, is sent, the pathChange() advice of the ContextAwareness is executed. This pointcut is not shown since it is similar to the one shown in Fig. 10.

The countdown of the specific version of the ErrorHandler aspect woven that is currently woven must be reset each time the GPS sends the data for the next vehicle position, which is specified by the GPSDataReception pointcut, as shown in Fig. 11. It indicates that BEFORE the Coordinator RECEIVEs the nextPosition message, the method resetTimer of the ErrorHandler aspect must be executed.

Depending on the context, a specific version of the abstract ErrorHandler aspect must be invoked. Figure 11 represents a context where a conservative error-handling strategy is applied.

This last pointcut needs to be updated at model execution time or at run time each time the context changes, in order to invoke the version of the abstract ErrorHandler aspect corresponding to the new context.

The next section explains how a Reconfigurator aspect deals with this task.

3.5   The Reconfigurator **Aspect**

A third aspect, named Reconfigurator is identified for this system. This aspect is responsible for detecting or observing changes in the context object and switching the error-handler aspects as necessary.

The Reconfigurator aspect must switch between different versions of the ErrorHandler aspect according to the changes in the context. Therefore, the Reconfigurator is also an *observer* that monitors changes in the Context object and reacts accordingly. The Reconfigurator aspect (Fig. 12 (left)) has a reference (cencibel) to the Cencibel platform, a reference (context) to the context object and a reference (pointcut) to the GPSDataReception pointcut (see Fig. 11).

The pointcut for composing the Reconfigurator aspect with the classes it cross-cuts is depicted in Fig. 12 (right). This pointcut specifies after a setter method of the Context object is executed, i.e. each time the Context object is updated, the switchErrorHandler aspect needs to be invoked, for unweaving the current ErrorHandler aspect and weaving a new one.

Figure 13 shows how the switchErrorHandler advice carries out this task. To change the current specific ErrorHandler aspect associated with the GPSData Reception pointcut, the Reconfigurator aspect uses a special service of the Cencibel platform (called changeAspect), which allows the advice value of a specific pointcut to be changed.

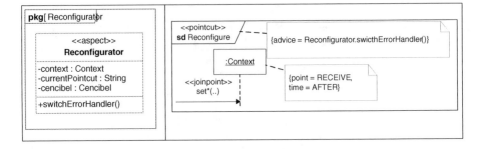

Fig. 12. (left) Reconfigurator aspect (right) Reconfigure pointcut

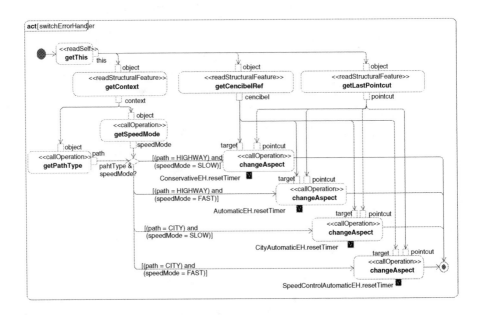

Fig. 13. Reconfigurator.switchErrorHandler advice

This is equivalent to unloading the pointcut with the old advice value and loading a pointcut equal to the most recent one, but with a different advice value. The changeAspect service is a shortcut to achieve this task.

According to Fig. 13, the swicthErrorHandler advice first gets a reference to itself (getThis) and using this reference, it reads the context, cencibel and pointcut attributes (getContext, getCencibel, and getPointcut actions, respectively). Using the reference to the Context object, it recovers the new values for the tuple (pathType, speedMode). Then, a specific call to the changeAspect service of the Cencibel platform is performed requesting the update of the current advice associated with the pointcut for error handling, i.e. the GPSDataReception pointcut. A call to this service results in the unweaving of the previously associated aspect and the weaving of the newly specified one. The name of the new advice is provided as a literal value in UML terminology, which varies for each combination of values of the (pathType, speedMode) tuple. Literal values passed as arguments to an action are modelled in UML 2.0 as *value pins*. A value pin is one which contains a literal expression that provides the value for an input of an action. Value pins have been coloured black in order to distinguish them more easily from common pins. The literal value for each one of them appears beside them (e.g. AutomaticEH.resetTimer). After calling the changeAspect service with the proper advice value, which results in the unweaving of an error-handler aspect and the weaving of a different one, the switchErrorHandler advice ends.

This section has shown how the application is able to dynamically change the error-handling strategy used by means of unweaving and weaving aspects at run time. The next section explains how this dynamic weaving can be achieved at the modelling level.

4   Aspect-Oriented Dynamic Weaving

This section describes how the aspect-oriented model created in the previous section can be executed using a dynamic model weaving strategy.

4.1   Dynamic Weaving Process

Using a dynamic weaving strategy, aspects can be woven and unwoven at run time by adding/removing/updating composition rules, i.e. pointcuts. Since the addition, updating or removal of pointcuts at model execution time is valid, it is not possible to know whether an aspect advice will be executed or not until just before the joinpoint interception happens. Therefore, just before a joinpoint is going to be executed (e.g. a method call), the dynamic weaving platform, called Cencibel, intercepts it. The platform checks according to the pointcuts currently loaded, some advice(s) must be executed. If so, the advice(s) and the joinpoint are executed in the order specified by the pointcut. Thus, according to the joinpoint model of the AOEM Profile [14], when an object needs to execute a call action, instead of calling the target object directly, this call is delegated to the dynamic weaving platform.

The structure of our Cencibel dynamic weaving platform is depicted in Fig. 14. The Cencibel platform contains a set of aspect composition rules (i.e. pointcuts). A CompositionRule indicates that when a specific message is delegated to the weaving platform, at a certain time (i.e. BEFORE, AROUND or AFTER) and at a certain point of execution of that message (i.e. either the sending SEND or the reception RECEIVE), a specific advice must be executed. A Message specifies the callerType, the receiverType and the message name. Cencibel also contains information about dynamic constraints (FlowConstraints) imposed on the composition rules. More specifically, it is allowed to discard messages if they are (active=true) or not (active=false) in the control flow of other messages. The included attribute specifies whether the message must be considered or not during the joinpoint flow (i.e. the counterpart in AspectJ would be cflow for included=true and cflowbelow for included=false).

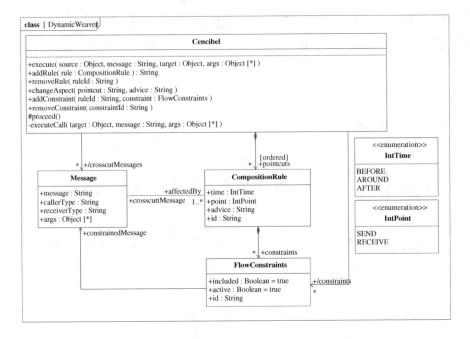

Fig. 14. Cencibel structure

The Cencibel interface offers an execute(source: Object, message: String, target: Object, args:Object[*]) method for executing call actions. It also provides methods for loading (addRule) and unloading (removeRule) aspect composition rules at run time, as well as for changing the value of the advice associated with one pointcut (changeAspect). Constraints to composition rules can also be added (addConstraint) and removed (removeConstraint) at run time.

When a call to a method is delegated to the Cencibel platform by means of the execute(aSource, aOperation, aTarget, aArgs) operation, Cencibel searches for all the crosscutMessages tuples that match the specific tuple (asource, aOperation, aTarget, aArgs) and that satisfy the associated constraints. All the resulting tuples are grouped by the (point, time) values of the composition rules associated with each message. Each group is then ordered by the advice execution priority (note that the collection of pointcuts contained in Cencibel is ordered). Next, the process depicted in Fig. 15[5] is executed:

1. Initially, Cencibel checks if there are any aspects applicable before the call action. If so, they are executed in order (Fig. 15, step 1). According to the AOEM Profile, neither BEFORE nor AFTER advices can contain proceed actions; thus, they can be simply executed in sequence by execution priority.
2. Cencibel then checks if there are any aspects applicable around the sending of the call action (Fig. 15, step 2). If so, the AROUND SEND advice with the

---

[5] This figure is a not a UML-compliant precise specification of the weaving process; it is only a high level description.

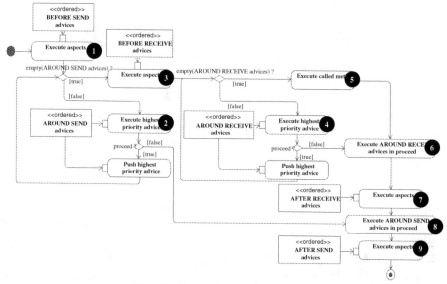

Fig. 15. Dynamic weaving process

highest priority is executed. During this execution, a call to the proceed action is performed, the advice is added to a stack for AROUND SEND advices in the "proceed" state, removed from the AROUND SEND advices collection, and the dynamic weaving process continues at step 2, checking if further AROUND SEND advices need to be executed. If an around call advice did not contain a call to proceed, it means the call has to be discarded, and the weaving process continues at step 8, skipping the execution of the called method (as well as the execution of other around advices with a lower execution priority, as well as any BEFORE RECEIVE, AROUND RECEIVE or AFTER RECEIVE advices).

3. After executing the aspects around the sending of the call (and if all of them have invoked a proceed action), the BEFORE RECEIVE advices are executed (Fig. 15, step 3). As in the BEFORE SEND case, they can be simply executed in order, since they do not contain proceed actions.

4. Then, the advices around the reception of the call are executed (Fig. 15, step 4). This process is the same as for the around send advices, but in this case, the process returns to step 4 when a proceed action is invoked, or goes to step 6 in the case where the execution of the method is skipped and the advices that have invoked a proceed action are stored in the stack for AROUND RECEIVE advices in the "proceed" state.

5. Next, the call is forwarded to the target object (just in case all the AROUND SEND advices have *proceeded*), which dispatches it (Fig. 15, step 5). To carry out this task, the Cencibel platform invokes its private function executeCall.

6. After the execution of the method, the AROUND RECEIVE advices pushed in the corresponding stack are popped out and executed (Fig. 15, step 6).

7. Then, the **AFTER RECEIVE** advices are executed (Fig. 15, step 7). They do not contain proceed actions, and so they can be simply executed in order.
8. The **AROUND SEND** advices pushed in the corresponding stack are popped and executed (Fig. 15, step 8).
9. Finally, the **AFTER SEND** advices, which do not contain proceed actions, are executed (Fig. 15, step 9) and the weaving process finishes.

In order to illustrate this algorithm, let us consider the execution trace of the sending of a nextPosition(pos) message from the GPS to the Coordinator (see Fig. 3):

1. First, the GPS executes a ≪CallOperation≫ action, invoking the operation nextPosition of the Coordinator object, with the data of the next position of the vehicle.
2. This call, instead of being executed directly, since it is a potential joinpoint, is delegated to the Cencibel platform (see Sect. 4.3 for further details about how this call is redirected to the platform).
3. Then, the Cencibel platform executes the algorithm described above:
   (a) The platform searches for all the advices applicable at this joinpoint. The applicable advices are those which are bound to the current joinpoint by a composition rule, and they also satisfy the dynamic conditions (e.g. cflow constraints), if these exist. In our case, one composition rule matches the current joinpoint. This composition rule is GPSDataReception (see Fig. 11). It specifies a **BEFORE RECEIVE** advice, which is a ConservativeEH.resetTimer[6].
   (b) Therefore, the two steps of the algorithm do not have any effect on the joinpoint because there are neither **BEFORE SEND** nor **AROUND SEND** advices.
   (c) Then, the ConservativeEH.resetTimer operation is executed because it is a **BEFORE RECEIVE** advice bound by a composition rule that matches the current joinpoint.
   (d) Step 4 of the algorithm is skipped because no **AROUND RECEIVE** advices are applicable at this joinpoint.
   (e) The current joinpoint is executed. Cencibel calls its private function executeCall, which invokes the operation delegated to the platform.
   (f) Steps 6, 7, 8 and 9 do not have any effect because there are no **AROUND RECEIVE** advices applicable, nor are **AROUND** advices pushed in the corresponding stacks, nor are there **AFTER RECEIVE** advices or **AFTER SEND** advices that should be executed.

With the current UML Action language, the execution of the delegated call action to Cencibel, i.e. step 5 of the weaving process, or according to the previous example, the invocation of the nextPosition method by the Cencibel platform, has a limitation. This is illustrated in Fig. 16. The target object (target) and the arguments (arg1, arg2, arg3, etc.) are provided to the call action at model

---

[6] Let us suppose for simplicity that the ConservativeEH is the concrete version of the error-handler aspect currently woven in the application.

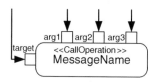

Fig. 16. Call operation action limitation

execution time, but the message name and the number of input pins must be statically specified at modelling time (i.e. hard-coded into the action); so the complete call action cannot be composed dynamically at model execution time.

Using the previous example, the exact problem is that the Cencibel platform cannot dynamically construct a CallOperation action at run time for invoking the nextPosition method of the Coordinator object (step 3.e of the previous example). The Coordinator object and the parameter can be supplied at model execution time, but the called operation, the number and type of arguments would have to be previously specified at design time.

This issue could be easily resolved using reflection mechanisms not currently supported by the UML Action language. We have extended the current UML Action language to provide the reflective support that we need. This extension is explained in the next section.

4.2   Reflective Executable UML

This section explains how reflective support can be smoothly incorporated into UML 2.0 based on previous ideas presented by Sunyé et al. [31]. The basic idea behind this work is that the UML Action language is a language for carrying out activities over object-oriented models, such as creating objects or setting attributes. The UML metamodel is itself an object-oriented model, and so the UML Action language can be used for executing actions over the UML meta-model, i.e. for changing a model at model execution time.

Following these ideas, we have created a simple UML 2.0 Profile for adding reflection to executable UML models. This profile contains only the ≪reflective≫ stereotype, which can be applied to any action. It means that an action stereotyped as ≪reflective≫ does not refer to the objects that are instances of the UML model; instead, it refers to the UML model itself as a set of instances of the metaclasses of the UML metamodel. For instance, a CreateObject action, stereotyped as ≪reflective≫, means we are creating a new instance of a metaclass of the UML metamodel. Then, using the reflective version of CreateObject, either a new UML class, a new UML activity, a simple final node of an activity or any other UML element can be created.

Using this slight extension to the UML Action language, the problem of constructing a call to an operation dynamically at model execution time can be solved using the executeCall procedure (depicted in Fig. 17), which is contained in the Cencibel class. This procedure accepts as input the called object, the name

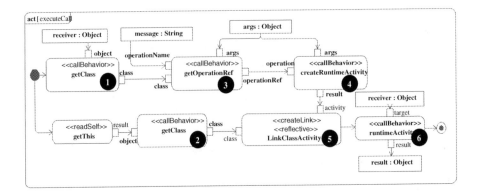

Fig. 17. Procedure for constructing a call to an operation at model execution time

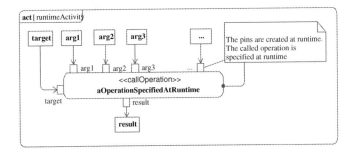

Fig. 18. Activity created at run time

of the called operation and the collection of arguments. This procedure uses three subprocedures: (1) getClass; (2) getOperationRef; and (3) createRuntimeActivity.

The getClass procedure returns a reference to the definition of the object class that is passed as an argument to the procedure. For instance, if getClass receives an object of type A, it returns a reference to the definition of class A (thinking reflectively, it would be a reference to the object A of the metaclass Class).

The getOperationRef procedure obtains a reference to the definition of an operation, given: (1) a reference to a class definition; (2) the name of the operation as a string; and (3) a collection of arguments that serves to select an operation with a specific signature (just in case there were several operations with the same name and different signature). These elements are passed as arguments to the getOperationRef procedure.

The createRuntimeActivity procedure creates the activity or procedure (called runtimeActivity), at model execution time that calls the operation delegated to the Cencibel platform. A general sketch of this procedure is shown in Fig. 18. The runtimeActivity is created entirely at run time using reflective UML actions. Its unique task is to invoke the operation whose call has been delegated to the Cencibel platform. The most interesting part of this activity is that the name of the callOperation action is specified at run time, and the corresponding attribute of the metaclass CallOperationAction is set by means of reflective UML actions. The input pins for this action are also created at run time, and their types are dynamically specified using reflection.

Using the example of the invocation of the nextPosition method used in the previous section, the runtimeActivity is dynamically created in that case in step 3.e. This activity contains only a ≪CallOperation≫ action that invokes the nextPosition operation of the Coordinator object, with the data of the next position of the vehicle as a parameter.

Using these three subprocedures, we come back to the executeCall procedure, which works as follows:

The goal is to add an activity at model execution time, as shown in Fig. 18, which executes the call delegated to the Cencibel platform, as part of the Cencibel platform behaviour. Then, the upper part of the Fig. 17 specifies the process to create the runtimeActivity reflectively (labels 1, 3 and 4) and the lower part models how this new activity is linked to the Cencibel platform object (label 2 and 5) and executed returning a result (label 6). This process is detailed below:

1. References to the definition of the class of the called object (Fig. 17, label 1) and to the definition of the Cencibel class (Fig. 17, label 2) are obtained.
2. A reference to the definition of the called operation is obtained (Fig. 17, label 3).
3. The runtimeActivity is created (Fig. 18) using the reference to the definition of the operation previously obtained and the collection of arguments for the called operation (Fig. 17, label 4).
4. The newly created activity is linked with the Cencibel platform using a UML reflective action, i.e. a new activity is added to the Cencibel class definition (Fig. 17, label 5).
5. This newly added behaviour is invoked (Fig. 17, label 6) and the result collected.

This section has shown how the problem regarding the execution of the delegated action can be solved using reflective UML, this being one of the contributions of this paper.

4.3 Running the Aspect-Oriented Model

Previous sections have described how a dynamic weaving process for executable models can be designed (or implemented) at the modelling level. However, before starting the execution of an aspect-oriented model with dynamic weaving, some preliminary tasks must be carried out to convert the aspects and the pointcuts modelled using the AOEM Profile into plain Executable UML elements that can be run in conjunction with the Cencibel platform. These preliminary actions are described in this section.

First, we need to ensure that each potential joinpoint is not directly executed by the model; instead, it is replaced with a call to the Cencibel platform requesting the execution of such a joinpoint. For instance, the GPS should not call the nextPosition method of the Coordinator object directly; instead, the GPS should delegate this call to the Cencibel platform. In order to avoid the designer needing to be aware of this indirection level, each potential joinpoint is automatically replaced with its equivalent call to the Cencibel platform by means of a model transformation provided by the Cencibel preprocessor. In this way, designers can work as usual, being only required to execute these model transformations before running the aspect-oriented model.

Second, the information specified in the pointcuts must be transformed into a sequence of calls (addRule and addConstraint) to the Cencibel platform in order to load these pointcuts 'programmatically' into the Cencibel platform. Another set of model transformations performs this task, avoiding the extra task of having the designer perform it manually. At design time, the designer can just use a special addPointcut action, which contains a reference to the sequence diagram that specifies the required pointcut as an argument. The set of model transformations replaces this special action with a set of calls to the Cencibel platform.

Finally, aspect advices need to be converted to plain Executable UML, which means we need to replace the special aspect-oriented actions of the AOEM Profile with common UML actions. All the information about the joinpoint context that could be required by a special aspect-oriented action (e.g. the message target and the message caller) is already loaded in the Cencibel platform; thus, each aspect-oriented action can be substituted by a proper action requesting this information from the Cencibel platform. In the case of the proceed action, this is substituted by a call to the Cencibel.Proceed method, which executes the original call action, according to the process described in Fig. 15. This transformation process is also implemented by means of a set of automatic model transformations.

The complete set of model transformations to be executed before running the model can be viewed as a compilation process at the modelling level. Once these transformations have been executed, the model is ready to be executed with the appropriate tool-support, which is described in the next section.

5   Tool Support

This section describes the tools required to reproduce our experiments.

The set of reflective actions presented in the previous section are not contained in the UML 2.0 standard. This implies that current tools able to execute UML models need to be extended with an implementation of these reflective actions in order to support our approach. At the time we faced this task, there were no tools available with these characteristics, as all the UML tools with execution capabilities were proprietary and non-extensible[7].

Due to the evident lack of effective tool support for our approach, we have developed a UML execution engine, called Pópulo, a kind of UML Virtual Machine that is provided as an Eclipse plugin [35,36]. This UML Virtual Machine

---

[7] Recently, a UML model debugger, in the form of an IBM Rational plugin, with similar characteristics to our requirements has been released. The interested reader can refer to [34].

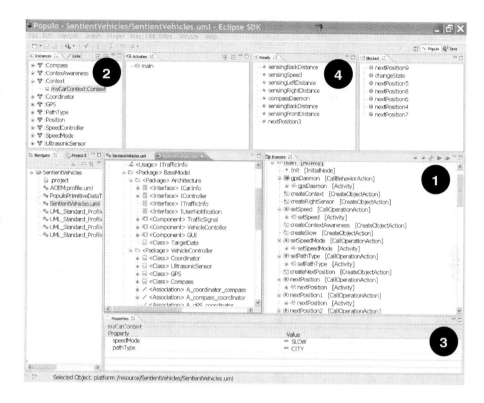

Fig. 19. The Pópulo UML Virtual Machine

is easily extensible with new actions (it was one of our main goals when developing Pópulo). Thus, the set of reflective actions required to run the Cencibel platform were built-in as part of this virtual machine. The Cencibel platform was therefore constructed as a model library that aspect-oriented applications can import and use. Aspect-oriented applications can then be executed, following a dynamic weaving strategy, using Pópulo.

Figure 19 shows a screenshot of Pópulo. This tool allows designers to visualise the behaviour of an (aspect-oriented) executable UML model by interpreting the UML actions. It works as a model debugger and provides four views for observing: (1) the execution trace of the model (Fig. 19, label 1); (2) the current status of the objects created by the application (Fig. 19, label 2); (3) the values of the attributes of such objects (Fig. 19, label 3); and (4) the current status of the stack of method calls, i.e. the status of the queue of actions and activities ready for execution and the status of the set of actions and activities that are blocked waiting for some object or control flows (Fig. 19, label 4). The Pópulo UML Virtual Machine supports breakpoints and step-by-step execution[8].

---

[8] Interested readers can find information about the Pópulo tool at
http://caosd.lcc.uma.es/populo/index.htm

For designing aspect-oriented UML models, any UML tool supporting the UML action language can be used. To the best of our knowledge, at least four tools support this feature: MagicDraw, Rational, Topcased and Eclipse UML2. XMI serialisations of UML models can differ depending on the the the UML tool used. Pópulo accepts as input UML models serialised in the flavour of the XMI standard supported by Eclipse UML2. Therefore, the selected tool must be able to export the models in an XMI format compatible with this XMI version. We opted for using this version, as it is becoming the de-facto standard for XMI serialisations, and a wide range of UML tools (e.g. MagicDraw, Rational, Together and Topcased) are compatible with this version.

Using these tools, Pópulo, the Cencibel model library and the AOEM Profile, the motivating example presented in this paper has been modelled, executed and simulated. In addition, an Online Book Store system presented in [14], which was already modelled in an aspect-oriented fashion using the AOEM Profile, has also been executed using this dynamic weaving strategy. Positive and negative aspects of this experience are discussed in the next section.

6   Discussion

Several approaches have recently appeared, such as Motorola WEAVR [13] or AOEM [14], which allow the execution, testing and/or debugging of aspect-oriented models. However, these approaches (one provided by the authors) only consider static weaving. Our experience trying to use these aspect-oriented model weavers in pervasive systems revealed to us that a static weaving strategy is not always sufficient and that we needed some dynamic weaving support at the modelling level to adequately simulate adaptive applications, i.e. those able to reconfigure themselves by dynamic aspect weaving and unweaving.

The goal of this paper is to present the infrastructure required for executing aspect-oriented models with a dynamic weaving process that allows an application to reconfigure itself. However, a systematic process for designing the test cases that allow designers to verify their models, such as described by Xu and Xu [37] or Baker and Jervis [38], is beyond the scope of this paper and has been left as future work. Currently, using our approach, an aspect-oriented model can be debugged by means of its execution. We comment on scenarios using the cooperating sentient vehicles system where our approach is useful for detecting potential errors using aspect-orientation.

Figure 12 (right) shows the pointcut for triggering the reconfiguration aspect. This pointcut intercepts all the executions of any setter method of the Context object (actually, what is intercepted is any call to a method whose name starts with 'set', independently if this method sets any attribute or not). By means of executing the model, we could discover that this pointcut is intercepting the execution of setter methods for contextual variables that do not affect the error-handling strategy. Thus, the current ErrorHandler aspect does not need to be unwoven, and the Reconfigurator aspect should not be executed.

Using the approach presented in this paper, the previous issue and other ones inherent to aspect-oriented applications, such as the problem of checking the correctness of aspect-interactions, can be analyzed at the modelling level by observing the trace of a model execution. When defects are discovered, the model can be fixed at design time without moving into a implementation. Industrial reports have revealed that fixing these defects at design time can contribute greatly to reducing the effort required for solving these errors (the Motorola experience [18] shows a 30–70x reduction on this effort).

Nevertheless, for analysing the previous issues, a dynamic weaving strategy is not strictly required. As a novel contribution of this approach, specific issues of dynamic system reconfiguration can also be analysed at the modelling level.

The experienced reader in adaptive systems will know that an extra piece of code/model behaviour must be specified to ensure the system behaves correctly during the dynamic reconfigurations (see, for instance, [22,39,40]). This piece of behaviour depends on each application. It has not been modelled in this paper for the cooperating sentient vehicle example, as the construction of these *safe reconfigurators* often involves a lot of technical details on the adaptive systems domain. This domain usually contains complex formalisms that are not essential for the goal of this paper. Readers interested in these topics can refer to the work of Rasche et al. [22], Zhang and Cheng [40] or a recent survey [39]. The goal of this paper is to provide the infrastructure to be able to simulate aspect-oriented adaptive applications and check that these *safe reconfigurators* work as expected. An adequate simulation of such *reconfigurators* cannot be properly addressed using a static weaving strategy.

In this respect, even developers unfamiliar with adaptive systems can realize that the reconfigurator presented in this paper does not work correctly simply by running the aspect-oriented model of this system. The aspect-oriented designer could easily find several bugs contained in the model, such as: (1) in the case where the GPS signal is lost just during the reconfiguration process, no aspect is executed; or (2) the countdowns may be longer than specified due to reconfigurations.

An additional contribution of this work is that different alternative solutions can be analysed without the necessity of implementing them, simply by observing the behaviour of the models.

We would also like to comment that the reader familiar with aspect-oriented technologies and especially with aspect-oriented modelling approaches, might miss in this paper advanced aspect-oriented mechanisms that go beyond method interception based on a pointcut plus advice scheme, such as multidimensional separation of concerns based on hyperslices [41] or the merge operator provided by Theme/UML [6]. This paper focuses on method interception because this is the aspect-oriented technique most often applied to the systems that use dynamic weaving strategies, such as adaptive systems or context-aware systems. The reason is that the kind of concern separated by means of method interception (e.g. encryption), it is also the same that requires being woven/unwoven dynamically. The kind of concerns using other methods, such as the Theme/UML merge operator, rarely require dynamic weaving strategies. In comparison with middleware platforms for component-based applications, the concerns separated by method interception are the ones that are most likely to be managed by the component containers. The concerns separated by other mechanisms are those that are most likely to be placed in the business logic of the component. While the former ones can normally be added or removed from the container at run time by application servers, it is rarely the case when the same dynamism applies to the latter ones.

In our experience, concerns composed by means of some kind of merge operator might require dynamic weaving strategies mainly in a Software Product Line (SPL) context [42]. In this case, the different features of a product are designed as separate models that are later composed in order to get a specific product. If we want to make a product of the SPL dynamically reconfigurable, dynamic weaving strategies could be of interest. However, this is a new topic that is beyond the scope of this paper and one that involves a lot of new challenges [43,44]. One possible solution would be as follows: the result of the composition of several modules by means of a merge operator may be a set of components. Thus, in order to dynamically reconfigure a model, the new set of features we want to include in our product would be selected, and a new set of common or base components would be generated as a result. These newly created components could be added to the application, and the old ones removed. Dynamic loading and unloading of components is nowadays feasible and it could be simulated at the modelling level.

It is reasonable therefore to think that the construction of fully executable models in UML provides benefits from a software engineering point of view. These executable models are so highly-detailed that it could be argued we are just programming in UML instead of using a conventional programming language and hence, there is no difference between programming and modelling.

We would like to point out that in order to analyse some critical parts, or different alternatives, of an aspect-oriented model, designers do not need to specify the model completely. They only need to model the behaviour of those parts they want to analyse, and the non-critical behaviours, such as trivial getters, setters or simple numeric algorithms, can be simply filled with dummy specifications, which will be refined at the implementation level.

Regarding the benefits of executable modelling, they rely mainly on three factors: (1) abstraction; (2) code generation; and (3) platform-independence.

First, in order to provide benefits from a software engineering point of view, models are supposed to be more abstract than programming languages, hiding irrelevant details of the implementation languages and helping software engineers to focus on the relevant details of the problem. In this respect, modelling languages often provide a richer set of abstractions (e.g. state-machine diagrams, sequence diagrams) than traditional programming languages, such as Java or C++. Software for certain domains (e.g. reactive systems which are mainly state-based) can be more easily specified using the high-level abstractions (e.g. state-machines) provided by modelling languages. On the other hand, for the kind of applications where the set of abstractions provided by programming languages is sufficient, such as purely numerical algorithms, the abstraction benefit of executable modelling is perhaps not so clear.

The effort associated with executable modelling is extremely beneficial when combined with code generation. One of the goals of the UML Action language is to allow 100% of the code to be automatically generated if desired (this feature is currently supported by several tools, such as Rhapsody, TAU G2 or Rational RT). Currently, powerful code generators, such as Motorola Mousetrap [45], can produce strongly optimised applications (which often perform better than hand-written code) [18,46], as reported in the Motorola experience. Code generation also serves to hide some particularities of the target language or platform from the developers, at the same time helping to ensure target code quality by automatically and systematically applying code generation patterns considered as best-practices [18].

Finally, models produced using the AOEM Profile are platform-independent, which means they are not dependent on any target language or platform. This implies that changes in the target language or platform (which unfortunately are more frequent than desired) would not affect these models, making them more stable than code. In addition, the same model could specify the same system for different target languages. Platform-independency when combined with code generation improves reusability, as the same model can be used to generate the same system for different target languages or platforms [47].

In general, the major benefits of executable modelling can be obtained from the combination of the three previously commented factors: abstraction, platform-independency and code generation [48]. A deeper discussion on when it is faster, cheaper and more desirable to model instead of going directly to code is not the goal of this paper. Interested readers can consult the Saturn experience [16], the work of Mellor and Balcer [49], the Motorola case [18] and also the Cottenier et al. [19,50]. Counter positions can be found in Bell [51] and Kleppe et al. [52], and a critical discussion of these issues is available in Hailpern and Tarr [53].

7   Related Work

To the best of our knowledge, this is the first work in the literature describing how to execute aspect-oriented models using a dynamic weaving strategy. Nevertheless, there is some work on aspect-orientation and executable models in the literature on static aspect-oriented model weaving, which are described in this section.

Ho et al. [54] present a framework for modelling aspect-oriented applications. It serves to construct AOEMs, but the weaving is postponed until the implementation phase and thus the execution of the complete model, including aspects, is not possible at modelling time. The weaving process is implemented as a model transformation from design to implementation, which generates the code from the UML actions.

C-SAW [55] is a framework for generating model weavers for aspect-oriented domain models. C-SAW is integrated with the GME[9] modelling environment.

---

[9] http://www.isis.vanderbilt.edu/projects/gme/

It focuses mainly on consistently adding constraints and properties to very large models rather than encapsulating crosscutting behaviours in aspects. In C-SAW, pointcuts and advices are modelled using the ECL (Embedded Constraint Language) language, defined by the authors, which is a subset of OCL (Object-Contraint Language). This kind of declarative and OCL-based textual languages might be cumbersome for specifying pointcuts, as demonstrated by Stein et al. [56]. Advices are also modelled using the ECL language; therefore aspect and base models are expressed in different notations, which could generate some comprehension problems. A more optimal solution, in our humble opinion, is to use the same notation for the aspect and the base model, and so the learning curve could decrease for those designers that are already familiar with the notation of the base model but not with aspect-oriented concepts. In addition, the behaviour of the advices is not modelled in a strict sense; instead, it is specified in a syntax similar to C++.

Theme/UML [6] is an extension of UML for aspect-oriented modelling. It supports all the UML 2.0 diagrams. Therefore, using Theme/UML, we should be able to weave UML executable models, which specify procedures using the UML Action language. However, although Theme/UML specifies the weaving semantics of the approach, until now, the weaving must be done manually, since no tool support is available. We tried to implement a Theme/UML weaver, but without fruitful results since it is quite complex and it is not precisely defined beyond sequence and class diagrams.

KerTheme [12] is an extension to Theme/UML which adds execution capabilities to common 'themes' by integrating them with the Kermeta language[10] [57]. This Kermeta language enables the definition of precise behaviour for metamodels (and models) by means of an action language. The main goal of KerTheme is to test models. A KerTheme comprises a sequence diagram, which describes a test case, and an *executable* class diagram. This diagram is executable since the behaviour of the class method is precisely specified using the Kermeta language. After specifying KerThemes, they are woven. The weaving process generates both woven executable class diagrams and woven test cases that can be used to check the correctness of the executable class diagrams. The main drawback of this approach is the use of the Kermeta language for providing model execution. Kermeta is a language designed for breathing life into metamodels, i.e. for specifying behaviour at the metamodel level (M2 level), but not for specifying behaviour at the modelling level (M1 level). Hence, it is aligned with MOF (M3 level) instead of the UML metamodel or any other metamodel (M2 level). This has several consequences: First, it forces designers to switch between their preferred UML editor and the corresponding tool for the Kermeta language in order to create their designs, unless their preferred UML editor provides a seamless integration with Kermeta, such as is the case for the Topcased tool[11]. Second, because Kermeta was designed for working at the metalevel, the Kermeta action language is less expressive and more restrictive than the UML action language.

---

[10] http://www.kermeta.org/
[11] http://topcased-mm.gforge.enseeiht.fr

Signals, forks or data store nodes that represent data streams are some examples of elements of the UML action language that are not supported by Kermeta. Finally, KerTheme behaviour is modelled using the Kermeta action language, which imposes an imperative and procedural style of specifying behaviour. Other modelling alternatives, such as state-machines, which could be more suitable for certain kinds of applications such as reactive systems, are simply discarded.

Cottenier et al. [13,50,58] present a powerful aspect-oriented static model weaver called Motorola WEAVR [19]. Currently, Motorola WEAVR can be considered the most mature model weaver, since it has been adopted by Motorola. This model weaver is integrated with the TAU G2 tool and it enables the use of powerful code generators provided by these tools. In addition, it provides an interesting joinpoint model based on states, which allows the specification of semantic pointcuts in reactive systems [59]. However, Motorola WEAVR is based on the Telelogic TAU G2 implementation of the Executable UML principles. Cottenier et al. define an aspect-oriented profile that extends the Telelogic SDL metamodel for the Action Semantics. This notation is not compatible with the current UML Action language and introduces some proprietary features that reduce its interoperability and tool-independence. The aspect-oriented model weaver is implemented as a Telelogic add-in [50]; therefore, it is not portable and tool-independent. In addition, the weaving process is not clearly described in their work.

Reedy et al. [11] present a model composition approach that is used for aspect-oriented model weaving. In this work, an aspect-oriented model comprises a primary model plus a number of aspect models that crosscut the primary model. Aspect models are presented as patterns that describe generic forms of crosscutting features. These patterns are instantiated and then merged with the primary model. The merging process is carried out using a composition metamodel and special composition directives that enable designers to tune it. These ideas have been implemeted in the Kompose tool. This composition metamodel only works once the aspect patterns have been instantiated, which implies designers need to instantiate the aspects manually for each joinpoint they crosscut. In our work, selected joinpoints are automatically found by the weaver and aspect models are automatically instantiated for each selected joinpoint. In addition, the composition metamodel presented by Reddy et al. only applies to class diagrams, the composition of behavioural diagrams not being addressed.

Groher and Völter [60] present a model weaver, called XWeave, which allows the weaving of models and metamodels based on the Eclipse Modelling Framework[12]. However, this model weaver is mainly focused on the structural definition of models and metamodels instead of their behaviour. In addition, it does not contain any mechanism to model the precise behaviour of aspects. Ubayashi et al. [61] propose MMAP (metamodel access protocol), which can be viewed as a reflection mechanism for manipulating a model as an instance of its metamodel. MMAP provides interesting benefits for the construction of model weavers for

---

[12] http://www.eclipse.org/modeling/emf/

aspect-oriented models. However, MMAP is limited to structural models (e.g. class diagrams), and so the handling of crosscutting behaviours is not possible.

MATA [15] is an aspect-oriented model weaving tool based on graph transformation, which supports weaving of sequence diagrams [62] and/or state machines [44]. This tool provides some interesting extra features, such as Critical Pair Analysis (CPA) for detecting some kind of problems due to aspect-interaction. Nevertheless, MATA does not currently support, weaving of activity diagrams; therefore, the weaving of highly-detailed UML executable models as presented in this paper is still not possible. In addition, because the weaving process of MATA is based on graph transformation, both the pointcut and advice models must be expressed using the same kind of diagram or conceptual model. In our case, advices are described using activity diagrams containing actions because we want to specify the precise behaviour of a method, and this seems to be the conceptual model that best fits in with our needs. Pointcuts are modelled using sequence diagrams because we want to represent execution traces that must trigger a crosscutting behaviour. In this case, sequence diagrams are the conceptual model most in accordance with our requirements. Our weaver is responsible for interpreting and composing this information coming from different conceptual models adequately.

SmartAdapter [63] is a generic aspect-oriented modelling approach that, as a novel contribution, uses an *adaptation model* in addition to the traditional advice and pointcut models for modelling aspects. This adaptation model specifies options and directives for composing an aspect with a module it crosscuts. For instance, when a class A, belonging to an aspect, and a class B, belonging to a crosscut model, must be combined, the adaptation model specifies how to do it. This adaptation model could specify that these classes must be simply merged, such as in Theme/UML, or we could opt for making that B inherits from A. This introduces some variability in the weaving process, which allows aspects and base model to be combined not always in the same way, supporting certain customisations for each case, which improves aspect reusability. Nevertheless, as in MATA, both the pointcut and advice models must be expressed using the similar kind of diagrams, the specification of pointcuts using sequence diagrams and the advices using activity diagrams being difficult.

In conclusion, we would like to point out that all these aspect-oriented model weavers are static, as already commented at the beginning of this section, and are unsuitable for the dynamic weaving requirements presented throughout this paper.

Finally, as already commented, the highly detailed models used in this paper are close to the implementation level. Therefore, it is also related to aspect-oriented languages with dynamic weaving, such as JAsCo [25], DAOP [26] or Prose [64]. This work is intended to be an aspect-oriented version (based on method interception) of executable UML [49]. Hence, the AOEM Profile adapts several concepts of aspect-oriented implementation level languages to the executable UML approach. The AOEM Profile borrows concepts from several aspect-oriented implementation languages, but there is not a one-to-one mapping between the AOEM Profile and any aspect-oriented language.

For instance, in the AOEM Profile, pointcuts are defined outside aspects, such as in JAsCO, where a pointcut is defined in a *connector* or DAOP, where a pointcut is defined in a composition rule placed in a XML file. In Prose, however, pointcuts are defined inside aspects. Our approach does not support introductions or intertype declarations, such as DAOP, and unlike JAsCo. The AOEM Profile supports dynamic joinpoints based on "cflow", which are included in the JAsCo language but are not supported by the DAOP platform. JAsCo supports stateful aspects [65], where pointcuts are enabled or disabled depending on the state where an aspect is. Each pointcut is responsible for indicating which pointcuts are enabled once it has been matched. The AOEM Profile supports this feature by means of UML 2.0 state machines that specify the reactive behaviour of an aspect. Nevertheless, UML 2.0 state machines used by the AOEM Profile are more expressive than stateful aspects of JAsCo, since elements such as nested states, orthogonal regions, timers or guard conditions in the transitions are available in the AOEM Profile but not in JAsCo. State machines of the AOEM Profile can also react to events different to pointcut satisfaction, such as time consumption or invocation of normal methods. Contrary to these aspect-oriented implementation languages, a pointcut can invoke either a common method or an advice.

In summary, the AOEM Profile adapts those concepts we have found most interesting from each aspect-oriented implementation language to the modelling level. Therefore, it has both differences and similarities with each aspect-oriented implementation language.

8   Conclusions and Future Work

This paper has presented the infrastructure and the process required for executing aspect-oriented models with dynamic weaving requirements, as a stepping stone towards the simulation and testing of this kind of model. The infrastructure comprises of: (1) a UML 2.0 Profile, named AOEM (a previous work of the authors), for Aspect-Oriented Executable Modelling, (2) a reusable model library, called Cencibel, which plays the role of a dynamic weaving platform at the modelling level and is able to weave aspects at model execution time; and (3) an extensible UML Virtual Machine, called Pópulo, which has allowed us the implementation of a set of UML reflective actions as a precondition for achieving aspect-oriented dynamic weaving at the modelling level. Using these three elements, aspect-oriented applications with dynamic weaving requirements can be executed, and thus their behaviour observed and debugged.

As future work, it is our intention to incorporate more aspect-oriented features to the AOEM Profile. One of the main drawbacks of this profile is that it is not able to access context beyond the intercepted joinpoint. For instance, arguments of messages considered in control flow constraints cannot be accessed from the aspect advices in a straightforward way. In order to overcome this shortcoming, we are now integrating Joinpoint Designation Diagrams (JPDDs) [66] into the AOEM Profile and our weaving process [67].

We will also continue working on the implementation of the Pópulo UML Virtual Machine and the reflective UML actions. We will focus particularly on the development of user interfaces for Pópulo which enable a user-friendly model simulation. Opportunities for integrating Pópulo with available UML tools, such as IBM Rational or Topcased, will also be explored.

Finally, we will also address dynamic weaving using advanced aspect-oriented mechanisms that goes beyond method interception. More specifically, we have found that dynamic weaving of concerns separated by some kind of *merge* operator could be of interest in the context of Software Product Lines (SPL) [42]. In this context, the CaesarJ [68] and ObjectTeams [69] languages provide a technique similar to the Theme/UML merge operator, called *family polymorphism*. Family polymorphism have a similar expressiveness to merge operators, but it involves fewer conflicting situations. Therefore, it is our intention to study how to incorporate mechanisms similar to family polymorphism at the modelling level (the work by Laguna et al. [70] could be considered a first step towards this goal). Subsequently, we will examine how to dynamically weave concerns separated by this technique at model execution time.

References

1. Colyer, A., Clement, A., Harley, G., Webster, M.: Eclipse AspectJ: Aspect-Oriented Programming with AspectJ and the Eclipse AspectJ Development Tools. Addison-Wesley Professional, Reading (2004)
2. Kiczales, G., Hilsdale, E., Hugunin, J., Kersten, M., Palm, J., Griswold, W.G.: An Overview of AspectJ. In: Knudsen, J.L. (ed.) ECOOP 2001. LNCS, vol. 2072, pp. 327–353. Springer, Heidelberg (2001)
3. Stein, D., Hanenberg, S., Unland, R.: A UML-based Aspect-Oriented Design Notation for AspectJ. In: Proc. of the 1st Int. Conference on Aspect-Oriented Software Development (AOSD), Enschede, The Netherlands, April 2002, pp. 106–112 (2002)
4. Aldawud, O., Elrad, T., Bader, A.: UML Profile for Aspect-Oriented Software Development. In: Proc. of 3rd Int. Workshop on Aspect-Oriented Modelling (AOM), 2nd Int. Conference on Aspect-Oriented Software Development (AOSD), Boston, Massachusetts, USA (March 2003)
5. Evermann, J.: A Meta-Level Specification and Profile for AspectJ in UML. Journal of Object Technology (JOT), Special Issue on Aspect-Oriented Modelling 6(7), 27–49 (2007)
6. Clarke, S., Baniassad, E.: Aspect-Oriented Analysis and Design: The Theme Approach. Addison-Wesley Professional, Reading (2005)
7. Wagelaar, D., Jonckers, V.: A Concept-Based Approach to Software Design. In: Hamza, M. (ed.) Proc. of the 7th Int. Conference on Software Engineering and Applications (SEA), Marina del Rey, California, USA (November 2003)
8. Grundy, J.: Multi-Perspective Specification, Design and Implementation of Components using Aspects. International Journal of Software Engineering and Knowledge Engineering 10(6), 713–734 (2000)

9. Clifton, C., Leavens, G.T.: A Design Discipline And Language Features For Modular Reasoning In Aspect-Oriented Programs. Technical Report TR #05-23, Department of Computer Science, Iowa State University (December 2005)
10. Kiczales, G., Mezini, M.: Aspect-Priented Programming and Modular Reasoning. In: Proc. of the 27th Int. Conference on Software Engineering (ICSE), St. Louis, Missouri, USA, May 2005, pp. 49–58 (2005)
11. Reddy, Y.R., Ghosh, S., France, R.B., Straw, G., Bieman, J.M., McEachen, N., Song, E., Georg, G.: Directives for Composing Aspect-Oriented Design Class Models. In: Rashid, A., Aksit, M. (eds.) Transactions on Aspect-Oriented Software Development I. LNCS, vol. 3880, pp. 75–105. Springer, Heidelberg (2006)
12. Jackson, A., Klein, J., Baudry, B., Clarke, S.: KerTheme: Testing Aspect Oriented Models. In: Proc. of the Workshop on Integration of Model Driven Development and Model Driven Testing, 2nd European Conference on Model-Driven Architecture-Foundations and Applications (ECMDA-FA), Bilbao, Spain (July 2006)
13. Cottenier, T., van den Berg, A., Elrad, T.: Motorola WEAVR: Aspect Orientation and Model-Driven Engineering. Journal of Object Technology (JOT), Special Issue on Aspect-Oriented Modelling 6(7), 51–88 (2007)
14. Fuentes, L., Sánchez, P.: Designing and Weaving Aspect-Oriented Executable UML models. Journal of Object Technology (JOT), Special Issue on Aspect-Oriented Modelling 6(7), 109–136 (2007)
15. Whittle, J., Jayaraman, P.: MATA: A Tool for Aspect-Oriented Modeling based on Graph Transformation. In: Proc. of the 11th Int. Workshop on Aspect-Oriented Modelling (AOM), 11th Int. Conference on Model Driven Engineering Languages and Systems (MoDELS), Nashville, Tennessee, USA (October 2007)
16. Long, E., Misra, A., Sztipanovits, J.: Increasing Productivity at Saturn. Computer 31(8), 35–43 (1998)
17. Doldi, L.: Validation of Telecom Systems with SDL: The Art of SDL Simulation and Reachability Analysis. Wiley, Chichester (2003)
18. Baker, P., Loh, S., Weil, F.: Model-Driven Engineering in a Large Industrial Context-Motorola Case Study. In: Briand, L.C., Williams, C. (eds.) MoDELS 2005. LNCS, vol. 3713, pp. 476–491. Springer, Heidelberg (2005)
19. Cottenier, T., van den Berg, A., Elrad, T.: Motorola WEAVR: Model Weaving in a Large Industrial Context. In: Proc. of the 6th Int. Conference on Aspect-Oriented Software Development (AOSD), Industry Track, Vancouver, British Columbia, Canada (March 2007)
20. Kon, F., Costa, F., Blair, G., Campbell, R.H.: The Case for Reflective Middleware. Communications of the ACM 45(6), 33–38 (2002)
21. Grace, P., Truyen, E., Lagaisse, B., Joosen, W.: The Case for Aspect-Oriented Reflective Middleware. In: Proc. of the 6th Workshop on Adaptive and Reflective Middleware (ARM), 8th Int. Conference on Middleware, Newport Beach, California, USA (November 2007)
22. Rasche, A., Schult, W., Polze, A.: Self-Adaptive Multithreaded Applications - A Case for Dynamic Aspect Weaving. In: Proc. of the 4th Workshop on Adaptive and Reflective Middleware (ARM), 6th International Conference on Middleware, Grenoble, France (November 2005)
23. Sivaharan, T., Blair, G., Friday, A., Wu, M., Duran-Limon, H., Okanda, P., Sørensen, C.: Cooperating Sentient Vehicles for Next Generation Automobiles. In: Proc. of the 1st Workshop on Applications of Mobile Embedded Systems (WAMES), 2nd Int. Conference on Mobile Systems, Applications and Services (MobiSys), Boston, Massachusetts, USA (June 2004)

24. Verissimo, P., Cahil, V., Casimiro, A., Cheverst, K., Friday, A., Kaiser, J.: Cortex: Towards Supporting Autonomous and Cooperating Sentient Entities. In: Proc. of the European Wireless Conference, Florence, Italy (February 2002)
25. Suvée, D., Vanderperren, W., Jonckers, V.: JAsCo: An Aspect- Oriented Approach Tailored for Component Based Software Development. In: Proc. of the 2nd Int. Conference on Aspect-Oriented Software Development (AOSD), Boston, Massachusetts, USA, March 2003, pp. 21–29 (2003)
26. Pinto, M., Fuentes, L., Troya, J.M.: A Dynamic Component and Aspect-Oriented Platform. The Computer Journal 48(4), 401–420 (2005)
27. Popovici, A., Gross, T., Alonso, G.: Dynamic Weaving for Aspect-Oriented Programming. In: Proc. of the 1st Int. Conference on Aspect-Oriented Software Development (AOSD), Enschede, The Netherlands, pp. 141–147 (2002)
28. Fuentes, L., Jiménez, D.: An Aspect-Priented Ambient Intelligence Middleware Platform. In: Proc. of the 3rd Int. Workshop on Middleware for Pervasive and Adhoc Computing (MPAC), 6th International Conference on Middleware, Grenoble, Grenoble, France, pp. 1–8 (2005)
29. Object Management Group (OMG): Semantics of a Foundational Subset for Executable UML Models, Request For Proposal (ad/2005-04-02) (April 2005)
30. Object Management Group (OMG): Unified Modelling Language: Superstructure v2.0 (formal/05-07-04), ch. 5: Actions (July 2005)
31. Sunyé, G., Pennaneac'h, F., Ho, W.M., Guennec, A.L., Jézéquel, J.M.: Using UML Action Semantics for Executable Modeling and Beyond. In: Dittrich, K.R., Geppert, A., Norrie, M.C. (eds.) CAiSE 2001. LNCS, vol. 2068, pp. 433–447. Springer, Heidelberg (2001)
32. Object Management Group (OMG): Unified Modelling Language: Superstructure v2.0 (formal/05-07-04) (August 2005)
33. Gamma, E., Helm, R., Johnson, R., Vlissides, J.: Design Patterns: Elements of Reusable Object-Oriented Software. Addison-Wesley Professional, Reading (1994)
34. Dotan, D., Kirshin, A.: Debugging and Testing Behavioral UML Models. In: Companion to the 22nd Int. Conference on Object Oriented Programming Systems and Applications, Montreal, Quebec, Canada, October 2007, pp. 838–839 (2007)
35. Fuentes, L., Manrique, J., Sánchez, P.: Pópulo: A tool for debugging uml models. In: Proc. of the 30th Int. Conference on Software Engineering (ICSE), Companion Volume (Research demonstration), Leipzig, Germany, May 2008, pp. 955–956 (2008)
36. Lidia Fuentes, J.M., Sánchez, P.: Execution and Simulation of (Profiled) UML models using Pópulo. In: Proc. of the 2nd Int. Workshop on Modelling in Software Engineering (MISE), 30th Int. Conference on Software Engineering (ICSE), Leipzig, Germany, May 2008, pp. 75–81 (2008)
37. Xu, D., Xu, W.: State-based Incremental Testing of Aspect-Oriented Programs. In: Proc. of the 5th Int. Conference on Aspect-Oriented Software Development (AOSD), Bonn, Germany, March 2006, pp. 180–189 (2006)
38. Baker, P., Jervis, C.: Testing UML 2.0 Models Using TTCN-3 and the UML 2.0 Testing Profile. In: Gaudin, E., Najm, E., Reed, R. (eds.) SDL 2007. LNCS, vol. 4745, pp. 86–100. Springer, Heidelberg (2007)
39. Bradbury, J.S., Cordy, J.R., Dingel, J., Wermelinger, M.: A Survey of Self-Management in Dynamic Software Architecture Specifications. In: Proceedings of the 1st Workshop on Self-managed Systems (WOSS), Newport Beach, California, USA, October-November 2004, pp. 28–33 (2004)

40. Zhang, J., Cheng, B.H.C.: Model-based Development of Dynamically Adaptive Software. In: Proc. of the 28th Int. Conference on Software Engineering (ICSE), Shanghai, China, May 2006, pp. 371–380 (2006)
41. Tarr, P., Ossher, H., Sutton, S.M., Harrison, W.: N Degrees of Separation: Multi-Dimensional Separation of Concerns. In: Filman, R.E., Elrad, T., Clarke, S., Akşit, M. (eds.) Aspect-Oriented Software Development, pp. 37–61. Addison-Wesley, Reading (2005)
42. Pohl, K., Böckle, G., van der Linden, F.J.: Software Product Line Engineering: Foundations, Principles and Techniques. Springer, Heidelberg (2005)
43. Nejati, S., Sabetzadeh, M., Chechik, M., Easterbrook, S., Zave, P.: Matching and Merging of Statecharts Specifications. In: Proc. of the 29th Int. Conference on Software Engineering (ICSE), Minneapolis, Minnesota, May 2007, pp. 54–64 (2007)
44. Whittle, J., Moreira, A., Araújo, J., Jayaraman, P.K., Elkhodary, A.M., Rabbi, R.: An Expressive Aspect Composition Language for UML State Diagrams. In: Engels, G., Opdyke, B., Schmidt, D.C., Weil, F. (eds.) MODELS 2007. LNCS, vol. 4735, pp. 514–528. Springer, Heidelberg (2007)
45. Dietz, P., Weigert, T., Weil, F.: Formal Techniques for Automatically Generating Marshalling Code From High-Level Specifications. In: Proc. of the 2nd Workshop on Industrial-Strength Formal Specification Techniques (WIFT), Boca Raton, Florida, USA, October 1998, pp. 40–47 (1998)
46. Weigert, T., Dietz, P.: Automated Generation of Marshaling Code from High-Level Specifications. In: Reed, R., Reed, J. (eds.) SDL 2003. LNCS, vol. 2708, pp. 374–386. Springer, Heidelberg (2003)
47. Mellor, S.J., Scott, K., Uhl, A., Weise, D.: MDA Distilled. Addison-Wesley, Reading (2004)
48. Selic, B.: The Pragmatics of Model-Driven Development. IEEE Software 20(5) (September 2003)
49. Mellor, S., Balcer, M.: Executable UML: A Foundation for Model Driven Architecture. Addison-Wesley Professional, Reading (2002)
50. Cottenier, T., van den Berg, A., Elrad, T.: Model Weaving: Bridging the Divide between Elaborationists and Translationists. In: Proc. of 9th Int. Workshop on Aspect-Oriented Modelling (AOM), 9th Int. Conference on Model Driven Engineering, Languages and Systems (MoDELS), Genova, Italy (October 2006)
51. Bell, A.E.: Death by UML Fever. ACM Queue 2(1), 72–80 (2004)
52. Kleppe, A., Warmer, J., Bast, W.: MDA Explained: The Model Driven Architecture–Practice and Promise. Addison-Wesley Professional, Reading (2003)
53. Hailpern, B., Tarr, P.: Model-Driven Development: The Good, The Bad, and The Ugly. IBM Systems Journal 45(3), 451–461 (2006)
54. Ho, W.M., Jézéquel, J.M., Pennaneac'h, F., Plouzeau, N.: A Toolkit for Weaving Aspect-Oriented UML designs. In: Proc. of the 1st Int. Conference on Aspect-oriented Software Development (AOSD), Enschede, The Netherlands, pp. 99–105 (2002)
55. Gray, J., Bapty, T., Neema, S., Schmidt, D.C., Gokhale, A., Natarajan, B.: An Approach for Supporting Aspect-Oriented Domain Modelling. In: Pfenning, F., Smaragdakis, Y. (eds.) GPCE 2003. LNCS, vol. 2830, pp. 151–168. Springer, Heidelberg (2003)
56. Stein, D., Hanenberg, S., Unland, R.: A Graphical Notation to Specify Model Queries for MDA Transformations on UML Models. In: Aßmann, U., Aksit, M., Rensink, A. (eds.) MDAFA 2003. LNCS, vol. 3599, pp. 77–92. Springer, Heidelberg (2005)

57. Muller, P.A., Fleurey, F., Jézéquel, J.M.: Weaving Executability into Object-Oriented Meta-languages. In: Briand, L.C., Williams, C. (eds.) MoDELS 2005. LNCS, vol. 3713, pp. 264–278. Springer, Heidelberg (2005)

58. Cottenier, T., de Berg, A.V., Elrad, T.: Modelling Aspect Oriented Compositions. In: Bruel, J.-M. (ed.) MoDELS 2005. LNCS, vol. 3844, pp. 100–109. Springer, Heidelberg (2006)

59. Cottenier, T., van den Berg, A., Elrad, T.: Joinpoint Inference from Behavioral Specification to Implementation. In: Ernst, E. (ed.) ECOOP 2007. LNCS, vol. 4609, pp. 476–500. Springer, Heidelberg (2007)

60. Groher, I., Völter, M.: XWeave: Models and Aspects in Concert. In: Proc. of 10th Int. Workshop on Aspect-Oriented Modelling (AOM), 6th Int. Conference on Aspect-Oriented Software Development (AOSD), Vancouver, British Columbia, Canada, March 2007, pp. 35–40 (2007)

61. Ubayashi, N., Sano, S., Otsubo, G.: A Reflective Aspect-Oriented Model Editor Based on Metamodel Extension. In: Proc. of the 1st Int. Workshop on Modelling in Software Engineering (MISE), 29th Int. Conference on Software Engineering (ICSE), Minneapolis, Minnesota, USA (May 2007)

62. Jayaraman, P.K., Whittle, J., Elkhodary, A.M., Gomaa, H.: Model Composition in Product Lines and Feature Interaction Detection Using Critical Pair Analysis. In: Engels, G., Opdyke, B., Schmidt, D.C., Weil, F. (eds.) MODELS 2007. LNCS, vol. 4735, pp. 151–165. Springer, Heidelberg (2007)

63. Lahire, P., Morin, B., Vanwormhoudt, G., Gaignard, A., Barais, O., Jézéquel, J.M.: Introducing Variability into Aspect-Oriented Modeling Approaches. In: Engels, G., Opdyke, B., Schmidt, D.C., Weil, F. (eds.) MODELS 2007. LNCS, vol. 4735, pp. 498–513. Springer, Heidelberg (2007)

64. Popovici, A., Alonso, G., Gross, T.R.: Just-In-Time Aspects: Efficient Dynamic Weaving for Java. In: Proc. of the 2nd Int. Conference on Aspect-Oriented Software Development (AOSD), Boston, Massachusetts, USA, pp. 100–109 (2003)

65. Vanderperren, W., Suvée, D., Cibrán, M.A., Fraine, B.D.: Stateful Aspects in JAsCo. In: Gschwind, T., Aßmann, U., Nierstrasz, O. (eds.) SC 2005. LNCS, vol. 3628, pp. 167–181. Springer, Heidelberg (2005)

66. Stein, D., Hanenberg, S., Unland, R.: Expressing Different Conceptual Models of Joinpoint Selections in Aspect-Oriented Design. In: Proc. of the 5th Int. Conference on Aspect-Oriented Software Development (AOSD), Bonn, Germany (March 2006)

67. Sánchez, P., Stein, D., Hanenberg, S.: Statecharts as an Intermediate Representation of JPDDs which Help Developers to Map Them to Executable Artifacts. In: Proc. of the 12th Workshop on Aspect-Oriented Modelling (AOM), 7th Int. Conference on Aspect-Oriented Software Development (AOSD), Brussels, Belgium, March-April (2008)

68. Aracic, I., Gasiunas, V., Mezini, M., Ostermann, K.: An Overview of CaesarJ. In: Rashid, A., Aksit, M. (eds.) Transactions on Aspect-Oriented Software Development I. LNCS, vol. 3880, pp. 135–173. Springer, Heidelberg (2006)

69. Herrmann, S.: Object Teams: Improving Modularity for Crosscutting Collaborations. In: Aksit, M., Mezini, M., Unland, R. (eds.) NODe 2002. LNCS, vol. 2591, pp. 248–264. Springer, Heidelberg (2003)

70. Laguna, M.A., González-Baixauli, B., Marqués, J.M.: Seamless Development of Software Product Lines. In: Consel, C., Lawall, J.L. (eds.) Proc. of the 6th Int. Conference on Generative Programming and Component Engineering (GPCE), Salzburg, Austria, October 2007, pp. 85–94 (2007)

On Language-Independent Model Modularisation

Florian Heidenreich[1], Jakob Henriksson[1], Jendrik Johannes[1], and Steffen Zschaler[2]

[1] Technische Universität Dresden
Institut für Software- und Multimediatechnik
D-01062, Dresden, Germany
{florian.heidenreich,jakob.henriksson,
jendrik.johannes}@tu-dresden.de
[2] Lancaster University
szschaler@acm.org

Abstract. As model-driven software development covers additional parts of the development process, the complexity of software models increases as well. At the same time, however, many modelling languages do not provide adequate support for modularising models. For this reason, there has been an increasing interest in the topic of model modularisation, often under the heading of aspect-oriented modelling (AOM). The approaches range from techniques that closely mimic concepts from aspect-oriented programming (AOP), such as AspectJ, to very powerful composition techniques for specific types of models—for example, state machines.

We believe that AOM is more than just copying the concepts of AOP at the modelling level and should rightly include a large number of other model-composition techniques. However, developing model composition techniques and tooling is costly. To minimise the effort required, this paper presents a generic technique for model composition. The technique is based on invasive software composition and our Reuseware tooling and can be used with arbitrary modelling languages. The basic technique itself is language independent, but it can be adapted to construct language- and purpose-specific composition techniques for specific modelling languages and situations. Hence, it can be used both as a tool for developing specific model-modularisation techniques and as an instrument of research for studying basic properties and concepts of model modularisation. The paper gives a detailed description of our approach and evaluates it using a number of examples.

1 Introduction

Model-driven development (MDD) [1] is increasingly viewed as one way of dealing with the complexity of modern-day software. Its promise is that by making models our primary development artefacts and generating the final application code from them, we can achieve a higher level of abstraction in development, and thus, achieve an improved understanding of more complex systems. MDD requires all models to completely describe the specific part and property of a system for which they have been constructed. This completeness requirement leads to an increasing size of models used. Therefore, it is often no longer possible to provide and use one single monolithic model of a system. Rather, we need to be able to split complex models into less complex, partial models that can be independently developed, maintained and studied.

S. Katz et al. (Eds.): Transactions on AOSD VI, LNCS 5560, pp. 39–82, 2009.

Modern modelling notations used in the context of MDD, such as the Unified Modeling Language (UML) [2], already provide some modularisation support. This support—for example UML's packages, hierarchical classifiers and hierarchical state machines—however, typically follows a dominant decomposition of the system to be developed. For some formal specification techniques—for example, state machines [3] or Petri nets [4]—other decomposition techniques are defined, but these are not typically supported by modern modelling languages. Even worse, in the context of MDD, domain-specific modelling languages (DSMLs) for very specific purposes are often developed in one or a number of projects.

This situation has led to a lot of interest in model-modularisation techniques apart from the dominant decomposition of a system. As the model modules studied in this context often cross-cut the dominant decomposition, this research has typically been performed under the heading of *aspect-oriented modelling* (AOM) [5,6]. AOM covers a quite large range of approaches, from those, for example [7], mimicking aspect-oriented programming (AOP) approaches (such as AspectJ [8]) to those, for example [9,10], providing very powerful composition techniques for specific purposes and languages using specific properties of modelling languages.

Developing such modularisation techniques and the supporting technology is costly and error prone. At the same time, it needs to be repeated for every new DSML to be enriched with such concepts. Therefore, a generic approach is required that can be applied efficiently to realise different specific model modularisation techniques. We discuss existing approaches that support modularisation techniques for DSMLs in Sect. 7.

To close this gap, in this paper, we present such a generic approach based on Invasive Software Composition (ISC) [11] and implemented in our tool Reuseware [12]. ISC is a generic, grey-box composition technique based on rewriting source code. It was formalised in the Reuseware approach [11,13] to be applicable to arbitrary context-free, textual languages. In this paper, we extend that work to cover graph-structured, possibly graphical languages. This paper is an extension of [14]. In that paper, we enhanced Reuseware by introducing the notion of *fragment queries* to group model or source code fragments. This enabled us to implement the concept of quantification [15], which is at the heart of aspect orientation. Fragment queries and standard Reuseware composition concepts, however, provide a rather crude set of tools for expressing model compositions. This paper extends and refines these simple concepts by adding the notions of ports, port groups and composition steps, greatly reducing the complexity of composition programs and enhancing the flexibility and expressiveness of the language-independent composition technique. Furthermore, we discuss how arbitrary modelling languages can be extended to integrate with our approach and how such an extension can be designed such that existing tooling for the language can still be used.

The rest of this paper is structured as follows: We begin in the following section by giving two motivating examples. Section 3 discusses requirements on a language-independent solution for model modularisation. This is followed by a presentation of our proposed solution in Sect. 4. In Sect. 5, we briefly discuss our tool Reuseware, which implements the concepts presented in this paper. Section 6 shows how our initial examples can be solved by our approach to support our claim of language independence.

2   Motivating Examples

This section introduces two examples that we will use in the paper to explain our approach. The first example is based on UML activity diagrams, outlining a real-world scenario. The second example is based on a toy DSL, explaining modularisation issues in DSLs in an illustrative manner. It should be noted that we not only present examples of concrete models but also of languages in which they are written. Our approach can be applied to any language expressible by a metamodel.

2.1   Business Process Extension

Business processes can be described by behaviour modelling, for instance, using UML activity diagrams. Often, general processes (e.g. a process for ordering goods in a shopping system) can be defined once and specialised for a concrete system with special requirements.

Although UML activity diagrams can be modularised into partitions in single models, reusing and combining parts of activities modelled separately is not well supported by UML itself. We would like to define general processes with activity diagrams and keep them extensible with specific activities for concrete application use-cases.

As an example, we look at the order processing activity modelled in Fig. 1. The process contains a checking activity (the *CustomerDataCheck* action together with the decision node below) that determines whether certain data (here customer data) are consistent. We want to keep the order processing activity extensible such that additional checks can be inserted in parallel to the customer data check.

To perform the extension, a developer need not to know anything about the ordering process, but should know that check activities can be inserted. What this developer needs to know is that a *check activity* has to have one incoming control flow (from the *checkFork* node) and two outgoing flows (to the *checkMerge* and *checkJoin* nodes). With this knowledge, the developer can design additional check activities, for instance, the one from Fig. 2 that determines the customer's credit card liquidity.

Such extensibility can be realised by thinking about models as components. Treating the ordering process model (cf. Fig. 1) as a model component, almost the whole activity should be encapsulated. Only the *checkFork*, *checkMerge* and *checkJoin* nodes (grey boxes), to which the incoming and outgoing flows of additional checks can connect, should be reflected in the composition interface. Looking at the credit card check (cf. Fig. 2) as a model component, we can again hide the internal activity. We only think of the initial (*InitialNodeCREDIT*) and final nodes (*FINISH* and *CANCEL*) as *open spots* in the model which need to be manipulated through the composition interface.

Our approach will enable us to look at UML models as model components by utilising UML language specifics to define composition interfaces on UML models. With our language-independent composition tooling, we can then easily define and execute a composition of both presented activities resulting in the model shown in Fig. 3, where only parts belonging to the composition interface of the model components (grey boxes) were manipulated.

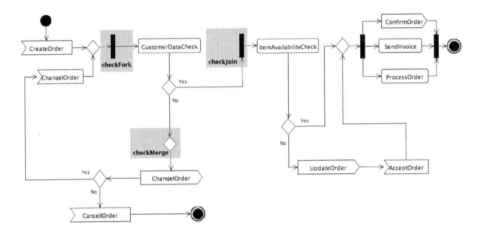

Fig. 1. An activity diagram for the control flow of an order process

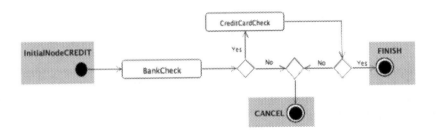

Fig. 2. An activity diagram for credit-card checks that can extend the order process with an additional check

2.2 Modular Ship and Cargo Distribution

In this example, we utilise the toy DSL *TaiPan*[1] that was created to demonstrate features of the Eclipse Graphical Modeling Framework [16]. Figure 4 shows a model defined in the TaiPan language. The language can be used to model a configuration of an *Aquatory* consisting of *Ports*, *Routes* between ports and *Ships* that may hold *Items* as cargo. Ships travel on a *Route* and have a *Port* as destination. A special kind of ship is a *Warship* that has the additional ability to execute *EscortOrders* (escorting another ship on its route) or *AttackOrders* (besieging a port).

Let us assume that *Ports*, *Ships* and *Items* are complex model parts that consist of several model elements and that there are many relations (*Routes*) between ports and many relations (*EscortOrders*) between *Ships*. Then, it becomes obvious that certain parts of a model can be reused in other models: the ports on the sea are always the same, while the ships on it can be different. The part that models a certain item can be reused everywhere it represents the cargo of a ship. We identified three different model parts in a TaiPan model, which can be individually reused in other TaiPan models.

---

[1] Available from http://wiki.eclipse.org/index.php/GMF_Tutorial#Quick_Start

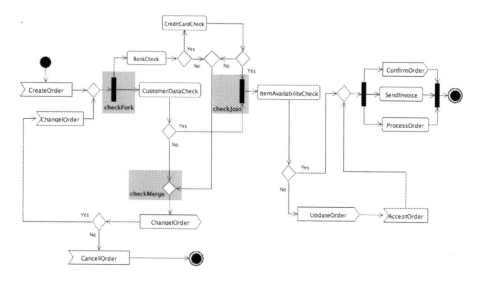

Fig. 3. A composition of the order process and the credit card check activity

1. *Port model* (Fig. 5). Here, the ports and routes between them are modelled. The number of ports and routes and their names seldom change in this model. However, details of the ports (e.g. its size and capacity) can change over time.
2. *Flotilla model* (Fig. 6). This models a flotilla of ships with their specifics and relations between them. Again, the number of ships and their names do not change so often in one flotilla, while the escort orders between ships might do so often.
3. *Cargo model* (Fig. 7). Here, individual items of cargo are modelled. Assuming that the model of a single item is not simple, this separation makes sense: only one item type needs to be modelled once and can be reused for several ships.

We want to look at these partial models as model components and compose them into a single TaiPan model, like the one in Fig. 4. We identify the following three components:

1. The port model should encapsulate details about the ports and routes, such as the size of the ports. It should offer an interface that allows access to the port and route names, such that they can be assigned to ships.
2. The flotilla model should encapsulate details about the ships and the relations between them (e.g. which war ship escorts which cargo ship). It should offer a composition interface that allows modification of port and route assignments, as well as a composition interface to fill the load of a cargo ship.
3. The cargo model should encapsulate details about the different cargo types. It should offer a composition interface that allows access to extract specific items from the cargo model.

Through such a component-oriented way of thinking about the models, benefits are gained over conventional model integration approaches (such as model transformations). Through encapsulation, two advantages are gained: First, it ensures that certain

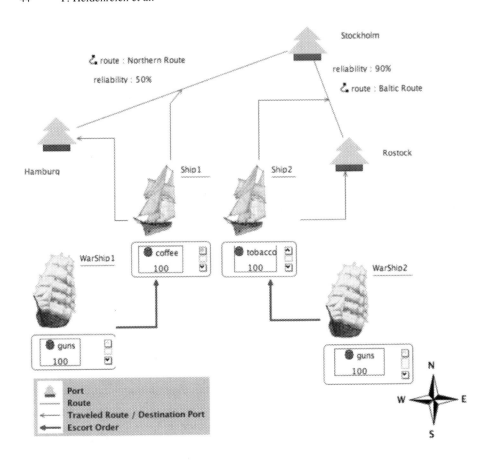

Fig. 4. A TaiPan model

elements are not changed during composition, which increases the understanding of relations between the components and the composition. The author of a component knows and can control which elements are changed during composition through defining the composition interface together with the component. Second, by knowing the encapsulated details, the component author can change them without the risk of breaking the composition. Through the clearly defined interfaces, composition becomes easier. One has to bother only about the interface and not the internals of the models (in contrast to model transformations, where extensive knowledge about the details of the involved models is often required).

Our model composition approach will allow to easily introduce the notion of composition interfaces into the TaiPan language and use our language-independent composition tooling to quickly define compositions of TaiPan model components. Thus, we can extend the language with new features that were not originally supported.

Were we to implement support for the two kinds of model compositions presented above manually into the activity diagram and the TaiPan language, we would face a daunting task indeed. For each language, we would have to design a modularisation

route : Northern Route

reliability : 50%

Stockholm

reliability : 90%

route : Baltic Route

Rostock

Hamburg

Fig. 5. A port model

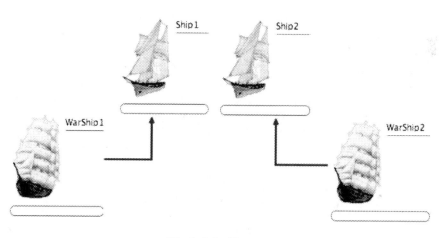

Ship 1

Ship2

WarShip 1

WarShip 2

Fig. 6. A flotilla model

tobacco	coffee	guns
100	100	100

Fig. 7. A cargo model

mechanism, manually adjust the language metamodel and implement the transformations necessary to make it work. Having done so for one language, we would not be able to reuse the effort spent once we move on to another language. Furthermore, whenever the original language changes (for example, when the representation of ships in TaiPan is modified to give more details of the internal structure of the ships), we would have to manually redo the implementation of the modularisation mechanism—a sheer maintainance nightmare. In this paper, we will provide generic concepts that can be used to easily implement a variety of composition approaches for arbitrary languages, including for the TaiPan and activity-diagram examples.

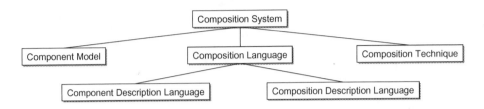

Fig. 8. Terms relevant in describing composition systems

3   Requirements for a Language-Independent Modularisation Technique

We can clearly see the need for generic support to implement modularisation techniques for arbitrary domain-specific languages. This section discusses the requirements such a generic support system needs to fulfil. We base our discussion on a classification defined in [11], where a composition system is sub-divided into a *component model,* explaining what components and their interfaces are, a *composition technique,* determining how components can be composed, and finally, a *composition language,* which allows composition programs to be formulated and concrete compositions to be described. Following this classification—an extended overview of which can be seen in Fig. 8—we will consequently discuss our requirements on the component model, the composition technique and the composition language.

3.1   Requirements on the Component Model

The purpose of a component model in a composition system is to define the units of composition that should be usable for modularising a program or model. This requires that the component model defines the notions of components, composition interfaces and consistent compositions.

A definition of the term *component* identifies the units of composition. This can range from a notion of binary, pre-compiled and immutable "black-box" components as defined, for example, for Enterprise Java Beans [17] and CORBA Components [18] to freely modifiable pieces of (structured) text ("white-box" components) as is, for example, the case for some hypermedia document components [19]. Since, in this paper, we are looking for a composition system that is independent of specific component description languages[2], we, of course, require a component definition that is independent of the specific language used in expressing components. In particular, components should be editable, analysable and maintainable by tools already available for the language in which they are expressed, while should also be recognizable as components of the composition system.

A *composition interface* makes explicit what parts of a component can be accessed during composition, i.e. what information about the internal structure of a component can be used when describing and executing compositions and how, if at all, this internal

---

[2] A component description language is a language used to write components.

structure can be adjusted. This is very much related to the different types of components ranging from black-box to white-box. In particular, the composition interface of a component defines whether the component is black-box or white-box or somewhere in-between. For example, the interface of the black-box components of EJB is essentially an operational interface, i.e. a list of signatures of operations that can be invoked on the component to interact with it plus a technique for resolving a component name into a component reference. For white-box, structured-text components, the interface is defined by the structure of the text and the possibility to freely edit this text. We believe that a completely language-independent composition system must necessarily be more open than a black-box system. Note that systems such as CORBA components are language independent only to some degree in that they still restrict components to those being expressed in programming languages that can be hidden behind an operational interface. We want to be more generic and also include modelling languages and other techniques. At the same time, completely white-box systems give too little control to component authors, and therefore we require a "grey-box" approach, i.e. an approach where the structure of components can be inspected and manipulated during composition, but the component author can control, through explicitly defined composition interfaces, the amount of inspection and manipulation possible. A similar idea has recently been advocated in AOP through the concept of explicit pointcut interfaces (XPIs) [20].

Consistent composition refers to conditions that must be fulfilled for two components to be composable in a certain manner. In effect, this refines the constraints imposed by composition interfaces, expressing not only what parts of a component's structure can be manipulated, but also how much these parts can be manipulated. We can distinguish syntactic and semantic consistency. For example, the structure of text in the white-box hypermedia systems discussed above provides syntactic consistency by asking that the result of any composition (however much the individual components are modified) must respect the structural constraints of the hypermedia language; that is, the composition result must be syntactically well formed. Semantic consistency requires that semantic constraints induced by one component must not be weakened when the component is used in a composition. For example, for black-box operation components (such as CORBA components), we require that no behaviours that are not acceptable for a component in isolation become acceptable simply by the component being used in a composition. Semantic consistency very much depends on the specific semantics of the component language. As semantics can differ very widely, we will restrict ourselves to syntactic consistency in this paper.

3.2   Requirements on the Composition Language

The composition language of a composition system provides means of expressing *composition programs,* that is, of describing concrete compositions of concrete components. Therefore, it needs to provide syntactic constructs denoting components and their interfaces as well as for denoting individual steps in a composition. As other formal languages, composition languages can be either declarative or imperative in nature. Because they allow more freedom in actually executing the composition, we prefer declarative composition languages.

Composition languages can be sub-divided into two parts:

1. *Component Description Language:* This is a language used to describe components and their interfaces. It can be used either in addition to the component language or can be used as an extension of the component language. In any case, because we are looking for a technique independent of the component language, it must provide its constructs with minimum impact on the component language. In particular, if tools exist for analysing, editing or compiling components, these must not be affected by the component description language.
2. *Composition Description Language:* This language is used to describe compositions of existing components. It should provide generic constructs for referencing components and their externally visible interfaces, and for expressing their composition. When using a composition description language, it should not be necessary to know what language components are expressed in. As a relaxation of this requirement, in this paper, we restrict ourselves to compositions of components that are all written in the same language. In the future, it should also be possible to compose components of different languages.

3.3 Requirements on the Composition Technique

The purpose of a composition technique in a composition system is to provide semantics to the composition language. The composition technique defines the basic composition operators that can be used in the composition description language and explains their effects in terms of the composition result. Furthermore, it explains how composition programs are interpreted.

We need a composition technique that can be defined independent of the language in which components are written. We find that, in this case, it is easiest to provide a composition technique based on rewriting of components.

4   Extending Invasive Software Composition for Model Composition

This section presents our solution to the requirements for a language-independent system for model composition described in the previous section.

4.1 A Language-Independent Component Model for Model Composition

As indicated in Sect. 3.1, a component model needs to define what the components and their interfaces are. In addition, a *generic* component model needs to do so independent of the language used for expressing the individual components. Our component-model definition is based on concepts from ISC [11,12,13]. Figure 9 gives a graphical overview of the main concepts of our component model. In the following, we will present and discuss these concepts. We will begin by discussing our notion of components—fragments or fragment components—followed by a discussion of the interface of such components.

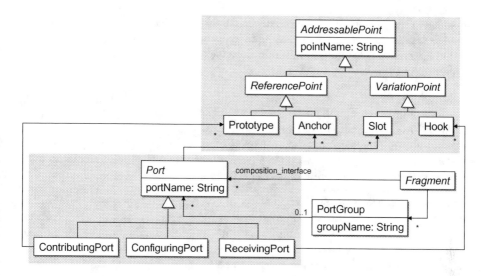

Fig. 9. Component model. These are the concepts available for describing components and their interfaces.

Fragment Components. We introduce the concept of a *fragment component*—or *fragment* for short—as our notion of a component. A fragment is a partial expression in some formal language. This underlying language is called the *core language*. A fragment can be partial in two ways:

1. A fragment can be *incomplete*. For textual languages, this means the fragment is derived from a non-terminal other than the start symbol of the core-language grammar. For a graphical language with a metamodel whose instances are not necessarily trees, incompleteness means that the fragment only represents a sub-graph of a valid metamodel instance. In our activity-diagram example, any combination of activities and transitions would be an incomplete fragment unless they were also embedded in an activity diagram and had at least one start and one stop activity.
2. A fragment can be *generic*. This means that some part of the fragment (whether incomplete or not) is (intentionally) missing. For textual core languages, we can potentially leave open any non-terminal defined in the core-language grammar. For graphical languages, we can make almost any metamodel class generic.

To express genericity of a fragment, we introduce *variation points*. These are elements within a fragment that can be used as place-holders for other fragments leaving some part of a fragment unspecified. Further, we also need to be able to address fragments or parts thereof. To this end, we introduce fragment *reference points*. Reference points address fragments or sub-fragments and give them a name so that they can be used in compositions. Hence, in general, a composition occurs when a variation point in one fragment is replaced by another fragment addressed through some reference point. Thus, variation points can be likened to formal parameters of procedures in imperative programming, while reference points are similar to actual parameters for a composition.

Taking this analogy one step further, we need to distinguish between two cases that are very similar to the passing of parameters "by value" or "by reference" that we often find in imperative programming: We introduce the following two pairs of variation and reference points:

1. *Hook–Prototype.* This corresponds to the intuitive notion of binding a fragment to a variation point: The fragment, addressed by a *prototype* reference point, is copied and then replaces the *hook* variation point.
2. *Slot–Anchor.* In analogy to the concept of passing by reference, no new copies of any fragment are created when an *anchor* is bound to a *slot*. Instead, references to the *slot* are replaced by references to the *anchor*.

It should be noted that when we say "replace" above, this does not necessarily imply that the variation point is removed from its fragment. Whether a variation point is removed after a composition step depends only on the maximum multiplicity of the references pointing at it. A variation point is only removed after its maximum multiplicity has been reached. Therefore, variation points can be bound multiple times as long as their maximum multiplicity allows it.

Composition Interfaces. A fragment is addressed during composition through its *composition interface*. Before we describe the details of fragment composition interfaces, we have to be aware that these interfaces are seen from two different perspectives.

1. *Fragment developer viewpoint.* The fragment developers (persons who write fragments) look at the interfaces from "inside" of the fragment components. They define the interfaces and link them to the fragment's contents.
2. *Fragment user viewpoint.* The fragment user (persons who reuse fragments defined earlier) look at the composition interfaces from the "outside". They address the fragments in composition programs, without looking at the internal details of the fragments.

A fragment composition interface is a collection of *port*s. Fragment developers define the ports and assign them unique names. Furthermore, they link each port to a set of variation and reference points in the fragment. Fragment users can then write composition programs in which they describe a composition by linking ports of different fragments.

In addition to the grouping of addressable points into ports, ports can be organised in port groups. A port group indicates to the fragment user that a set of ports should be addressed together in a composition program. Fragment developers can decide how they apply the two abilities of grouping addressable points according to the task at hand. The more addressable points are grouped into a port, the more abstract the interface becomes: details are hidden from the fragment user. If the grouping is shifted into port groups with several ports, the interface becomes less abstract and more responsibility is transferred to the fragment developer, as well as more flexibility.

The two important properties of a fragment's composition interface are that it is *quantifying* and *typed*. The former supports the high abstraction of interfaces, the latter the consistent composition:

- *Quantifying* refers to the fact that a port collects a set of variation and reference points that are handled together during composition. The linkage between ports and addressable points can be expressed not only by explicitly assigning points to a port but also by giving a quantifying query expression over the set of addressable points in a fragment. This grouping is independent of any structure dictated by the fragment's content.
- The *typing* of a port is determined by the typing of its associated addressable points. These are typed in two dimensions: First, as discussed above, we distinguish four different types of addressable points: namely hooks, prototypes, slots, and anchors. Since these types are given by the generic component model we call this the *language-independent type* of the addressable point. Second, each variation point represents a specific metaclass and each reference point references an instance of a specific metaclass; hence, all addressable points are also typed by the metaclass they are associated with. Such a metaclass is given by a concrete language and is therefore the *language-dependent type* of the addressable point. The language-independent (language-dependent) type of a port is the set of all the language-independent (language-dependent) types of its associated addressable points.

Ports are categorised into three different categories by their language-independent types:

1. *Configuring Ports* contain only slots and anchors. They are used to configure a fragment (by re-routing references from slots to anchors) and not to extend it with additional model elements. Notice that using only configuration ports in a composition description makes no sense, as they can only be used to configure the composition result.
2. *Contributing Ports* contain prototypes (but no hooks). They offer content (i.e. addition model elements) as extension to a fragment. They may also contain slots or anchors for configuration.
3. *Receiving Ports* contain hooks (but no prototypes). They allow a fragment to be extended with additional model elements. They may also contain slots or anchors for configuration.

The distinction made above has conceptual and technical reasons. Conceptually, the fragment user can easily recognise whether a port contributes new elements or expects a contribution of elements without looking at the addressable points behind the port. Since slots and anchors cannot be used to add new model elements to fragments, they do not influence the contributing/receiving character of a port. The technical reason for the distinction is that our composition technique needs to know, at each point of the composition process between two fragments, which fragment is contributing and which one is receiving model elements. The reasons for this will be explained in the context of our composition technique in Sect. 4.3.

Configuring ports should be grouped with receiving or contributing ports into port groups. The reason is that configuration (i.e. cross-referencing) makes no sense before fragments are actually integrated. Thus, addressing configuring ports independently in a composition program is not useful. Furthermore, the more abstract the interface, the less often configuring ports are required—the slots and anchors are contained directly in the contributing and receiving ports.

4.2   A Generic Composition Language for Model Composition

As stated in Sect. 3.2, the composition language can be split into the *Component Description Language* and the *Composition Description Language*. A component description language is used by the *fragment developer* to describe fragments and their interfaces. A composition description language is used by the *fragment user* to define fragment composition programs. Thus, both languages inherit concepts of the component model defined in the last section.

In our setting, the component description language can be any existing (or just developed) modelling language (a *core language*), extended to support the definition of fragment composition interfaces. We call such an extended language a *reuse language*. If this extension is done following the same formalism for any language, the composition description language can be defined independent of any specific component description language. This is because the composition description language only relies on the extended part of the reuse language, which is based on the concepts of the language-independent fragment component model.

This section first describes the possibilities and the formalism to extend a core language by extending its metamodel to make it usable as a component description language. It then describes the (language-independent) composition description language.

Component Description Language. To turn an arbitrary core language into a reuse language, which is usable as a component description language in our approach, we need to perform a language extension. Two methods are applicable for this:

1. *Extending the Core Language Metamodel.* This method can be used to inject constructs for variation and reference point definitions into the core language. This enables the fragment author to declare the interface of each fragment individually by defining variation points and marking model elements as reference points. A drawback, in some cases, is that tools which are already implemented on the basis of the original metamodel might break[3]. For example, models containing variation points may not be accepted by tooling based on the original metamodel. Alternatively, such new metamodel constructs may be ignored by the tooling, or in the worst case, even removed from the model.

2. *Defining OCL Expressions over the Component Language Metamodel.* In this approach, we define how the composition interface is extracted from fragments defined in the core language. This approach can be used for two purposes: First, it avoids the need for language extension because original language concepts can be selected to represent addressable points (e.g. through naming conventions). Second, it can be used to define a default interface for fragments which does not require explicit declaration by the fragment developer. Note that structural queries over metamodel instances, as enabled by OCL, are sufficient because we only consider static compositions of development artefacts.

---

[3] As will be explained later, the extension is restricted and does not harm existing language constructs. If the language tools are build openly and allow for extension, the language extension approach may still be feasible.

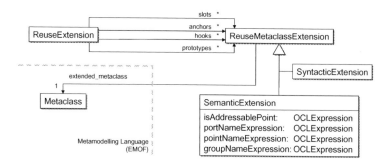

Fig. 10. Metamodel of the reuse-extension language

Effectively, both approaches extend the core language. The first one syntactically and semantically—by introducing new meaningful constructs into the core language. The second one only semantically—by giving additional meaning to existing constructs. In the following, we will refer to the first approach as a *syntactic language extension* and to the second approach as a *semantic language extension*. Both concepts can also be combined when extending a metamodel.

We call all such metamodel extensions *reuse extensions*. Figure 10 shows the metamodel of a small language we use to describe reuse extensions. Reuse extensions can be performed to provide constructs for expressing each of the four types of addressable points. Hence, a `ReuseExtension` collects four sets of `ReuseMetaclassExtensions`, one for each type of addressable point (`hook`, `prototype`, `slot` and `anchor`). Each `ReuseMetaclassExtension` defines the extension on the basis of a metaclass of the core metamodel[4].

For each type of metamodel extension, there is a specific subclass of `ReuseMetaclassExtension`. Semantic language extensions are captured by the `SemanticExtension` metaclass. The specific extension is defined by the following four attributes, of which two are mandatory and two optional:

1. *isAddressablePoint (required).* This is a constraint expressed on instances of the core metaclass. It results in true for those instances that should be interpreted as addressable points. Note that the language-independent type of the addressable point is already determined by the association from `ReuseExtension`.
2. *portNameExpression (required).* If the *isAddressablePoint* constraint holds, this expression is used to extract the name of the port this addressable point belongs to.
3. *pointNameExpression (optional).* If the addressable point has a specific name, this expression is used to extract it.
4. *groupNameExpression (optional).* If the addressable point and its port should belong to a specific port group, this expression is used to extract the name of the group.

Syntactic language extensions are more involved, because we also need to modify the metamodel of the core language itself. Specifically, we need to introduce specific

---

[4] Throughout the paper, we refer to the core metamodel as the metamodel representing the core language.

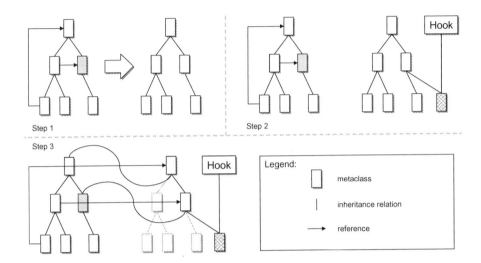

Fig. 11. Steps of the language extension algorithm

metaclasses to be used for expressing addressable points. Such addressable-point meta-model instances should be substitutable for their corresponding core metaclass every-where in the extended language. For example, in the TaiPan example, we want to be able to place a cargo hook wherever we would be able to place a specific piece of cargo. At the same time, however, addressable points should not share any features specific to core language elements. For example, for a cargo hook, we need not to express a cargo name and amount. Typically, in metamodels, we use inheritance to express sub-stitutability. However, we also use inheritance to share features between language el-ements. Therefore, simply inserting new elements into the inheritance structure of the core language would not fit our requirements. Instead, we need to use a slightly more involved algorithm. Figure 11 illustrates the steps of this algorithm using a symbolic example. In the following, we explain each step in turn:

1. *Type hierarchy extraction.* To separate the use of inheritance for substitutability from its use for feature sharing, we duplicate the hierarchy of metamodel elements of the core metamodel. For each core metaclass, we create a new abstract metaclass and call it the *type metaclass* of the core metaclass. For each inheritance relation-ship between two core metaclasses, an inheritance relationship between the corre-sponding type metaclasses is introduced. (This is represented in Fig. 11 by simple lines connecting two boxes. The upper box represents the super class of the lower box.) In step 1 of Fig. 11, we show a symbolic core metamodel on the left and the derived corresponding type hierarchy on the right. Notice that the type hierarchy contains only classes and inheritance relations, but no references or other features within these classes.

2. *Addressable point introduction.* For each `ReuseMetaclassExtension`, we introduce an *addressable point metaclass* into the type hierarchy. The address-able point metaclass inherits from the type metaclass of the core metaclass that is

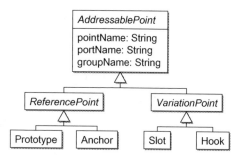

Fig. 12. Common metamodel that is integrated into reuse languages with syntactical extensions

extended. In the figure, we show how one core metaclass (the grey one) is extended. To this end, we introduce a new class in the type hierarchy, represented by a hashed box in the figure.

In addition, we integrate into each reuse language the metamodel from Fig. 12 introducing the different types of addressable points available. Depending on the type of addressable point that is to be introduced for the core metaclass, the new class in the type hierarchy also inherits from the corresponding class from Fig. 12. For our TaiPan example from above, this would be the Hook metaclass. For prototype and anchor metaclasses, a reference (*content*) to the core metaclass is also added to hold the actual model element that is referenced.

3. *Reference redirection.* Finally, the two hierarchies of metaclasses need to be integrated so that the new metaclasses from the type hierarchy are used instead of the original core metaclasses. To this end, every reference to an extended core metaclass (or to a superclass of an extended core metaclass) is redirected to the corresponding type metaclass. Each core metaclass to which references existed that have been redirected is made a subclass of its type metaclass. As a result, instances of the extended core metaclass are substitutable by addressable points.

After the metamodel extension for a specific core language, fragments can be written and their interfaces can be defined in the extended language. A composition system can extract interfaces from the fragments to make them explicit by analysing the model elements of the fragment. All elements that are either instances of a subclass of a metaclass from Fig. 12 or on which an *isAddressablePoint* constraint holds define the composition interface of the fragment.

Composition Description Language. Figure 13 depicts the concepts of our Composition Description Language. A *CompositionProgram* consists of several *Fragment*s and their composition interface that is represented by *Port*s. A Port can either be a *ConfiguringPort*, a *ContributingPort* or a *ReceivingPort*. Composition is realised through different *CompositionStep*s where each CompositionStep consists of *CompositionLink*s between two ConfiguringPorts (a *ConfigurationLink*) or one ContributingPort and one ReceivingPort (a *ContributionLink*).

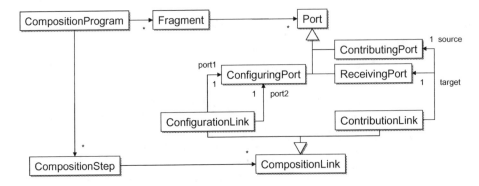

Fig. 13. Metamodel of the Composition Description Language

We defined a graphical syntax for expressing compositions of fragments that includes concepts for representing fragments, their composition ports and composition links between those. In addition, means for defining composition steps are provided. This syntax is supported by a graphical editor that is built on top of the Eclipse Platform [21] and the Graphical Modeling Framework (GMF) [16]. An example of a fragment composition program written in our editor is shown in Fig. 14. The pallette on the right offers means to create composition links, composition steps, participations of composition links in composition steps and so-called fragment queries, which will be examined later.

In our editor, a fragment is represented by a rectangle that has its composition ports attached as circles, where contributing ports are depicted as black circles, receiving ports as white circles and configuring ports as white circles with a dashed line. The composition ports are automatically extracted from the fragment when the fragment is dropped onto the editor canvas. Composition links are represented as lines between composition ports. A configuring link is shown as a dashed line and a contributing link, which defines a direction of composition from the contributing to the receiving port, as an arrow visualising this direction. Within the fragment, a composition port group— represented by a small rectangle—is connected to its participating composition ports. To allow for grouping of composition links to steps, syntax for defining composition steps is necessary. A composition step is represented by an ellipse that references all associated composition links by dashed lines.

Sometimes, multiple fragments need to be composed in essentially similar ways. In our activity-diagram example, there may be more than one check activity fragment to be woven into the core activity. Although we could express each such composition individually, this would require a lot of duplication in the composition code. To avoid such duplication, we introduce the syntactical concept of *fragment queries*. An example of a fragment query is the dashed box named FragmentA.* in Fig. 14. Note that this is purely a concept of the composition language as every composition including a fragment query can be transformed into a set of compositions without queries.

Fragment queries group a set of fragments and treat the complete group like a single fragment. Figure 15 shows an overview of the essential syntactical concepts involved in

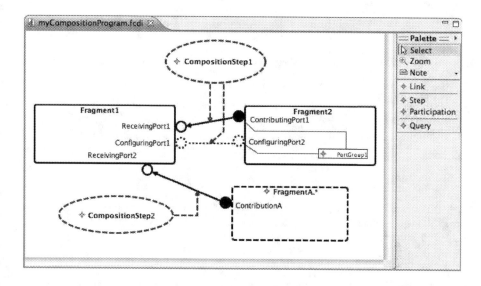

Fig. 14. Fragment Composition Editor

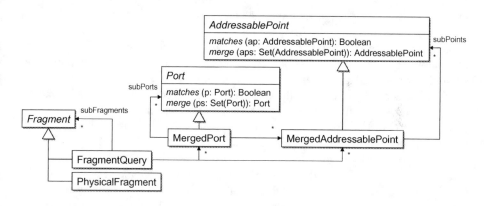

Fig. 15. Essential concepts of fragment queries

expressing fragment queries. It can be seen that fragment queries can be nested hierarchically inside each other. An elemental fragment, as defined in the component model, is represented by the `PhysicalFragment` class in the figure.

Fragment queries can be defined in essentially two ways: a) by enumerating the fragments to be encompassed by the query and b) by providing an expression describing the set of fragments to be included. Both approaches are supported by our composition language using regular expressions as query expressions. Fragment queries add an additional level of quantification to the composition. It is interesting to see that this enables us to distinguish quantification introduced by fragment developers (using groupings between variation and reference points) and fragment users (using fragment queries).

```
1   context AddressablePoint::matches (ap: AddressablePoint) : Boolean
2   post: result = (typeMatch (ap)) and
3                   (pointName = ap.pointName) and
4                   (apElements.type->forAll (t1 |
5                       ap.apElements.type->forAll (c2 | c2 = c1)
6                   ))
7
8   context AddressablePoint::typeMatch (ap: AddressablePoint) : Boolean
9   post: result = (self.oclIsKindOf (Prototype) and ap.oclIsKindOf (Prototype)) or
10                  (self.oclIsKindOf (Anchor)    and ap.oclIsKindOf (Anchor)) or
11                  (self.oclIsKindOf (Slot)      and ap.oclIsKindOf (Slot)) or
12                  (self.oclIsKindOf (Hook)      and ap.oclIsKindOf (Hook)) or
13                  (self.oclIsKindOf (MergedAddressablePoint) and
14                   subPoints->forAll(ape | ap.typeMatch(ape))) or
15                  (ap.oclIsKindOf (MergedAddressablePoint) and
16                   ap.elements->forAll(ape | self.typeMatch(ape)))
```

Listing 1. Definition of matching between addressable points. Two addressable points should be merged if they have the same name, are of the same type, and the type of the elements they are associated with is the same.

This adds a new level of control not supported by typical AOP/AOM realisations in the literature.

To be able to view a fragment query as a fragment again, we need to define how the fragment query's composition interface is determined. Basically, the composition interface of a fragment query reflects the interfaces of its element fragments. However, variation and reference points of the same name and type that occur in different element fragments are merged into one variation or reference point for the fragment query and similarly for ports and port groups. To precisely define how the composition interface of a fragment query is derived from the composition interfaces of its element fragments, we need to introduce a few helper concepts. To do so, in the following, we use the Object Constraint Language (OCL) [22] to formally express additional concepts for our metamodel classes. The OCL constraints we will show in Listings 1 to 5 are hence an integral part of the metamodel of our composition description language.

First, we need to define which variation or reference points should be merged. To this end, in Fig. 15, we have introduced the operation `matches()` on addressable points that returns `true` if two addressable points are sufficiently equal to be merged into one. Listing 1 shows the definition of `matches()`. Note that these functions make use of a—previously unshown—association from addressable points to elements of a fragment. This association is accessed through its association end `apElements`.

The merging of matching addressable points is represented by another operation: `merge()`. Listing 2 shows its specification. This operation always creates a `Merged-AddressablePoint` collecting all the merged addressable points. Note that anchors can only be merged with anchors, slots with slots, hooks with hooks and prototypes with prototypes. The introduction of a `MergedAddressablePoint` allows composition interfaces of fragment queries to be viewed in two ways:

1. From the outside, the addressable points in the composition interface of a fragment query look just like any other addressable point. In particular, the elements they refer to can be accessed through the `apElements` association end.

```
1   context AddressablePoint::merge (aps: Set(AddressablePoint)): AddressablePoint
2   pre:  aps->forAll (ap | self.matches (ap))
3   post: (typeMatch (result)) and
4         (result.oclIsKindOf (MergedAddressablePoint)) and
5         (result.pointName = pointName) and
6         (result.subPoints = aps->collect (ap |
7             if (ap.oclIsKindOf(MergedAddressablePoint)) then
8                 ap.subPoints
9             else
10                ap
11            endif
12        )->union (
13            if (self.oclIsKindOf (MergedAddressablePoint)) then
14                self.subPoints
15            else
16                self
17            endif
18        )) and
19        (result.apElements = result.subPoints.apElements)
```

Listing 2. Merge operation defined for addressable points

```
1   context Port::matches (p: Port) : Boolean
2   post: result = (portName = p.portName) and
3             (addressablePoint->size () = p.addressablePoint->size ()) and
4             (addressablePoint->forAll(ap | p.addressablePoint
5                         ->exists (ap2 | ap.match(ap2)))) and
6             (p.addressablePoint->forAll(ap | addressablePoint
7                         ->exists (ap2 | ap.match(ap2))))
```

Listing 3. Definition of matching between ports. Two ports should be merged if they have the same name and group matching addressable points.

2. The composition system can further inspect merged addressable points and identify for each sub-point the fragment it came from and the elements it refers to. This will be used in describing the composition technique later in this section.

Based on these definitions of how to merge addressable points, we can now define how ports are to be merged: We begin, again, by defining which ports may be merged. We do so in the `matches()` operation of `Port`. Its definition can be seen in Listing 3.

Merging ports is done by merging all matching addressable points in the ports and creating a new `MergedPort` of the same name and with all the merged addressable points inside it. We refrain from expressing this in OCL as it is quite straightforward.

There are various ways of defining a fragment query's composition interface from the composition interfaces of its element fragments:

1. *Maximal interface.* Intuitively, the maximal interface is the union of all composition interfaces of all element fragments where matching ports have been merged as defined by the `merge()` operation.
2. *Minimal interface.* The minimal interface contains only those ports that exist in *all* element fragments. Merging applies as for the maximal interface.
3. *Merging function.* Such a merging function allows to merge ports fulfilling some condition into one port, possibly with a new name. This approach can be combined freely with the two above.

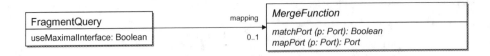

Fig. 16. Metamodel of merge functions

Figure 16 shows the additional metamodel elements required for supporting merge functions and minimal vs. maximal fragment-query interfaces. For each fragment query, we can provide one additional merge function, which will handle all port merges for this query. The merge function provides two query operations: `matchPort` is used to determine if a given port is to be subject to treatment by the merge function and `mapPort` is used to identify the port that is the result of applying the merge function.

Listing 4 shows how the composition interface of a fragment query is derived from the composition interfaces of its element fragments. Lines 4–19 produce the maximal interface, with lines 5–10 taking into account an optional merge function. The remainder from line 20 restricts the interface to the minimal interface if required. Finally, we need to ensure that merged ports in a fragment query respect all the rules imposed by any port groups in the participating fragments. This is shown formally in Listing 5.

Fragment queries expressed in our prototypical graphical composition description language will always use the minimal composition interface. In addition, a merging function can be provided, using regular expressions over port names to express the `matchPort` operation. `mapPort` is implemented implicitly by creating a port with a generated name. Fragment queries are represented by a rectangle with dashed lines (cf. Fig. 14). Accompanying query expressions can be edited via a properties view in the editor.

4.3 A Language-Independent Composition Technique for Model Composition

Once a composition program is defined over a set of fragments, it can be executed, merging the involved fragments into bigger fragments or complete models. In this process, each composition step is executed individually, transforming the fragments involved. We will first look at the overall processing of composition programs and steps and then look into the details of how fragments are merged. The processing of a composition is sketched in Fig. 17 to support the explanations below. At the end, we will shortly discuss the interpretation of fragment queries.

Executing composition steps and programs. A composition program consists of composition steps; each of them is executed individually. Before this can be done, the execution order of the steps has to be determined. This order is controlled by the contribution links. Such a link gives a certain role to the two fragments involved: one fragment (defining the receiving port of the link) is the *receiving fragment,* the other (defining the contributing port of the link) is the *contributing fragment.* Receiving fragments can be compared to *cores* and contributing fragments to *aspects* in AOP. This means that we can weave in a contributing fragment into several receiving fragments. In each composition step, the role of each fragment (involved through one or several links) has to

```
 1   context FragmentQuery
 2   inv compositionInterface =
 3       elementFragments. compositionInterface
 4         ->iterate (p: Port; cmpIntf: Set(Port) = Set{} |
 5           if (mapping->notEmpty() and mapping. matchPort (p)) then
 6             — merge using merging function
 7             cmpIntf->reject (p1 | p1. matches (mapping. mapPort (p)))
 8                   ->including (p. merge (
 9                       cmpIntf->select (p1 | p1. matches (mapping. mapPort (p))))
10                       . rename (mapping. mapPort (p) . name))
11           else
12             if (cmpIntf->exists (p1 | p. matches (p1))) then
13               — merge implicitly matching ports
14               cmpIntf->excluding (p1 | p. matches (p1))
15                     ->including (p. merge (cmpIntf->select (p1 | p. matches (p1))))
16             else
17               cmpIntf->including (p)
18             endif
19         )
20         ->reject (p: Port |
21           (not useMaximalInterface) and
22           elementFragments->exists (f | not f. compositionInterface->exists (
23               p1 | p. matches (p1) or
24                   (mapping->notEmpty() and mapping. matchPort (p1) and
25                     p. matches (mapping. mapPort (p1)))
26             )
27         )
28       )
```

Listing 4. Composition interface of a fragment query

```
 1   context FragmentQuery
 2   inv: subFragments. portGroup->forAll (pg |
 3         self. portGroup->exists (pg2 |
 4           pg2. port. oclAsType (MergedPort). subPorts->containsAll (pg. port)
 5         )
 6       )
```

Listing 5. Port merges must additionally maintain any port groups set up on any contained fragments

be clear. Otherwise, the composition step is invalid. The following restrictions for a composition step can be derived from this:

1. The involvement of a fragment in a composition step has to be defined through at least one contribution link. The other way around: A fragment cannot be involved in a composition step through configuration links only. If it would be, it would neither be receiving nor contributing.
2. If a fragment is involved in a composition step through more than one composition link; all these links have to have the same direction, because a fragment cannot be contributing and receiving within one composition step.

The composition program CP in Fig. 17 defines a composition of the three fragments $F1$, $F2$ and $F3$ by declaring two composition steps, $Step1$ and $Step2$. $F2$ is involved in both steps, because both have links to ports of $F2$. In the context of $Step1$, $F2$ is a receiving fragment while $F3$ is a contributing fragment (and $F1$ is not involved). In

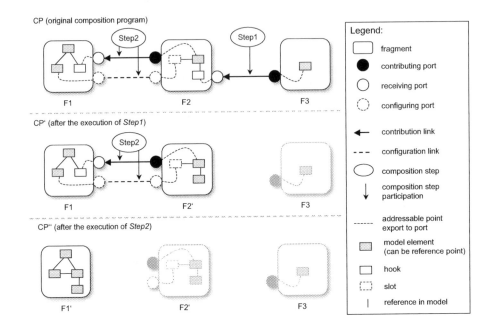

CP (original composition program)

F1   F2   F3

Legend:

fragment

contributing port

receiving port

configuring port

contribution link

configuration link

composition step

composition step participation

addressable point export to port

model element (can be reference point)

hook

slot

reference in model

CP' (after the execution of *Step1*)

F1   F2'   F3

CP'' (after the execution of *Step2*)

F1'   F2'   F3

Fig. 17. Stepwise processing of a composition program

the context of $Step2$, however, $F2$ is a contributing fragment while $F1$ is a receiving fragment (and $F3$ is not involved).

Executing a composition step means that all contributing fragments are integrated into the receiving fragments—resulting in a new set of *composed fragments* of similar size as the set of receiving fragments. During this process, the contributing fragments are not directly integrated, but a *fragment copy* of them. Thus, the original contributing fragments remain available as contributions for other steps executed at a later point.

When a composition step is successfully executed, it is removed from the program and the receiving fragments of the step are replaced by the composed fragments. Thus, the processing of the whole composition program is an iterative process in which eventually all steps have been executed and the set of composed fragments of the last executed step is the result set.

When $Step1$ of CP (cf. Fig. 17) is executed, the result can be visualised as a modified composition program CP': The content of $F3$ (the only contributing fragment) is copied and integrated into $F2$ (the only receiving fragment), leading to $F2'$. $F2$ is replaced by $F2'$ and $Step1$ is removed.

As we have seen, only receiving fragments are modified and contributing ones remain unchanged by the execution of a step. This property determines the execution order of steps. The next step to execute is always one where all contributing fragments are not receiving fragments of any other remaining step in the composition program. Thus, they can be safely copied because further modification cannot occur. Note that—because the execution of a step modifies its receiving fragments and removes the step from the program—fragments that were receiving at the beginning of the composition process lose this property at some point.

In the composition program CP of Fig. 17, $Step1$ can be executed, because its only contributing fragment $F3$ is never a receiving fragment in the context of any step of CP. On the other hand, $Step2$ cannot be executed, because its only contributing fragment $F2$ is a receiving fragment in the context of another step ($Step1$). In CP' however, where $Step1$ has been removed, $Step2$ can be executed resulting in CP''. $F1'$ in CP'' is the resulting model of the complete composition.

It is obvious that invalid composition programs can be defined where no step fulfils the required property—which basically means that they define cyclic dependencies between the fragments. It might also be that such a situation is reached during the iterative execution process if the program is not analysed beforehand. We believe that such invalid programs are counter intuitive and will seldom occur in practice. Should they occur, however, invalid programs can be detected by our tool.

Matching addressable points and merging fragments. Until now, we have described the general process of executing composition steps. What we have not discussed yet is how receiving and contributing fragment are merged concretely when a step is executed.

A merging is done per composition link and involves only the addressable points behind the two ports the link connects. The first thing that has to be done, before the actual merge, is to determine which variation point of a port can be replaced by which reference point of the other port. The first requirement is that anchors can only replace slots and prototypes can only replace hooks (this is the language-independent typing). The second necessary requirement for such a replacement is that the language-dependent types (i.e., the metaclasses for which the addressable points were introduced) of both points *match*. This means the language-dependent type of a reference point has to be the same as, or a subclass of, the language-dependent type of variation point. This ensures that the composed model, where the reference points replaced the variation points, is still a syntactically valid instance of the metamodel of the used component description language.

If, for each prototype involved in a composition step, a hook with a matching type can be found, the composition is executable. This is necessary to physically integrate the fragments. If some hooks, anchors or slots are not addressed, this is in general no problem. It is also possible to address the same hook or slot multiple times if the multiplicity of the affected references allow it. Sometimes also different matches are possible. In such non-deterministic situations, the composition step is not valid.

To increase determinism, further matching strategies for addressable points are needed. We use the naming of addressable points for this purpose: if a reference point could be bound to different variation points, the names of the points are taken into account. This was sufficient for the examples we inspected so far. However, with respect to reuse, the names of the points might not match directly, additional matching strategies—for example based on regular expressions—could be used.

For some compositions, it might well be required that not only the binding of prototypes but also of other kinds of addressable points should be enforced when two ports are linked. These questions, however, very much depend on the concrete language and modularisation approach at hand. Therefore, further experiences are needed to learn about the problems and requirements.

Once all pairs of hook–prototype and slot–anchor bindings are determined, the merging of fragments is simple. For a hook–prototype pair, the *containing reference*[5] to the hook is re-routed to the prototype or, in cases where the prototype concept was introduced by a syntactic metaclass extension, to the element referenced in the *content* reference of the prototypes (cf. Sect. 4.2). This effectively adds content to the fragment that contains the hook. A slot–anchor pair is resolved by taking all *non-containment references* to the slot and re-routing them to the anchor (or to the element referenced in its *content* reference). It should be noted that re-routing references means that a hook or slot can stay referenced for further addressing, if the multiplicities of all affected references allow that.

Note that in the composition illustrated in Fig. 17, each port has only one addressable point. Thus, the matching is straightforward. It is assumed in the figure that the language-dependent types match in all three cases. When $Step1$ and $Step2$ are executed, variation points are replaced with reference points.

Our implementation of the composition technique also enforces that all ports addressed on a contributing fragment in one composition step must be grouped into one port group. While this is redundant for the execution of the composition—the grouping can be assumed by the fact that the ports are addressed together in one step—it is essential information for the developer. If a fragment comes with a large composition interface where different ports should be addressed in different composition steps, the developer would have little chance to know which configuring ports are to be addressed together with which contributing ports.

Executing fragment queries. As mentioned, fragment queries are solely constructs of the composition definition language to ease composition program development. In the general composition program execution process, fragment queries are treated as usual fragments (i.e., they have a receiving or contributing character).

If a composition step is to be executed that involves a fragment query the query is expanded. One can think of this process as drawing each fragment that is grouped by the query individually into the composition program and then defining composition steps for all possible compositions of the single fragments. If we define, for instance, a composition step that involves one fragment query, which groups k fragments, as receiving "fragment" and another fragment query, which groups l fragments, as contributing "fragment" the transformation would produce $l * k$ composition steps. Each of these steps composes one fragment from the first query with one from the second query. Then, all the steps are executed.

If receiving fragments belonged to a fragment query, the corresponding composed fragments are again grouped into a fragment query that replaces the original query in the composition program.

---

[5] A containing reference is a reference that holds the actual definition of an element. Each element in a model (with the exception of one root node) has exactly one. Which references are containing is defined in the metamodel.

In this section, we have demonstrated our language-independent model composition approach in detail. In the next section, we explain how the approach and its concepts have been implemented in a tool that can be used to solve the problems shown in the introductory examples: the Reuseware Composition Framework.

5 Tooling: The Reuseware Composition Framework

The previous section demonstrated our language-independent model composition approach and its concepts. These concepts were implemented in the Reuseware Composition Framework, available from [12]. The implementation is based on the Eclipse Modelling Framework (EMF) [23]. In this section, we briefly describe the architecture of the tool, which we use in the next section to realise concrete solutions for the problems shown in the introductory examples.

The tooling is split into a developer kit, which is used to instantiate the framework for concrete languages, and run time tooling, which is used by the end-users of composition systems. Section 5.1 describes the developer tooling and Sect. 5.2 the run time functionality.

5.1 CoMoGen: The Reuseware Development Kit

The development kit is named *CoMoGen*, which stands for *Component Model Generator*. The name was given by the central functionality provided by the tool—generating a new component model for a given language based on its metamodel. CoMoGen offers the *reuse extension* metalanguage in which a developer can express syntactic as well as semantic reuse extensions (cf. Sect. 4.2).

Figure 18 shows the architecture of CoMoGen. On the lowest layer, it uses the functionality of EMF: EMF's resource management is used to load and store metamodels; EMF's code generation is applied to generate metamodel code; EMF's metamodeling facilities—arranged around the metalanguage *Ecore*[6]—are utilised to construct, modify and annotate metamodels.

Next, CoMoGen interacts with other EMF-based metamodeling tools that provide metamodels and other specifications, for instance, about a language's syntax. Examples of such tools are Ecore metamodel editors (such as the one contained in [25]), the mentioned GMF [16] or tools for defining textual syntax (such as *EMFText* [26]).

Our implementation then offers facilities to define composition systems (e.g., an editor for the reuse extension language) and the component model generator itself, which modifies Ecore metamodels following the algorithm from Sect. 4.2 and adds annotations with OCL expressions to the metamodels using Ecore's annotation mechanism.

5.2 CoCoNut: The Reuseware Run Time

CoCoNut, the *Composition Core Runtime*, implements the composition algorithm and provides tooling to define concrete model compositions. Due to the language independence of our approach, the tooling, which is based on the language-independent concepts only, can be reused in any composition system defined with Reuseware.

---

[6] Ecore implements the OMG's EMOF standard [24].

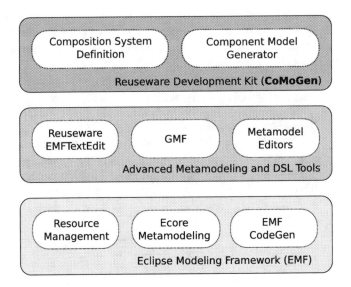

Fig. 18. Overview of the Reuseware Development Kit (CoMoGen) architecture

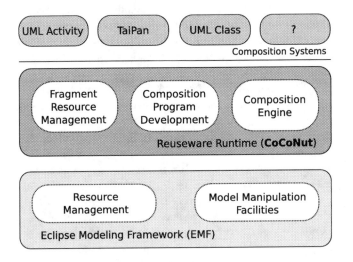

Fig. 19. Overview of the Reuseware Runtime (CoCoNut) architecture

The CoCoNut architecture is shown in Fig. 19. Again, we use EMF's model resource management and Ecore-based model manipulation facilities to load, save and compose model fragments. On top of this, CoCoNut implements an extended resource management, which explicitly knows about model fragments. This means that it can identify fragments by unique identifiers and can present them—for instance, in a fragment browser—by showing only their composition interfaces. Furthermore, CoCoNut includes composition program development tools such as the editor presented in

Sect. 4.2. The composition engine implements the composition algorithm described in Sect. 4.3 by using EMF facilities to copy and compose fragments in memory.

All components of CoCoNut are aware of the concepts of our composition approach. They know that a certain element of a model fragment belongs to the fragment's composition interface by inspecting its metaclass and evaluating OCL expressions annotated to the fragment's metamodel. Thus, a new composition system can be plugged into Co-CoNut by providing a metamodel that has been extended and annotated by CoMoGen. No additional implementation effort is required.

Latest information about the Reuseware Composition Framework and the available tooling can be found on the Reuseware website [12].

6   Examples

In this section, we take up the examples introduced in Sect. 2. For each example, we will demonstrate how the language extension (cf. Sect. 4.2) is performed to make the applied modelling language a suitable component description language. Next, we show how the composition interfaces for the example components are defined and discuss the composition programs producing the desired results. Then, we briefly look at possible variations of the composition programs to highlight the advantages of using fragment model components rather than monolithic models.

6.1   Implementation of a Simple Business Process Extension System

To extend the UML activity diagram language, we perform only semantic extensions to maintain tool support. However, to give the fragment developer control over defining addressable points, we apply a small UML profile and use semantic extensions to map applied stereotypes to addressable points. The profile (*reuseuml*) is tailored for the activity diagram scenario and is simplistic: it defines two stereotypes *Anchor* and *Slot* each with the tagged values *portName*, *groupName* and *pointName*.

Table 1 enumerates all semantic extensions we defined. In (1) and (3), we define that each activity offers an implicit extension point: one of the nodes (edges) is, in addition to its native semantics, also a hook. We group them together into a port named after the activity's name such that they appear as a single extension point for the activity (a receiving port). In (2) and (4), all elements contained in an activity (i.e. its nodes and edges) are identified as prototypes and associated with a port named after the activity's name. Only nodes that have the *Slot* stereotype applied are ignored here. At last, (5) and (6) define that nodes with a *Slot* (or *Anchor*) stereotype are treated as slots (or anchors respectively). The properties of the addressable point are derived from the tagged values of the stereotype application[7].

We are now ready to prepare the order processing model from Fig. 1 and the credit card check model from Fig. 2 for composition. The order processing model now implicitly offers a receiving port *OrderProcessingExtensionPoint* (cf. 1 and 3 in Table 1).

---

[7] The operation *self.getValue (stereotypeApplication, 'taggedValue')* can be used in the Eclipse UML2 [27] implementation, which we use in our tool to obtain a tagged value of an applied stereotype.

Table 1. Semantic UML language extension in the following format: (*ref. number*) (*type of variation point*) extension: (*metaclass*)

(1) hook extension: ActivityNode

isAddressablePoint	self = self.activity.node–>any (true)
portNameExpression	self.activity.name.concat('ExtensionPoint')

(2) prototype extension: ActivityNode

isAddressablePoint	self.getAppliedStereotype('reuseuml::Slot').oclIsUndefined()
portNameExpression	self.activity.name.concat('Definition')
groupNameExpression	self.activity.name

(3) hook extension: ActivityEdge

isAddressablePoint	self = self.activity.edge–>any (true)
portNameExpression	self.activity.name.concat('ExtensionPoint')

(4) prototype extension: ActivityEdge

isAddressablePoint	true
portNameExpression	self.activity.nam.concat('Definition')
groupNameExpression	self.activity.name

(5) slot extension: ActivityNode

isAddressablePoint	not self.getAppliedStereotype('reuseuml::Slot').oclIsUndefined()
portNameExpression	self.getValue(self.getAppliedStereotype('reuseuml::Slot'), 'portName')
groupNameExpression	self.getValue(self.getAppliedStereotype('reuseuml::Slot'), 'groupName')
pointNameExpression	self.getValue(self.getAppliedStereotype('reuseuml::Slot'), 'pointName')

(6) anchor extension: ActivityNode

isAddressablePoint	not self.getAppliedStereotype('reuseuml::Anchor').oclIsUndefined()
portNameExpression	self.getValue(self.getAppliedStereotype('reuseuml::Anchor'),'portName')
groupNameExpression	self.getValue(self.getAppliedStereotype('reuseuml::Anchor'),'groupName')
pointNameExpression	self.getValue(self.getAppliedStereotype('reuseuml::Anchor'),'pointName')

In addition, the *checkFork*, *checkJoin* and *checkMerge* nodes should be addressable to connect additional check activities to them. We do that by applying stereotypes to these nodes and setting the tagged values *portName* and *pointName* as shown in Table 2.

The credit card check model implicitly exports its content, i.e. its two actions and all control flows—to a contributing port *CreditCardCheckDefinition* (cf. 2 and 4 in Table 1). To connect the edges correctly to the nodes of the order processing model later, we apply the slot stereotype on the initial and final nodes of the credit card check model. We add them to the *CreditCardCheck* group and give them the same point names (cf. Table 3) as used for the anchors (cf. Table 2) in the order processing model. This enables the composition engine to match the anchors and slots as desired.

We now load the fragments into the composition program editor that displays their composition interfaces only. In the composition program, we link the contributing port *CreditCardCheckDefinition* with the receiving port *OrderProcessExtensionPoint* and the two configuring ports *CreditCardCheck* and *CheckActivitiesExtension*. The two links are assigned to the step *ActivityComposition*. When we execute the composition program using our implementation of the composition technique from Sect. 4.3, we obtain a composed model as shown in Fig. 3.

Table 2. Anchor stereotype applications on the process order model (cf. Fig. 1) in the following format: << (*stereotype*) >> (*targeted model element*) : (*metaclass*)

<<**reuseuml::Anchor**>> **checkFork : ForkNode**

portName	CheckActivity
pointName	IN
groupName	

<<**reuseuml::Anchor**>> **checkJoin : JoinNode**

portName	CheckActivity
pointName	OUT_YES
groupName	

<<**reuseuml::Anchor**>> **checkMerge : MergeNode**

portName	CheckActivity
pointName	OUT_NO
groupName	

Table 3. Slot stereotype applications on the credit card check model (cf. Fig. 2)

<<**reuseuml::Slot**>> **InitialNodeCREDIT : InitalNode**

portName	CheckActivity
pointName	IN
groupName	CreditCardCheck

<<**reuseuml::Slot**>> **FINISH : FinalNode**

portName	CheckActivity
pointName	OUT_YES
groupName	CreditCardCheck

<<**reuseuml::Slot**>> **CANCEL : FinalNode**

portName	CheckActivity
pointName	OUT_NO
groupName	CreditCardCheck

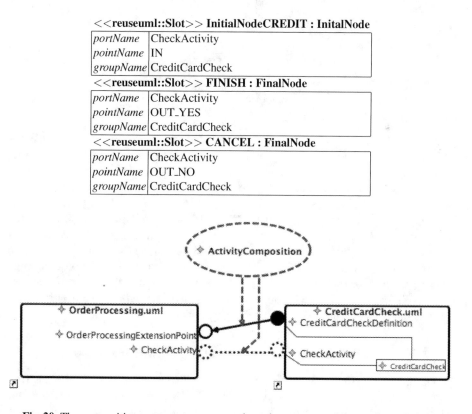

Fig. 20. The composition program to compose the order process and the credit card check

Table 4. Taipan language extension

(1) hook extension: Ship

isAddressablePoint	self = self.aquatory.ships–>any (true)
portNameExpression	'shipExtension'

(2) prototype extension: Ship

isAddressablePoint	true
groupNameExpression	flotilla
portNameExpression	ships

(3) slot extension: Port

syntactic extension

(4) anchor extension: Port

isAddressablePoint	true
portNameExpression	self.location.concat('Port')

(5) slot extension: Route

syntactic extension

(6) anchor extension: Route

isAddressablePoint	true
portNameExpression	self.description

(7) hook extension: LargeItem

syntactic extension

(8) prototype extension: LargeItem

isAddressablePoint	true
portNameExpression	self.article

This example has demonstrated how a system for the desired activity diagram composition can be defined. With this system, similar activity extensions and variations can be defined and executed. For instance, imagine a scenario where a large set of check activities that all declare a contributing port with an *IN*, an *OUT_YES* and an *OUT_NO* slot (i.e. offer a similar composition interface) are available in a library. There might be checks related to software products (*CheckSW*.uml*) and checks related to hardware products (*CheckHW*.uml*). Companies want to incorporate checks according to the products they sell into their ordering process. We can use a fragment query to tailor the process by selecting a set of activities and composing them into the ordering process. By varying the query, we can adjust the defined system to the customer's needs: *CheckSW*.uml* for a software selling company, *CheckHW*.uml* for a hardware selling company and *Check*.uml* for a company selling both (Fig. 20).

6.2   Implementation of a Modular Ship and Cargo Distribution System

To add modularisation to the TaiPan language, we also use *syntactic* extensions. This is possible because the tooling is generated with GMF and can be regenerated and extended. Nevertheless, we also define some semantic metaclass extensions to introduce a default composition interface for certain model components.

Table 4 enumerates all extensions performed. Extensions (1), (4) and (6) are defined to make an aquatory model component extensible. Note that these are all semantic

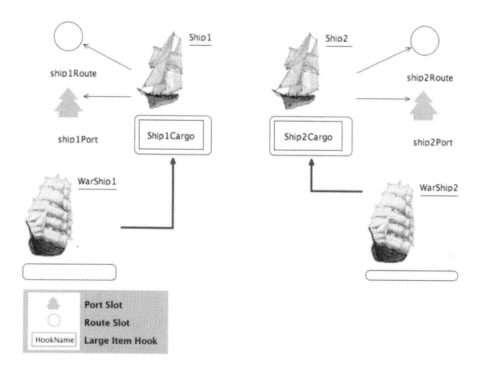

Fig. 21. The flotilla model with slots and hooks

extensions that define hooks (to put ships into the aquatory) and anchors (to enable ships to address ports and routes). Thus, they define a default (or implicit) interface for aquatory models and save the developer of such models the effort of defining each hook and anchor explicitly. Still, the developer should be aware of the existence of the default interface, which he can always inspect in our composition program editor. All the syntactic extensions, (3), (5) and (7), are intended for the developers of *flotilla* model components. They can use slots for the ports and routes of ships. Inside the cargo bays of ships, they can define hooks for large items. In addition, extension (2) will automatically export each individual ship to the composition interface. Extension (8) defines all large items in *cargo* model components to be prototypes such that they can be addressed for composition with flotilla models.

The port and cargo models (cf. Figs. 5 and 7) do not require any further editing, because they only offer a default interface. The flotilla is extended with defined slots and hooks. We extended the TaiPan graphical editor to support the declaration of these elements and used them in Fig. 21[8].

---

[8] This was a surprisingly easy task, because the editor was generated from a very abstract model (called *sketch model* in GMF) that assigns graphical representations to metaclasses. So we only had to select graphics for slot and hook representations and assign them to the slot and hook metaclasses of the reuse metamodel and then regenerate the editor.

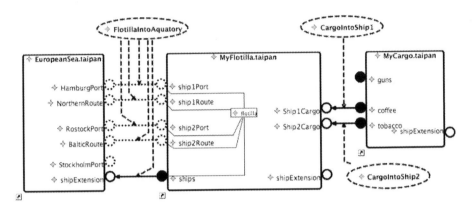

Fig. 22. The composition program to compose the aquatory, flotilla and cargo model components

Figure 22 displays the composition program that composes the example aquatory, flotilla and cargo model components into a single TaiPan model as shown in Fig. 4. The composition is separated into three independent composition steps that are executed one after another. It demonstrates how the flotilla model first receives—through the two composition steps *CargoIntoShip1* and *CargoIntoShip2*—and then contributes—through the composition step *FlotillaIntoAquatory*. Interpreting the composition as an aspect-weaving, the flotilla model first plays the role of a core and then of an aspect.

We can further use aspect-oriented concepts, when we replace the flotilla model in the example by a fragment query grouping many such models as shown in Fig. 23. Assuming that we have a second flotilla model *MyFlottillaB.taipan* in our repository, the fragment query *MyFlottilla.*.taipan* groups the two flotilla models *MyFlottilla.taipan* and *MyFlottillaB.taipan*. *MyFlottillaB.taipan* defines an additional ship with the ports *Ship3Port*, *Ship3Route* and *Ship3Cargo*. Using regular expressions, we merge the ports from the different flotilla models as follows:

– *Ship(2|3)Port* merges *Ship2Port* and *Ship3Port*.
– *Ship(2|3)Route* merges *Ship2Route* and *Ship3Route*.
– *ships* merges *ships* from *MyFlottilla.taipan* and *ships* from *MyFlottillaB.taipan*.
– *Ship(2|3)Cargo* merges *Ship2Cargo* and *Ship3Cargo*.

Similar to distributing an aspect over a core, we load the same cargo (*tobacco*) into two ships in the *CargoIntoShip2+3* composition step. Through the merged ports *Ship(2|3)Port* and *Ship(2|3)Route*, we ensure that the two ships get the same route and destination assigned in the *FlotillaIntoAquatory* composition step.

The composition step *CargoIntoShip2+3* resembles an aspect-weaving: The fragment query *MyFlottilla.*.taipan* and the port merge *Ship(2|3)Cargo* quantify over a set of *core* flotilla models and the tobacco cargo *aspect* is distributed over it in a cross-cutting manner.

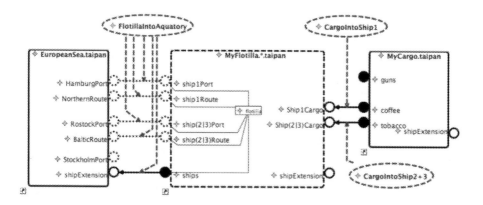

Fig. 23. The composition program to compose the aquatory, two flotilla and cargo model components by applying a fragment query

6.3 Other Examples

In this section, we briefly discuss additional applications we were and are still working on. More details and examples can be found on the Reuseware website [12].

Class Diagram Weaving. In this application, we introduced aspect-oriented concepts into *Ecore* (which could similarly be done for UML or other languages with a class concept). The idea is to distinguish between core classes, which are complete classes that offer an interface for extension, and advice classes, which define operations and features (possibly referring other advice classes) to be reused as extensions for core classes. Advice classes can be woven into core classes, which means that all their operations and features are injected into the core class. If an advice class has references to other advice classes, all these classes have to be bound in one composition step.

The composition system is defined in terms of semantic extensions only. To distinguish between core and advice classes, a name convention on the package that contains the classes is used: a package with *advice* in its name contains advice, others contain core classes. A core class has hooks for both its lists of operations and features. In addition, the class itself is an anchor. The two hooks and the anchor of each core class are exported to a receiving port that is named like the class itself. An advice class, on the contrary, defines two lists with prototypes, its operations and features, and itself as a slot. The two prototype lists and the anchor of each advice class are exported to a contributing port that is named like the class itself.

As an example, one can consider the, rather technical, aspect of a subject–observer relationship that can be modelled in two related advice classes: *Observer* and *Subject*. The two classes appear as contributing ports on the composition interface of the advice fragment and can be linked individually to two classes of a core fragment in a composition step. A more detailed example and the complete definition of the composition system can be found on the Web[9].

---

[9] http://reuseware.org/index.php/Ecore_Aspect_Weaving

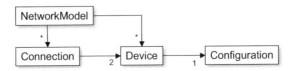

Fig. 24. Excerpt from the metamodel of a network configuration DSL

Weaving Java Classes. As mentioned in the above application, the composition system for class weaving can be ported to other languages that have a class concept. This is not limited to graphical languages, but can also be done for textual languages, as long as a proper metamodel exists (and a tool that can parse textual model definitions). We defined such a metamodel for (a subset of) Java and then realised the class weaving composition system for Java. We have already used this as an example in [14]. There, we applied syntactic extension.

We modified the composition system to work with semantic extensions, similar to the Ecore weaving system. Interestingly, we can reuse the composition programs defined for Ecore fragments above for similar examples based on Java fragments, without having to change the composition programs at all. In MDD, one can benefit from this, for instance, in code generation: model fragments can be translated to code individually—reducing complexity of generation and keeping the separation of concerns from the models down to the code, which is important when the code is manually modified after generation. To integrate the code fragments, one can reuse the composition program already defined on the modelling level. This is one direction of future work, where we investigate how our approach can help in broader MDD settings, where different languages and composition systems are involved. More information about our experiments with Java can be found on the Web[10].

Including Modularisation and Aspect-Orientation in a DSL under development
When a DSL is developed, our approach can be used to add modularisation capabilities to the language and profit from our existing tools for composition definition and execution. This example demonstrates this on a DSL for network configuration. Figure 24 shows an excerpt from the metamodel: A *network model* consist of *connections* and *devices* that have a *configuration* attached. Now, independent definition and reuse of *configurations* should be supported. Hence, we add hooks and prototypes for *configurations*, and we are done with the definition.

Networks with hooks instead of concrete configurations and configuration prototype fragments can now be modelled. Configurations can be bound to hooks using the composition editor. Because of the support for quantification through fragment queries and merged ports, we can also distribute one configuration over a large network model. More details about this example can be found on the Web[11].

Query Modularisation. A complex composition system we built based on our earlier, grammar-based, work [13] is a module system for the XML query language Xcerpt

---

[10] http://reuseware.org/index.php/Java
[11] http://reuseware.org/index.php/CIM_DSL_Extension

[28]. Details about this systems are published in [13] and [29]. The system extends a language that previously included no notion of modularisation with a module system that performs encapsulation and enables the developer to import modules and to control the data flow between modules.

The system was not defined through concepts introduced in this paper, but uses our previous grammar-based approach. Information about the Xcerpt module system can also be found on the Web[12].

Managing Variability in Software Product Line Engineering. In Software Product Line Engineering (SPLE), one of the main challenges is expressing and managing the variable parts in product lines. Although there already exist different variability concepts and patterns, all of them are tied to a specific level of abstraction in the software development process (e.g. models or code).

Due to its language independence and its built-in concept for expressing variability, ISC is an interesting technique to express and manage variability on each stage of a multi-staged software development process, which we examined in a case study where we developed a simple product line of time-sheet applications.

In this case study, we used Reuseware's modularisation concepts to decompose the variable parts of the product line on both the modelling level and code level. We created fragments for each feature realisation and used Reuseware's graphical composition language to specify the composition of those variable parts of the product line with the core. Since we aim at an automated product-instantiation process, we created a mapping between conceptual variability models and composition steps of the composition programs using our tool *FeatureMapper*[13] [30]. This mapping is interpreted by a dedicated product-instantiation workbench we developed in the context of the case study, which only executes the actual composition if the corresponding feature from the variability model should be included in the concrete product variant.

7 Related Work

In [31], Klint et al. identify the need for an engineering approach to language development. Our Reuseware tool, presented in this paper, can be viewed as a form of meta-grammarware in their sense that is, as a "software that supports concrete grammar use cases by some means of meta-programming, generative programming or domain-specific language implementation" [31, p. 342]. Our approach uses metamodels (which are grammars in the sense of Klint et al., who use the term grammar in a slightly more general sense essentially as 'anything describing a language') to generate composition systems and enable the execution of compositions through model or program transformation for languages that originally did not support composition.

As Reuseware and invasive software composition have originally been developed for textual languages, in the following, we first discuss a number of related work in the area of textual languages before also discussing some related work in modelling. For space

---

[12] http://xcerpt.reuseware.org/

[13] http://featuremapper.org

reasons, neither discussion is meant to be complete, but rather to give an insight into some of the manifold research approaches in the expanding field of grammarware engineering. We will particularly focus on approaches in the aspect-oriented community.

Several approaches exist that provide aspect orientation for the .NET platform and claim that this makes their approaches language agnostic or independent. For example, Aspect.NET [32] uses static weaving based on binary assemblies to provide AspectJ-like AOP for .NET, Compose* [33] is an implementation of Composition Filters for .NET. These approaches work on the level of the Common Language Infrastructure (CLI) and hence are independent of specific programming languages. At the same time, however, working at the CLI level also means that these approaches cannot provide language-specific modularisation concepts. Our approach works at the level of each individual language itself. While this makes it more complicated to mix modules of different languages, it enables us to build custom modularisation techniques for each language.

Fractal Aspect Components (FAC) [34] is an extension of the Fractal Component Model [35] to support AOP. It aims at bridging the gap between Component-Based Software Engineering and AOP. FAC introduces several additional concepts to the Fractal Component Model to compose Aspectisable Components and Aspect Components. FAC is similar to the Reuseware approach, because the component model is designed in a language-independent way. This allows for conceptual reuse within different implementations. It is, however, also different in many ways. For example, aspect binding and composition programs do not abstract from the implementation of the component model in FAC. With the graphical fragment composition editor, the Reuseware approach provides a general-purpose way to express compositions independent of the fragment component's core language.

In [36], Gray and Roychoudhury present a technique for constructing aspect weavers for arbitrary languages. They define an aspect-weaving language (called *Aspect Domain*), which can be used to define weavings for different languages. They argue that a common superset of weaving operations can be applied to arbitrary languages, while certain languages require specific extensions. The weaving language is comparable to our composition language. One important difference is that Gray and Roychoudhury do not extend languages, because their components (i.e. *core* and *advice* artefacts) only have implicit composition interfaces—which is reasonable, since they focus on legacy systems written in existing languages—while we focus on programs and models under development. Furthermore, our approach can also deal with non-textual languages described by a metamodel.

The *Mjølner System* and the *Beta language* [37] were the first to introduce the concept of slots. In Beta, any programming construct can be replaced by a slot typed with the non-terminal corresponding to that construct. Beta also supports a notion of inheritance of grammar types. Binding of slots happens when the name of a fragment and the name of a slot in the same project match. Our approach extends the Beta approach in two ways:

1. We introduce additional types of variation points, such as anchors, hooks and prototypes. In addition, we introduce the new (language-independent) abstraction of ports that gives more control to the fragment developer when defining an interface.

The linking of ports is also an explicit operation allowing the definition and variation of composition programs, while Beta uses implicit matching of names only.

2. We extend the concept to any language that can be described by a metamodel. Different from Beta, our tool allows arbitrary languages to be extended with a composition system.

The *Software COMPOsition SysTem* (COMPOST) [38], the demonstrator system of [11], is a predecessor of our current system, which introduced many of the concepts available in our approach, but was limited to Java and XML. For each new language that should be supported by COMPOST, a large amount of implementation work is required. In [13], we introduced the first version of the Reuseware system, which was capable of extending grammar-based textual languages and performing compositions of syntax trees, without the requirement for manual implementations. We took first steps in extending these concepts towards metamodel-based (possibly graphical) languages in [14]. There, we introduced the concept of fragment queries but did not elaborate on the details of metamodel extension or the composition algorithm. Novel in the current work are also the concepts of ports, composition links and composition steps, which were not required in the syntax-tree composition approach [13] and were not yet applied in the compositions presented in [14].

Our notion of fragment components is comparable to the notion of *syntactic units* presented in [39]. Syntactic units are arranged in *syntactic unit trees* that can be likened to composition programs. In this approach, the so-called extension spots can be defined as alternatives for any fragment of code derivable from a non-terminal. Compared to our approach, there is no formalisation of language extensions, which allows for tailored extension of a language (to only allow the desired amount of variability) and generation of language-specific tooling.

In the area of model-based approaches, Model Weaving is strongly related to the work presented in this paper. It allows for combining two or more models to form a composed or woven model. AMW, the Atlas Model Weaver [40], is a tool that allows generating model transformations based on a so-called *Weaving Model*. The Weaving Model consists of links between two or more models that are used to generate model transformations and model weavings.

Another approach to model weaving presented in [9] by Heidenreich and Lochmann stems from Product-Line Engineering and provides means to express *Aspectual Features* in separate models, which are woven into a core model according to the feature selection of the product line. The authors are using graph-rewrite systems to weave the Aspectual Features to the core model. This idea was adopted in the design of the XWeave [41] tool by Groher and Völter. XWeave is integrated in the openArchitectureWare tool chain and uses name correspondence and regular expressions for model weaving as our composition language does.

However, the work presented in this paper goes beyond existing model weaving. It unifies weaving and composition operations on both model and text artefacts through the general concepts of addressable points and fragment queries.

The Generic Modeling Environment (GME) [42,43] offers generic means to build UML-based DSMLs and also allows for defining concrete syntax for those languages. It supports partitioning of models according to *aspects* that are defined on the metamodel level. While this increases understandability and maintainability of complex models, it does not address the issue of reusability of language modules, the goal of Reuseware. In [44], the authors introduce the concept of metamodel composition to GME, where existing language modules and newly developed languages can be composed by dedicated composition operators. This fosters reuse of modularisation techniques, which is the driving force behind our work. Compared with the Reuseware approach, metamodel composition as presented within GME does not allow for language-agnostic interpretation of the reused language modules.

Many aspect-oriented approaches to modelling have been developed, most of which are specific to one particular modelling language. A large number of these approaches are inspired by aspect technology as introduced in the area of AOP—for example, Zhang et al. [7] present an approach to aspect-orientation for state machines that is closely inspired by AspectJ technology. At the same time, approaches are beginning to appear that show composition techniques differing from aspect-oriented ideas. For example, in [10], Whittle et al. present an approach that uses pattern matching on state-machine concrete syntax and graph transformation to describe aspects on state machines.

Fleurey et al. [45, and references therein] present a generic framework for composing different views on a model. The approach distinguished a *matching* and a *merging* phase. The matching phase determines which model elements in two models should be merged together, while the merging phase performs the actual merging. Merging is implemented in a completely language-independent fashion. Matching is language dependent and the match rules must, therefore, be provided in a specialisation of the framework. However, the framework defines an interface for the match rules, which is, to our understanding, based on matching metaclasses and signatures. Our approach can also be seen to distinguish a matching and a merging phase. However, both phases are expressed language-independently by composition diagrams in our composition description language. Specialisation to specific languages is only necessary to identify how addressable points, etc. can be expressed for model components. In our approach, matching must be done for each composition individually. In contrast, Fleurey et al. [45] use matching rules that are defined once for a specific language and then applied to multiple combinations of models. We are planning, however, to extend the approach presented in this paper to support concepts similar to such matching rules. For textual languages, we have already presented such an approach in [46] under the name of a *light-weight dedicated composition system* (LWDCS).

C-SAW [47] is a general model transformation tool that also supports some form of AOM independent of the specific modelling language. Developers write so-called *aspects* or *strategies*, model transformations expressed in the Embedded Constraint Language (ECL), querying for a number of model elements and then modifying these. Reuseware also is based on model transformation. However, the collection of model elements to be transformed is encapsulated in an explicit construct—the model fragment—rather than implicitly represented in a query inside the composition program.

8   Conclusions and Outlook

Modularising models is becoming increasingly important, especially due to the fact that MDD approaches are requiring richer and more complex models to be constructed. Not only are models growing in complexity and becoming harder to overview, but many different modelling languages—domain-specific modelling languages—are being developed alongside general-purpose ones such as UML. As we have demonstrated with use-cases for both kinds of languages, it is important to be able to construct larger models from smaller and better understood ones. The first use-case concerned the modularisation of UML activity diagrams, while the second use-case described how models of a domain-specific language (called TaiPan) can be split into different concerns. We have in this paper presented a language-independent approach to enable component-oriented thinking and development for modelling languages.

We proposed two ways of extending modelling languages with component capabilities. The first involves an extension of the underlying modelling language's metamodel in order to define components' interfaces, while the second can extract such interfaces implicitly. Avoiding metamodel extension has the benefit that already developed editors and tools will not break. However, for certain domain-specific modelling languages, an extension of the language metamodel can make sense and be an easier approach, as we have demonstrated on the TaiPan modelling language. Hence, both approaches can be useful depending on the particulars of the addressed language and the desired modularisation.

We would not have been able to reach our solution without implementing the ideas and applying them on examples. Our current implementation [12] is based on the Eclipse Modeling Framework and offers GUI tooling as plug-ins for the Eclipse platform. The main components of our tool are the graphical composition program editor presented and a fragment management system that extends the general resource management of the Eclipse Modeling Framework [23]. Because of the integrated Eclipse platform [21], on which many modelling tools are based, our tool can directly interact with tooling of the used component description languages. These tools are used to define fragments and view composition results. In the examples, for instance, we used the TOPCASED UML Editor [25] and the TaiPan editor. The importance of providing such a tool should not be underestimated for future research: It enables us to do case-studies more quickly and the good integration with existing modelling tools may improve acceptance in the community.

For the future, we plan to do further case-studies to clarify the open questions of what additional matching concepts are needed in composition program definitions to match the ports of composition links and in fragment queries. This issue is also related to the concepts of *complex composition operators*, which we introduced as means to define composition systems for grammar-based languages [13,46]. Such operators allow for the grouping of several composition operations that work together on a set of fragments and variation points. This grouping is similar to the grouping of addressable points into ports but defines the binding between variation and reference points explicitly. We believe that both concepts can be unified and that complex composition operators can be translated into composition programs of the approach presented in this paper. Doing this would unite our grammar-based and our metamodel-based approaches.

In the future, we will formalise our composition technique, which we described in this paper and implemented in the tool. This will give a formal definition of what a *valid* and an *invalid* composition program is and will enable an analysis of the limits of our approach.

We also see potential in applying our approach in a larger MDD process, where different languages are utilised. We believe our approach will show its advantages in such a scenario, that is, where modularisation issues of all involved languages can be solved with a common base component model and a language-independent composition description language. In general, it becomes easier to relate artefacts even when they are written in different languages, because they share certain parts of their component models. Composition programs can, for instance, be reused at different abstraction levels of an MDD process, where only details, but not the architecture, of a system change. We took a first step in this direction in [14], where we used the same composition program to compose UML and Java fragments.

Acknowledgments

This research has been co-funded by the European Commission and by the Swiss Federal Office for Education and Science within the 6th Framework Programme project REWERSE number 506779 (http://rewerse.net) as well as the 6th Framework Programme project MODELPLEX contract number 034081 (http://www.modelplex.org) and by the German Ministry of Education and Research (BMBF) within the project feasiPLe (http://www.feasiple.de).

References

1. Ritsko, J.J., Seidman, D.I.: Preface. IBM Systems Journal – Special Issue on Model-Driven Software Development 45(3) (2006)
2. Object Management Group: UML 2.0 infrastructure specification. OMG Document (October 2004), http://www.omg.org/cgi-bin/doc?ptc/04-10-14
3. Nejati, S., Sabetzadeh, M., Chechik, M., Easterbrook, S., Zave, P.: Matching and merging of statecharts specifications. In: 29th International Conference on Software Engineering (ICSE 2007), Minneapolis, MN, USA, pp. 54–63. IEEE Computer Society, Los Alamitos (2007)
4. Peterson, J.L.: Petri nets. ACM Computing Surveys 9(3), 223–252 (1977)
5. Aldawud, O., Cazzola, W., Elrad, T., Gray, J., Kienzle, J., Stein, D. (eds.): 10th Workshop on Aspect-Oriented Modeling (AOM at AOSD 2007) co-located with the 6th International Conference on Aspect-Oriented Software Development (AOSD 2007), Online Proc. (March 2007), http://www.aspect-modeling.org/aosd07/
6. Aldawud, O., Cazzola, W., Elrad, T., Gray, J., Kienzle, J., Stein, D. (eds.): 11th International Workshop on Aspect-Oriented Modeling (AOM at MoDELS 2007) co-located with ACM/IEEE 10th International Conference on Model Driven Engineering Languages and Systems MODELS 2007, Online Proc. (September 2007),
http://www.aspect-modeling.org/models07/
7. Zhang, G., Hölzl, M., Knapp, A.: Enhancing UML state machines with aspects. In: [48], pp. 529–543
8. Colyer, A., Clement, A., Harley, G., Webster, M.: Eclipse AspectJ: Aspect-Oriented Programming with AspectJ and the Eclipse AspectJ Development Tools (The Eclipse Series). Addison-Wesley, Reading (2004)

9. Heidenreich, F., Lochmann, H.: Using graph-rewriting for model weaving in the context of aspect-oriented product line engineering. In: 1st Workshop on Aspect-Oriented Product Line Engineering (AOPLE 2006) co-located with the International Conference on Generative Programming and Component Engineering (GPCE 2006), Portland, Oregon, Online Proc. (October 2006), http://www.softeng.ox.ac.uk/aople/aople1/

10. Whittle, J., Moreira, A., Araújo, J., Jayaraman, P., Elkhodary, A., Rabbi, R.: An expressive aspect composition language for UML state diagrams. In: [48], pp. 514–528

11. Aßmann, U.: Invasive Software Composition. Springer, Secaucus (2003)

12. Software Technology Group, Technische Universität Dresden: Reuseware Composition Framework (April 2008), http://www.reuseware.org

13. Henriksson, J., Heidenreich, F., Johannes, J., Zschaler, S., Aßmann, U.: Extending grammars and metamodels for reuse: the reuseware approach. IET Software 2(3), 165–184 (2008)

14. Heidenreich, F., Johannes, J., Zschaler, S.: Aspect orientation for your language of choice. In: [6], http://www.aspect-modeling.org/models07/

15. Filman, R., Friedman, D.: Aspect-oriented programming is quantification and obliviousness. In: Workshop on Advanced Separation of Concerns co-located with OOPSLA 2000, Minneapolis, MN, USA (October 2000)

16. The Eclipse Foundation: Graphical Modeling Framework (April 2008), http://www.eclipse.org/gmf/

17. Sun Microsystems: Enterprise JavaBeans Specification, version 2.0. Final Release (August 2001)

18. Object Management Group: CORBA 3.0 new component chapters. OMG Document (October 1999), http://www.omg.org/cgi-bin/doc?ptc/99-10-04

19. Fiala, Z.: Design and Development of Component-based Adaptive Web Applications. PhD thesis, Technische Universität Dresden, Dresden, Germany (February 2007)

20. Sullivan, K., Griswold, W.G., Song, Y., Cai, Y., Shonle, M., Tewari, N., Rajan, H.: Information hiding interfaces for aspect-oriented design. In: 10th European Software Engineering Conference held jointly with 13th ACM SIGSOFT International Symposium on Foundations of Software Engineering, Lisbon, Portugal, pp. 166–175. ACM Press, New York (2005)

21. The Eclipse Foundation: The Eclipse Platform (April 2008), http://www.eclipse.org

22. Object Management Group: UML 2.0 OCL specification. OMG Document (October 2003), http://www.omg.org/cgi-bin/doc?ptc/03-10-14

23. Budinsky, F., Brodsky, S.A., Merks, E.: Eclipse Modeling Framework. Pearson Education, London (2003)

24. Object Management Group: MOF 2.0 core specification. OMG Document (January 2006), http://www.omg.org/spec/MOF/2.0

25. The Topcased Project Team: TOPCASED (April 2008), http://www.topcased.org

26. Software Technology Group, Technische Universität Dresden: EMFText Tool (January 2008), http://www.emftext.org

27. The Eclipse Foundation: UML2 Project (April 2008), http://www.eclipse.org/modeling/mdt/?project=uml2tools

28. Bry, F., Schaffert, S.: The XML query language Xcerpt: Design principles, examples, and semantics. In: Chaudhri, A.B., Jeckle, M., Rahm, E., Unland, R. (eds.) NODe-WS 2002. LNCS, vol. 2593, pp. 295–310. Springer, Heidelberg (2003)

29. Aßmann, U., Berger, S., Bry, F., Furche, T., Henriksson, J., Johannes, J.: Modular web queries – from rules to stores. In: Meersman, R., Tari, Z., Herrero, P. (eds.) OTM-WS 2007, Part II. LNCS, vol. 4806, pp. 1165–1175. Springer, Heidelberg (2007)

30. Heidenreich, F., Kopcsek, J., Wende, C.: FeatureMapper: Mapping Features to Models (Informal Research Demonstration). In: Companion Proceedings of the 30th International Conference on Software Engineering (ICSE 2008), Leipzig, Germany (May 2008)

31. Klint, P., Lämmel, R., Verhoef, C.: Toward an engineering discipline for grammarware. ACM Transactions on Software Engineering 3(14), 331–380 (2005)
32. Safonov, V., Gratchev, M., Grigoryev, D., Maslennikov, A.: Aspect.NET – aspect-oriented toolkit for Microsoft.NET based on Phoenix and Whidbey. In: Knoop, J., Skala, V. (eds.) 4th International Conference .NET Technologies, Plzen, Czech Republic, University of West Bohemia, May 2006, pp. 19–30 (2006)
33. García, C.F.N.: Compose* – a runtime for the.Net platform. Master's thesis, Vrije Universiteit Brussel, Belgium (August 2003), http://composestar.sf.net/
34. Pessemier, N., Seinturier, L., Coupaye, T., Duchien, L.: A model for developing component-based and aspect-oriented systems. In: Löwe, W., Südholt, M. (eds.) SC 2006. LNCS, vol. 4089, pp. 259–274. Springer, Heidelberg (2006)
35. The Fractal Project Team: The Fractal Project (April 2008), http://fractal.objectweb.org/
36. Gray, J., Roychoudhury, S.: A technique for constructing aspect weavers using a program transformation engine. In: Murphy, G.C., Lieberherr, K.J. (eds.) 3rd International Conference on Aspect-Oriented Software Development (AOSD 2004), Lancaster, UK, pp. 36–45. ACM Press, New York (2004)
37. Madsen, O.L., Møller-Pedersen, B., Nygaard, K.: Object-Oriented Programming in the BETA Programming Language. Addison-Wesley, Reading (1993)
38. The COMPOST Consortium: The COMPOST system (April 2008), http://www.the-compost-system.org
39. Majkut, M., Franczyk, B.: Generation of implementations for the model driven architecture with syntactic unit trees. In: Crocker, R., Steele Jr., G.L. (eds.) 2nd Workshop Generative Techniques in the context of MDA co-located with OOPSLA 2003, Anaheim, CA, USA, Online Proc. (October 2003)
40. The AMW Project Team: Atlas Model Weaver (April 2008), http://eclipse.org/gmt/amw/
41. Groher, I., Völter, M.: XWeave: Models and aspects in concert. In: [5], http://www.aspect-modeling.org/aosd07/
42. Vanderbilt University, Institute for Software Integrated Systems: GME: The Generic Modeling Environment (2008), http://www.isis.vanderbilt.edu/Projects/gme/
43. Ledeczi, A., Maroti, M., Bakay, A., Karsai, G., Garrett, J., Thomason, C., Nordstrom, G., Sprinkle, J., Volgyesi, P.: The generic modeling environment. Technical report, Vanderbilt University, Institute for Software Integrated Systems, Nashville, TN, USA (2000)
44. Ledeczi, A., Nordstrom, G., Karsai, G., Volgyesi, P., Maroti, M.: On metamodel composition. In: IEEE International Conference on Control Applications 2001 (CCA 2001), Mexico City, Mexico, September 2001, pp. 756–760 (2001)
45. Fleurey, F., Baudry, B., France, R., Ghosh, S.: A generic approach for automatic model composition. In: [6], http://www.aspect-modeling.org/models07/
46. Henriksson, J., Aßmann, U., Heidenreich, F., Johannes, J., Zschaler, S.: How dark should a component black box be? The Reuseware Answer. In: Weck, W., Reussner, R., Szyperski, C. (eds.) 12th International Workshop on Component-Oriented Programming (WCOP) co-located with 21st European Conference on Object-Oriented Programming (ECOOP 2007). LNCS, vol. 4906, Berlin, Germany (July 2007)
47. Gray, J., Lin, Y., Zhang, J.: Automating change evolution in model-driven engineering. IEEE Computer 39(2), 51–58 (2006)
48. Engels, G., Opdyke, B., Schmidt, D.C., Weil, F. (eds.): 10th International Conference on Model Driven Engineering Languages and Systems (MoDELS 2007). LNCS, vol. 4735. Springer, Heidelberg (2007)

Aspects across Software Life Cycle: A Goal-Driven Approach

Nan Niu[1], Yijun Yu[2], Bruno González-Baixauli[3], Neil Ernst[1],
Julio Cesar Sampaio do Prado Leite[4], and John Mylopoulos[1]

[1] Dept. of Computer Science, University of Toronto, Canada
{nn,nernst,jm}@cs.toronto.edu
[2] Computing Dept., The Open University, UK
y.yu@open.ac.uk
[3] Dept. de Informática, Universidad de Valladolid, Spain
bbaixauli@infor.uva.es
[4] Dept. de Informática, PUC-Rio, Brazil
julio@inf.puc-rio.br

Abstract. Goal modeling fits model-driven engineering (MDE) in that
it captures stakeholder concerns and the interdependencies using concepts that are much less bound to the underlying implementation technology and are much closer to the problem languages. Aspect-oriented
software development (AOSD) provides language constructs to facilitate
the representation of multiple perceptions and to alleviate tangling and
scattering concerns. Synthesis of AOSD and MDE not only manages
software complexity but also improves productivity, as well as model
quality and longevity. In this paper, we propose a model-driven framework for tracing aspects from requirements to implementation and testing, where goal models become engineering assets and straightforward
model-to-code transformation bridges the gap between domain concepts
and implementation technologies. We test our hypotheses and evaluate
the framework's applicability and usefulness with a case study of an
open-source e-commerce platform written in PHP.

1 Introduction

We use models when we try to understand phenomena, when we think about
problems, when we construct mechanisms, when we describe solutions, and when
we communicate to each other. The role of modeling in engineering is similar:
Models help in developing artifacts by providing information about the consequences of building those artifacts before they are actually made [20]. The use
of models in engineering software is pervasive across different phases, from requirements and design to verification and validation. It is the emerging paradigm
of model-driven engineering (MDE) [36], which advocates the systematic use of
models as primary engineering artifacts throughout the software life cycle.

Model-driven engineering is simply the notion that we can construct a model
of a system that we can then transform into the real thing [36]. One of the

S. Katz et al. (Eds.): Transactions on AOSD VI, LNCS 5560, pp. 83–110, 2009.

challenges faced in MDE is the escalating complexity of software and system models [13]. For large-scale software development, the sheer size of models, the intertwining relationships between intra- and inter-model elements, and the concerns expressed across different models present a high adoption barrier to MDE practice. A fundamental principle in addressing complexity is separation of concerns [32]. Maintaining a clear separation of concerns throughout the software life cycle has long been a goal of the software community. Aspect-oriented software development (AOSD) provides explicit means to model concerns that crosscut multiple system components. It is argued that the synthesis of MDE and AOSD can not only provide effective support for managing software complexity but also improve model quality and productivity [13].

In this paper, we propose a framework for tracing aspects from requirement goal models to implementation and testing. Goal-oriented requirements engineering (RE) uses goal models to elicit, specify, and analyze requirements [41]. We provide language support for modeling goal aspects and mechanisms for transforming models to aspect-oriented programs. Test cases are derived from requirements models to guide verification and validation of aspects. The benefits of leveraging our framework are twofold. By separating crosscutting concerns throughout requirements, implementation, and testing phases, we achieve a high degree of modularity and traceability in software development. By driving implementation and validation from stakeholder goals, we achieve a high level of software quality and user satisfaction.

Our aim is to lay a foundation for goal-driven development techniques that exploit aspect orientation to modularize concerns and to compose them into the system implementation. We are also interested in exploring the extent to which early aspects [1] can be traced and validated across software life cycle. To demonstrate the idea, we present an exploratory case study showing the approach's application to an open-source e-commerce platform written in PHP. The purpose is to describe our initial investigation into designing a model-driven framework for capturing and implementing goal aspects, instantiate the framework to engineer a real-world system, discuss the findings and preliminary results, examine costs, benefits, and the scope of applicability of the proposed framework, and open up new research avenues arising from our investigation. Our work also helps replace hype with sound technical insights and lessons learned from experience with complex systems.

Preliminary work on goal aspects was published in [45,46,47]. The emphasis of [45] was to discover candidate aspects during goal-oriented requirements analysis, while the idea of tracing and validating the early identified goal aspects was sketched in [47] and detailed in [46]. This paper brings together the essentials from our earlier work, integrates the full-fledged aspect tracing method, and describes a systematic empirical study, to offer a more complete treatment and a more critical evaluation of our framework. Section 2 lays the background and provides the context of our research. Section 3 articulates and discusses the goal-oriented model-driven aspect framework. Section 4 presents the case study and reports

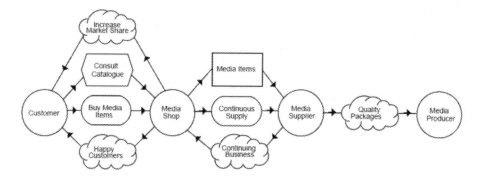

Fig. 1. A strategic dependency model for media shop

our experience. Section 5 reviews related work. Section 6 draws some concluding remarks and outlines future work.

2   Background

This section aims to situate our research within the existing literature on RE, MDE and AOSD.

2.1   Goal Models

Recent research in RE has generated a number of notations for modeling stakeholder goals and the relationships between them. Goals express, at various levels of abstraction, stakeholders' many objectives for the system under consideration. Goal-oriented RE uses goal models to elicit, elaborate, structure, specify, analyze, negotiate, document, and modify requirements [41].

Goal modeling shifts the emphasis in requirements analysis to the actors in an organization, their goals, and the interdependencies between those goals, rather than focusing on processes and objects, as in, for example, object-oriented analysis [2]. This helps us understand why a new system is needed and lets us effectively link software solutions to business needs. The i^* framework [44] uses goal models to provide criteria for justifying the presence of requirements, for determining requirements completeness and trade-offs, and for validating stakeholder concerns.

In i^*, stakeholders are represented as (social) actors who depend on each other for goals to be achieved, tasks to be performed, and resources to be furnished. Two types of models are involved in i^*: the strategic dependency model for describing the network of relationships among actors and the strategic rationale model for describing and supporting the reasoning that each actor goes through concerning its relationships with other actors [44].

As an example, a strategic dependency model for media shop is shown in Fig. 1. Media shop is a store selling different kinds of media items such as books, newspapers, magazines, audio CDs, and videotapes. The goal models developed for media shop were presented in detail in [5]. As shown in Fig. 1, actors are represented as circles, dependums—goals, softgoals, tasks, and resources—are respectively, represented as ovals, clouds, hexagons, and rectangles, and dependencies have the form *depender* → *dependum* → *dependee*. In Fig. 1, for instance, customer depends on media shop to buy media items and media shop, in turn, depends on customer to increase market share. Modeling such dependencies among organizational actors helps tease out the business goals of the intended software.

Goal-modeling frameworks such as i^* distinguish between *hard (functional) goals*—states that actors can attain—and *softgoals*, which can never be fully satisfied. Non-functional requirements (NFRs) [6] such as reliability and efficiency are typically expressed as softgoals to suggest that the intended software is expected to satisfy them within acceptable limits, rather than absolutely.

Extensive work on goal-oriented RE has been carried out for the past decade. A guided tour of this line of research is given in [41]. Experience shows that goal modeling is particularly useful in the early requirements analysis phase [44], which is concerned with the understanding of a problem by studying and modeling the intentions of stakeholders and the strategic relationships amongst those organizational actors. To make goal models a true engineering asset that drives software development beyond the early-RE phase, detailed design and implementation of goal models must be sought.

2.2   Engineering Goal Models Using Agent-Oriented Programming

An earlier effort to transform goal models into implementations was made in the *Tropos* project [5]. The intuition is that using an agent-oriented programming platform for the implementation seems natural, given that the requirements model is defined in terms of actors, goals, and interdependencies amongst them. An agent is an entity whose state is viewed as consisting of mental components (e.g., capabilities, choices, and commitments), and so agenthood is in the mind of the programmer [39]. The *Tropos* programming environment is supported by JACK, a commercial product based on the beliefs-desires-intentions (BDI) agent architecture rooted in artificial intelligence [3].

The natural and basic transformation from requirements to design and implementation is to map actors to agents. Then, resources and tasks in i^* models are mapped to beliefs and intentions, and both functional goals and softgoals are mapped to desires in the BDI architecture. Model refinement (e.g., decompositions and dependencies) and design generation are driven by the fulfillment of each actor's (agent's) obligations.

A set of stereotypes, tagged values, and constraints are proposed to accommodate *Tropos* concepts with UML [2]. As an example, Fig. 2a depicts a refined i^* strategic dependency model for media shop in UML using the stereotypes defined in [5], notably ≪ i^*actor ≫ and ≪ $i^*dependency$ ≫. Such mapping in UML could also be done in a similar way for strategic rationale or goal analysis models. Making further design decisions requires the introduction of additional details

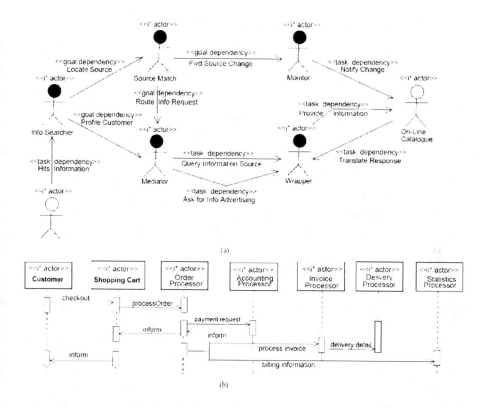

Fig. 2. Representing i^* models for media shop in UML with stereotypes. **a** Strategic dependency model. **b** Sequence diagram for ordering media items.

for each strategic actor and architectural component of a system. In *Tropos*, this involves actor communication and actor behavior. Figure 2b presents such a design model for media shop: A sequence diagram that provides basic specification for an intra-agent order processing protocol.

Despite the effort made by *Tropos* to implement i^* models via agent-oriented programming paradigm, a number of problems remain to be addressed. First, agent-oriented programming has yet to prove its constructability and applicability in mainstream software development, partly due to the lack of support for underlying programming constructs and integrated development environments [4]. To overcome these deficiencies, the JACK intelligent agents development environment adopts the widespread object-oriented (OO) concepts and extends the popular Java language with the BDI model.

A second problem thus refers to the mismatch between agent and object orientations, which can adversely affect design refinement and model transformation [4]. For example, the parameters for defining an object are unconstrained, whereas those for defining an agent must be constrained by the notions of beliefs, commitments, and choices. Another example is that no constraint needs to be specified on object message passing and responding, but honesty constraints on agent methods must be specified [39]. A workaround solution used in *Tropos*, to mitigate the mismatch, is to treat each actor as a single class, and then model the behavior and communications among actors, as indicated in Fig. 2. However, such an "actor↔class" mapping is rarely the case in OO modeling and design. For instance, to effectively encapsulate information [2], we might design a single "processor" abstract class, rather than having five distinct "processor" classes in Fig. 2b. In this way, the specialized classes may be implemented as interfaces at the code level.

Third, the distinction between hard goals and softgoals made in the early-RE phase is blurred in design and implementation because both are transformed to desires in *Tropos* BDI. As we shall see, this distinction needs to be preserved throughout the software life cycle. Our proposed approach aims at addressing the above limitations by leveraging ideas and techniques from AOSD.

2.3   Goal Aspects

Aspect-oriented software development applies the principle of separation of concerns [32] to make systems modular so that the intended software is easier to produce, maintain, and evolve [17]. The AOSD community has recognized the importance of considering aspects early on in the software life cycle during analysis and design, as opposed to only at the implementation stage [31]. Aspects at the requirements level present stakeholder concerns that crosscut the problem domain, with the potential for a broad impact on questions of scoping, prioritization, and architectural design [26]. Discovering aspects early can help detect conflicting concerns early, when trade-offs can be resolved more economically [1].

Aspects in goal models can be discovered using the correlations from hard goals to softgoals along with a goal elicitation and refinement process based on the V-graph model [45]. The formal process can be briefly explained as follows. Initially, the stakeholders' high-level concerns are elicited as abstract goals. The functional ones are represented by hard goals and the non-functional ones are represented by softgoals. Relations are also elicited as abstract contribution (correlation) links from the hard goals to the softgoals that must be fulfilled by the prescribed system-to-be.

During the refinement process, these abstract goals are recursively decomposed into more concrete ones through AND/OR decomposition rules [44]. When a goal g is AND-decomposed into $g_1, \ldots, g_n$ then g is satisfied if and only if g_i are satisfied for all $1 \leq i \leq n$. If g is OR-decomposed, it is satisfied if and only if there exists an i such that g_i is satisfied. As a result, several hierarchies of the goal trees are derived. One must make sure that the abstract contribution (correlation) links are maintained by introducing contribution links from more concrete hard goals to the high-level softgoals.

At the end of the model refinement, all abstract goals are decomposed into a set of goals that no longer need further decompositions. A model is well refined if all intentional goals are operationalized, i.e. specific operations are defined for the intended software to fulfill the goals [8]. These leaf-level operations are

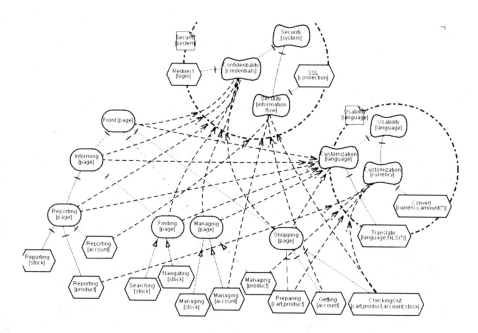

Fig. 3. Illustration of goal aspects in media shop i^* model. Goal aspects, together with their advising tasks, are represented as first-class modules in the upper-right corner of the goal model. The contribution links, from hard goals and functional tasks to goal aspects, modularize the crosscuts that would otherwise be tangled and scattered in the goal model.

called tasks that can be carried out by certain functions of the system-to-be. The set of tasks are further categorized into functional and non-functional one, depending on whether they are at the bottom of the decomposition hierarchy of an abstract hard goal, or of an abstract softgoal. This model refinement must be validated to maintain the abstract contribution links, which can often be fulfilled by weaving the concrete non-functional (operationalized) tasks into the functional tasks. As such, every OR-decomposed subgoal must fulfill the same commitment to the softgoals as their parent goal does. It is often the case, if not always, that non-functional tasks crosscut several functional ones that belong to different OR-decomposed subtrees.

Figure 3 illustrates goal aspects for media shop. The top level softgoals, such as "Security [system]" and "Usability [language]", are captured as goal aspects, which are represented as cloud-shape entities in Fig. 3. The softgoals are decomposed and eventually operationalized into advising tasks (hexagons in Fig. 3). For modularization purposes, we represent the model entities that are relevant to a goal aspect inside a dash-dotted circle, as shown in the upper-right corner of Fig. 3.

The weaving of goal aspect is achieved by composing the advising tasks with the functional tasks of effected hard goals. Such a weaving is similar to the weaving defined in aspect-oriented programming [17] in that it is the aspect's responsibility to specify the conditions (e.g. where and when) and the content (advice) of weaving. Since a (weaved) goal model need not be executed, goal aspect weaving is simpler than program aspect weaving. As an example, the goal aspect "Customization [language]" is operationalized into an advising task "Translate [language, NLS]", meaning that the media shop is advised to translate occurrences of natural language strings (NLS) into the desired language. This advice crosscuts all hard goals that display Web pages and is intended to enhance system usability for native users of the desired language. While the weaving affects certain hard goals in the usability aspect, the basic functionalities (e.g. "Informing", "Reporting", and "Shopping") defined by these hard goals via functional tasks shall remain functioning as expected.

It is crucial to represent and use NFRs during the development process because the quality concerns captured by NFRs are often regarded as architectural drivers that evoke trade-off analysis among design alternatives [21]. However, NFRs are hard to be allocated into independent modules and usually represent tangled and scattered concerns; therefore they have huge potential to become candidate early aspects [24]. The V-graph model [45] provides an effective way to identify NFR-related goal aspects. Next, we introduce an approach to tracing the aspects throughout software development.

3   Tracing Aspects across Software Life Cycle

The goal model not only captures stakeholder intentions and strategic dependencies but also represents design decisions during goal decomposition and refinement. These decisions, such as the advising tasks related to softgoals, can be transformed into concrete aspect-oriented implementations, thereby elevating the goal model to be a primary artifact of development.

3.1   Framework Overview

Figure 4 gives an overview of our aspect-tracing framework. As in most MDE approaches, two kinds of model transformation are present: model-to-model and model-to-code [38]. Model-to-model transformation refers to the refinement of goal models (Sect. 2.3). Model-to-code transformation, in our framework, refers to the mapping from a goal model construct (e.g., goal aspect, advising task, etc.) to some artifact in the code base.

The upper part of Fig. 4 highlights the early aspects discovery process discussed in Sect. 2.3. Aspect-oriented concepts are modeled explicitly in requirements at the beginning of the development process. Advising tasks, which operationalize softgoals and relate to hard goals, are modularized as aspects and weaved into the goal model to enable aspect-oriented requirements analysis [31]. The resulting model, notably the goal model augmented with aspects, is amenable to be transformed into aspect-oriented programs (AOP) [17]. To ease this transformation, we provide language support for modeling goal aspects in

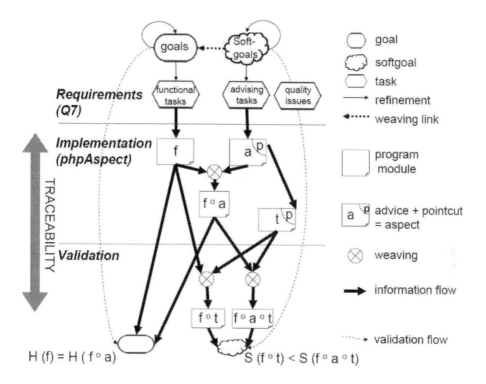

Fig. 4. Process overview of the aspect-tracing framework

Q7 (Sect. 3.2). It is worth bearing in mind that the requirements goal model provides a cornerstone for system validation.

Key concepts of AOP implementation are depicted in the middle of Fig. 4. Functional modules (f) and code aspects (advice + pointcut) are derived from functional and advising tasks, respectively. The distinction between functional goals and softgoals made in the requirements model is respected and preserved. We choose different subject matters to include into program modules and ignore others. Namely, the f modules focus on functionalities, whereas aspects modularize crosscutting NFR concerns in terms of operationalized advising tasks. Such a separation-of-concern strategy results in an uncluttered structure. It also mandates the separated concerns to be weaved together in the implementation.

The weaved system $(f \circ a)$ is obtained by composing advice (a) with bases according to the pointcut expression (p). Some aspects identified at the requirements level may not be mapped to code at all. For example, a typical performance requirement might state that the system shall complete a specific task within 2 seconds. These early identified aspects play a key role in monitoring the system's behavior. We record them as quality issues to establish their traceability throughout the software life cycle. Deciding whether to implement a goal aspect or to record it as an issue depends on two activities: prioritizing softgoals [21] and defining quantitative measures [35]. While handling quality issues is important, we consider it to be our future work and discuss related research in Sect. 5. The success criteria for aspects are specified in a test case (t), which gathers quality metrics and shares with a the same pointcut (p). In another word, p is reused from goal aspects to implementation (a) and testing (t). It is important to incorporate the metrics t so that one can measure system qualities with $(f \circ a \circ t)$ and without $(f \circ t)$ aspects. Note that our framework is viable for applying different programming languages and weaving mechanisms such as AspectC, AspectJ or HyperJ. We use phpAspect to illustrate our approach in Sect. 3.3.

System validation is shown in the lower part of Fig. 4 and is further discussed in Sect. 3.4. The weaved system $(f \circ a)$ is subject to two tests. The first test ensures that systems with and without aspects have the same functionality defined by hard goals: $H(f) = H(f \circ a)$. Existing testing mechanisms, such as unit testing, can be reused to validate whether the weaved system satisfies the functional requirements. The second test checks whether the weaved system indeed improves system qualities in terms of the degree of softgoal satisfaction: $S(f \circ t) < S(f \circ a \circ t)$. It is evident that validation is directed by stakeholder goals and the many concerns emerged in design and implementation.

Our goal-driven framework enables not only forward mapping of crosscutting concerns (e.g. from requirements to implementation) but also backward tracing of aspects (e.g. from implementation to requirements). The case study presented in Sect. 4 shows examples of both kinds. We intend a straightforward model transformation scheme [38]—the heart and soul of our MDE framework—to easily capture the application domain knowledge. In most cases, the relationship between goal aspects and program aspects is a one-to-one mapping or is at least intuitively clear from goal model refinement. Our framework currently focuses on one-to-one mappings, trying to work out the basic scenarios. We plan to extend the framework to deal with more complex cases that may involve many-to-many mappings.

3.2   Goal Aspects in Q7

Q7, or 5W2H—why, who, what, when, where, how, how much—is a pseudo programming language that captures the structure of requirements goal graphs, including the major entities of the NFR framework [6]. The syntax of the language is designed to facilitate the reuse of solutions in the non-functional domains [18]. The semantic domain is formally depicted in GRL [12]. We exploit the Q7 language to support the description of aspects in goal models.

The answers to the **why** and **how** questions respectively indicate the composition and decomposition relations between abstraction and implementation. Adapted from the goal model of Fig. 3, the following example shows the AND/OR decomposition relations among the hard goals for media shop. The front page of the shop has the functionality for "informing" the end-users and administrators. This goal is decomposed into "finding" *and* (&) "reporting" relevant information. To find information, a user is allowed to "search" *or* (|) "navigate" the shop. The nesting structure of curly braces helps visualize the decomposition hierarchy of the goals.

```
Informing { &
  Finding { |
    Searching
    Navigating
  }
  Reporting
    ...
}
```

The answers to the **how much** question show the degree of contributions between hard goals and softgoals. Q7 uses the labels "++", "+", "−", and "−−" to indicate the "make", "help", "hurt", and "break" relations between the goals. The answers to the **what** question connect the goal to its subject matter [48]. In Q7, such information is placed inside square brackets as topics of the goals or softgoals. For example, when the system meets the media shop's "Front [page]" goal, it also *makes* (++) major top-level softgoals ("⇒"), such as "Security [system]" and "Usability [language]".

```
Front [page] {
    ...
} => ++ Security [system],
     ++ Usability [language] ...
```

The answers to the **when** question indicate the feasibility of the goals [18], and those to the **who** question attribute a goal to an encapsulating module. In the i^* terminology [44], such a module is called an actor that either processes or delegates a goal or a task to other actors via strategic dependencies. In Q7, we use the idea of "namespaces" to represent the actor names. For example,

```
<MediaShop>::Front [page] { &
  Managing [page]
    ...
}
```

Here, "MediaShop" is the actor that processes the goal "Front [page]". If the actor is not explicitly specified, a goal inherits the namespace from its parent goal. Thus, "Managing [page]" belongs to the same "MediaShop" actor.

As an extension of the encapsulating actors, we create a new namespace to modularize the aspect that cuts across multiple entities in the goal model. As an example, the security aspect in Fig. 3 is represented as follows.

```
<aspect>::Security [system] { &
  Confidentiality [credentials] <=+ [page] { &
    Redirect [login]
  }
  Security [information flow] <=+ [account] { &
    SSL [connection]
  }
}
```

The goal hierarchy within the aspect module is an *advice* and the leaf-level tasks in the hierarchy are called *advising tasks*. These tasks do not exist by themselves, since they have to be weaved into the functional goals by indicating where to attach the advice. The answers to the **where** question are designed to express the pointcut of an aspect, indicating which functional goals are suitable for applying the advice. For example, the following Q7 statements show a point-cut expression after the "$\Leftarrow$" symbol: + * [page], which matches the hard goals of any name (indicated by the wildcard *), of the subject matter Web "page", and those helping (+) achieve the usability softgoal. The advising task translates the "natural language string" (NLS) appeared in the Web page into the desired language (e.g. Spanish or German). Note that a pointcut can also be specified by enumerating the effected hard goals.

```
<aspect>::Usability [language] { &
  Customization [language] <= + * [page] { &
    Translate [language, NLS]
  }
}
```

All matched goals are therefore the *joinpoints* of the aspect. A weaving algorithm at the requirements level [18] has been implemented in the OpenOME modeling tool [28] to identify the joinpoints and attach the advising tasks as siblings to the joinpoint tasks. Both joinpoint tasks and advising tasks then share the same parent, which is called the *weaved goal*. The weaving algorithm implemented in Q7 makes it possible to analyze the weaved goal model through a goal analysis tool, e.g. a goal reasoning algorithm [11]. It is important to articulate the advice and pointcut of a goal aspect. Such an exercise not only supports aspect-oriented requirements analysis [31] but also provides reusable information for implementing and validating aspects, as shown in Fig. 4.

As we can see from the examples presented above, Q7 provides a quality-based reuse mechanism for representing and modularizing crosscutting concerns in the goal model. The Q7 language is capable of not only handling the characteristics of the quality knowledge but also relating those with functional descriptions. In addition, the textual form of Q7 greatly facilitates the tracing of stakeholder concerns throughout the software life cycle, as we shall demonstrate via a case study in Sect. 4.

3.3   Implementation in phpAspect

The early candidate aspects discovered in the goal model are suited to be engineered as code aspects, but developers may choose other means to address these crosscutting concerns (e.g. recorded as quality issues to monitor the resulting system), as previously stated. Nevertheless, our approach explores the possibility to equip developers with a full-fledged aspect-oriented framework so that a clear separation of concerns is promoted throughout software development.

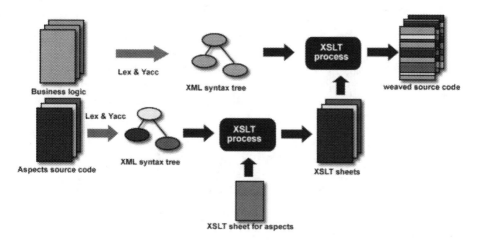

Fig. 5. The weaving process implemented in phpAspect

As one can see from Fig. 4, functional and advising tasks from the requirements model are transformed into functional and aspectual modules in the implementation, respectively. Since the subject in our case study—osCommerce [29]—is implemented in PHP, we select a solution for AOP in this language, phpAspect[1], to facilitate the discussion in implementing early aspects.

The phpAspect language is designed as an extension to PHP. It adds new constructs, such as aspects, pointcuts, advices, and inter-types declarations, inspired by AspectJ for expressing aspects relating to objects and classes while embracing specific features for Web-based applications. It provides pointcut expressions for constructions used in these applications, such as function call and execution, Web-based variable access, XML/HTML enclosing context identification, and the like. Moreover, phpAspect is able to weave aspect components in portions of code that are embedded into XML or HTML elements.

Figure 5 shows how the weaving is performed in phpAspect. It uses a static weaving process that performs source code transformation of a PHP program with aspect extensions into a standard PHP program. The full implementation is based on YAXX [42], which first converts the PHP program into a YACC parsing tree in XML, then weaves the XML representation of the components with the XML representation of the aspects through a customized XSLT stylesheet. The weaved XML representation of the program is then transformed into the source code through another reusable XSLT stylesheet that does the inverse of parsing (unparsing).

The following code snippet shows an example of the security aspect for a Web application. This aspect first introduces a credential checking around all Web pages that require access authentication (captured with the `checkCredentials` pointcut on `goto` method call). This checking prevents users from accessing a

---

[1] Developed by William Candillon during the Google Summer of Code, see
http://code.google.com/soc/php/about.html

Web page if they are not logged in or do not have the right credentials. In these cases, users are redirected to a more appropriate page, either the login or index page. Second, the security aspect checks that all cart operations performed by the client are done in an HTTPS (SSL) mode and deny them otherwise.

```php
<?php
aspect Security {
  //Intercept all instantiations of a page
  pointcut checkCredentials:call(Page->goTo($arg2));

  //Intercept all method execution of the cart
  pointcut checkSSL:exec(Cart->*(*));

  //Around all page instantiations, check the credentials
  around(User $user) checkCredentials {
      if($user->hasCredentials($_GET['page'],
                                $_GET['action'])) {
          proceed();
      } elseif (!$user->isLoggedIn()) {
          $thisJoinPoint->getObject()->goTo('login.php');
      } else {
          $thisJoinPoint->getObject()->goTo('index.php');
      }
  }

  //Around all method execution of the Cart,
  //We check whether the connection is SSL
  around checkSSL {
      if(!$_SERVER['https']) {
          header("Location: https://{$_SERVER['HTTP_HOST']}
                             {$_SERVER['REQUEST_URI']}");
      } else {
          proceed();
      }
  }
}
?>
```

The above example not only demonstrates phpAspect's competence in working out the implementation of goal aspects in question but also shows its capacity to build the model-to-code transformation of interdependent concerns in the system.

3.4 Aspects Validation

It is crucial to validate the implementation against stakeholder requirements to check the faithfulness and appropriateness of the model transformation. We propose a goal-based testing approach to ensure that system functionalities are preserved and system qualities are enhanced by weaving aspects into base modules. This concept is highlighted by the validation flows in Fig. 4.

When it is concrete enough to express the function of a task in terms of input and the expected output, a unit test case can be created to check whether the function is violated by comparing the output of the implemented function with the expected output of the required function. Therefore, the leaf-level functional task in the goal model corresponds to a set of unit test cases that tells whether the base program delivers the required functionality. Having enough unit test cases in terms of the coverage of the input domain, the functional task can be labeled "tested".

Aspects discovered in the goal model provide a baseline for code aspects validation. If an advising task cuts across multiple functional tasks, the unit test cases of the functional tasks at the joinpoints can be reused to test the functionality of the weaved system. This is because goal aspects must not change basic functionalities defined by hard goals and functional tasks. The implementation of aspects, therefore, has to preserve this property.

On the other hand, the degree of certain softgoal satisfaction must be enhanced by the weaved system. In other words, certain qualities in the system with weaved aspects must outperform the one without aspects so that the effort of managing aspects in MDE can be justified. Measuring quality attributes typically presents an obstacle to traditional testing mechanisms, since NFRs are not always easy to be quantitatively measured. Our effort of modeling aspects early in the requirements pays off here. The results from goal-oriented analysis, including the quality metrics, the advising task and pointcut of goal aspects, can be reused and extended to test softgoal satisfaction.

For example, the media shop keeps users from accessing a Web page if they are not logged in or do not have the right credentials. We model this requirement as a security aspect, and transform it to a code aspect in phpAspect, as explained in Sect. 3.3. We can define a set of unit test cases that act as unauthorized agents and try to break into the system. The expected output would be redirecting these malicious visits to the login or index page. Since these security-related test cases crosscut the ones devoted to testing system functionalities (e.g. shopping and searching), they can be regarded as *unit testing aspects* [19], thereby reusing the security aspect's pointcut description to perform the test case weaving.

Note that validating goal aspects can be carried out by other means than defining unit testing aspects. For example, typical Web layer components do not lend themselves to unit testing, unless proper frameworks such as HttpUnit or PHPUnit are employed. In order to ensure that shopping is done securely, testing scripts can be developed to automatically verify that all cart operations are performed in an HTTPS (SSL) mode. Even though such a test may not manifest itself as a testing aspect, it takes full advantage of the early aspects analysis results to check whether the desired level of softgoal satisfaction is achieved.

Another point worth noting is that to separate concerns in functional and non-functional requirements, our use of goal aspects avoids changing basic functionalities defined by hard goals and functional tasks. If one has to constrain a hard goal due to a goal aspect, such as "controlling certain access privilege to a user", then the hard goal is the same; yet it is constrained by an additional condition caused by aspect weaving. As a result, the softgoal associated with access control, namely security, is helped. A side effect of our weaving mechanism is that the original function test must be extended, in this case, by constraining the precondition of the function of the original hard goal. Thus, for those instances that satisfy the constrained precondition, the hard goal functionality is still satisfied; for the instances that fail the new precondition, the postcondition of the composed function is undefined, i.e. they are not comparable to the postcondition of the original functions. The above example also explains the necessity of generating testing aspects from goal aspects and their related functionalities.

3.5   Evolving Requirements Aspects

An important component of working with requirements models is adapting to change: We do not expect our models to be valid for all situations. Consequently, we have been developing a framework for managing requirements models much like configuration management (CM) of source code. Our system consists of an object-oriented version control system, named Molhado [22]; a query language in OCL; and custom code to provide configuration support: temporal query, commit, checkout, reporting and so on. Our implementation is implemented in Eclipse, using the EMF modeling framework.

Changes to a model's entities are mirrored and updated to the graph structures in the model-driven CM repository. The mirror maintains a mapping between the model in memory and the model in persistent storage. The mirror mapping is necessary as the EMF-generated model does not use the Molhado-specific in-memory data structure. Our mapping is implemented as follows.

For each modeling project, the mirror contains (with decreasing granularity): 1) a folder object, representing the project name; 2) leaf folders containing model objects that are uniquely identified by name of goal model files; and 3) model objects containing Molhado graph structure objects (i.e. nodes and edges) that maintain a one-to-one mapping with the model objects in the EMF model. In other words, not only the versions of files but also the versions of individual objects are being maintained.

We have validated the tool using both aspect and aspect-less requirements models. We convert the models from the textual Q7 language losslessly to our EMF-derived metamodel. This allows us to leverage the suite of modeling tools in the Eclipse project. Once the model is in the EMF format, we can edit it in our custom graphical editor, and commit versions of that model to Molhado's file-based storage. The versioning system is fine-grained, with each object in the model—goal, aspect, relation—getting a separate version.

How well does this configuration management system support changes in aspect-oriented requirements models? We committed a version of our example models using both aspects and no aspects to see how the tool performed. Version 1 of each model is a goal model with two aspects: usability and security. Version 2 adds the notion of language customization to the usability aspect as advice (Goal:

Usability [language], children Goal: Customization, Task: Translate). In the non-woven model, this advice is separate, but in the non-aspectual context, the advice is tightly integrated. From version 1 to version 2 of the non-woven model, a mere three changes are made, reflecting the new advice. In the non-aspectual model, in contrast, there are now those three advice elements, as well as the contribution links between the functional elements and the aspects, amounting to six additional linkages, which is nearly 15% more linkages in our small proof-of-concept model (for reference, version 1 of the aspect model contains 22 links and 26 nodes). There are 11 added links between version 1 of the aspect model and version 1 of the non-aspectual model. We conclude that maintaining an evolving aspect version of the model places less demand on the modeler than its non-aspectual counterpart.

4   Case Study

Case studies are an empirical inquiry to investigate a contemporary phenomenon within its real-life context. We used an exploratory case study [43] as the basis for our empirical evaluation. An exploratory case study is an in-depth exploration of one particular case (situation or subject) for the purpose of gaining depth of understanding into the issues being investigated. The design of a case study, in the most elementary sense, is the logical sequence that connects the empirical data to a study's initial research questions, and ultimately, to its conclusions. Our research questions focus on leveraging our framework in a real-world setting and examining the consequences. Specifically, we derive the following hypotheses to guide the study design:

1. Tracing broadly-scoped non-functional concerns across the software life cycle is enabled by our framework;
2. The goal model, together with its refinement and transformation defined in our framework, becomes a primary artifact in the development and validation process; and
3. Software complexity is addressed by the synthesis of MDE and AOSD.

4.1   Data Collection

The subject in our study is osCommerce [29], an open-source platform written in PHP, on which a Web-based media shop [5] development can be fully based. In our previous work [45], we used osCommerce to show how to discover aspects from media shop goal models. In particular, seven goal aspects were identified in [45], among which we choose security and usability aspects as two embedded units of analysis within the current case study. Such a selection is guided by the previous work in a familiar e-commerce domain, and represents a typical case and units of analysis since both security and usability are commonly discussed early aspects in the literature [31].

The data collection in our study consisted of three parts. First, the goal model with aspects for media shop was presented in [45] and further represented in

Table 1. Tracing security ($\mathcal{S}$) and usability ($\mathcal{U}$) aspects in an osCommerce media shop

Concept	Q7		phpAspect	Validation
aspect ($\mathcal{S}$)	`<aspect>::Security [system]`		`aspect Security`	Use PHPUnit to verify
pointcut ($\mathcal{S}$)	`<= + * [page]`		`call(Page->goTo($arg2))`	http authentication
	`<= + * [cart]`		`exec(Cart->*(*))`	and page redirection.
advice ($\mathcal{S}$)	`{ & Redirect [login] }`		`checkCredentials{...}`	Validation result:
	`{ & SSL [connection] }`		`checkSSL{...}`	security insured.
aspect ($\mathcal{U}$)	`<aspect>::Usability [language]`		`aspect Usability_Language`	Use pspell and native-
pointcut ($\mathcal{U}$)	`<= + * [page]`		`call(Page->*printf(*))`	speaker testers to check
	`<= + * [date]`		`call(Data->strftime($arg2))`	the correctness of lang-
	`<= + * [amount]`		`exec(Amount->display($arg2))`	uage translation, date
advice ($\mathcal{U}$)	`{ & Translate [language, NLS] }`		`translatePage{...}`	display, and currencies.
	`{ & Display [format, date] }`		`dateTimeFormat{...}`	Validation result:
	`{ & Convert [currency, amount] }`		`convertCurrency{...}`	usability enhanced.

Q7. Second, the implementation of osCommerce in PHP was accessible through open-source repositories. Our implementation of osCommerce's code aspects in phpAspect was available at [30]. Note that, currently, a human agent has to manually carry out the model-to-code transformation; automatic support is planned for future research. Third, the goal-based validation instrumentation was developed and gathered by some of the authors of this paper (also available at [30]).

It should be noted that case studies, like experiments, are generalizable to theoretical propositions and not to populations or universe. In this sense, the case study, like the experiment, does not represent a "sample", and in doing a case study, our goal will be to expand and generalize theories (*analytic* generalization) and not to enumerate frequencies (*statistical* generalization) [43]. To this end, we regard the selection of subject and units of analysis in our study sufficient. We explicitly formulated three plausible hypotheses for testing, and expect to make analytic generalization about these theoretical propositions.

4.2   Data Analysis

Table 1 summarizes the analysis results of tracing aspects in our subject osCommerce system. The mappings between goal aspects in Q7 and code aspects in phpAspect can be readily spotted in Table 1. Specifically, the name of a goal aspect corresponds to that of a code aspect. Moreover, we map goal's topics into parameterized pointcuts, and map softgoal's operationalizations into advices. The one-to-one correspondence between model aspect and code aspect presented in Table 1 is rather a coincidence due to the chosen units of analysis than the norm of our framework. In more general and complex cases, advanced many-to-many tracing mechanisms may be needed. Nevertheless, we favor a straightforward model-to-code transformation scheme to bridge the gap between domain concepts and implementation technologies. The results in Table 1 happen to illustrate this point.

We focus on the usability aspect in this section, as security is discussed in the previous section as an illustration of our approach. The goal aspect "Usability [language]" is AND-decomposed into 3 parts. One translates natural language strings (NLS) appearing in a Web page to the local language. Another deals with displaying date and time in the desired conventional format. The third converts money amounts from a country's currency into the local currency. The Q7 representations for each pointcut and advice of the usability aspect ($\mathcal{U}$) are given in the second column of Table 1. Correspondingly, Table 1's third column highlights these concepts' counterparts in the phpAspect implementation. The implemented aspects were weaved into osCommerce's base modules by the phpAspect weaver, as explained in Fig. 5.

The goal model plays a crucial role in system validation, and validation in turn justifies the effort of modeling aspects early in the requirements phase. We tested the weaved system in two respects: hard goal preservation and softgoal enhancement. Unit test cases existed for validating the functional requirements of the osCommerce system. Such test cases should not be affected by introducing the aspects that implemented the NFRs. Therefore, we *reused* the functional testing units without any change for checking the functionalities of the weaved system. For example, the shopping cart sum computation must be the same regardless of which natural language is used by the media shop customer. A unit test case using PHPUnit [33] was reused.

```php
require_once 'PHPUnit/Framework/TestCase.php';
require_once 'classes/cart.class.php';
class CheckoutTest extends
          PHPUnit_Framework_TestCase {
  private function getOrder(){
    $cart = new Cart();
    $cart->addItem('Bread', 2);
    // 2.20 each in USD
    $cart->addItem('Butter', 1);
    // 3.20 each in USD
    return $cart->getAmount();
  }
  public function testCheckoutTotal(){
    $this->assertEquals(Currency::convert(
      2*2.20+1*3.20, 'usd'), $this->getOrder());
  }
}
```

We reused 22 functional unit test cases for the weaved system to ensure that introducing goal aspects does not change the function of osCommerce. If one introduces an aspect that does change the functionality of the original system, we consider that either the function is not intended originally or new test case needs to be designed and weaved into the original set of test cases along with the code aspect. However, it is beyond the scope of this paper to discuss how

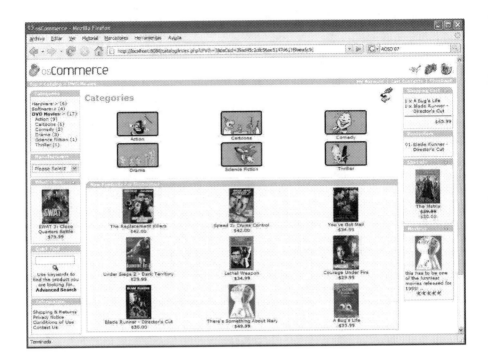

Fig. 6. Screenshot of an osCommerce media shop shown in default language (English)

an aspect should implement a functional requirement, and how such an aspect should be traced and validated.

Having checked that the weaved system preserved system functionalities, we wanted to test whether the aspects indeed addressed the quality concerns, and more importantly, whether they helped better achieve the original stakeholder softgoals. Such a validation was guided by the quality metrics derived from goal-oriented analysis. Taking "Usability [language]" for example, osCommerce currently supported English, German, Spanish, and Japanese users. Figure 6 shows a Web page in the default language—English. The usability aspect should render a Web page by using the language chosen by the user as natural as possible. This included showing textual strings, date, and currency in the desired language and format, as described earlier and indicated in Table 1. Figure 7 shows two screenshots of the weaved system after the language customization aspect is applied.

We validated the usability aspect via two means. Native-speaker (in our case Spanish and Japanese) testers confirmed that the language customization aspect worked very well, in that most Web page contents shown in the desired language, including date and currency, were semantically correct. To evaluate this result in a triangulating fashion [43], we also chose the pspell testing harness [34] to check the syntax of the resulting Web page texts automatically. The fact that all customized pages contained less than 5% syntactic errors increased our confi-

untranslated words

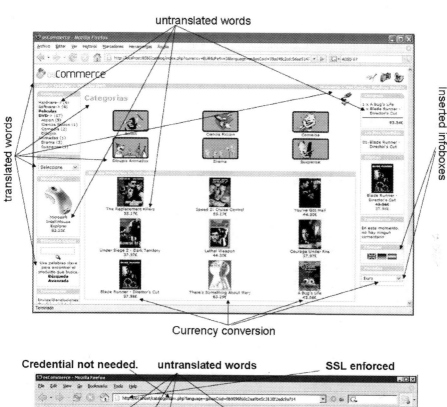

translated words

Inserted infoboxes

Currency conversion

Credential not needed.   untranslated words   SSL enforced

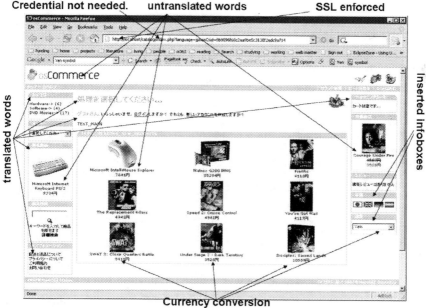

translated words

Inserted infoboxes

Currency conversion

Fig. 7. Screenshots of the weaved system that enhances usability for Spanish (upper) and Japanese (lower) users

dence that the aspects "weaved system indeed helped better meet stakeholders" usability requirements.

4.3   Validity Discussion

Several factors can affect the validity of our exploratory case study: construct validity, external validity, and reliability [43]. Construct validity concerns establishing correct operational measures for the concepts being studied. The key construct in our study is the idea of a goal aspect. Although softgoals have huge potential to become early aspects [24], others may argue that goal aspects can be functional as well. We believe that goal aspects are intended to enhance system qualities while preserving functionalities, and the early aspects community needs to address it more thoroughly. External validity involves establishing the domain to which a study's findings can be generalized. In regard to external validity, we chose Q7, phpAspect, and various testing mechanisms in tracing aspects across an e-commerce application. Further empirical studies are needed to examine the applicability and generality of our framework in coping with other modeling notations, programming languages, and application domains. To reduce the threats to reliability, which cares about demonstrating that the operations of a study can be repeated with the same results, we selected an open-source project and made all our empirical data publicly accessible [30]. Thus, our reported study is replicable, and we believe we would obtain similar results if we repeated the study.

When a developer needs to choose an approach to apply in (re-)engineering an application such as osCommerce, which approach is most appropriate will depend on the task at hand and what type of input is already available. We found out from our case study that our proposed framework could be particularly useful if multiple stakeholder roles were involved in the problem domain, intentionally relying on each other for achieving their individual goals and softgoals. In addition, goal-oriented modeling was preliminary to goal aspects discovery, tracing, and validation, which seemed to be a major cost of applying our approach. Some limitations also arose from the study that we plan to investigate further. First, deciding how to map a goal aspect, either to a code aspect or to a quality issue, turned out to be non-trivial, and the framework should provide guidelines or heuristics to facilitate the decision making. Second, the framework should be extended to allow multiple, possibly conflicting, aspects to be weaved at the same time. Third, automatic support for model transformation, especially complex many-to-many mappings, was necessary for the framework to be more scalable and extensible.

It is worthwhile discussing some experience from our study. When re-engineering osCommerce using aspects, we wanted to achieve a high degree of maintainability to facilitate modification and reuse. Aspects modularized code that would be tangled and scattered otherwise. This not only led to a cleaner code base but also addressed the complexity issue in that uncluttered views were modeled and preserved in the development process. For instance, in the original implementation, 603 natural language string variables were defined in each of the English, German, Spanish, and Japanese language header files to be included in specific Web pages. This caused scattered code duplication. We defined a single usability aspect to modularize these language customization concerns, and removed 3,990 lines of code, 7.6% from the whole code base. In addition to the reduced complexity at the implementation level, the goal model is much closer to the problem situation, which circumvents complexity at the conceptual level.

The above finding helped address the "maintainability" softgoal from the developer's perspective. However, "maintainability" was not originally an NFR concern in the media shop goal model presented in [45]. Thus, we successfully uncovered a missing part of the goal model during the engineering process. This effectively improved the model's quality and longevity because there were no conceptual discontinuities that precluded backtracking. In this sense, one shall not apply our framework in a strict forward-engineering way, but in an iterative fashion within an integrated MDE process. We, therefore, conclude that the exploratory case study presented positive empirical evidence for accepting our three initial hypotheses.

5   Related Work

Goal modeling has become a central activity in RE [41]. It expresses concepts that are fundamental for understanding and specifying stakeholder intentions and concerns. The resulting goal model is a critical mass that supports various kinds of analysis: trade-offs [6], completeness [8], propagation [11], semantics [12], NFRs [21], interferences [25], aspects [45], and many more [41]. Unfortunately, the literature has paid little attention to leveraging the goal model to drive the software development. As a result, practitioners often consider the goal model a nice-to-have artifact or document in the daily practice. Of course, if the model ends up merely as documentation, it is of limited value because documentation all too easily diverges from reality. Consequently, a key premise behind MDE is that programs are (automatically) generated from their corresponding models [37].

The *Tropos* project [5] avoided the shortsighted view of treating models merely as documentation, and used the goal model as a driving force in subsequent implementation. In particular, agent-oriented programming platform was used to develop the goal model, because it seemed natural to map actors to agents. As discussed in Sect. 2.2, several problems exist, among which the distinction between hard goals and softgoals is obscured in the software life cycle. Because these model constructs were not explicitly connected to the actual software, there was no way of ensuring that the developers followed the analysis and design decisions captured in the goal model during implementation. They would often change design intent during implementation—thereby invalidating the model. Unfortunately, because the mapping between models and code is implicit and the code is difficult to comprehend, such digressions would remain undetected and could easily lead to downstream integration and maintenance problems. Note that changing design intent is not necessarily a bad thing, but it is bad if the change goes unobserved [37]. In contrast, we fully appreciate the distinction between hard goals and softgoals, and have devised a full-fledged AOSD framework to transfer the design intent into implementations.

The straightforward model-to-code transformation proposed in our framework shall not de-emphasize the model-to-model transformation, which in our case is the refinement of goal models. It is well recognized that NFRs may not be aligned cleanly and they often depend on or contradict with each other [6]. A major advantage of modeling aspects in goal models is to gain insights into the interplays of NFRs and detect conflicting concerns early, when trade-offs can be resolved more economically [1]. In [23], we presented a rigorous approach to based on the repertory grid technique [9] and formal concept analysis [10], analyzing, refining, and prioritizing stakeholders' interrelated concerns. This concept-driven approach [23] deals with goal model transformation in-depth, and can be seamlessly integrated with our current framework to capitalize on the productivity improvements offered by MDE and AOSD.

When abstract NFRs (softgoals) are concretized, some concerns manifest themselves as quality issues rather than specific code fragments, as shown in Fig. 4. One way to handle these quality issues is to define the specification of *measurements* independent of specific applications. Aside from the structural transformation proposed in our framework, non-functional measurement refinement can be applied to support MDE [35]. The idea is to have definitions of measurements at different levels of abstraction, including provision of transformation rules. The measurement repository can be constructed independent of application development and preferably at a far earlier time, so that the application engineer can reuse the repository when addressing specific quality issues. Structural and measurement refinements are by no means orthogonal: they both connect to the functional models and their refinement [35]. Our approach complements quality measurement development by providing mechanisms to specify the joinpoints in the goal model and its transformations.

Aspects at the requirements level have been studied extensively in recent years. A requirements aspect has been *discovered* (or more accurately *made explicit*) in many RE frameworks: a collaboration in requirements for software components [14], an extension in a use case diagram [15], a softgoal in a goal model [45], an instance of terminological interference in viewpoint-based requirements models [24], an NFR in a software requirements specification [7], and more. A taxonomy of asymmetric requirements aspects is provided in [26]. Asymmetric approaches have made the base-aspect distinction clear, i.e. aspects are relative to the dominant decomposition criterion. On the contrary, a symmetric approach does not separate base from aspects: requirements are decomposed in a uniform fashion. This makes it possible to project any particular set of requirements on a range of other requirements and to support a multi-dimensional separation of concerns [40].

However, most work failed to take advantage of the early aspects model to direct software development. A notable exception is the work presented in [16], where proof obligations were introduced to formalize the validation of the aspectual requirements. Their approach can be applied to programs of well-defined axiomatic semantics. For the quality attributes that do not have a clear-cut answer to satisfaction, it is necessary to validate whether and how much the system can be improved after weaving the proposed aspects. For example, instead of proving that a word is Spanish, we show how well it is understandable by the Spanish-speaking users. Although we reuse unit testing for functional requirements, we believe a complementary approach based on generating proof obligations can better guide the validation of functional requirements.

6   Conclusions

Aspect-oriented software development offers *language* constructs to tackle software complexity. Aspects provides the mechanism that enables the source code to be structured to facilitate the representation of multiple perceptions and to alleviate tangling and scattering concerns. Many of these concerns often arise in the problem domain [27]. Therefore, it is important to identify and represent concerns that arise during the early phases of software development, and to determine how these concerns interact.

Model-driven engineering tackles *conceptual* complexity in software development. The major advantage of MDE is that we express models using concepts that are much less bound to the underlying implementation technology and are much closer to the problem languages [37]. Goal modeling fits in the MDE picture in that it captures stakeholder intentions, beliefs, commitments, and the relationships among the various concerns. This higher level of abstraction makes the goal model easier to specify, understand, and maintain.

In this paper, we have presented our initial investigation into designing a goal-based framework that synthesizes AOSD and MDE, thereby managing complexity in both language and conceptual dimensions. A goal aspect models a system from a stakeholder-defined viewpoint. The aspect is a slice of a system model that contains only information pertinent to the viewpoint. Our framework keeps a clear separation of concerns across software life cycle, and the straightforward model-to-code transformation helps bridge the gap between domain concepts and implementation technologies. The goal model plays a key role in system validation and becomes a primary artifact in software development. Evolving requirements aspects help increase the model's longevity. We evaluated the approach via an exploratory case study that re-engineered a public domain e-commerce platform. The study collected positive evidence to confirm the framework's applicability and usefulness, as well as our hypotheses. We also verified the initial AOP claim that it is natural to implement the globally concerned NFRs as aspects that cut across the subsystems [17].

Our work can be continued in many directions. More in-depth empirical studies are needed to lend strength to the preliminary findings reported here. Aspects other than security and usability can be carried out, and AOP languages other than phpAspect can be tried out. It would be useful to extend our framework's ability to handle conflicts and trade-offs when composing multiple aspects at the same time. Also of interest would be providing automation support for our framework. The future research agenda also includes investigating the framework's applicability to handle functional aspects, incorporating advanced many-to-many tracing mechanisms to cope with complex transformations, and integrating non-functional measurement refinement to deal with quality issues. Synthesis of AOSD and MDE has a rich value in tackling complexity and improving productivity. We hope our work can become a key enabler for more rigorous investigation in this area.

Acknowledgments. We would like to thank William Candillon, Steve Easterbrook, Gilles Vanwormhoudt, Robin Laney, Bashar Nuseibeh, Eric Yu, and Rick Salay for helpful discussions and for insightful comments on the osCommerce case study. We also thank the anonymous reviewers for their constructive suggestions.

References

1. Baniassad, E., Clements, P.C., Araújo, J., Moreira, A., Rashid, A., Tekinerdoğan, B.: Discovering early aspects. IEEE Software 23(1), 61–70 (2006)
2. Booch, G., Rumbaugh, J., Jacobson, I.: The Unified Modeling Language: User Guide. Addison-Wesley, Reading (1999)
3. Bratman, M.: Intention, Plans, and Practical Reason. Harvard Univ. Press, Cambridge (1987)
4. Bresciani, P., Giorgini, P., Giunchiglia, F., Mylopoulos, J., Perini, A.: Towards an agent oriented approach to software engineering. In: Wkshp on Objects and Agents (2001)
5. Castro, J., Kolp, M., Mylopoulos, J.: Towards requirements-driven information systems engineering: the Tropos project. Information Systems 27(6), 365–389 (2002)
6. Chung, L., Nixon, B.A., Yu, E., Mylopoulos, J.: Non-Functional Requirements in Software Engineering. Kluwer Academic Publishers, Dordrecht (2000)
7. Cleland-Huang, J., Settimi, R., Zou, X., Solc, P.: The detection and classification of non-functional requirements with application to early aspects. In: Intl. RE Conf., pp. 39–48 (2006)
8. Dardenne, A., van Lamsweerde, A., Fickas, S.: Goal-directed requirements acquisition. Sci. Comput. Programming 20(1-2), 3–50 (1993)
9. Fransella, F., Bell, R., Bannister, D.: A Manual for Repertory Grid Technique, 2nd edn. John Wiley & Sons, Ltd., Chichester (2004)
10. Ganter, B., Wille, R.: Formal Concept Analysis. Springer, Heidelberg (1996)
11. Giorgini, P., Mylopoulos, J., Nicchiarelli, E., Sebastiani, R.: Reasoning with goal models. In: Spaccapietra, S., March, S.T., Kambayashi, Y. (eds.) ER 2002. LNCS, vol. 2503, pp. 167–181. Springer, Heidelberg (2002)
12. Goal-oriented requirement language (GRL): http://www.cs.toronto.edu/km/GRL/ (last accessed on February 20, 2009)
13. Gray, J., Lin, Y., Zhang, J.: Automating change evolution in model-driven engineering. Computer 39(2), 51–58 (2006)
14. Grundy, J.: Aspect-oriented requirements engineering for component-based software systems. In: Intl. Symp. on RE, pp. 84–91 (1999)
15. Jacobson, I.: Use cases and aspects – working seamlessly together. Journal of Object Technology 2(4), 7–28 (2003)
16. Katz, S., Rashid, A.: From aspectual requirements to proof obligations for aspect-oriented systems. In: Intl. RE Conf., pp. 48–57 (2004)

17. Kiczales, G., Lamping, J., Menhdhekar, A., Maeda, C., Lopes, C., Loingtier, J.-M., Irwin, J.: Aspect-oriented programming. In: Aksit, M., Matsuoka, S. (eds.) ECOOP 1997. LNCS, vol. 1241, pp. 220–242. Springer, Heidelberg (1997)

18. Leite, J., Yu, Y., Liu, L., Yu, E., Mylopoulos, J.: Quality-based software reuse. In: Pastor, Ó., Falcão e Cunha, J. (eds.) CAiSE 2005. LNCS, vol. 3520, pp. 535–550. Springer, Heidelberg (2005)

19. Lesiecki, N.: Unit test your aspects – eight new patterns for verifying crosscutting behavior. IBM Developer Works (2005)

20. Ludewig, J.: Models in software engineering – an introduction. Softw. and Systems Modeling 2(1), 5–14 (2003)

21. Mylopoulos, J., Chung, L., Nixon, B.: Representing and using nonfunctional requirements: a process-oriented approach. IEEE Trans. Softw. Eng. 18(6), 483–497 (1992)

22. Nguyen, T., Munson, E., Boyland, J., Thao, C.: An infrastructure for development of object-oriented, multi-level configuration management services. In: Intl. Conf. Softw. Eng., pp. 215–224 (2005)

23. Niu, N., Easterbrook, S.: Analysis of early aspects in requirements goal models: a concept-driven approach. In: Rashid, A., Aksit, M. (eds.) Transactions on AOSD III. LNCS, vol. 4620, pp. 40–72. Springer, Heidelberg (2007)

24. Niu, N., Easterbrook, S.: Discovering aspects in requirements with repertory grid. In: Early Aspects Wkshp at ICSE, pp. 35–41 (2006)

25. Niu, N., Easterbrook, S.: So, you think you know others' goals? a repertory grid study. IEEE Software 24(2), 53–61 (2007)

26. Niu, N., Easterbrook, S., Yu, Y.: A taxonomy of asymmetric requirements aspects. In: Moreira, A., Grundy, J. (eds.) Early Aspects Workshop 2007 and EACSL 2007. LNCS, vol. 4765, pp. 1–18. Springer, Heidelberg (2007)

27. Nuseibeh, B.: Crosscutting requirements. In: Intl. Conf. on AOSD, pp. 3–4 (2004)

28. Open OME (organization modelling environment): http://www.cs.toronto.edu/km/openome/ (last accessed on February 20, 2009)

29. osCommerce: http://www.oscommerce.org/ (last accessed on February 20, 2009)

30. osCommerce's phpAspect portal: http://www.cs.toronto.edu/~yijun/aspectPHP (last accessed on February 20, 2009)

31. Rashid, A., Sawyer, P., Moreira, A., Araújo, J.: Early aspects: a model for aspect-oriented requirements engineering. In: Intl. RE Conf., pp. 199–202 (2002)

32. Parnas, D.: On the criteria to be used in decomposing systems into modules. Comm. ACM 15(12), 1053–1058 (1972)

33. PHPUnit: http://phpunit.sourceforge.net/ (last accessed on February 20, 2009)

34. pspell: http://php.net/manualen/ref.pspell.php (last accessed on February 20, 2009)

35. Röttger, S., Zschaler, S.: Tool support for refinement of non-functional specifications. Softw. and Systems Modeling 6(2), 185–204 (2007)

36. Schmidt, D.C.: Model-driven engineering. Computer 39(2), 25–31 (2006)

37. Selic, B.: The pragmatics of model-driven development. IEEE Software 20(5), 19–25 (2003)

38. Sendall, S., Kozaczynski, W.: Model transformation: the heart and soul of model-driven software development. IEEE Software 20(5), 42–45 (2003)

39. Shoham, Y.: Agent-oriented programming. Technical Report STAN-CS-1335-90, Stanford Univ. (1990)

40. Tarr, P.L., Ossher, H., Harrison, W.H., Sutton, S.M.: N degrees of separation: multi-dimensional separation of concerns. In: Intl. Conf. on Softw. Eng., pp. 107–119 (1999)
41. van Lamsweerde, A.: Goal-oriented requirements engineering: a guided tour. In: Intl. Symp. on RE, pp. 249–262 (2001)
42. YAXX: http://yaxx.sourceforge.net/ (last accessed on February 20, 2009)
43. Yin, R.: Case Study Research: Design and Methods. Sage Publications, Thousand Oaks (2003)
44. Yu., E.: Towards modelling and reasoning support for early-phase requirements engineering. In: Intl. Symp. on RE, pp. 226–235 (1997)
45. Yu, Y., do Prado Leite, J.C.S., Mylopoulos, J.: From goals to aspects: discovering aspects from requirements goal models. In: Intl. RE Conf., pp. 38–47 (2004)
46. Yu, Y., Niu, N., González-Baixauli, B., Mylopoulos, J., Easterbrook, S., do Prado Leite, J.C.S.: Requirements Engineering and Aspects. In: Lyytinen, K., Loucopoulos, P., Mylopoulos, J., Robinson, B. (eds.) Design Requirements Engineering: A Ten-Year Perspective (to appear, 2009)
47. Yu, Y., Niu, N., González-Baixauli, B., Candillon, W., Mylopoulos, J., Easterbrook, S., do Prado Leite, J.C.S., Vanwormhoudt, G.: Tracing and validating goal aspects. In: Intl. RE Conf., pp. 53–56 (2007)
48. Zave, P., Jackson, M.: Four dark corners of requirements engineering. ACM TOSEM 6(1), 1–30 (1997)

Aspect-Oriented Model-Driven Software Product Line Engineering

Iris Groher and Markus Voelter

Johannes Kepler University Linz, Austria
Independent Consultant, Goeppingen, Germany
Iris.Groher@jku.at, voelter@acm.org

Abstract. Software product line engineering aims to reduce development time, effort, cost, and complexity by taking advantage of the commonality within a portfolio of similar products. The effectiveness of a
software product line approach directly depends on how well feature variability within the portfolio is implemented and managed throughout the
development lifecycle, from early analysis through maintenance and evolution. This article presents an approach that facilitates variability implementation, management, and tracing by integrating model-driven and
aspect-oriented software development. Features are separated in models and composed of aspect-oriented composition techniques on model
level. Model transformations support the transition from problem to solution space models. Aspect-oriented techniques enable the explicit expression and modularization of variability on model, template, and code
level. The presented concepts are illustrated with a case study of a home
automation system.

Keywords: Software product line development, Aspect-oriented software
development, Model-driven software development.

1 Introduction

Most high-tech companies provide products for a specific market. Those products usually tend to have many things in common. An increasing number of
these companies realize that product line development [10] [41] fosters planned
reuse at all stages of the lifecycle, shortens development time, and helps staying
competitive.

Commonalities between products in the portfolio as well as the flexibility to
adapt to different product requirements are captured in so-called *core assets*.
Those reusable assets are created during domain engineering. During application engineering, products are either automatically or manually assembled using
the assets created during the domain engineering process and completed with
product-specific artifacts.

Products usually differ by the set of features they include to fulfill customer
requirements. A feature is defined as an increment in functionality provided by
one or more members of a product line [6]. The effectiveness of a software product line approach directly depends on how well feature variability within the

S. Katz et al. (Eds.): Transactions on AOSD VI, LNCS 5560, pp. 111–152, 2009.
© Springer-Verlag Berlin Heidelberg 2009

portfolio is managed from early analysis to implementation and through maintenance and evolution. Variability of features often has widespread impact on multiple artifacts in multiple lifecycle stages, making it a pre-dominant engineering challenge in software product line engineering.

Despite their crucial importance, features are rarely modularized and there is only little support for incremental variation of feature functionality. The reason is that feature-specific parts are often of crosscutting nature. On implementation level, often pre-processors are used to wrap feature-specific code fragments in #if-#endif statements. Listing 1 shows an implementation example of the eCos operating system [16]. The `Cyg_Mutex` constructor includes 29 lines of code. Four lines of code implement the actual business logic (lines 1, 3, 4, and 29), two lines set the tracing policy (lines 2 and 28), and 23 (almost unreadable) lines implement optional features in this case.

```
1  Cyg_Mutex::Cyg_Mutex() {
       CYG_REPORT_FUNCTION();    //tracing policy
3      locked = false;
       owner = NULL;
5  #if defined(CYGSEM_KERNEL_PRIORITY_INVERSION_PROTOCOL_DEFAULT) &&
           defined(CYGSEM_KERNEL_PRIORITY_INVERSION_PROTOCOL_DYNAMIC)
7  #ifdef CYGSEM_KERNEL_PRIORITY_INVERSION_PROTOCOL_DEFAULT_INHERIT
       protocol = INHERIT;
9  #endif
   #ifdef CYGSEM_KERNEL_PRIORITY_INVERSION_PROTOCOL_DEFAULT_CEILING
11     protocol = CEILING;
       ceiling = CYGSEM_KERNEL_PRIORITY_INVERSION_PROTOCOL_DEFAULT_PRI;
13 #endif
   #ifdef CYGSEM_KERNEL_PRIORITY_INVERSION_PROTOCOL_DEFAULT_NONE
15     protocol = NONE;
   #endif
17 #else // not (DYNAMIC and DEFAULT defined)
   #ifdef CYGSEM_KERNEL_PRIORITY_INVERSION_PROTOCOL_CEILING
19 #ifdef CYGSEM_KERNEL_PRIORITY_INVERSION_PROTOCOL_DEFAULT_PRIORITY
       // if there is a default priority ceiling defined, use that
21     // to initialize the ceiling.
       ceiling = CYGSEM_KERNEL_PRIORITY_INVERSION_PROTOCOL_DEFAULT_PRIORITY;
23 #else
       ceiling = 0; // Otherwise set it to zero.
25 #endif
   #endif
27 #endif // DYNAMIC and DEFAULT defined
       CYG_REPORT_RETURN();    //tracing policy
29 }
```

Listing 1. eCos implementation example [31]

Another pitfall is that features and architecture are often derived from requirements in a non-systematic, ad hoc way. For software product lines it is essential to know the relationship among requirements, the derived architecture, the design, and the implementation artifacts. Consequently, a systematic way to group requirements into features that are then related to architectural entities and a seamless tracing of requirements throughout the whole lifecycle is necessary.

As demonstrated, variability tends to crosscut multiple points in code as well as different other artifacts in the software development lifecycle. Moreover, the effects of variability and, in particular, new variations brought in by evolution tend to propagate in ways that cannot be easily modeled or managed. New requirements may necessitate changes to code, design, documentation, and user manuals among many other artifacts and assets that go into making a product line. Ensuring the traceability of requirements and their variations throughout the software life cycle is key for successful software development in general, and a successful product line in particular.

Also, the mapping between problem space and solution space is not trivial. The problem space is concerned with end-user understandable concepts representing the business domain of the product line. The solution space deals with the elements necessary for implementing the solution, typically IT relevant artifacts. There is a many-to-many relationship between entities in the problem space (requirements and features) to entities in the solution space (software components).

Aspect-oriented software development (AOSD) [18, 29] improves the way software is developed by providing means for modularizing crosscutting concerns. They are encapsulated as aspects and powerful mechanisms support their subsequent composition with other software artifacts. Aspects interact with other artifacts at so-called *joinpoints*, well-defined points in the structure, or execution flow of an artifact or a program. Pointcut expressions quantify over the joinpoints to select the set of actual composition points for a specific aspect. An aspect weaver automatically composes aspects with the rest of the system, either statically during compilation, dynamically at runtime, or at load-time.

Model-driven software development (MDSD) [21, 44] improves the way software is developed by capturing key features of a system in models which are developed and refined as the system is created. During the system's life cycle, models are synchronized, combined, and transformed between different levels of abstraction and different viewpoints. In contrast to traditional modeling, models do not only constitute documentation but are processed by automated tools. Thus models have to be formal. Every model is an instance of a metamodel. The metamodel defines the vocabulary and grammar, i.e. the abstract syntax used to build models. To be useful for MDSD, models have to be complete regarding the abstraction level or viewpoint they describe.

While AOSD and MDSD are different in many ways–MDSD adds domain-specific abstractions and AOSD offers improved support for concern modularization across the life cycle as well as powerful composition mechanisms–they also have many things in common, e.g. they help the developer to reason about one concern at a time. Essentially, AOSD and MDSD complement each other.

We propose an approach that facilitates variability implementation, management, and tracing from architectural modeling to implementation of product lines by integrating both AOSD and MDSD. When building product lines, our integrated approach increases productivity because

- Variability can be described more abstractly because in addition to the traditional mechanisms, variability is also described on model level.
- The mapping from problem to solution space can be formally described and automated using model-to-model transformations.

- Aspect-oriented techniques enable the explicit expression and modularization of crosscutting variability on model, code, and generator level.
- Fine-grained traceability is supported since tracing is done on model element level rather than on the level of code artifacts.

The presented concepts are illustrated with a case study of a home automation system. The case study is based on real-world system requirements from Siemens AG and demonstrates the benefits of the presented approach. We used data from the case study to answer our research question:

> *Where and how can software product line development benefit from AOSD, MDSD, and their combination?*

The remainder of this article is organized as follows: Section 2 provides an overview of our integrated aspect-oriented model-driven software product line development approach. In addition it gives an overview of openArchitecture-Ware, the MDSD framework our tools are based on. Section 3 illustrates the selective adaptation of models and provides an overview of XWeave and XVar. AO on model transformation level is discussed in Section 4. Section 5 discusses AO on code generation level. Variability on code level is addressed in Sect. 6. We report the case study we conducted at Siemens in Sect. 7. We conclude with a summary and a note on future work in Sect. 8.

2   Aspect-Oriented Model-Driven Software Product Line Engineering

This section gives an overview of what we call *Aspect-Oriented Model-Driven Software Product Line Engineering (AO-MD-PLE)*. The key parts are presented in this section while the separate building blocks and tools are demonstrated in detail in the subsequent sections.

Our approach [48] integrates AO and MDSD into product line development to facilitate variability implementation, management, and tracing from architectural modeling to implementation. We argue that because models are more abstract and hence less detailed than the code, variability on model level is inherently less scattered and therefore simpler to manage (cf. Fig. 1).

AO-MD-PLE uses models to describe product lines. Variants are defined on model level. Transformations generate running applications. AO techniques are used to help define the variants in the models as well as in the transformers and generators. We strongly believe that this is the case because domain-specific models are typically less detailed than the code. From one *piece of model*, usually several *pieces of the code* are generated that depend on that model via the generation rules. If one wants to change all the dependent locations in the code manually, then these are obviously more places compared to changing the model from which those code locations are generated. The fact that models are less scattered can be explained via a related reasoning process. As already

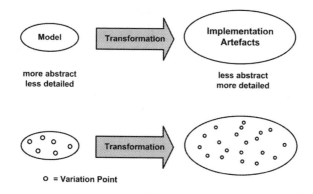

Fig. 1. Mapping abstract models to detailed implementations

explained, a generator typically creates several distinct pieces of code in different artifacts from the same model (e.g. data structures, database access code, database schema, or XML schema). This means that the generated code that belongs to a well-localized part of the model is scattered over different places in different artifacts.

The approach we propose is as follows:

– We express the different product line artifact types and their instances using models, i.e. we give them representations on model level. This allows for processing these artifacts using model transformations.
– Mappings from problem to solution space are implemented as model-to-model transformations. This enables to formally describe the mappings and automate their execution.
– Variable parts of the resulting system are assembled from pre-built assets generated from models. This is more efficient and less error prone than manual coding.
– Aspect-oriented modeling (AOM) [5, 9] is used to implement variability in models. This supports the selective adaptation of models.
– AO on model transformation and code generation level [47] is used to implement variability in transformers and generators.
– Aspect-oriented programming (AOP) [4, 28] is used to implement crosscutting features on code level that cannot be easily modularized in the generator.
– Certain parts of the product will still be implemented manually because, for economic reasons, developing a custom generator is too costly. The manually written code is integrated with the generated code in well-defined ways.

An overview of AO-MD-PLE is given in Fig. 2. Domain requirements are captured in a problem space metamodel. Based on product requirements, a problem space model is created that is an instance of the problem space metamodel. The problem space metamodel defines the vocabulary and grammar, i.e. the abstract syntax used to build the problem space model. The model itself is built using a

Domain-specific language (DSL) [44]. A DSL is a formalism for building models. It encompasses a metamodel (in this case, the problem space metamodel) as well as a definition of a concrete syntax that is used to represent the model. The concrete syntax can be textual, graphical, or can be using other means such as tables, trees, or dialogs. It is essential that the concrete syntax can sensibly represent the concepts the DSL is intended to describe. A suitable editor has to be provided that supports the creation of models using the DSL.

Both problem space metamodels and problem space models can be configured using either model weaving or model tailoring. In model weaving, optional parts are added to a minimal core, whereas in model tailoring, optional parts are removed from an overall model.

The tool developed to support model weaving is called XWeave, and the tool to support model tailoring is called XVar. Both allow the selective adaptation of models and metamodels based on feature selections in configuration models. The model configuration approach and the respective tools will be introduced in great detail in Sect. 3.

A formal mapping is defined between the problem space metamodel and the solution space metamodel. The defined mapping allows for an automatic transformation of the problem space model into the solution space model. This step can be repeated as desired. For example, one could first map the problem space metamodel to a platform-independent model and map this metamodel to a platform-specific model. This separation makes it possible to easily support different platform technologies. Model transformations can be configured using AO on transformation level.

We used an AO model transformation language called Xtend that supports the selective adaptation of transformation functions. Again, model transformation aspects can be linked to features defined in a feature model. AO on transformation level and the respective language will be illustrated in Sect. 4.

In order to create a running system, the code is generated from the solution space model. This step can also be configured using AO on template level and is supported by a language called Xpand. Code generation template weaving will be described in Sect. 5. As a 100% generation is not realistic, manually written code has to be integrated with the generated code in well-defined ways. Also, it might be necessary to integrate pre-built reusable components in the form of libraries into the generated system. Because in our approach all artifacts have representations on model level, we can process them using model transformations. Based on the information in the models, we can determine whether a given component (either manually written or pre-built) is part of a product and thus has to be integrated.

Because it is in most cases necessary to include manually written code, variability on source code level is an issue. We use AOP to implement positive variability on code level. In addition, we developed a tool called XVar that supports negative variability on code level. We will elaborate this in Sect. 6.

An important concern in software product lines is tracing, as stakeholders want to be able to trace how a given requirement results in a certain software

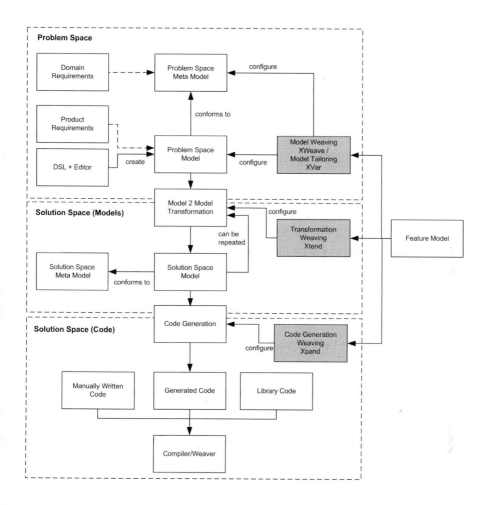

Fig. 2. Aspect-oriented model-driven product line engineering

configuration. Using our AO-MD-PLE approach, this is relatively easy to do. Since mappings between abstraction levels are based on formal model transformations, we can make sure that the mappings are made persistent in a trace model. It can either be built automatically by the transformation engine or it can be built manually by the transformation developer.

Since we trace between model elements, the trace is finer grained than in current approaches where tracing happens between artifacts [27, 33]. Also, since problem space concepts are also represented as models and these models have a defined mapping to solution space models, we gain traceability from the problem space over to the solution space.

In addition, tracing down to code level is an important issue. Specific regions of the code need to be associated with model elements. For generated code, this is straight forward since the generator knows which model elements are "in scope" when a given region of code is generated. For manually written code, it is more challenging since a piece of hand-written code may implement any number of requirements. This problem can be mitigated to some extent by clearly defining the locations where manually written code can be integrated. An alternative approach is to specify the trace from models to code manually. Tracing to library code is again relatively easy to do in our approach as every library component has some kind of representation on model level. We can then trace via model element relationships.

On the other end of the spectrum, we also need to trace requirements. These are different from problem space models as requirements are typically plain English text. To make them traceable, we need to somehow integrate them into the "modeling world". This can be done in various ways, depending on the tool that is used to capture the requirements. For example, it would be possible to create an EMF model [14] based on requirements managed with the DOORS [46] tool and use the EMF model for tracing purposes.

2.1   openArchitectureWare

This section introduces openArchitectureWare (oAW) [38, 39], a toolkit for all aspects of MDSD. The tools developed in the course of our work are all part of the oAW framework.

oAW is an open source MDSD framework implemented in Java and integrates a number of tool components. oAW supports arbitrary import model formats, metamodels, and output code formats. oAW is integrated into Eclipse and provides various plug-ins that support model-driven development. It contributes to and reuses components from the Eclipse Modeling Project [14].

At the core, there is a workflow engine that allows the definition of transformation workflows by sequencing various kinds of workflow components. oAW comes with pre-built workflow components for reading and instantiating models, checking them for constraint violations, transforming them into other models, and then finally, for generating code. oAW provides a family of specialized languages for specifying constraint checks, transformations, and code generators. All of those languages are built on a common OCL-like expression language. Editors and debuggers integrated into Eclipse are provided for all those languages.

Figure 3 provides an overview of oAW and its main building blocks. The list explains the different components (marked with numbers) as follows:

1. Model verification using constraints: Both models and metamodels can be checked for validity. In oAW, constraints are defined using the Checks language.
2. Artifact generation: Any textual artifact can be generated from models using the Xpand template language.
3. Integrating generated code with manually written code: The Recipe Framework can be used to enforce rules on the code base. For example, a generator

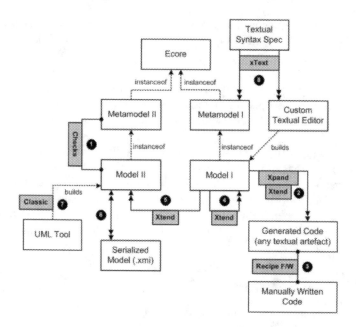

Fig. 3. Overview of openArchitectureWare [38]

can generate an abstract base class from which developers extend their implementation classes containing the business logic. Such rules can be specified using Recipes.

4. Model modification: Models can be modified or completed using the Xtend language.
5. Model transformation: Models can be transformed into other models using the Xtend language. Typically, input and output models are instances of different metamodels.
6. Loading and storing models: By default, EMF models are stored in XMI [36] files. oAW provides workflow components for loading and storing models from/to XMI files.
7. Model creation using UML tools: Models can be created and edited using familiar UML tools such as Rational Rose [25] or MagicDraw [35]. oAW provides adapters for various commonly used UML tools.
8. Textual model creation: oAW can also read textual models created with custom-built textual editors based on its Xtext framework. The DSL is described in EBNF, and the parser, metamodel, and customized editor is created automatically.
9. oAW also integrates with custom graphical editors built using Eclipse GMF [15]. oAW constraints can be evaluated inside GMF editors in real time, and oAW can process models created with GMF.

The transformation and generation workflow is described using the oAW workflow language. As of version 4.2, workflow files are XML files that describe the steps that need to be executed in a generator run. Each of these steps is specified with what is called a *workflow component*. A typical oAW workflow (Listing 2) consists of loading one or more models, checking constraints on them, transforming them into other models and then generating code from them.

The root element is named workflow, followed by the declaration of two workflow components. The first component has an attribute id and can be referenced throughout this id. The attribute class refers to the Java class that implements the workflow component. In the first component, an EMF model (inputModel.xmi) is read from its XMI-based serialization format. The top-level metamodel package is data.DataPackage. The read model is stored in a model slot named model, which is used to pass the instantiated model to the transformation component. In the second workflow component, the model is transformed by invoking a transformation function transform on the model. The function is defined in the file model2model. The transformed model is available for further processing in the transformedModel slot.

```
<workflow>
    <component  id="xmiParser"
          class="org.openarchitectureware.emf.XmiReader">
          <modelFile  value="inputModel.xmi" />
    <metaModelPackage value="data.DataPackage" />
    <outputSlot  value="model"/>
  </component>

    <transform  id="XtendComponent.model2model" >
          <invoke  value="model2model::transform(\${model})"/>
          <outputSlot  value="transformedModel"/>
    </transform>
</workflow>
```

Listing 2. oAW example workflow

In oAW, model-to-model transformations are implemented using a language called Xtend. It is a functional language for querying and navigating existing models as well as building new models. Listing 3 shows an example transformation that transforms a model element Interface defined in the metamodel sourceMM into a model element Service defined in the metamodel targetMM. It sets the name of the target element of type Service to the name of the source element of type Interface. The operations of the interface are copied from the source to the target element.

```
create targetMM::Service Interface2Service( sourceMM::Interface intf ):
    setName( intf.name ) ->
    setOperations( (List)intf.operations.clone() );
```

Listing 3. oAW example Xtend transformation

Code generation is done using a language called Xpand. It is an object-oriented template language that supports polymorphism. Listing 4 shows an example Xpand template file. First, the metamodel is imported. Second, a new file with the name of the entity `Class` including the class skeleton is generated. The template ≪name≫ is substituted with a concrete value (the name of the class) at generation time.

```
<<IMPORT metamodel>>

<<DEFINE javaClass FOR Class>>
    <<FILE name + ".java">>

        public class <<name>> {
                // add implementation of class here
        }

    <<ENDFILE>>
<<ENDDEFINE>>
```

Listing 4. oAW example Xpand template

Each oAW language (Check, Xtend, Xpand) is based on a common expression language and type system. This has the advantage that all the languages can operate on the same models, metamodels, and meta metamodels have a common look and feel to them, and are therefore easy to learn. The expressions framework provides a uniform abstraction layer over different meta metamodels [39].

Integrating oAW and pure::variants. This section illustrates how the variant management tool pure::variants [42] has been integrated into oAW to enable seamless and efficient aspect-oriented model-driven product line development.

pure::variants is a variant management tool that manages product line variability and assists in managing and assembling individual product variants. The basic idea of pure::variants is to realize product lines by feature models and family models. The problem space is captured with feature models and the solution space is captured with family models, separately and independently. A family model consists of so-called components. Components represent elements of the software solution and contain parts like classes, objects, functions, variables, and documentation. A feature model specifies the interdependencies of the features of a product line. They represent all variability of the products in the product line. pure::variants also supports the use of multiple feature models that are hierarchically linked.

Users can select features required for the desired product from the feature models. A configuration model represents such a selection of features. pure::variants checks the validity of this selection, and if necessary, automatically resolves dependency conflicts. A valid selection triggers an evaluation of the family models that contain component definitions consisting of logical and physical parts. The evaluation process results in an abstract description of the selected solution in terms of components.

Within the oAW tooling, global configuration models can be queried, and hence, MDSD activities can be performed based on the selection of features. Workflow components, model-transformations, and code generation templates can be linked to features. Their execution then depends on the presence or absence of features in the configuration model.

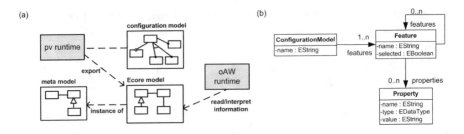

Fig. 4. Integration of pure::variants and oAW

As illustrated in Fig. 4(a), the data transfer between pure::variants and oAW is done using EMF Ecore. An automatic variant model export has been integrated into pure::variants. The oAW runtime reads this model and makes the variant information available for querying by oAW workflows, transformations and templates. In order for this integration to work, a metamodel for configuration models (Fig. 4(b)) has been defined. A ConfigurationModel contains a list of Features that again contain features (subfeatures). Features can contain attributes that have a name and a value.

The dependency between workflow steps and features is expressed by the surrounding < feature ... > tag. Listing 5 shows an example. If and only if the feature debug is selected in the global configuration model, code that implements the debug feature is generated.

```
<feature exists="debug">
    <component class='oaw.xpand2.Generator>
        ... invoke generator that generates debugging code
    </component>
</feature>
```

Listing 5. Dependency between workflow and features

It is also possible to access the configuration model directly from within transformations or code generation templates. In Listing 6, the transformation function handleDebugFeature is only called if the debug feature is selected in the configuration model.

```
create Service transformInterface2Service (Interface f) :
    ...
    hasFeature("debug") ? handleDebugFeature() -> this ) : this;

handleDebugFeature (System sys) :
    setValue( (String) getFeatureAttributeValue ("debug", "level") ) ->
    ...
```

Listing 6. Dependency between transformation and features

The integration of pure::variants and oAW also supports addressing properties or attributes of features. The values of properties and attributes can be read and used in the transformation or code generation templates. In Listing 6, the debug level is read and handled within the transformation.

The integration of variant management tools other than pure::variants is easily possible. As long as the tool provides an export of variant information to the defined metamodel in Fig. 4, oAW can read and interpret this information. The variant information is then automatically available to the workflow, transformation, and generation engine.

3 Expressing Variability in Structural Models

This section describes concepts and tools that support the definition of feature-based variability in structural models and hence the selective adaptation of models. Structural models are models built with a creative construction DSL. Features expressed in structural models can be linked to configuration models. This enables the adaptation of those structural models based on the feature selection in configuration models.

3.1 Positive Variability

The terms positive and negative variability have been initially introduced in [11]. As illustrated in Fig. 5, positive variability starts with a minimal core and selectively adds additional parts. The core represents the model parts that are common to all products within the product line. Varying model parts are attached to the core based on the presence or absence of features in the configuration models.

Negative variability selectively takes away parts of a creative construction model. It will be discussed in detail in Sect. 3.2

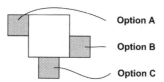

Fig. 5. Positive variability

When expressing variability in models, optional model elements have to be connected to the core at specific points. This is analogous to the concept of joinpoints in aspect-orientation. In AOP, joinpoints are those elements of the programming language semantics which the aspects coordinate with [2]. In modeling, joinpoints are elements of the modeling language which aspects coordinate with. In product lines, variation points represent variability subjects within domain artifacts [41]. Domain artifacts include all kinds of development artifacts such as requirements, architecture, design, code, and tests. This similarity in the concept of a variation point and a joinpoint makes AOM and specifically model weaving well-suited candidates for implementing positive variability in structural

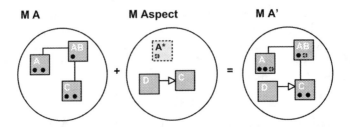

Fig. 6. Model weaving

models. Similar to weaving of code level aspects in traditional AO languages, aspects are defined on model level and are composed with a base model. Weaving is technically done by an aspect weaver at designated joinpoints.

In the field of AOP, there are various joinpoint models around and many are still under development. Joinpoint models heavily depend on the underlying programming language and AO language [2]. Hence, the joinpoint model of AOM depends on the underlying modeling language and the language used to express aspects on model level. We introduce a model weaving approach including a joinpoint model that supports the expression of aspects on model level and a composition technique for base models and aspect models.

Figure 6 illustrates the concept of model weaving. A given base model (M A) and an aspect model (M Aspect) are composed. The aspect model consists of pointcut definitions that capture the points where in the base model additional model elements should be added. In addition to the pointcut definitions, the aspect model contains advices that represent the elements to be added. The aspect model uses both name matching and pointcut expressions to select the desired joinpoints. Both techniques will be explained in great detail later in this section. In this case, the model element D of the aspect model M Aspect that is derived from element C is added to the result model. The weaving rule applied here is simple name matching. The elements named C in both models correspond, and so both elements are combined. This results in C having a new child D in the result model. The aspect element A* specifies that the dotted gray element within A* should be added to all base elements whose name starts with A, in this case, element A and element AB. This is an application of a pointcut expression. After the weaving process a result model (M A') is created that contains all the original base model elements plus the aspect elements added at the desired joinpoints.

A tool called XWeave[1] [22, 23] has been developed that implements the concepts presented above. It is based on Eclipse as a tool platform and Ecore as the meta metamodel. Since it is an oAW workflow component, it easily integrates into oAW-based model processing.

XWeave is a model weaver that can weave models that are either instances of Ecore (called metamodels) or instances of these metamodels (called models).

---

[1] XWeave is part of openArchitectureWare 4.2 and can be downloaded from http://www.openarchitectureware.org/

The tool takes a base model as well as one or more aspect models as input and weaves the content of the aspect model into the base model. Weaving an aspect element means that all properties of the element, including its child elements, are woven into the base model. Both aspect and base models must conform to the same metamodel. The aspect model consists of definitions that capture the points, where in the base model, the additional model elements should be added (the *pointcut* in AO terms). It also contains these additional model elements (the *advice* in AO terms). This is a form of asymmetric AO. During weaving, aspect elements are physically woven into the base model. The result of this process is an updated model. Subsequent tooling cannot tell the difference between a woven and a non-woven model.

The joinpoint model of XWeave is based purely on the metamodel of the base model and is thus generic. All elements of the base model are potential joinpoints. This means that any model element of an EMF model can serve as a joinpoint. Pointcuts select sets of those elements where additional elements can be attached.

XWeave provides two ways of specifying pointcuts: name matching and explicit pointcut expressions. The next sections will introduce both approaches in detail. For illustration purposes, all examples use the concrete syntax of UML.

Name Matching. Name matching means that if a model element in the aspect model has a corresponding element in the base model (both name and type have to be equal), the elements are combined. Combining the two elements means that all children of the aspect element are added to the base element. In case of a class, the woven class would hence include all attributes and operations from the base element as well as those from the aspect element.

Figure 7 shows an example of name matching in XWeave to specify the desired joinpoints. It is an application of metamodel weaving. The model in (a) shows the metamodel of a simple state machine. The state machine has a list of states linked by transitions. The metamodel only supports simple states. A variation of this metamodel is to not only support simple states but also dedicated start and stop states. The model in (b) illustrates the aspect model. StartState and StopState are derived from State and should be woven to the base model. The aspect element State has a corresponding element in the base model and is therefore the point at which StartState and StopState are added. The model in (c) shows the result model after weaving.

Pointcut Expressions. Another way of specifying pointcuts are explicit pointcut expressions. They can be defined using oAW's expression language. Expressions can select one or more elements of the base model and are defined externally to both aspect and base model in a separate expression file. Every expression has a name. The named expressions (pointcuts) can be used in the aspect model. If an aspect element's name starts with %, $, or ? followed by the name of a defined expression, the expression will be evaluated for this element. The % sign introduces an expression that returns a collection of elements. The $

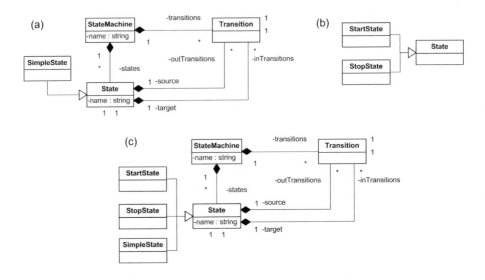

Fig. 7. Metamodel weaving using name matching

character introduces an expression that returns a single element. The ? character is followed by a String expression, i.e. it has to return a String. It can be used to add any kind of name to the elements. In addition, it is possible to use * (the asterisk) character as the name of an element. This matches all instances of that particular type.

Pointcut expressions make it possible to select several joinpoints in the model with only one declarative statement. This is referred to as the quantification principle of AO [19]. Expressions must be parameterized with the type that serves as the root for the base model. Whatever the expression returns, will be used as the target for the weaving process.

To express pointcuts, XWeave uses the oAW expression language [39], which is a syntactical mixture of OCL and Java. A complete reference of the language can be found in [39].

Figure 8 illustrates an example of pointcut expressions. In (a) a state machine model of an oven is presented. It is an instance of the metamodel presented in Fig. 7. The oven can be either open, closed, or in cooking state. The aspect models in (b) weave an emergency state into the base model including the respective transitions. The aspect model on the left uses a pointcut expression to select all states of type `SimpleState` using the pointcut expression `pc`. The right side of figure (b) is an alternative to using the pointcut expression. The asterisk matches all instances of a particular type, in this case, `SimpleState`. The model in (c) shows the result after weaving.

The XWeave approach can be applied to both problem space models and solution space models. This means that both domain models and software models can be configured.

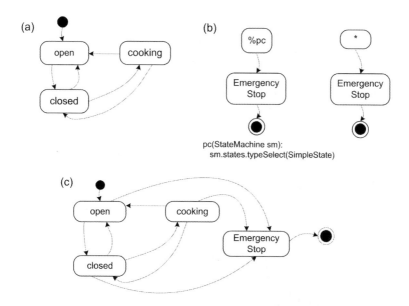

Fig. 8. Model weaving using pointcut expressions

Linking XWeave to Configuration Models. Model weaving assists in the composition of different separated models into a consistent whole. It allows capturing feature-dependent parts of models in aspect models. This technique supports a clear separation of variable model parts from the core and supports an automatic composition to create a complete model representing a member of the product line.

During domain engineering, the core[2] and the aspects are developed. The core represents model parts common to all products in the product line, and the aspects represent features that are increments in functionality provided by one or more members of the product line. During application engineering, the aspect models are composed with the core according to a selection of features in a configuration model. Consequently, the core is minimal in that it only contains elements common to all products in the portfolio. Product-specific parts are added when needed.

The dependency between aspect models and features is specified in the oAW workflow. Aspects that implement optional parts of structural models are linked to features defined in configuration models. Based on a selection of features, the corresponding aspect models are woven to the base model. This dependency between features and aspect models is illustrated in Fig. 9.

Listing 7 shows an example workflow. If the `EmergencyStateFeature` is present in the global configuration model, XWeave weaves the content of the aspect model into the oven model. Aspect and base model are illustrated in Fig. 8. The base model is already in a workflow slot.

---

[2] We will use the terms core and base model as synonyms.

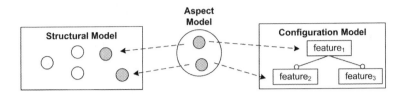

Fig. 9. Linking positive variability to configuration models

```
<feature exists="EmergencyStateFeature">
  <cartridge file="org/openarchitectureware/util/xweave/wf−weave−expr"
    baseModelSlot="ovenModel"
    aspectFile"emergencyStateAspect.xmi"
    expressionFile="expressions"/>
</feature>
```

Listing 7. XWeave workflow

3.2 Negative Variability

As illustrated in Fig. 10, negative variability selectively takes away parts of a creative construction model based on the presence or absence of features in the configuration models. This technique is fundamentally different to the technique introduced in the previous section. When using negative variability to implement feature-based variability in structural models, one has to build the "overall" model manually and connect elements to certain features in a configuration model. The model is then tailored based on a certain feature selection, thus model elements are taken away from the full model.

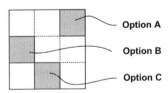

Fig. 10. Negative variability

Figure 11 illustrates how subtractive variability on model level works. It shows a simple feature model of a person database. A person can either have an international phone number or a local phone number. There is also an optional feature, namely, the possibility of adding state information for US citizens. Features of the feature model are linked to elements of the structural model below. In this case, attributes are connected to the features. Those elements are only present in the model if and only if the corresponding features are part of a configuration.

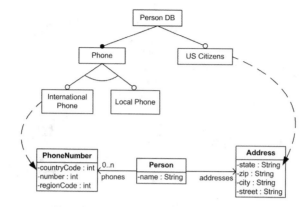

Fig. 11. Negative variability in structural models

A tool called XVar[3] [22] has been developed that implements the concepts presented above. Similar to XWeave, it is based on Eclipse as a tool platform, Ecore as the meta metamodel, and oAW as the tool for model processing.

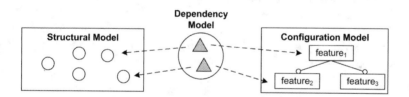

Fig. 12. Linking negative variability to configuration models

Figure 12 illustrates how XVar links structural models to configuration models. A dependency model captures the relationships between model elements and features. Depending on the selection of features, the structural model is tailored to only contain the model elements needed for the respective configuration by deleting model elements whose features are not selected. Deleting means that the element itself and all references to this element are removed from the model.

Figure 13(a) shows the dependency model for the person database example. Every element describes a dependency between a feature and the linked model elements. The international phone feature is linked to the countryCode attribute in class PhoneNumber, and the US citizens feature is linked to the state attribute in class Address. According to this dependency model, the structural model is tailored based on a concrete selection of features. Figure 13(b) illustrates a model that results if only the optional US Citizens and the Local

---

[3] XVar is part of openArchitectureWare 4.2 and can be downloaded from http://www.openarchitectureware.org/

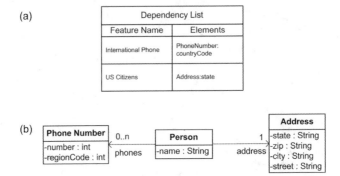

Fig. 13. Dependency model and result model

Phone features are selected. The `International Phone` feature is not part of this configuration. Thus, the attribute `countryCode` of class `PhoneNumber` is deleted from the structural model in Fig. 12.

XVar can tailor models that are either instances of Ecore (called metamodels) or of these models (called models). The dependency between features and model elements is specified in a separate dependency model. The advantage of defining feature dependencies in an external model is that no invasive changes to the model are required. All dependencies are explicitly listed in the dependency model. The XVar approach can be applied to both problem space models and solution space models.

3.3   Related Work

Positive Variability in Structural Models. The Atlas Model Weaver (AMW) [17] is a tool created as part of the Atlas Model Management Architecture. It's primary goal is to establish links between models. In the first phase of working with AMW, a number of links are established between two or more models. This process can be done manually or semi-automatic. The result is called a weaving model. Based on that model, one can generate model transformations that merge models. AMW is similar to XWeave as both tools can weave or merge models. There is, however, an important difference. AMW contains an interactive tool to build weaving models, whereas XWeave uses name correspondence or pointcut expressions.

C-SAW [20] is a general transformation engine for manipulating models based on aspect specifications using ECL (a variant of OCL). The weaver traverses the model and selects a set of elements to which the aspects should be applied. The advice then modifies the selected element in some way, for example, by adding a precondition or changing the element's structure. C-SAW has been developed to tackle the challenge of evolving large models in a consistent way. Instead of applying a set of changes manually, one merely writes an aspect that applies the changes to all selected elements in the model. Comparing it to XWeave reveals that C-SAW does not weave models (in the sense of merging them) as XWeave does. Rather, it efficiently applies (crosscutting) changes to a collection of elements in a large model by automatically traversing the model and giving the advice code a change to modify an element if it sees fit.

The Motorola WEAVR [12] is a model weaver developed as a plug-in for Telelogic TAU. It supports weaving of UML statecharts that include action semantics and are thus executable. There are two different types of joinpoints: action and transition. Advices are encapsulated in a construct called connector. Similar to XWeave, the Motorola WEAVR weaves aspects based on pointcut specifications. The main difference between the two approaches is that XWeave provides a generic EMF-based solution that can weave arbitrary models and metamodels. The Motorola WEAVR only supports weaving of UML statecharts.

XJoin [39] is a tool for establishing links between metamodels. The tool takes two or more existing metamodels as input and adds relationships to join them. The partial metamodels still keep their own identities and do not need to know about the other ones. Using XJoin, different architectural viewpoints [30] can be separately described and later combined. The difference to XWeave is that XJoin does not weave models; it only establishes links between them. Both tools are part of the oAW framework and thus integrate very well.

General AOM approaches [9] are also related to XWeave. Theme/UML [5], for example, provides an extension to UML that supports concern modeling and composition. Most AOM techniques are based on UML, which is an important difference to XWeave. Also, most approaches lack tool support, which is essential for a successful application of the technique in an industrial product line context.

Negative Variability in Structural Models. In [13], structural models are connected to feature models to implement negative variability. A feature model is linked to a UML model via stereotypes. Depending on the selected features, the UML model changes. XVar also implements negative variability for structural models, but in contrast to [13], it provides a generic EMF-based solution. Another important difference is that in XVar the links between model elements and features are managed in a separate dependency model. In [13], the links are managed using stereotypes, which requires invasive changes to the model that should be tailored.

In [24], a tool is presented that supports linking features to parts of EMF models. Changes made to structural models are recorded and can be associated to features in the feature model. At product creation time, only the model elements that belong to the currently selected features are present in the model. This approach is similar to XVar in the way how it tailors models according to a specific configuration. An important advantage of XVar is that it models dependencies between features and model elements explicitly in a dependency model. The tool presented in [24] only observes changes to the core, but the mapping information is hidden in the tool.

The Gears variant management tool, [8] provides a plug-in for the Rhapsody modeling tool. Models can become Gears core assets and thus include variation points. Different variants for model elements can be created and are selected according to a specific configuration. The model does not change; only the generated code varies. XVar actually changes the model, which is the main difference to the Gears/Rhapsody bridge. Also, Rhapsody only supports UML models.

4   Expressing Variability in Model Transformations

This section describes concepts and tools that support the definition of feature-based variability in model transformations. Transformations can thus be selectively adapted.

In model transformations, a model is transformed into another model, and the input model is typically left unchanged. In Fig. 14a model M is transformed into a model K. Both models are instances of different metamodels. The small circle on the right symbolizes the unchanged model M. An important advantage of model transformations is that a clean separation between models and also between metamodels can be achieved. Also, different metamodels can evolve independently.

There is also the notion of a model modification, where a model is modified "in place", i.e. the input model is changed, and no additional output model is created. Since such a model modification is technically almost identical to a model transformation as defined above, this section focuses exclusively on model transformations.

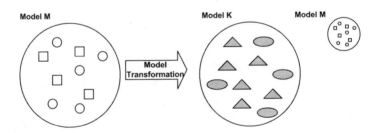

Fig. 14. Model transformations

As demonstrated in the previous section, both models and metamodels can vary using the concepts and tools we developed. This directly leads us to the need of varying model transformations. New metamodel elements brought by additional features must be added to the transformation workflow. Again, the adaptation of model transformations is only required in case the respective features are selected in the current configuration.

We solve this problem by applying AO to model transformations. The transformation language Xtend [39] has been extended with support for aspects.

Xtend supports the application of advices to model transformation functions. Only around advices are supported. Listing 8 shows the syntax of advices in

Xtend. The keyword **around** is followed by a pointcut that selects the points where the advice should be applied. Any number of expressions can be executed within the advice. By calling **proceed()**, the original transformation function is executed.

```
around [pointcut] :
    expression;
```

Listing 8. Around advices in Xtend

A pointcut consists of a fully qualified name and a list of parameter declarations. The asterisk character is used to specify wildcards. Listing 9 shows some examples of how pointcuts are specified. Parameter-type polymorphism is considered when matching the pointcut.

```
my::Extension::definition        /* matches extensions with the
                                    specified name */
org::oaw::*                      /* matches extensions prefixed
                                    with 'org::oaw::' */
*Operation*                      /* matches extensions containing
                                    'Operation' */
*                               /* matches all extensions */
```

Listing 9. Pointcut specifications in Xtend

As we want to apply advices only in case a certain feature is selected in the current configuration, we need to link advices to features. Figure 15 illustrates how this is done. Transformation aspects are connected to features in the oAW workflow. The advice is then only applied to the transformation in case the respective feature is selected.

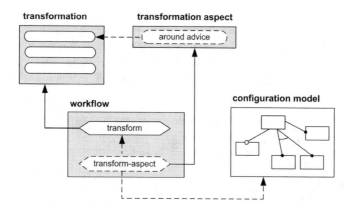

Fig. 15. Variability in model transformations

Imagine one wants to deploy an optional tracing interceptor to a system. The runtime infrastructure supports the use of interceptors for any component. Interceptors are available in libraries. Listing 11 shows the advice that is applied

```
<transform id="xtendComponent.trafos">
    <invoke value="trafos::transformSystem(inputModel)"/>
    <outputSlot value="outputModel.xmi"/>
</transform>

<transformationAspect adviceTarget="xtendComponent.trafos">
    <extensionAdvices value="tracing"/>
</transformationAspect>
```

Listing 10. Adding transformation aspects to the workflow

to the transformation function `transformSystem` defined in the extension file `trafos`. The advice is defined in a separate extension file named `tracing`. First, the original transformation function is executed (by calling `ctx.proceed()`). A local variable s is defined that stores the return value of the original transformation function. Then, a tracing interceptor is looked up in the library and added to the list of deployed interceptors. At the end of the around advice, the variable s is returned. Note that it is not necessary to explicitly list the return type in the signature of the around advice as it is known from the signature of the original transformation.

For the aspect to be applied to the transformation, it has to be added to the workflow. Listing 10 shows how this works. The original transformation is executed by invoking the top-level function (`transformSystem`) in the `trafos` extension file. Model transformation functions are defined in extension files and are thus called extensions. The output of the transformation is stored in the `outputModel.xmi` model file. The transformation aspect is configured below. The target of the advice has to be specified (transformation with id `xtendComponent.trafos`), including the extension file that contains the actual advice (`tracing`).

Applying aspects to model transformations realizes positive variability on transformation level. As an alternative, one could also develop the overall transformation and exclude transformation steps in case a certain feature is selected. This can be realized by calling the `hasFeature(featureName)` function from within transformations and can be considered negative variability on transformation level.

```
around trafos::transformSystem( System sys ):
    let s = ctx.proceed(): (
        deployedInterceptors.addAll(
            library().interceptors.findByName("TracingInterceptor"))
        -> s
);
```

Listing 11. Optional tracing interceptor advice

4.1   Related Work

The approach presented in [37] includes an aspect-oriented extension to a model-to-text transformation language. Those so-called high-order transformations can be used to represent variability in product line engineering. The approach is similar to our approach as an existing transformation language has been extended with support for aspects. An important difference is that our approach supports linking these aspects to features defined in a feature model. The approach in [37] does not include this capability.

5   Expressing Variability in Code Generation Templates

This section describes concepts and tools that support the definition of feature-based variability in code generation templates. Generators can thus be selectively adapted.

A generator generates some textual output (e.g. code, build scripts, and XML configuration files) from a model. The generator operates on the metamodel of the DSL and thus has to know this metamodel. Figure 16 illustrates the relationship among model, metamodel, and generator.

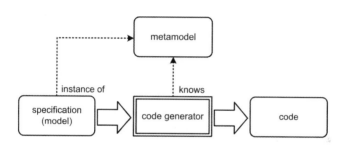

Fig. 16. Code generation

A template language including a suitable template engine is used to generate the output. Templates support the generation of any text-based output.

In our approach, the code is generated from the final solution space model. As metamodel, models, and the respective transformations can vary, we also need to incorporate variability into the code generation process. We use AO on code generation level for this purpose. The template language Xpand [39] provides support for template aspects.

Xpand supports around advices whereby any execution of a template definition can be a joinpoint. The definition name part of a pointcut must match the fully qualified name of the joinpoint's definition. The asterisk character is used to specify wildcards. Listing 12 shows the syntax of Xpand advices. The original template definition can be called with `proceed()`.

```
<<AROUND qualifiedDefinitionName(parameterList) FOR type>>
        a sequence of statements
<<ENDAROUND>>
```

Listing 12. Xpand around advice

The parameters of the definitions we want to add our advice to can also be specified in the pointcut. The rule is that the type of the specified parameter must be the same or a super type of the corresponding parameter type of the definition to be called (i.e. polymorphic dispatch is used on all arguments). In addition, one can set the wildcard at the end of the parameter list to specify that there might be none or more parameters of any kind. Listing 13 shows some examples.

```
my::Templ::def()           /* template definition without parameters */
my::Templ::def(String s)   /* template definition with exactly one
                              parameter of type String */
my::Templ::def(String s,*) /* template definition with one or more
                              parameters where the first parameter
                              is of type String */
my::Templ::def(*)          /* template definition with any number of
                              parameters */
```

Listing 13. Wildcards in parameter definitions

As it is the case with model transformation aspects, we want generator advices only to be applied in case a certain feature is selected in the current configuration. The dependency between template aspects and features is specified in the workflow (cf. Fig. 17).

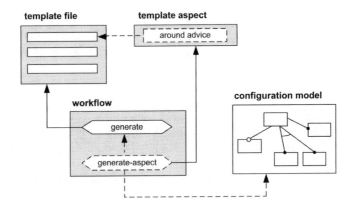

Fig. 17. Variability in code generation templates

Imagine, one wants to add a reflection layer to inspect a generated system. Specifically, if component instance states should be inspected, the data structures representing the state need to be *reflective*. Of course, since this functionality is for debugging purposes only, it is optional, i.e. it depends on whether the Debug feature is selected or not.

In the following, we will only show the code generator aspect that is used to add the reflection layer to generated state data structures. The code generator for the data structures contains the following templates: typeClass generates a

Java class that represents the state data structure (basically a bean with getters and setters). That template in turn calls the imports and body templates. Listing 14 shows the templates that will be adviced by the template aspect.

```
<<DEFINE typeClass FOR ComplexType>>
    <<FILE fileName()>>
        package <<implClassPackage()>>;
        <<EXPAND imports>>
        public class    {
            <<EXPAND body>>
        }
    <<ENDFILE>>
<<ENDDEFINE>>

<<DEFINE imports FOR ComplexType>>
    . . .
<<ENDDEFINE>>
<<DEFINE body FOR ComplexType>>
    . . .
<<ENDDEFINE>>
```

Listing 14. Templates to be adviced

The piece of Xpand code in Listing 15 is the template aspect that adds the reflection layer to the generated data structures. Note how the AROUND declarations reference existing DEFINEs to advice them. targetDef.proceed() calls the original template.

```
<<AROUND data::api::data::body FOR ComplexType>>
    <<targetDef.proceed()>>
    <<EXPAND reflectionImplementation>>
<<ENDAROUND>>

<<AROUND data::api::data::imports FOR ComplexType>>
    <<targetDef.proceed()>>
    import smarthome.common.platform.MemberMeta;
    import smarthome.common.platform.ComplexTypeMeta;
<<ENDAROUND>>

<<DEFINE reflectionImplementation FOR ComplexType>>
    private transient ComplexTypeMeta _meta = null;
    public ComplexTypeMeta _metaObject() {

    }
    public void _metaSet( MemberMeta member, Object value ) {

    }
    public Object _metaGet( MemberMeta member ) {

    }
<<ENDDEFINE>>
```

Listing 15. Template aspect

Of course, to make this work as desired, we have to couple the aspect to the configuration model. This dependency is specified in the workflow.

Applying aspects to code generation templates realizes positive variability on generation level. Again, as an alternative, one could also develop the overall generator and exclude templates in case a certain feature is selected. This can be realized by calling the `hasFeature(featureName)` function from within the templates and can be considered negative variability on generator level.

5.1 Related Work

In [32], a generative approach called Framed Aspects is proposed. Framed Aspects combine AOP with frame technology to modularize crosscutting feature implementations and improve evolution of product lines. In contrast, our approach includes aspects directly into code generation templates to incorporate features into the code generation process. The approach presented in [32] only parameterizes aspects.

The transformation engine of ArcStyler, CARAT [26], supports the specialization of cartridges. It allows to override generator code specified in a super cartridge. While this kind of specialization is also possible with our approach. However, our approach is more generic because it also supports quantification—the ability to select a set of joinpoints using a pointcut to add generator behavior in several places at once.

6   Expressing Variability in Code

For some features, developing a custom generator might be too costly. Thus, for economic reasons, certain parts of the product will still be implemented manually. In this case, variability has to be considered at code level.

We use AO on code level to realize positive variability. AspectJ [28] and CaesarJ [4] are popular candidates for implementing features on code level.

Sometimes, a feature might be requested for which the product line architecture may not provide the required configuration or customization hooks. Either one has to manually tweak the generated code to accommodate the variant or the product line architecture has to be adapted to include the additional hooks. The latter approach is desirable, but for reasons of versioning, coordination, or time pressure it is often not realistic. AOP can be very useful in this case. One can hook into generated (or manually written) code at places where the product line architecture does not provide hooks. Thus, the necessary change can be accommodated without changing the product line architecture and without manually changing the generated code—the change is external in the aspect.

To support negative variability on code level, we extended XVar [22, 39] with additional capabilities. It is possible to include special comments to the code that define the dependencies to features. In case the respective feature is not part of the current configuration, the code implementing this feature is removed from the code base. Listing 16 shows an example. A light switch can switch both normal lights and dimmable lights. The feature `Dimmable Lights` is optional. The example illustrates how special comments (starting with #) specify the dependency to the feature. In case the feature is selected, the first statement is part of the code base; in the other case, the second statement is included.

The XVar approach works well for simple, well-modularized features. For example, an optional method call can depend on a feature and pruned from the code base using XVar. Also, the approach can be used to first develop the overall system that includes all options. Later, the code implementing the feature can be refactored as an aspect.

```
public void execute() {
    ...
    //# dimmableLights
    parseLightsToSwitch(changedLights, status.getStatusLightLevel());
    //~# dimmableLights

    //# !dimmableLights
    parseLightsToSwitch(changedLights);
    //~# !dimmableLights
}
```

Listing 16. Negative variability on code level

6.1 Related Work

The main focus of research on AOSD in SPLE is targeted toward variability implementation using AOP languages.

In [34], it is demonstrated how CaesarJ helps to overcome the deficiencies of feature-oriented programming (FOP) and AOP for implementing variability. CaesarJ supports both multi-abstraction modules and joinpoint interception.

The approach described in [3] introduces Aspectual Mixin Layers (AML) which integrate both AOP and FOP by introducing aspects into mixin layers and providing aspect refinement.

In [1], the capabilities of AO to implement variability are evaluated according to defined criteria. The evaluation has shown that AOP is especially suitable for variability across several components, i.e. crosscutting variability.

In [7], it was demonstrated how AspectC++ can be employed in a weather station product line. The use of AspectC++ simplified the development process since crosscutting product line features could be directly mapped to aspects. Aspect C++ enabled configuring the appropriate level and therefore enhanced the code reusability.

7 Home Automation Case Study

The case study to illustrate our approach is a home automation system (see also [41]) called *Smart Home*. In homes, you will find a wide range of electrical and electronic devices such as lights, thermostats, electric blinds, fire, and smoke detection sensors, white goods such as washing machines, as well as entertainment equipment.

Smart Home connects those devices and enables inhabitants to monitor and control them from a common UI. The home network also allows the devices to coordinate their behavior to fulfill complex tasks without human intervention.

Sensors are devices that measure physical properties of the environment and make them available to Smart Home. Controllers activate devices whose state can be monitored and changed. All installed devices are part of the Smart Home network. The status of devices can either be changed by inhabitants via the UI or by the system using predefined policies. Policies let the system act autonomously in case of certain events. For example, in case of smoke detection, windows get closed and the fire brigade is called. Varying types of houses, different customer demands, the need for short time-to-market, and cost savings drive the need for a Smart Home product line and are the main causes of variability.

The case study includes six metamodels that each consist of more than 30 elements. The feature model of the home automation product line allows creating 314,250 different valid product instances. Smart Home consists of about 100 generated artifacts and about 180 hand-written artifacts including transformers and generators.

The remainder of this section will explain how the techniques introduced in Sect. 2 were used to implement the Smart Home product line.

7.1 Problem Space Modeling

In the problem space, Smart Home systems are formally described. A problem space metamodel is defined as that contains entities such as buildings, floors, rooms, the various kinds of sensors, and actuators. Note that this model does not contain anything concerned with software or computing hardware. It formally describes domain requirements. Figure 18 shows parts of the problem space metamodel of Smart Home. Buildings contain floors and floors contain rooms. Staircases connect the different floors in the house. Different kinds of devices are located in rooms.

Using this metamodel, a DSL is built, which supports modeling Smart Home systems from the perspective of a building architect or a home owner. The syntax is semi-graphical and a customized tree view is developed. Figure 19 shows an example of a house that is modeled using the DSL. This DSL is a creative construction DSL. Note that in a real-world system, the building data would be extracted from a CAD system.

7.2 Solution Space Modeling

The solution space comprises a component-based architecture. Figure 20 shows the types viewpoint of this component metamodel. Additional viewpoints are defined to express component instances, their connections, hardware structure as well as the mapping of software component instances onto hardware nodes. There is no need to provide a sophisticated concrete syntax for that domain since the models are created by model transformations from problem space models. Note that this metamodel is platform independent in that the generic component architecture can be mapped onto various target platforms such as OSGi [40], Spring [43], or JEE [45]. The case study implementation uses OSGi.

To a large extent, Smart Home systems consist of a specific arrangement of pre-built sensors and actuators (although a specific system can have custom devices). It therefore makes sense to keep a library of software components that control certain types of hardware. We use a combination of manually written

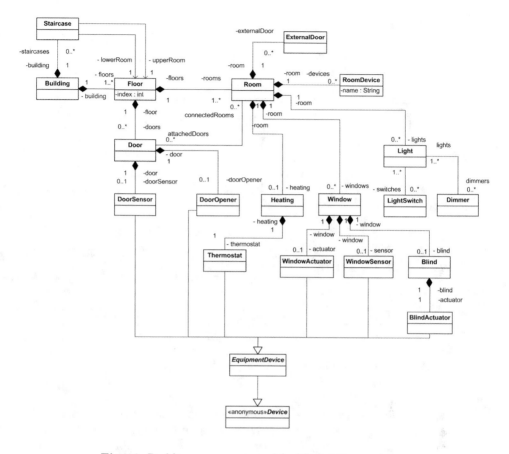

Fig. 18. Problem space metamodel of Smart Home

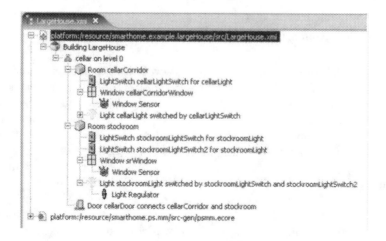

Fig. 19. Example house

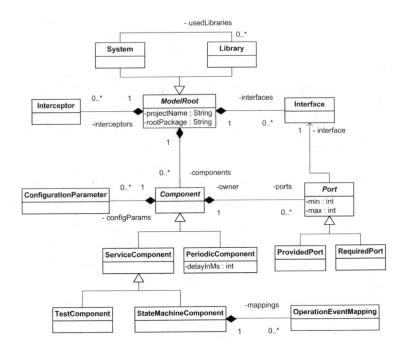

Fig. 20. Platform-independent component metamodel: Types viewpoint

code (i.e. the business logic) and models to represent these components to be able to use them to define a given system. Based on the problem space model, the transformation instantiates, wires, and deploys those library software components in the context of the software system generated for a particular building.

7.3   Solution Space Implementation

In realistic Smart Home scenarios, there are several target implementation technologies. For example, computing platforms and networking/bus technologies change depending on the level of sophistication of a product. In our case study, we selected OSGi as a target platform. We defined an extended OSGi metamodel (cf. Fig. 21) and mapped the platform-independent component metamodel to the OSGi metamodel using a model-to-model transformation.

The formally defined mappings allow us to automatically transform a problem space model (cf. Fig. 19) into a platform-independent component model and in turn into an OSGi model. Finally, we generate code from the OSGi model.

Figure 22 provides an overview of the metamodels, models, and transformations used in the Smart Home case study. Metamodel parts common to the component metamodel and the OSGi metamodel were modeled in separate metamodels. Common parts include data types and operations. We developed a tool

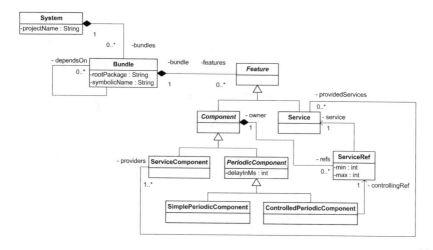

Fig. 21. OSGi metamodel

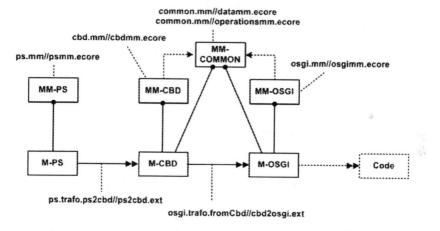

Fig. 22. Smart Home models and transformations overview

called XJoin[4] which supports adding relationships between metamodels to join them. The separate metamodels keep their own identities, and the partial models do not need to know about the other ones. Sharing elements between metamodels has the obvious advantage of reducing duplication. However, there are other more important benefits: Because the types of the model elements are literally the same, the transformation is reduced to a simple cloning operation. Also, one can share the same code generation templates, which typically simplifies the volume of the templates significantly.

---

[4] XJoin is part of openArchitectureWare 4.2 and can be downloaded from
http://www.openarchitectureware.org/

7.4   Orthogonal Variability

We use a global feature model to incorporate features that are orthogonal to the house structure. Those features require configuring the entities of the house, the transformation, and generation process in one way or the other. For implementing this orthogonal variability we use the concepts and tools described in Sect. 2 and subsequent sections. We use pure::variants [42] for feature modeling.

Figure 23 shows parts of the feature model of Smart Home. It provides several automation features that let the house act autonomously according to defined policies. In addition, it provides debugging features and several alternatives with respect to deployment. Optional features are indicated by a question mark, and mandatory features are indicated by an exclamation point. Alternative features are represented by arrows.

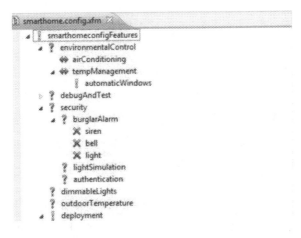

Fig. 23. Smart Home feature model

Due to space limitations, we can only provide details for two of these features, namely the automation feature *Automatic Windows* and the debugging feature *Reflective Data Structures*.

Automatic Windows. The `Automatic Windows` feature automatically opens the windows if the temperature in a room raises above a certain threshold and closes them if the temperature falls below a certain threshold. For this feature to be included in a configuration, the necessary devices have to be woven into the building model.

Figure 24 shows the aspect model that is responsible for weaving the respective devices into the example house shown in Fig. 19. It weaves a thermometer in every room that has at least one window and adds a window actuator to the windows. The pointcut expressions used in the aspect model are shown in Listing 17. `rooms` returns all rooms that have windows. This pointcut expression is referenced with %rooms in the aspect model. The % sign is used because the expression rooms returns a set of elements. To all of them, a thermometer should be added and thermoName is a helper function that creates a sensible name for this thermometer. The thermoName expression is referenced with ?thermoName in the aspect model. The ? sign is used because the thermoName expression returns a String expression. windows returns all windows of these rooms and a window actuator is added to them. The windows expression is referenced with %windows in the aspect model. The % sign is used because the expression windows returns a set of elements.

Fig. 24. Window automation aspect

```
rooms(Building this) :  floors.rooms.select(e|e.windows.size >0);
windows(Building this) :  rooms().windows;
thermoName(Thermometer this) :  ((Room)eContainer.name.toFirstLower() +
                                 "Thermometer";
```

Listing 17. Window automation pointcut expressions

The resulting (woven) model has a thermometer in each room to measure the current temperature and a window actuator for each window to be able to automatically open it. If the Automatic Windows feature is present in the configuration model, XWeave [22, 23] weaves the content of the aspect model into the house model. This dependency is specified in the workflow.

The additional devices have to be transformed into platform-independent components. Also, the component that includes the business logic (i.e. the logic that periodically checks the temperature and triggers the opening and closing of the windows) has to be taken from the library and added to the platform-independent component model. These additional transformation steps are implemented as a model transformation aspect. Parts of the transformation aspect and the original transformation function are shown in Listing 18. The function createConfig transforms a floor into an object of type Configuration. The around advice first calls the original function (cf. ctx.proceed()) and then handles the additional devices. It creates an instance of a window actuator and adds it to the list of component instances owned by the configuration. If a room has at least one window and at least one thermometer, the handleWindowCoordinator function is called. This function establishes a connection between windows and thermometers.

There is no need to change the code generator as the variability is purely handled on model and transformator level.

```
around ps2cbd::createConfig( Floor f ):
    let config = (Configuration)ctx.proceed():
        config.instances.addAll(
            f.rooms.windows.actuator.createInstance() ) ->
        (f.rooms.windows.size > 0 &&
        f.rooms.devices.typeSelect(Thermometer).size > 0 )?
            config.handleWindowCoordinator(f) : null -> config;

create Configuration createConfig( Floor f ):
    createTrace( f, "floor2configuration" ) ->
    setName( f.name+"FloorConfiguration" );
```

Listing 18. Window automation transformation advice

The business logic of the **Automatic Windows** feature (the actual opening or closing of the windows in case the temperature reaches or falls below a certain threshold) is pre-built in the form of a library component and included into the final product in case the feature is selected. Since all pre-built components have representations on model level, we can process them using model transformations (cf. the handling of the window coordinator in Listing 18). Based on the information in the models, it is possible to determine whether the window automation component is part of a product or not.

Light Simulation. The **Light Simulation** feature periodically turns on the lights in the house. Its purpose is to simulate inhabitants being at home in case they are on holiday. This feature should prevent burglars from breaking into the house as it seems to be occupied.

```
around ps2cbd::createConfig( Floor f ):
    let res = (Configuration)ctx.proceed():
        (f.rooms.lights.size > 0)? res.handleLightSimulator(f) : null ->
        res;

private handleLightSimulator( Configuration this, Floor f ):
    let c = f.createLightSimulator(): (
        instances.add( c ) ->
        connectors.add( f.createLightConnector( c ) )
    );
```

Listing 19. Light simulation transformation advice

The business logic of the light simulation feature (the actual turning on of the lights) is pre-built in the form of a library component. A transformation aspect (shown in Listing 19) optionally transforms this component. In this case, the variability is purely handled on model transformation level. The house model and the code generator remain untouched. If the **Light Simulation** feature is selected in the current configuration, the transformation aspect is woven into the transformation from the problem space model to the platform-independent component model. This dependency is specified in the workflow.

7.5   Tracing

In our approach, tracing is straightforward. Since mappings between abstraction levels are based on formal model transformations, we make sure the mappings are made persistent in a trace model. It can be built either automatically by the transformation engine or manually by the transformation developer. We implement the second approach since it allows developers to control the trace granularity.

Our approach to traceability has two main advantages:

- Since we trace between model elements, the trace is finer grained than in currently used approaches, where tracing happens between complete artifacts [27, 33].
- Since problem space concepts are also represented as models, we gain traceability from the problem space over to the solution space.

To be able to control the trace granularity, the trace model is built manually by calling a createTrace (toElement, fromElement, traceKind) function at the appropriate locations within the transformation functions and generation templates. The trace conforming to the trace model is then emitted automatically when the transformation and generation steps are done for a concrete input model.

Since problem domain concepts are also represented as models, we gain full traceability from the application domain over to the implementation domain.

Listing 20 illustrates how tracing data is collected in model to model transformation functions. The function transform translates a system on component level into a system on OSGi level. The call to createTrace creates a trace link of kind *cbdSystem2osgiSystem* between the object sys of type cbdmm:System and the newly created object of type osgimm:System.

```
create osgimm::System transform( cbdmm::System sys ):
    createTrace( sys , "cbdSystem2osgiSystem" ) ->
    setName(sys.name) ->
    ...
```

Listing 20. Tracing in model transformation functions

Listing 21 shows how tracing is done on code generation template level. A trace link of kind *componentImplementationClass* is created between a service component and its implementation class. Tracing links can be established by calling VTRACE within the templates.

Based on the trace information collected in model transformation functions and code generation templates, we can automatically build a trace model that is available in memory as an EMF [14] model. It can be used by subsequent transformation steps or analyzed in any way required. The trace model can also be exported and made persistent for a given product variant as an XMI [36] file. We also support an export of the trace information to HTML to make the trace information more accessible for human reading.

```
<<DEFINE componentBaseClass FOR ServiceComponent>>
    <<FILE baseClassFileName()>>
        package <<baseClassPackageName()>>;
        // <<VITRACE(this, "componentImplementationClass")>>
        public abstract class <<baseClassName()>> extends
                              <<platformBaseClassName()>>
        ...

    }
    <<ENDFILE>>
<<ENDDEFINE>>
```

Listing 21. Tracing in code generation templates

8   Summary and Future Work

8.1   Research Questions Revisited

In Sect. 1, we define the research question we aim to answer based on data from the case study we conducted at Siemens AG.

This research question is:

> *Where and how can software product line development benefit from AOSD, MDSD, and their combination?*

We started by modeling the problem space, i.e. by creating a metamodel of the domain requirements. Next, we defined a metamodel of a platform neutral component-based architecture and mapped the domain entities to components. We then defined a metamodel of OSGi, created the mapping from the component-based architecture metamodel, and developed the code generator.

The metamodels, mappings, and generator already provided the appropriate means for dealing with all variability concerning the structure of the house. Developers are now able to model different instances of houses and automatically generate the appropriate OSGi code from them.

This leads us to the first important benefit: By integrating MDSD into SPLE, creative construction DSLs can handle variability with respect to the structure or behavior the DSL intends to model. A DSL allows to create models that are instances of a defined metamodel, which is the metamodel of the domain. Variability with respect to domain entities and their relations can be efficiently handled using a MDSD approach. Although DSLs only deal with structural variability and in product lines, configurative variability is an important issue as well.

In our case study, we used AO concepts and techniques on model, transformator, generator, and code level to handle *orthogonal variability*. By orthogonal, we mean variability that affects multiple domain entities and their subsequent processing (i.e. transformation) steps. We used a feature model to describe the configurative variability of the home automation system and realized the features using AO at the appropriate levels.

This leads us to the second important benefit: Variability that is orthogonal (and usually configurative) to the structure the DSL intends to model can be efficiently addressed using AO techniques. Features can thus be localized in aspects and combined with the core as desired. The higher the abstraction level, the fewer variation points exist. Features expressed on models level are thus inherently simpler than features expressed on code generation level. We therefore argue to always express features on the highest possible level.

In AO systems, whenever more than one aspect is applied to a system, aspect precedence is an issue, i.e. the advice ordering in case more than one advice is applied at the same joinpoint. We solve this by explicitly coding the order in which aspects are applied in the workflow. Workflow steps are executed in sequential order, which means that the weaving process is strictly sequential. One aspect is applied after the other in the order specified in the workflow. In the case of XWeave, woven models can be the input of a weaving process again as XWeave does not distinguish between a woven and a non-woven model. The fact that one can actually look at the woven model has a positive impact on understandability and usability.

Another important contribution of our approach is the integration of a variant management tool (in this case, pure::variants) into the MDSD tool chain. Within our tooling, configuration models can be queried, and hence, activities can be performed based on the presence or absence of features in a configuration model.

In general, our approach is best suited for the development of new systems. This is because of the inherent forward-engineering approach, i.e. the detailed low-level code is generated from more abstract domain-specific models. Therefore, a natural question is, how the presented approach can be used in scenarios, where a system is already present. First, it is possible to apply the approach to a part of a legacy system and leave the rest of the system as is. Second, an MDSD approach can be used to define the overall architecture and generate implementation skeletons, copying the implementation code from the old system manually and adapting it to the new architectural structure. Finally, one can try to *extract* models from the legacy system code base and then develop the new system against those (this is, however, not very practical in many cases).

8.2   Future Research

In future we will work on the improvement of the tooling we introduced in this article. We will work on a better visualization of the dependencies between MDSD artifacts and features. For example, the workflow components, transformation steps, and templates that depend on a feature can be highlighted in the same color. This facilitates maintainability of features.

Also, XWeave currently only supports additive weaving. In future, we extend XWeave to support changing or overriding existing base model elements using aspects. Another possible extension of XWeave is support for symmetric model weaving. This kind of weaving does not distinguish between aspect and base models. Models are woven together according to defined rules to form the final system. Our observations show that in SPLE, typically, a core capturing the commonality within a portfolio of similar products can be identified. Features are increments in functionality and thus match well with the idea of weaving in aspect-orientation.

Currently, we do not deal with any issues related to runtime variability. This is important as domain experts often want to customize the product on-site. Also, the specific hardware configuration of the customer could be detected automatically. In the future, we will tackle the question of how to use runtime weaving of aspects to implement this diversity.

In addition, we will apply our approach in a second industrial case study to further validate the developed concepts and tools.

Acknowledgments. This work is supported by AMPLE Grant IST-033710. The authors would like to thank Christa Schwanninger for her valuable comments on earlier drafts of this article.

References

[1] Anastasopoulos, M., Muthig, D.: An evaluation of aspect-oriented programming as a product line implementation technology. In: Bosch, J., Krueger, C. (eds.) ICOIN 2004 and ICSR 2004. LNCS, vol. 3107, pp. 141–156. Springer, Heidelberg (2004)

[2] AOSD Community Wiki. Glossary (2007), http://www.aosd.net/wiki/

[3] Apel, S., Leich, T., Saake, G.: Aspectual mixin layers: aspects and features in concert. In: ICSE, pp. 122–131 (2006)

[4] Aracic, I., Gasiunas, V., Mezini, M., Ostermann, K.: An overview of CaesarJ. In: Rashid, A., Aksit, M. (eds.) Transactions on Aspect-Oriented Software Development I. LNCS, vol. 3880, pp. 135–173. Springer, Heidelberg (2006)

[5] Baniassad, E.L.A., Clarke, S.: Theme: An approach for aspect-oriented analysis and design. In: ICSE, pp. 158–167 (2004)

[6] Batory, D., Sarvela, J.N., Rauschmayer, A.: Scaling step-wise refinement. In: ICSE 2003: Proceedings of the 25th International Conference on Software Engineering, Washington, DC, USA, pp. 187–197. IEEE Computer Society, Los Alamitos (2003)

[7] Beuche, D., Spinczyk, O.: Variant management for embedded software product lines with pure: : consul and aspectc++. In: OOPSLA Companion, pp. 108–109 (2003)

[8] BigLever. Gears (2007), http://www.biglever.com/

[9] Chitchyan, R., Rashid, A., Sawyer, P., Garcia, A., Alarcon, M.P., Bakker, J., Tekinerdogan, B., Clarke, S., Jackson, A.: Report synthesizing state-of-the-art in aspect-oriented requirements engineering, architectures and design. Tech. Rep. AOSD-Europe Deliverable D11, AOSD-Europe-ULANC-9, Lancaster University (May 18, 2005)

[10] Clements, P.C., Northrop, L.M.: Software Product Lines: Practices and Patterns. Addison Wesley, Reading (2001)

[11] Coplien, J.O.: Multiparadigm Design for C++. Addison Wesley, Reading (1998)

[12] Cottenier, T., van den Berg, A., Elrad, T.: Joinpoint inference from behavioral specification to implementation. In: Ernst, E. (ed.) ECOOP 2007. LNCS, vol. 4609, pp. 476–500. Springer, Heidelberg (2007)

[13] Czarnecki, K., Antkiewicz, M.: Mapping features to models: A template approach based on superimposed variants. In: Glück, R., Lowry, M. (eds.) GPCE 2005. LNCS, vol. 3676, pp. 422–437. Springer, Heidelberg (2005)

[14] Eclipse. Eclipse modeling framework (EMF) (2007),
     http://www.eclipse.org/emf
[15] Eclipse. Graphical Modeling Framework (GMF) (2007),
     http://www.eclipse.org/gmf/
[16] ECos. Operating system (2007), http://ecos.sourceware.org/
[17] Fabro, M.D.D., Valduriez, P.: Semi-automatic model integration using matching transformations and weaving models. In: SAC, pp. 963–970 (2007)
[18] Filman, R.E., Elrad, T., Clarke, S., Aksit, M.: Aspect-Oriented Software Development. Addison-Wesley Longman, Amsterdam (2004)
[19] Filman, R.E., Friedman, D.P.: Aspect-oriented programming is quantification and obliviousness. Tech. rep. (2000)
[20] Gray, J., Lin, Y., Zhang, J.: Automating change evolution in model-driven engineering. IEEE Computer 39(2), 51–58 (2006)
[21] Greenfield, J., Short, K., Cook, S., Kent, S.: Software Factories: Assembling Applications with Patterns, Models, Frameworks, and Tools. Wiley, Chichester (2004)
[22] Groher, I., Voelter, M.: Expressing feature-based variability in structural models. In: Workshop on Managing Variability for Software Product Lines (2007)
[23] Groher, I., Voelter, M.: XWeave: Models and Aspects in Concert. In: AOM 2007: Proceedings of the 10th international workshop on Aspect-oriented modeling, pp. 35–40. ACM Press, New York (2007)
[24] Heidenreich, F., Wende, C.: Bridging the gap between features and models. In: Second Workshop on Aspect-Oriented Product Line Engineering (2007)
[25] IBM. Rational Rose (2007),
     http://www-128.ibm.com/developerworks/rational/
[26] Interactive Objects. Arcstyler (2007), http://www.interactive-objects.com/
[27] Kannan, M., Ramesh, B.: Managing variability with traceability in product and service families. In: HICSS, p. 76 (2002)
[28] Kiczales, G., Hilsdale, E., Hugunin, J., Kersten, M., Palm, J., Griswold, W.G.: An overview of AspectJ. In: Knudsen, J.L. (ed.) ECOOP 2001. LNCS, vol. 2072, pp. 327–353. Springer, Heidelberg (2001)
[29] Kiczales, G., Lamping, J., Mendhekar, A., Maeda, C., Lopes, C.V., Loingtier, J.-M., Irwin, J.: Aspect-oriented programming. In: Aksit, M., Matsuoka, S. (eds.) ECOOP 1997. LNCS, vol. 1241, pp. 220–242. Springer, Heidelberg (1997)
[30] Kruchten, P.: The 4+1 view model of architecture. IEEE Software 12(6), 42–50 (1995)
[31] Lohmann, D., Scheler, F., Tartler, R., Spinczyk, O., Schröder-Preikschat, W.: A quantitative analysis of aspects in the ecos kernel. In: EuroSys 2006: Proceedings of the ACM SIGOPS/EuroSys European Conference on Computer Systems 2006, pp. 191–204. ACM, New York (2006)
[32] Loughran, N., Rashid, A.: Framed aspects: Supporting variability and configurability for AOP. In: Bosch, J., Krueger, C. (eds.) ICOIN 2004 and ICSR 2004. LNCS, vol. 3107, pp. 127–140. Springer, Heidelberg (2004)
[33] Maeder, P., Riebisch, M., Philippow, I.: Traceability for managing evolutionary change. In: SEDE, pp. 1–8 (2006)
[34] Mezini, M., Ostermann, K.: Variability management with feature-oriented programming and aspects. In: SIGSOFT FSE, pp. 127–136 (2004)
[35] No Magic. Magicdraw (2007), http://www.magicdraw.com/
[36] Object Management Group. XML Metadata Interchange (XMI) specification (2007), http://www.omg.org/mof/
[37] Oldevik, J., Haugen, O.: Higher-order transformations for product lines. In: SPLC, pp. 243–254 (2007)

[38] OpenArchitectureWare (2007), http://www.openarchitectureware.org
[39] OpenArchitectureWare. User guide version 4.2 (2007), http://www.eclipse.org/gmt/oaw/doc/4.2/openArchitectureWare-42-reference.pdf
[40] OSGi Alliance. Osgi framework (2007), http://osgi.org/
[41] Pohl, K., Böckle, G., van der Linden, F.: Software Product Line Engineering: Foundations, Principles, and Techniques. Springer, Berlin (2005)
[42] Pure systems. pure::variants (2007), http://www.pure-systems.com/
[43] Spring Framework (2007), http://www.springframework.org/
[44] Stahl, T., Völter, M.: Model-Driven Software Development: Technology, Engineering, Management. Wiley & Sons, Chichester (2006)
[45] Sun Microsystems. Java Enterprise Edition (2007), http://java.sun.com/javaee/
[46] Telelogic. DOORS (2007), http://www.telelogic.com/products/doors
[47] Voelter, M., Groher, I.: Handling variability in model transformations and generators. In: 7th OOPSLA Workshop on Domain-Specific Modeling (2007)
[48] Voelter, M., Groher, I.: Product line implementation using aspect-oriented and model-driven software development. In: SPLC, pp. 233–242 (2007)

Constraint-Based Model Weaving

Jules White[1], Jeff Gray[2], and Douglas C. Schmidt[1]

[1] Vanderbilt University
Nashville, TN, USA
{jules,schmidt}@dre.vanderbilt.edu
[2] University of Alabama, Birmingham
Birmingham, AL, USA
gray@cis.uab.edu

Abstract. Aspect-oriented modeling (AOM) is a promising technique for untangling the concerns of complex enterprise software systems. AOM decomposes the crosscutting concerns of a model into separate models that can be woven together to form a composite solution model. In many domains, such as multi-tiered e-commerce web applications, separating concerns is much easier than deducing the proper way to weave the concerns back together into a solution model. For example, modeling the types and sizes of caches that can be leveraged by a Web application is much easier than deducing the optimal way to weave the caches back into the solution architecture to achieve high system throughput.

This paper presents a technique called constraint-based weaving that maps model weaving to a constraint satisfaction problem (CSP) and uses a constraint-solver to deduce the appropriate weaving strategy. By mapping model weaving to a CSP and leveraging a constraint solver, our technique (1) generates solutions that are correct with respect to the weaving constraints, (2) can incorporate complex global weaving constraints, (3) can provide weaving solutions that are optimal with respect to a weaving cost function, and (4) can eliminate manual effort that would normally be required to specify pointcuts and maintain them as target models change. The paper also presents the results of a case study that applies our CSP weaving technique to a representative enterprise Java application. Our evaluation of this case study showed a reduction in manual effort that our technique provides.

Keywords: Model Weaving, Aspect Oriented Programming, Constraint Satisfaction, Global Constraints.

1 Introduction

Developers of complex enterprise applications are faced with the daunting task of managing not only numerous functional concerns, such as ensuring that the application properly executes key business logic, but also meeting challenging non-functional requirements, such as end-to-end response time and security. Enterprise domain solutions have traditionally been developed using large monolithic models that either provide a single view of the system or a limited set of views [20]. The result of using a limited set of views to build the system is that certain concerns are not cleanly separated by the dominant lines of decomposition and are scattered throughout the system's models.

S. Katz et al. (Eds.): Transactions on AOSD VI, LNCS 5560, pp. 153–190, 2009.
© Springer-Verlag Berlin Heidelberg 2009

Aspect-oriented modeling (AOM) [7,17,38] has emerged as a powerful method of untangling and managing scattered concerns in large enterprise application models [21,19]. With AOM, any scattered concern can be extracted into its own view. For example, caching considerations of an application can be extracted into an aspect. Once caching is separated into its own aspect, the cache sizes and types can be adjusted independent of the application components where the caches are applied. When a final composite solution model for the application is produced, the various aspects are woven back into the solution model and the numerous affected modeling elements are updated to reflect the independently modeled concerns.

Although concerns can often be separated easily into their own aspects or views, it is hard to correctly or optimally merge these concerns back into the solution model. Merging the models is hard because there are typically numerous competing non-functional and functional constraints, such as balancing encryption levels for security against end-to-end performance, that must be balanced against each other without violating domain constraints (such as maximum available bandwidth). Manual approaches for deriving solutions to these types of constraints do not scale well.

Most current model weavers [9,16,21,38,45] rely on techniques such as specifying queries or patterns to match against model elements, which are ideal for matching advice against methods and constructors in application code, but are not necessarily ideal for static weaving problems. Many enterprise applications require developers to incorporate global constraints into the weaving process that can only be solved in a static weaving problem. As discussed in Sect. 3.2, the techniques used to match against dynamic joinpoints, such as pattern matching, cannot capture global constraints, such as resource constraints (*e.g.* total RAM consumed < available RAM), which are common in enterprise applications. Because global constraints are not honored by the model weaver, developers are forced to expend significant effort manually deriving weaving solutions that honor them.

When weavers cannot handle global constraints, optimization, or dependency-based constraints, traditional model weaving becomes a manual four stage process, as shown in Fig. 1. The left-hand column shows the steps involved in model weaving problems with global constraints in general. The right-hand column shows how these steps manifest themselves in the cache weaving example. First, the advice and joinpoint elements (*e.g.* caches and components) available in the solution model are identified in step 1. Second, as shown in steps 2 and 3, because a weaver cannot handle global constraints or optimization, developers manually determine which advice elements should be matched to which model elements (*e.g.* the cache types, cache sizes, and the components to apply the caches to). This second step requires substantial effort because it involves deriving a solution to a complex set of global constraints.

In terms of deriving cache placements in an enterprise application, the second step involves determining cache architectures that fit within the required memory budget and respect the numerous dependency and exclusion constraints between caches. After viable cache architectures are identified, a developer must use the expected request distribution patterns and queueing theory to predict the optimal cache architecture. As the examples in Sect. 3 show, even for a small set of caches and potential cache locations, the cache placement process requires significant work.

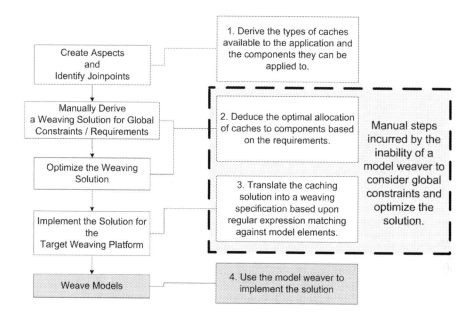

Fig. 1. The Model Weaving Process

In the third step, developers take this manually-derived solution and translate it into pointcut definitions that match against model elements using regular expressions or queries (*e.g.* a specification of how to insert the caching model elements into the models to implement the caching architecture). In some cases, the manually derived solution needs to be translated into the pointcut specification languages of multiple model weavers so that the architecture can be implemented in a set of heterogeneous models spanning multiple modeling tools. The model weavers then take these final specifications and merge the models. Each time the underlying solution models change (*e.g.* the available memory for caching changes), the global constraints can cause the entire solution to change (*e.g.* the previously used caches no longer fit in the budgeted memory) and the entire three steps must be repeated from scratch.

This paper shows that the manual steps of deriving a weaving solution that meets the global application requirements (steps 2 and 3) can be automated in many cases by creating a weaver capable of handling global constraints and optimization. Creating a weaver that can honor these constraints and optimize weaving allows developers to translate the high-level application requirements into pointcut specifications and optimization goals that can be used by the weaver when producing a weaving solution. Finally, because the weaver is responsible for deducing a weaving solution that meets the overall application requirements, as the individual solution models change, the weaver can automatically update the global weaving solution and re-implement it on behalf of the developer for multiple model weaving platforms.

This paper shows how model weaving can be mapped to a constraint satisfaction problem (CSP) [13,34,44]. With a CSP formulation of a model weaving problem, a constraint solver can be used to derive a correct—and in some cases optimal—weaving solution. Using a constraint solver to derive a correct weaving solution provides the following key benefits to model weaving:

- It ensures that the solution is correct with respect to the various modeled functional and non-functional weaving constraints.
- A constraint solver can honor global constraints when producing a solution and not just local regular expression or query-based constraints.
- A constraint solver automates the deduction of the correct weaving and saves considerable effort in manual solution derivation.
- The weaving solution can automatically be updated by the solver when the core solution models (and hence joinpoints) change.
- The solver can produce a platform-independent weaving solution (a symbolic weaving solution that is not coupled to any specific pointcut language) where model transformations [8,15] are applied to create a weaving solution for each required weaving platform and
- The solver can derive an optimal weaving solution (with respect to a cost function) in many cases.

The remainder of this paper is organized as follows: Section 2 presents the multi-tiered Web application used as a case study throughout the paper; Section 3 shows current challenges in applying existing model weaving techniques to our case study; Section 5 describes how constraint solving can be used to derive a correct weaving solution and how it addresses the gaps in existing solutions; Section 4 presents a mapping from model weaving to a CSP; Section 7 summarizes empirical results obtained from applying constraint-based weaving to our case study; Section 8 compares constraint-based weaving with related work; and Section 9 presents concluding remarks and lessons learned.

2   Case Study: The Java Pet Store

This paper uses a case study based on Sun's Java Pet Store [5] multi-tiered e-commerce application. The Pet Store is a canonical e-commerce application for selling pets. Customers can create accounts, browse the Pet Store's product categories, products, and individual product items (*e.g.* male adult Bulldog vs. female adult Bulldog).

The Pet Store application was implemented by Sun to showcase the capabilities of the various Java 2 Enterprise Edition frameworks [43]. The Pet Store has since been re-implemented or modified by multiple parties, including Microsoft (the .NET Pet Store) [4] and the Java Spring Framework [6]. The Spring Framework's version of the Pet Store includes support for aspects via AspectJ [2] and Spring Interceptors and is hence the implementation that we base our study on.

2.1   Middle-Tier Caching in the Pet Store

Our case study focuses on implementing caching in the middle-tier (*i.e.* the persistent data access layer) of the Pet Store through caching aspects. The business logic and views in the Pet Store are relatively simple and thus the retrieval and storage of persistent data is the major performance bottleneck. In performance tests that we ran on the Pet Store using Apache JMeter [1], the average response time across 3,000 requests for viewing the product categories was 3 times greater for a remotely hosted database than a remotely hosted database with a local data cache (25% hit rate). The same tests also showed that caching reduced the worst case response time for viewing product categories by a factor of 2.

Our experiments tested only a single middle-tier and back-end configuration of the Pet Store. Many different configurations are possible. The Spring Pet Store can use a single database for product and order data or separate databases. Data access objects (DAOs) are provided for four different database vendors. Choosing the correct way of weaving caches into the middle-tier of the Pet Store requires considering the following factors:

- The workload characteristics or distributions of request types, which determine what data is most beneficial to cache [32]. For example, keeping the product information in the cache that is most frequently requested will be most beneficial.
- The architecture of the back-end database servers providing product, account, and order data to the application determines the cost of a query [31]. For example, in a simple Pet Store deployment where the back-end database is co-located with the Pet Store's application server, queries will be less expensive than in an arrangement where queries must be sent across a network to the database server.
- The hardware hosting the cache and the applications co-located with it will determine the amount of memory available for caching product data. If the Pet Store is deployed on small commodity servers with limited memory, large caches may be undesirable.
- The number of possible cache keys and sizes of the data associated with each cache item will influence the expected cache hit rate and the penalty for having to transfer a dataset across the network from the database to the application server [35]. For example, product categories with large numbers of products will be more expensive to serialize and transfer from the database than the information on a single product item.
- The frequency that the data associated with the various middle-tier DAOs is updated and the importance of up-to-date information will affect which items can be cached and any required cache coherence schemes [35]. For example, product item availability is likely to change frequently, making product items less suitable to cache than product categories that are unlikely to change.

2.2   Modeling and Integrating Caches into the Pet Store

Aspect modeling can be used effectively to weave caches into the Pet Store to adapt it for changing request distribution patterns and back-end database configurations. We used this scenario for our case study to show that although caches can be woven into the code and models to adapt the Pet Store for a new environment, creating and maintaining a cache weaving solution that satisfies the Pet Store's global application requirements takes significant manual effort due to the inability of model weavers to encode and automate weaving with the global application constraints. Each time the global application requirements change, the manually deduced global cache weaving solution must be updated. Updating the global cache weaving solution involves a number of models and tools. Figure 2 shows the various models, code artifacts, and tools involved in implementing caching in the Pet Store.

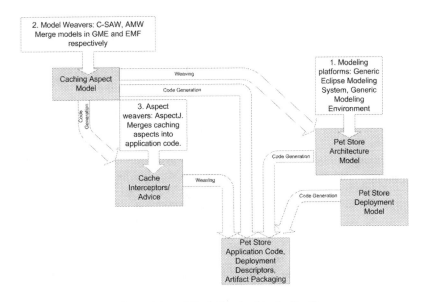

Fig. 2. Models and Tools Involved in the Pet Store

1. Modeling platforms. We have implemented models of different parts of the Pet Store in two different modeling tools: the Generic Eclipse Modeling System (GEMS) [48] and the Generic Modeling Environment (GME) [30]. GME was chosen due to its extensive support for different views, while GEMS was selected for its strengths in *model intelligence*, which was used for automating parts of the deployment modeling process. Using different tools simplifies the derivation of the deployment plan and the understanding of the system architecture but also requires some level of integration between the tools.

Generic Eclipse Modeling System is a graphical modeling tool built on top of Eclipse [41] and the Eclipse Modeling Framework (EMF) [12]. GEMS allows developers to use a Visio-like graphical interface to specify metamodels and generate domain-specific modeling language (DSML) tools for Eclipse. In GEMS, a deployment modeling tool has been implemented to capture the various deployment artifacts, such as required Java Archive Resources (JAR) files and their placement on application servers. Another Neat Tool (ANT) [24] build, configuration, and deployment scripts can be generated from the GEMS deployment model.

Generic Modeling Environment [30] is another graphical modeling tool similar to GEMS that allows developers to graphically specify a metamodel and generate a DSML editor. A modeling tool for specifying the overall component architecture of the Pet Store has been implemented in GME. The GME architecture model is used to capture the component types, the various client types, back-end database architecture, and expected distribution of client requests to the Pet Store. The GME architecture model is shown in Fig. 3.

2. Model weaving tools. The caching aspect of the Pet Store is modeled separately from the GEMS deployment model and GME architecture model. Each time the caching model is updated, model weaving tools must be used to apply the new caching architecture to the GEMS and GME models. For the GME models, the C-SAW [42] model weaver is used to merge the caching architecture into the architecture model. C-SAW relies on a series of weaving definition files to perform the merger. Each manually derived global cache weaving solution is implemented in C-SAW's weaving definition files to apply to the GME architecture models. Again, because we need two separate modeling tools to produce the best possible deployment and architecture models, we must also utilize and integrate two separate model weavers into the development process.

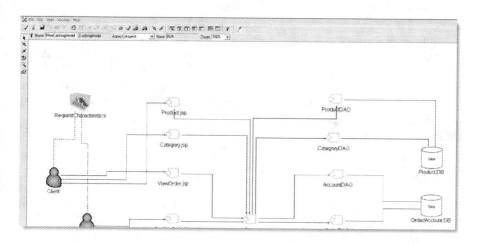

Fig. 3. GME Pet Store Architecture Model

The deployment models in GEMS need to be updated via a model weaver, such as the Atlas Model Weaver (AMW) [16], which can interoperate with models based on EMF. With AMW, developers specify two EMF models and a series of merger directives (*i.e.* a weaving specification). AMW produces a third merged EMF model from the two source models. Each global cache weaving solution must also be implemented as a weaving specification for AMW. Once the AMW specification is implemented, the cache weaving solution can be merged into the GEMS EMF-based deployment model to include any required JAR files and cache configuration steps.

3. Code weaving tools. Finally, to apply the cache weaving solution to the legacy Pet Store code, the Java cache advice implementations must be woven into the Pet Store's middle-tier objects using AspectJ [2], which is a framework for weaving advice into Java applications. Although the Spring framework allows the application of AspectJ advice definitions to the Pet Store, it requires that the Spring bean definition files for the Pet Store be updated to include the new AspectJ pointcuts and advice specifications. A final third implementation of the global cache weaving solution must be created and specified in terms of Spring bean definitions and AspectJ pointcuts.

Overall, there are three separate tool chains that the Pet Store cache weaving solution must be implemented. First, C-SAW weaving specifications must be created to update the GME architectural models. Second, AMW weaving specifications must be produced to update the GEMS deployment models. Finally, the weaving solution must be turned into AspectJ advice/pointcut definitions for weaving the caches into the Pet Store at run time.

3   Model Weaving Challenges

One of the primary limitations of applying existing model weavers to the Pet Store case study described in Sect. 2 is that the existing model weaver pointcut specifications cannot encode global application constraints, such as memory consumption constraints, and also cannot leverage global constraints or dependency-based weaving rules to produce an overall global weaving solution. Developers must instead document and derive a solution for the overall global application constraints and implement the solution for each of the numerous modeling and weaving platforms for the Pet Store. Moreover, each time the underlying global application constraints change (*e.g.* the memory available for caches is adjusted), the overall global weaving solution must be recalculated and implemented in the numerous modeling tools and platforms.

3.1   Differences between Aspect Weavers and Model Weavers

To understand why model weavers do not currently support global constraints and how this can be rectified, we first must evaluate aspect weavers at the coding level, which have influenced model weavers. Aspect weavers, such as AspectJ and HyperJ [3], face an indeterminate number of potential joinpoints (also referred to as *joinpoint shadows* [23]) that will be passed through during application execution. For example, late-binding can be used in a Java application to dynamically load and link multiple libraries for different parts of the application.

Each library may have hundreds or thousands of classes and numerous methods per class (each a potential joinpoint). An aspect weaver cannot identify which classes and methods the execution path of the application will pass through before the process exits. The weaver can therefore never ascertain the exact set of potential joinpoints that will be used ahead of time. Although the weaver may have knowledge of every joinpoint shadow, it will not have knowledge of which are actually used at run time. Model weaving, however, faces a different situation than a run time aspect weaver. The key differences are

- Model weaving merges two models of finite and known size.
- Because models have no thread of execution, the weaver can exactly ascertain what joinpoints are used by each model.
- Model weaving speed is less critical than aspect weaving speed at run time and adding additional seconds to the total weaving time is not unreasonable.

Because a model weaver has knowledge of the entire set of joinpoints used by the models at its disposal, it can perform a number of activities that are not possible with runtime weaving where the entire used set of target joinpoints is not known. For example, a model weaver can incorporate global constraints into the weaving process. A runtime weaver cannot honor global constraints because it cannot see the entire used joinpoint set at once. To honor a global constraint, the weaver must be able to see the entire target joinpoint set to avoid violating a global constraint.

Runtime aspect weaving involves a large number of potential joinpoints or joinpoint shadows and is not well-suited for capturing and solving global application constraints as part of the weaving process. When weaving must be performed on an extremely large set of target joinpoints, the weaver must use a high-efficiency technique for matching advice to joinpoints (every millisecond counts). The most common technique is to use a query or regular expression that can be used to determine if a pointcut matches a joinpoint. The queries and regular expressions are independent of each other, which allows the weaver to quickly compare each pointcut to the potential joinpoints and determine matches.

If dependencies were introduced between the queries or expressions (*e.g.* only match pointcut A if pointcut B or C do not match), the weaver would be forced to perform far less efficient matching algorithms. Moreover, since the weaver could not know the entire joinpoint set passed through by the application's execution thread ahead of time, it could not honor a dependency, such as match pointcut A only if pointcuts B and C are *never* matched, because it cannot predict whether or not B and C will match in the future. Finally, when dependencies are introduced, there is no longer necessarily a single correct solution. Situations can arise where the weaver must either choose to apply A or apply B and C.

3.2   Challenge 1: Existing Model Weaving Poinctut Specifications Cannot Encode Global Application Constraints

Most model weavers, such as C-SAW, AMW, and the Motorola WEAVR [14], have adopted the approach of runtime weavers and do not allow dependencies between pointcuts or global constraints. Because the model weaver does not incorporate these types of constraints, developers cannot encode the global application constraints into the weaving specification. Figure 4 presents the manual refactoring steps (the first six steps) that must be performed when the modeled distribution of request types to the Pet Store changes.

In the Pet Store case study, there are a number of dependencies and global constraints that must be honored to find a correct weaving. We created caching advice implementations that capture all product queries and implementations that are biased towards, specific data items such as the FishCache. The biased cache is used when the majority

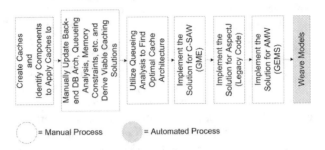

Fig. 4. Solution Model Changes Cause Weaving Solution Updates

of requests are for a particular product type. The `FishCache` and the generic product cache should be mutually exclusive. The use of the `FishCache` is excluded if the percentage of requests for fish drops below 50%. Moreover, the generic product cache will then become applicable and must be applied.

A small change in the solution model can cause numerous significant ripple effects in the global application constraints and hence weaving solution. This problem of changes to the solution models of an applicaiton causing substantial refactoring of the weaving solution is well-known [22]. The problem becomes even more complex, however, with the global weaving solution, where significant refactoring causes multiple implementations of the weaving specification to change.

The problem with managing this ripple effect with existing model weavers is that both the `FishCache` and the generic product cache have a pointcut that matches the same model element, the `ProductDAO`. With existing pointcut languages based on regular expressions or queries, there is no way to specify that only one of the two pointcut definitions should be matched to the `ProductDAO`. The pointcut definitions only allow the developer to specify matching conditions based on joinpoint properties and not on the matching success of other pointcuts.

Developers often need to restrict the overall cache selection to use less than a specified amount of memory. For example, rather than having the `FishCache` and `GenericCache` be mutually exclusive, the two caches could be allowed to be applied if there is sufficient memory available to support both. Requiring that the woven caches fit within a memory budget is a resource constraint on the total memory consumed by the weaving solution and relies on specifying a property over the entire weaving solution. Existing regular expression and query-based pointcut languages usually do not capture these types of rules.

Another challenge of producing this weaving constraint on the memory consumed by the caches is that it relies on properties of both the advice objects (*e.g.* the memory consumed by the cache) and the joinpoint objects (*e.g.* the memory available to the hosting object's application server). Most model weaving pointcut languages allow specifying conditions only against the properties of the target joinpoints and not over the advice elements associated with the pointcut. To circumvent this limitation, developers must manually add up the memory consumed by the advice associated with the pointcut and encode it into the pointcut specification's query (*e.g.* find all elements hosted by an application server with at least 30 MB of memory).

3.3   Challenge 2: Changes to the Solution Model Can Require Significant Refactoring of the Weaving Solution

As the solution models of the application that determine the set of joinpoints change, each manual step in Fig. 4 may need to be repeated. The caching solution relies on multiple solution models, such as the server request distribution model, the cache hit ratio and service times model, and the PetStore software architecture model. A change in any of these models can trigger a recalculation of the global weaving solution. Each recalculation of the global weaving solution involves multiple complex caculations to determine the new targets for caches. After the new cache targets are identified, the implementation of the solution for each weaving platform, such as the C-SAW weaving definition files, must be updated to reflect the new caching architecture.

For example, the correct weaving of caches into the Pet Store requires considering the back-end organization of the product database. If the database is hosted on a separate server from the Pet Store's application server, caching product information can significantly improve performance, as described in Sect. 2. The cache weaving solution is no longer correct; however, if biased caches are applied to various product types that are being retrieved from a remote database and the database is co-hosted with the Pet Store's application server. A developer must then update the weaving solution to produce a new and correct solution for the updated solution model.

As seen in Fig. 5, not only are numerous manual steps required to update the weaving solution when solution model changes occur but each manual step can be complex. For example, re-calculating the optimal placement of caches using a queueing model is non-trivial. Moreover, each manual step in the process is a potential source of errors that can produce incorrect solutions and requires repeating the process. The large numbers of solution model changes that occur in enterprise development, and the complexity of updating the weaving solution to respect global constraints, make manually updating a global weaving solution hard.

3.4   Challenge 3: Existing Model Weavers Cannot Leverage a Weaving Goal to Find an Optimal Concern Merging Solution

Another challenge of encoding global application constraints into a weaving specification is that global constraints create situations where there are multiple correct solutions. Existing model weavers do not allow situations where there are multiple possible weaving solutions. Because the weaver cannot choose between weaving solutions, developers must manually deduce the correct and optimal solution to use.

Optimizing a solution bound by a set of global constraints is a computationally intensive search process. Searching for an optimal solution involves exploring the solution space (the set of solutions that adhere to the global constraints) to determine the optimal solution. This type of optimization search can sometimes be performed manually with numerical methods, such as the Simplex [37] method, but is typically hard. In particular, each time the solution models change, developers must manually derive a new optimal solution from scratch.

For example, to optimize the allocation of caches to DAOs in the Pet Store, developers must:

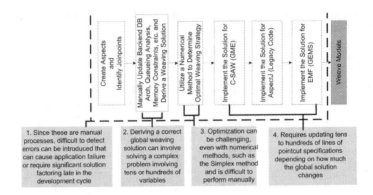

Fig. 5. Challenges of Updating a Weaving Solution

- Evaluate the back-end database configuration to determine if product, account, or other data must be cached to reduce query latency.
- Derive from the cache deployment constraints what caches can be applied to the system and in what combinations.
- Determine how much memory is available to the caches and how memory constraints restrict potential cache configurations.
- Exhaustively compare feasible caching architectures using queuing analysis to derive the optimal allocation of caches to DAOs based on DAO service rates with and without caching and with various cache hit rates.

It is hard to manually perform these complex calculations each time the solution models change or caching constraints are modified.

4   CSP-Based Model Weaving

To address the challenges described in Sect. 3, we have developed *AspectScatter*, which is a static model weaver that can:

1. Transform a model weaving problem into a CSP and incorporate global constraints and dependencies between pointcuts to address Challenge 1 from Sect. 3.2.
2. Using a constraint solver, automatically derive a weaving solution that is correct with respect to a set of global constraints, eliminating the need to manually update the weaving solution when solution models change, as described in Challenge 2 from Sect. 3.3.
3. Select an optimal weaving solution (when multiple solutions exist) with regard to a function over the properties of the advice and joinpoints, allowing the weaver rather than the developer to perform optimization, thereby addressing Challenge 3 from Sect. 3.4.
4. Produce a platform-independent weaving model and transform it into multiple platform-specific weaving solutions for AspectJ, C-SAW, and AMW through model transformations, thus addressing the problems associated with maintaining the weaving specification in multiple weaving platforms.

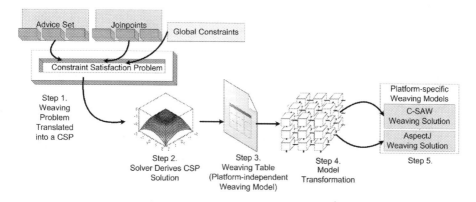

Fig. 6. Constraint-based Weaving Overview

Figure 6 shows an overview of AspectScatter's weaving approach. In Step 1, developers describe the advice, joinpoints, and weaving constraints to AspectScatter using its domain-specific language (DSL) for specifying aspect weaving problems with global constraints. In Step 2, AspectScatter transforms the DSL instance into a CSP and uses a constraint solver to derive a guaranteed correct and, if needed, optimal weaving solution. In Step 3, AspectScatter transforms the solution into a platform-independent weaving model. Finally, in Step 4, model transformations are used to transform the platform-independent weaving model into specific implementations, such as C-SAW weaving definition files, for each target weaving platform.

The remainder of this section presents a mapping from model weaving to a CSP. By producing a CSP for model weaving, a constraint solver can be used to deduce a correct, and in many cases, optimal solution to a weaving problem.

4.1   CSP Background

A CSP is a set of variables and a set of constraints over those variables. For example, $A < B < 100$ is a CSP over the integer variables A and B. A solution to a CSP is a set of values for the variables (called a labeling) that adheres to the set of constraints. For example, $A = 10, B = 50$ is a valid labeling (solution) of the example CSP.

Solutions to CSPs are obtained by using *constraint solvers*, which are automated tools for finding CSP solutions. Constraint solvers build a graph of the variables and constraints and apply techniques, such as arc-consistency, to find the ranges that variable values can be set to. Search algorithms then traverse the constraint network to hone in on a valid or optimal solution.

A constraint solver can also be used to derive a labeling of a CSP that maximizes or minimizes a specific goal function (*i.e.* a function over the variables). For example, the solver could be asked to maximize the goal function $A + B$ in our example CSP. A maximal labeling of the variables with respect to this goal function would be $A = 98, B = 99$.

4.2 Mapping Cache Weaving to a CSP

Cache weaving can be used as a simple example of how a CSP can be used to solve a weaving problem. In the following example, we make several assumptions, such as the hit ratio for the caches being the same for both joinpoints, to simplify the problem for clarity. Real weaving examples involving optimal caching or other types of global constraints are substantially more difficult to solve manually and hence motivate our constraint solver weaving solution.

Assume that there are two caches that can be woven into an application, denoted as $C1$ and $C2$. Furthermore, assume that there are two joinpoints that the caches can be applied to, denoted as $J1$ and $J2$. Let there be a total of 200K of memory available to the caches. Furthermore, the two caches are mutually exclusive and cannot be applied to the same joinpoint. Let the time required to service a request at $J1$ be 10 ms and the time at $J2$ be 12 ms.

Each cache hit on $C1$ requires 2 ms to service and each cache hit on $C2$ requires 3 ms to service. All requests pass through both $J1$ and $J2$, and the goal is to optimally match the caches to joinpoints and set their sizes to minimize the total service time per request. The size of each cache, $C1_{size}$ and $C2_{size}$, determines the cache's hit ratio. For $C1$, the hit ratio is $C1_{size}/500$, and for $C2$, the hit ratio is $C2_{size}/700$. Let us assume that cache $C1$ is woven into joinpoint $J1$ and $C2$ is woven into joinpoint $J2$, the service time per request can be calculated as

$$SvcTime = 2(C1_{size}/500) + 10(1 - C1_{size}/500) + 3(C1_{size}/700) + 12(1 - C1_{size}/700)$$

With this formulation, we can derive the optimal sizes for the caches subject to the global weaving constraint:

$$C1_{size} + C2_{size} < 200$$

The problem, however, is that we want to know not only the optimal cache size but also where to weave the caches and the above formulation assumes that cache $C1$ is assigned to $J1$ and $C2$ to $J2$. Thus, instead, we need to introduce variables into the service time calculation to represent the joinpoint that each cache is actually applied to so that we do not assume an architecture of how caches are applied to joinpoints. That is, we want to deduce not only the cache sizes but also the best allocation of caches to joinpoints (the caching architecture). Let the variable M_{jk} have value 1 if the j_{th} cache C_j is matched to joinpoint J_k and 0 otherwise. We can update our service time formula so that it does not include a fixed assignment of caches to joinpoints:

$$SvcTime = 2(M_{11} * C1_{size}/500) + 3(M_{21} * C2_{size}/700) +$$

$$10(1 - ((M_{11} * C1_{size}/500) + (M_{21} * C2_{size}/700))) +$$

$$2(M_{12} * C1_{size}/500) + 3(M_{22} * C2_{size}/700) +$$

$$12(1 - ((M_{12} * C1_{size}/500) + (M_{22} * C2_{size}/700)))$$

The new formulation of the response time takes into account the different caches that could be deployed at each joinpoint. For example, the service time at joinpoint $J1$ is defined as

$$J1SvcTime = 2(M_{11} * C1_{size}/500)$$

$$+3(M_{21} * C2_{size}/700)+$$

$$+10(1 - ((M_{11} * C1_{size}/500) + (M_{21} * C2_{size}/500)))$$

In this formulation the variables M_{11} and M_{21} influence the service time calculation by determining if a specific cache's servicing information is included in the calculation. If the cache $C1$ is applied to $J1$, then $M_{11} = 1$ and the cache's service time is included in the calculation. If the cache is not woven into $J1$, then $M_{11} = 0$, which zeros out the effect of the cache at $J1$ since:

$$J1SvcTime = 2(0)\ldots 10(1 - (0 + (M_{21} * C2_{size}/500)))$$

Thus, by calculating the optimal values of the M_{ij} variables, we are also calculating the optimal way of assigning the caches (advice) to the joinpoints.

To optimally weave the caches into the application, we need to derive a set of values for the variables in the service time equation that minimizes its value. Furthermore, we must derive a solution that not only minimizes the above equation's value but respects the constraints:

$$C1_{size} + C2_{size} < 200$$

$$(M_{11} = 1) \Rightarrow (M_{21} = 0)$$

$$(M_{21} = 1) \Rightarrow (M_{22} = 0)$$

because the cache sizes must add up to less than the alloted memory (200K) and both caches cannot be applied to the same joinpoint.

When the constraint solver is invoked on the CSP, the output will be the values for the M_{ij} variables. That is, for each Advice i and joinpoint j the solver will output the value of the variable M_{ij}, which specifies if Advice, A_i, should be mapped to joinpoint, B_j. The M_{ij} variables can be viewed as a table where the rows represent the advice elements, the columns represent the joinpoints, and the values (0 or 1) at each cell are the solver's solution as to whether or not a particular advice should be applied to a specific joinpoint. Furthermore, any variables that do not have values set, such as the cache sizes ($C1_{size}$ and $C2_{size}$), will have optimal values set by the constraint solver.

Even for this seemingly simple weaving problem, deriving what joinpoints the caches should be applied to and how big each cache should be is not easy to do manually. However, by creating this formulation of the weaving problems as a CSP, we can use a constraint solver to derive the optimal solution on our behalf. The solution that the solver creates will include not only the optimal cache sizes but also which joinpoints each cache should be applied to, which would be very difficult to derive manually.

4.3   A General Mapping of Weaving to a CSP

Section 4.2 showed how a CSP could be used to solve a weaving problem involving optimization and global constraints. This section presents a generalized mapping from

Table 1. An Example Weaving Table

	ProductDAO	ItemDAO
$ProductsCache$	$M_{00} = 1$	$M_{01} = 0$
$FishCache$	$M_{10} = 0$	$M_{11} = 0$

a weaving problem to a CSP so that the technique can be applied to arbitrary model weaving problems with global constraints.

We define a solution to a model weaving problem as a mapping of elements from an advice set α to a joinpoint set β that adheres to a set of constraints γ. To represent this mapping as a CSP, we create a table, called the *weaving table*, where for each advice A_i in α and joinpoint B_j in β, we define a cell (*i.e.* a variable in the CSP) M_{ij}. If the advice A_i should be applied to the joinpoint B_j, then $M_{ij} = 1$ (meaning the table cell <i,j> has value 1). If A_i should not be applied to B_j, then $M_{ij} = 0$. The rules for building a weaving solution are described to the constraint solver as constraints over the M_{ij} variables. An example weaving table where the ProductsCache is applied to the ProductDAO is shown in Table 1.

Some weaving constraints are described purely in terms of the weaving table. For example, Challenge 1 from Sect. 3.2 introduced the constraint that the FishCache should only be used if the ProductsCache is not applied to any component. This constraint can be defined in terms of a constraint over the weaving table. If the FishCache is A_0 and the ProductsCache is A_1, then we can encode this constraint as for all joinpoints, j:

$$\left(\sum_{j=0}^{n} M_{0j} > 0 \right) \to \left(\sum_{j=0}^{n} M_{1j} = 0 \right)$$

Some examples of dependency constraints between advice elements that can be implemented as CSP constraints on the weaving table are:

$Advice_0$ requires $Advice_1$ to always be applied to the same joinpoint:

$$\forall B_j \subset \beta, (M_{0j} = 1) \to (M_{1j} = 1)$$

$Advice_0$ excludes $Advice_1$ from being applied to the same joinpoint:

$$\forall B_j \subset \beta, (M_{0j} = 1) \to (M_{1j} = 0)$$

$Advice_0$ requires between $MIN \ldots MAX$ of $Advice_1 \ldots Advice_k$ at the same joinpoint:

$$\forall B_j \subset \beta, (M_{0j} = 1) \to \left(\sum_{i=1}^{k} M_{ij} \geq MIN \right) \wedge \left(\sum_{i=1}^{k} M_{ij} \leq MAX \right)$$

4.4 Advice and Joinpoint Properties Tables

Other weaving constraints must take into account the properties of the advice and joinpoint elements and cannot be defined purely in terms of the weaving table. To incorporate constraints involving the properties of the advice and joinpoints, we create two

Table 2. An Example Joinpoint Properties Table

	%Fish Requests	%Bird Requests
ProductDAO	65% ($PT_{00} = 0.65$)	20% ($PT_{01} = 0.2$)
ItemDAO	17% ($PT_{10} = 0.17$)	47% ($PT_{11} = 0.47$)

additional tables: the *advice properties table* and *joinpoint properties table*. Each row P_i in the advice properties table represents the properties of the advice element A_i. The columns of the advice table represent the different property types. Thus, the cell <i,j>, represented by the variable PA_{ij}, contains A_i's value for the property associated with the j_{th} column. The joinpoint properties table is constructed in the same fashion with the rows being the joinpoints (*i.e.* each cell is denoted by the variable PT_{ij}). An example joinpoint properties table is shown in Table 2.

Challenge 1 from Sect. 3.2 introduced the constraint that the FishCache should only be applied to the ProductDAO if more than 50% (the majority) of the requests to the ProductDAO are for fish. We can use the advice and joinpoint properties tables to encode this request distribution constraint. Let the joinpoint properties table column at index 0 be associated with the property for the percentage of requests that are for Fish, as shown in the the joinpoint properties table shown in Table 2. Moreover, let A_1 be the FishCache and B_0 be the ProductDAO. The example request distribution constraint can be encoded as $M_{10} \rightarrow (PT_{00} > 50)$.

4.5   Global Constraints

In enterprise systems, global constraints are often needed to limit the amount of memory, bandwidth, or CPU consumed by a weaving solution. Global constraints can naturally be incorporated into the CSP model as constraints involving the entire set of variables in the weaving table. For example, the memory constraint on the total amount of RAM consumed by the caches, described in Challenge 1 from Sect. 3.2, can be specified as a constraint on the weaving and properties tables.

Let the joinpoint property table column at index 5, as shown in Table 3, represent the amount of free memory available on the hosting application server of each joinpoint. Moreover, let the advice property table column at index 4, as shown in Table 4, contain the amount of memory consumed by each cache. The memory consumption constraint can be specified as:

$$\forall B_j \subset \beta, \left(\sum_{i=0}^{n} PA_{i4} * M_{ij} \right) < PT_{j5}$$

If an advice element is matched against a joinpoint, the corresponding M_{ij} variable is set to 1 and the advice element's memory consumption value PA_{i4} is added to the total consumed memory on the target application server. The constraint that the consumed memory be less than the available memory is captured by the stipulation that this sum be $< PT_{j5}$, which is the total amount of free memory available on the joinpoint's application server.

Table 3. An Example Joinpoint Properties Table with Available Memory

	. . .	RAM on Application Server
ProductDAO	. . .	1024K ($PT_{05} = 1024$)
. . .	. . .	. . .

Table 4. An Example Advice Properties Table with RAM Consumption

	. . .	RAM Consumed
ProductCache	. . .	400K ($PA_{04} = 400$)
FishCache	. . .	700K ($PA_{14} = 700$)

4.6   Joinpoint Feasibility Filtering with Regular Expressions and Queries

Some types of constraints, such as constraints that require matching strings against regular expressions, are more naturally represented using existing query and regular expression techniques. The CSP approach to model weaving can also incorporate these types of constraint expressions. Regular expressions, queries, and other pointcut expressions that do not have dependenices can be used as an initial filtering step to explicitly set zero values for some M_{ij} variables. The filtering step reduces the set of feasible joinpoints that the solver must consider when producing a weaving solution.

For example, the FishCache should only be applied to DAOs with the naming convention "Product*". This rule can be captured with an existing pointcut language and then checked against all possible joinpoints, as shown in Fig. 7. For each joinpoint j that the pointcut does not match, the CSP variable M_{ij} for each advice element i associated with the pointcut is set to 0. Layering existing dependency-free pointcut languages as filters on top of the CSP-based weaver can help to increase the number of labeled variables provided to the solver and thus reduce solving time.

4.7   CSP-Weaving Benefits

Challenge 3 from Sect. 3.4 showed the need for the ability to incorporate a weaving goal to produce an optimal weaving. Using a CSP model of a weaving problem, a weaving goal can be specified as a function over the M_{ij}, PA_{ij}, and PT_{ij} variables. Once the goal is defined in terms of these variables, the solver can be used to derive a weaving solution that maximizes the weaving goal. Moreover, the solver can set optimal values for attributes of the advice elements such as cache size.

Allowing developers to specify optimization goals for the weaver enables different weaving solutions to be obtained that prioritize application concerns differently. For example, the same Pet Store solution models can be used to derive caching solutions that minimize response time at the expense of memory, balance response time, and memory consumption, or minimize the response time of particular user actions, such as adding items to the shopping cart. To explore these various solution possibilities, developers update the optimization function provided to AspectScatter and not the entire weaving

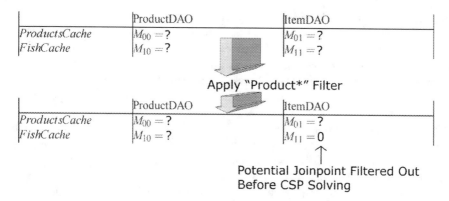

	ProductDAO	ItemDAO
ProductsCache	$M_{00} = ?$	$M_{01} = ?$
FishCache	$M_{10} = ?$	$M_{11} = ?$

Apply "Product*" Filter

	ProductDAO	ItemDAO
ProductsCache	$M_{00} = ?$	$M_{01} = ?$
FishCache	$M_{10} = ?$	$M_{11} = 0$

Potential Joinpoint Filtered Out
Before CSP Solving

Fig. 7. Joinpoint Feasibility Filtering

solution calculation process. With the manual optimization approaches required by existing model weavers, it is typically too time-consuming to evaluate multiple solution alternatives.

Mapping aspect weaving to a CSP and using a constraint solver to derive a weaving solution addresses Challenge 1 from Sect. 3.2. CSPs can naturally accomodate both dependency constraints and complex global constraints, such as resource or scheduling constraints. With existing model weaving approaches, developers manually identify and document solutions to the global weaving constraints. With a CSP formulation of weaving, conversely, a constraint solver can perform this task automatically as part of the weaving process.

Manual approaches to create a weaving solution for a set of constraints have numerous points where errors can be introduced. When AspectScatter is used to derive a weaving solution, the correctness of the resulting solution is assured with respect to the weaving constraints. Moreover, in cases where there is no viable solution, AspectScatter will indicate that weaving is not possible.

A further benefit of mapping an aspect weaving problem to a CSP is that extensive prior research on CSPs can be applied to deriving aspect weaving solutions. Existing research includes different approaches to finding solutions [27], incorporating soft constraints [40], selecting optimal solutions or approximations in polynomial time [11,18,39], and handling conflicting constraints. Conflict resolution has been singled out in model weaving research as a major challenge [49]. Numerous existing techniques for over-constrainted systems [10,25,?,46] (*i.e.* CSPs with conflicting constraints), such as using higher-order constraints, can be applied by mapping model weaving to a CSP.

5   The AspectScatter DSL

Manually translating an aspect weaving problem into a CSP using the mapping presented in Sect. 4 is not ideal. A CSP model can accomodate global constraints and dependencies but requires a complex mapping that must be performed correctly to produce a valid solution. Working directly with the CSP variables to specify a weaving problem is akin to writing assembly code as opposed to Java or C++ code.

AspectScatter provides a textual DSL for specifying weaving problems and can automatically transform instances of the DSL into the equivalent CSP model for a constraint solver. AspectScatter's DSL allows developers to work at the advice/joinpoint level of abstraction and still leverage a CSP and constraint solver for deriving a weaving solution.

The CSP formulation of an aspect weaving problem is not specific to any one particular type of joinpoint or advice. The construction and solving of the CSP is a mathematical manipulation of symbols representing a set of joinpoints and advice. As such, the joinpoints could potentially be Java method invocations or model elements. In Sect. 6, we discuss how these symbols are translated into platform-specific joinpoints and advice. For this section, however, it is important to remember that we are only declaring and stating the symbols and constraints that are used to build the mathematical CSP weaving problem.

For example, in the context of the cache weaving example, there are two different types of platform-specific joinpoints. First, there are the joinpoints used by C-SAW, which are types of model elements in a GME model. Second, there are AspectJ-type joinpoints, which are the invocation of various methods on the Java implementations of the ProductDAO, OrderDAO, etc. In the platform-independent model used by the CSP, the joinpoint definition OrderDAO is merely a symbolic definition of a joinpoint. When the platform-specific solution is translated into a platform-specific weaving solution, OrderDAO is mapped to a model element in the GME model used by C-SAW and an invocation of a query method on the Java implementation of the OrderDAO.

The basic format for an AspectScatter DSL instance is shown below:

```
ADVICE_1_ID
{
  (DIRECTIVE;)*
}
...
ADVICE_N_ID
{
  (DIRECTIVE;)*
}
JOINPOINT_1_ID
{
  (VARIABLENAME=EXPRESSION;)*
}
...
JOINPOINT_N_ID
{
  (VARIABLENAME=EXPRESSION;)*
}
```

The JOINPOINT declaration specifies a joinpoint, an element $B_j \subset \beta$, which ADVICE elements can be matched against. The JOINPOINT_ID is the identifier, such as "Order-DAO," which is given as a symbolic name for the joinpoint. Each JOINPOINT element contains one or more property declarations in the form of VARIABLENAME=EXPRESSION. The columns for the joinpoint properties table are created by traversing all of the JOINPOINT declarations and creating columns for the set of VARIABLENAMEs. The *EXPRESSION that a JOINPOINT specifies for a VARIABLENAME becomes the entry for that JOINPOINT's row in the specified VARIABLENAME column, PT_{ij}.

Table 5. AspectScatter DSL Directives

DIRECTIVE	Applied To	Description
Requires : ADVICE+	one or more other ADVICE elements	Ensures that all of the specified ADVICE elements are applied to a JOINPOINT if the enclosing ADVICE element is
Required : (true|false)	an ADVICE element	The enclosing ADVICE element must be applied to at least one JOINPOINT (if true).
Excludes : ADVICE+	one or more other ADVICE elements	Ensures that none of the specified ADVICE are applied to the same JOINPOINT as the enclosing ADVICE
Select : [MIN..MAX],ADVICE+	a cardinality expression and one or more other ADVICE	Ensures that at least MIN and at most MAX of the specified ADVICE are mapped to the same JOINPOINT as the enclosing ADVICE
Target : CONSTRAINT	an ADVICE element	Requires that CONSTRAINT hold true for the ADVICE and JOINPOINT's properties if the ADVICE is mapped to the JOINPOINT
Evaluate : (ocl|groovy), FILTER_EXPRESSION	an ADVICE element	Requires that FILTER_EXPRESSION defined in OCL or Groovy hold true for the ADVICE and JOINPOINT's properties if the ADVICE is mapped to the JOINPOINT
DefineVar : VARIABLENAME (= EXPRESSION)?	a weaving problem	Defines a variable. The final value for the variable is bound by the weaver and must cause the optional EXPRESSION to evaluate to true
Define : VARIABLENAME = EXPRESSION	a weaving problem	Defines a variable and sets a constant value for it
Goal : (maximize|minimize), VARIABLE_EXPRESSION	a weaving problem	Defines an expression over the properties of ADVICE and JOINPOINTS that should be maximized or minimized by the weaving

Table 6. AspectScatter DSL Expressions

EXPRESSION	$(CONSTANT\|VARIABLE\_EXPRESSION)$ $(+\|-\|\times)$ $(CONSTANT\|VARIABLE\_EXPRESSION)$	An expression
CONSTRAINT	$(VARIABLE\_EXPRESSION\|CONSTANT)$ $(<\|>\|=\|!=\|=<\|>=)$ $(VARIABLE\_EXPRESSION\|CONSTANT)$	Defines a constraint that must hold true in the final weaving solution.
VARIABLE_EXPRESSION	$(VARIABLE\_V\_EXPRESSION\|CONSTANT)$ $(+\|-\|\times)$ $(VARIABLE\_V\_EXPRESSION\|CONSTANT)$	An expression over a set of variables
VARIABLE_V_EXPRESSION	(Target|Source).VARIABLENAME	The value of the specified defined variable (VARIABLENAME) on a ADVICE or JOINPOINT element. *Target* specifies that the variable should be resolved against the JOINPOINT matched by the enclosing ADVICE. *Source* specifies that the variable should be resolved against the enclosing ADVICE element.

Each `ADVICE` declaration specifies an advice element that can be matched against the set of `JOINPOINT` elements, an element $A_i \subset \alpha$. The `DIRECTIVES` within the advice element specify the constraints that must be upheld by the weaving solution produced by AspectScatter and the properties of the `ADVICE` element (values for the PA_{ij} variables). The directives available in AspectScatter are shown in Table 5.

As an example, the AspectScatter ADVICE definitions:

```
GenericCache
{
  Excludes:FishCache;
  DefineVar:CacheSize;
}
FishCache
{
}
```

defines two advice elements called `GenericCache` and `FishCAche`. The `DIRECTIVEs` within the `GenericCache` declaration (between "{..}") specify the constraints that must be upheld by the joinpoint it is associated with and the properties the advice element defines. The `GenericCache` excludes the advice element `FishCache` from being applied to the same joinpoint as the `GenericCache`. The `GenericCache` declaration also specifies a property variable, called `CacheSize`, which the weaver must determine a value for.

Assume that the `GenericCache` is A_2 and the `FishCache` is A_1. The AspectScatter specification would be transformed into: the mapping variables $M_{20} \ldots M_{2n}$, the advice property variables $PA_{20} \ldots PA_{2k}$, an advice property table column for `CacheSize`, and the CSP constraint $\forall B_j \subset \beta, (M_2 j = 1) \rightarrow (M_1 j = 0)$.

The final part of an AspectScatter DSL instance is an optional set of global variable definitions and an optimization goal. The global variable definitions are defined in an element named `Globals`. Within the `Globals` element, properties can be defined that are not specific to a single `ADVICE` or `JOINPOINT`. Furthermore, the `Goal` directive key word can be used within the `Globals` element to define the function that the constraint solver should attempt to maximize or minimize.

The values for variables provided by the weaver are determined by labeling the CSP for the weaving problem. For example, the global constraints for the Pet Store weaving problem define the goal as the minimization of the response time of the `ItemDAO` and `ProductDAO`, as can be seen below:

```
Globals {
  Define:TotalFish = 100;
  Define:TotalBirds = 75;
  Define:TotalOtherAnimals = 19;
  Constraint:Sources.CacheSize.Sum < 1024;
  Goal:minimize, ProductDAO.RequestPercentage * ProductDAO.ResponseTime +
                 ItemDAO.RequestPercentage * ItemDAO.ResponseTime;
}
```

Each `Define` creates a variable in the CSP and sets its value. The variable created by the `Define` can then have a constraint bound to it. For example, the variable `TotalBirds` is used in the constraint $(\sum_{j=0}^{n} M_{0j} > 0) \rightarrow (TotalBirds < 80)$. This simple constraint states that the 0th advice element can only be applied to a joinpoint if there are less than 80 birds.

The `Constraint` directive adds a constraint to the CSP. In the example above, the specification adds a constraint that the sum of the cache sizes must be less than 1024. The statement "`Sources.CacheSize.Sum`" is a special AspectScatter language expression for obtaining a value from a properties table (the advice properties table), a column (`CacheSize`), and an operation (summation). Assuming `CacheSize` is the 0th column in the advice properties table, the statement adds the following constraint to the CSP:

$$\forall B_j \subset \beta, \left(\sum_{i=0}^{n} (M_{ij} * PA_{i0}) < 1024 \right)$$

Since no explicit values for each advice element's `CacheSize` is set, these will be variables that the solver will need to find values for as part of the CSP solving process. Because the response times of the DAOs are dependent on the size of each cache, the `CacheSize` variables will be set by the weaver to minimize response time. Developers can use the AspectScatter DSL to produce complex aspect weaving problems with both global constraints and goals.

AspectScatter's DSL also includes support for the filtering operations described in Sect. 4.6. Filters to restrict the potential joinpoints that an advice element can be mapped to can be defined using an object constraint language (OCL) [47] or Groovy [26] language expression that must hold true for the advice/joinpoint mapping (*i.e.* the choice of expression language is up to the user). Filters are defined via the `Evaluate` directive. For example, a Groovy constraint can be used to restrict the FishCache from being applied to any order-related DAOs via a regular expression constraint:

```
FishCache {
 ...
 Evaluate:groovy,{!target.name.contains("Order")};
}
```

An OCL constraint could be used to further restrict the FishCache to be only applied to DAOs that receive requests from a category listing page:

```
FishCache {
 ...
 Evaluate:ocl,(target.requestsFrom->collect(x | x.name = 'ViewCategories.jsp')->size() > 0};
}
```

As described in Sect. 4.6, the filter expressions defined via Evaluate are used to preprocess the weaving CSP and eliminate unwanted advice/joinpoint combinations.

6   AspectScatter Model Transformation Language

The result of solving the CSP is a platform-independent weaving solution that symbolically defines which advice elements should be mapped to which joinpoints. This symbolic weaving solution still needs to be translated into a platform-specific weaving model such as an AspectJ weaving specification. The platform-specific weaving specification can then be executed to perform the actual code or model weaving.

Each platform-independent weaving representation of the weaving solution can be transformed into multiple platform-specific weaving solutions, such as AspectJ, C-SAW, or AMW-specific weaving specifications. Producing a platform-independent weaving model of the solution and transforming it into implementations for specific tools allows AspectScatter to eliminate much of the significant manual effort required to synchronize multiple weaving specifications across a diverse set of models, modeling languages, and modeling tools. For example, when the modeled request distribution changes for the Pet Store, the C-SAW, AspectJ, and GEMS weaving specifications can automatically be re-generated by AspectScatter, as shown in Step 4 of Fig. 6.

AspectScatter's platform-independent weaving model can be transformed into a platform-specific model with a number of Java-based model transformation tools such as ATL [28]. AspectScatter also includes a simple model transformation tool based on pointcut generation templates that can be used to create the platform-specific weaving model. In this section, we show the use of the built-in transformation language in the context of the C-SAW weaving definition files needed for the GME model.

C-SAW weaves the caching specification into the GME architecture according to a set of weaving directives specified in a weaving definition file. The implementation of the C-SAW weaving definition file that is used to merge caches into the architecture model is produced from the platform-independent weaving solution model. To transform the platform-independent solution into a C-SAW weaving definition file, an AspectScatter model transformation is applied to the solution to create C-SAW *strategies* to update model elements with caches and C-SAW *aspects* to deduce the elements to which the strategies should be applied. For each cache inserted into the GME architecture model, two components must be added to the C-SAW weaving definition file. First, the *Strategy* for updating the GME model to include the cache and connect it to the correct component must be created, as shown below:

```
strategy ProductDAOAddGenericCache( ) {
    declare parentModel : model;
    declare component, cache : atom;
    parentModel := parent();
    component := self;
    cache := parentModel.addAtom("Cache", "GenericCacheForProductDAO");
    parentModel.addConnection("CacheInstallation",cache,component);
}
```

A root `Aspect` and `Strategy` must also be created that matches the root element of the GME model and invokes the weaving of the individual DAO caches. The root definitions are shown below:

```
aspect RootAspect()
{
  rootFolder().models()->AddCaches();
}
strategy AddCaches()
{
    declare parentModel : model;
    parentModel := self;
    parentModel.atoms("Component")->select(m|m.name() == "ProductDAO")->ProductDAOAddGenericCache ( );
    ....
}
```

For each advice/joinpoint combination, the `Strategy` to weave in the cache must be created. Moreover, for each advice/joinpoint combination, a weaving instruction must be added to the root `AddCaches` strategy to invoke the advice/joinpoint-specific weaving strategy.

To create the advice/joinpoint-specific cache weaving strategy, an AspectScatter template can be created as follows:

```
#advice[*](for-each[list=targets]){(#
strategy ${value}Add${advice}Cache( ) {
    declare parentModel : model;
    declare component, cache : atom;
    parentModel := parent();
    component := self;
    cache := parentModel.addAtom("Cache", "${advice}CacheFor${value}");
    parentModel.addConnection("CacheInstallation",cache,component);
}
#)#
```

The template defines that for all advice elements matched against joinpoints *"*advice*[*]*", iterate over the joinpoints that each advice element is applied to *"for-each[list=targets]*", and create a copy of the template code between "{#" and "#}" for each target joinpoint. Moreover, each copy of the template has the name of the advice element and target element inserted into the placeholders "${advice}" and "${value}", respectively. The "${advice}" placeholder is filled with the symbolic name of the advice element from its ADVICE declaration in the AspectScatter DSL instance.

The "${value}" placeholder is the symbolic name of the joinpoint, which is also obtained from its definition in the AspectScatter DSL instance that the advice element has been mapped to. The properties of an advice element can also be referred to using the placeholder "${PROPERTYNAME}." For example, the property CacheSize of the advice element could be referred to and inserted into the template by using the placeholder "${CacheSize}".

After deriving a weaving solution, AspectScatter uses the templates defined for C-SAW to produce the final weaving solution for the GME model. Invoking the generated C-SAW file inserts the caches into the appropriate points in the architecture diagram. A final woven Pet Store architecture diagram in GME can be seen in Fig. 8.

With existing weaving approaches, each time the global properties such as request distributions change, developers must manually derive a new weaving solution. When

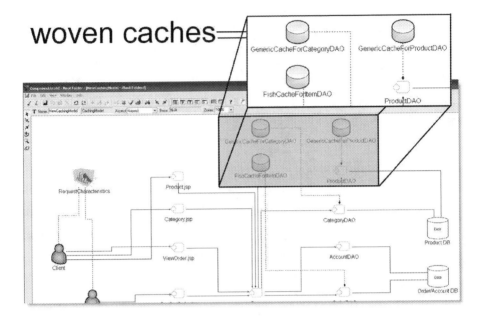

Fig. 8. The GME Architecture Model with Caches Woven in by C-SAW

the properties of the solution models change, however, AspectScatter can automatically solve for new weaving solutions, and then use model transformation to generate the platform-specific weaving implementations, thereby addressing Challenge 2 from Sect. 3.3. The CSP formulation of a weaving problem is based on the weaving constraints and not specific solution model properties. As long as the constraint relationships do not change, AspectScatter can automatically re-calculate the weaving solution and regenerate the weaving implementations. For example, if new request distributions are obtained, AspectScatter can re-calculate the weaving solution to accomodate the new information. Automatically updating the weaving solution as the solution model properties change can save substantial development effort across multiple solution model refactorings.

7 Applying Constraint-Based Weaving to the Java Pet Store

This section demonstrates the reduction in manual effort and complexity achieved by applying AspectScatter to the Spring Java Pet Store to handle global constraints and generate platform-specific weaving implementations. For comparison, we also applied the existing weaving platforms C-SAW and AspectJ to the same code base using a manual weaving solution derivation process. The results document the manual effort required to derive and implement a caching solution for the Pet Store's ItemDAO and ProductDAO.

7.1   Manual Complexity Overview

It is difficult to directly compare the manual effort required to execute two different aspect weaving processes. The problem is that there is no way of correlating the relative difficulty of the individual tasks of each process. Furthermore, the relative difficulty of tasks may change depending on the developer.

Although it is difficult to quantify the relative difficulty of the individual steps, we can define functions $M(WP)$ and $M'(WP)$ to calculate the total number of manual steps required for each process as a function of the size of the weaving problem (WP) input. That is, as more advice elements, joinpoints, and constraints are added to the weaving problem, how is the number of manual steps of each process affected? What we can show is that one process exhibits a better algorithmic O bound for the number of manual steps as a function of the input size.

Let us assume that each step in one process is E times harder than the steps in the second process. This gives the formula:

$$E * M_{step} = M'_{step}$$

Even if there is some unknown coefficient E, representing the extra effort of each step in the process yielding $M'(WP)$, if $M'(WP)$ posseses a better O bound, then there must exist an input, $wp_i \subset WP$ (WP is sorted in ascending order based on size), for which:

$$E * M'(wp_i) \leq M(wp_i)$$

and for all $wp_x \subset (wp_{i+1} \ldots wp_n)$:

$$E * M'(wp_x) < M(wp_x)$$

Once the size of the weaving problem reaches size wp_{i+1}, even though the steps in M' are E times more complicated than those in $M(WP)$, the faster rate of growth of the function $M(WP)$ makes it less efficient. If we can calculate O bounds for the number of manual steps required by each process as a function of the size of the weaving problem, then we can definitively show that for large enough problems, the process with the better O bound will be better.

In order to compare the AspectScatter-based approach to our original C-SAW and AspectJ approach, we provide an example weaving problem involving global constraints and optimization. We apply each process to the problem to show the manual steps involved in the two processes. Next, we calculate functions $M(WP)$ and $M'(WP)$ for the traditional and AspectScatter processes, respectively, and show that $M'(WP)$ exhibits a superior O bound.

7.2   Experimental Setup

We evaluated both the manual effort required to use the existing weaving solutions to implement a potentially non-optimal caching solution and the effort required to derive and implement a guaranteed optimal caching solution. By comparing the two different processes using existing weavers, we determined how much of the manual effort results

Activity	Step	Min Lines of Code	Max Lines of Code	Min Steps	Max Steps
Existing Model Weaving Approach w/o Optimization					
Initial Implementation					
Create Aspects				1	1
Identify/Define Joinpoints				1	1
Derive Caching Strategy				1	1
Implement Weaving Specification for C-SAW	Create AddCache Strategies	8	48	1	6
Implement Weaving Specification for C-SAW	Create Root AddCaches Strategy	1	6	1	1
Implement Weaving Specification for AspectJ	Add ProductDAO / ItemDAO Proxy	11	22	1	2
Implement Weaving Specification for AspectJ	Add Cache Beans	3	18	1	6
Implement Weaving Specification for AspectJ	Apply Cache Beans to ProductDAO/ItemDAO Methods	1	6	1	6
Totals		24	100	8	24
Refactoring for Request Distribution Change					
Derive New Caching Strategy				1	1
Implement Weaving Specification for C-SAW	Remove Unused AddCache Strategies	0	48	1	6
Implement Weaving Specification for C-SAW	Remove Unused AddCaches Strategy	0	6	1	1
Implement Weaving Specification for C-SAW	Create AddCache Strategies	8	48	1	6
Implement Weaving Specification for C-SAW	Create Root AddCaches Strategy	1	6	1	1
Implement Weaving Specification for AspectJ	Remove Previous Proxies	0	22	1	2
Implement Weaving Specification for AspectJ	Remove Previous Cache Beans	0	18	1	6
Implement Weaving Specification for AspectJ	Remove Unused Cache Beans from ProductDAO/ItemDAO Methods	0	6	1	6
Implement Weaving Specification for AspectJ	Add ProductDAO / ItemDAO Proxy	11	22	1	2
Implement Weaving Specification for AspectJ	Add Cache Beans	3	18	1	6
Implement Weaving Specification for AspectJ	Apply Cache Beans to ProductDAO/ItemDAO Methods	1	6	1	6
Totals		24	200	11	43

Fig. 9. Manual Effort Required for Using Existing Model Weaving Techniques Without Caching Optimization

from supporting multiple weaving platforms and how much results from the solution derivation process. Both processes with existing tools were then compared to a process using AspectScatter to evaluate the reduction in solution derivation complexity and solution implementation effort provided by AspectScatter.

7.3 Deriving and Implementing a Non-optimal Caching Solution with Existing Weaving Techniques

The results for applying existing weavers to derive and implement a non-optimal caching solution are shown in Fig. 9. Each individual manual set of steps is associated with an activity that corresponds to the process diagram shown in Fig. 4. The results tables contain minimum and maximum values for the number of steps and lines of code. The implementation of each step is dependent on the solution chosen. The minimum value assumes that only a single cache is woven into the Pet Store, whereas the maximum value assumes every possible cache is used.

The top table in Fig. 9 shows the effort required to produce the initial caching solution and implementation for the Pet Store. In the first two steps, developers identify and catalog the advice and joinpoint elements. Developers then pick a caching architecture (which may or may not be good or optimal) that will be used to produce a weaving solution. In the next three steps, developers must implement the weaving solution as a C-SAW weaving definition file. Finally, developers must update the Spring bean definition file with various directives to use AspectJ to weave the caches into the legacy Pet Store code base.

| Existing Model Weaving Approach w/ Optimization | | | | | |
| Initial Implementation | | | | | |
Activity	Step	Min Lines of Code	Max Lines of Code	Min Steps	Max Steps
Create Aspects				1	1
Identify/Define Joinpoints				1	1
Derive Optimal Caching Strategy	Arch			19	115
Implement Weaving Specification for C-SAW	Create AddCache Strategies	8	48	1	6
Implement Weaving Specification for C-SAW	Create Root AddCaches Strategy	1	6	1	1
Implement Weaving Specification for AspectJ	Add ProductDAO / ItemDAO Proxy	11	22	1	2
Implement Weaving Specification for AspectJ	Add Cache Beans	3	18	1	6
	Apply Cache Beans to				
Implement Weaving Specification for AspectJ	ProductDAO/ItemDAO Methods	1	6	1	6
Totals		24	100	26	138

Fig. 10. Manual Effort Required for Using Existing Model Weaving Techniques With Caching Optimization

| Existing Model Weaving Approach w/ Optimization | | | | | |
| Refactoring for Request Distribution Change | | | | | |
Activity	Step	Min Lines of Code	Max Lines of Code	Min Steps	Max Steps
Derive Optimal Caching Strategy				19	115
Implement Weaving Specification for C-SAW	Remove Unused AddCache Strategies	0	48	1	6
Implement Weaving Specification for C-SAW	Remove Unused AddCaches Strategy	0	6	1	1
Implement Weaving Specification for C-SAW	Create AddCache Strategies	8	48	1	6
Implement Weaving Specification for C-SAW	Create Root AddCaches Strategy	1	6	1	1
Implement Weaving Specification for AspectJ	Remove Previous Proxies	0	22	1	2
Implement Weaving Specification for AspectJ	Remove Previous Cache Beans	0	18	1	6
	Remove Unused Cache Beans from				
Implement Weaving Specification for AspectJ	ProductDAO/ItemDAO Methods	0	6	1	6
Implement Weaving Specification for AspectJ	Add ProductDAO / ItemDAO Proxy	11	22	1	2
Implement Weaving Specification for AspectJ	Add Cache Beans	3	18	1	6
	Apply Cache Beans to				
Implement Weaving Specification for AspectJ	ProductDAO/ItemDAO Methods	1	6	1	6
Totals		24	200	29	157

Fig. 11. Manual Effort Required for Using Existing Model Weaving Techniques to Refactor Optimal Caching Architecture

The bottom table in Fig. 9 documents the steps required to update the caching architecture and weaving implementation to incorporate a change in the distribution of request types to the Pet Store. In the first step, the developer derives a new caching architecture. In the next 12 steps, developers remove any caches from the original C-SAW and AspectJ implementations that are no longer used by the new solution and implement the new caching solution using C-SAW and AspectJ.

7.4 Deriving and Implementing an Optimal Caching Solution with Existing Weaving Techniques

Figure 10 presents the manual effort to derive and implement an optimal caching solution for the Pet Store using existing weavers. The change in this experiment is that it measures the manual effort required to derive an optimal solution for the Pet Store by calculating the Pet Store's response time using each potential caching architecture and choosing the optimal one. The steps for implementing the weaving solution are identical to those from the results presented in Fig. 9.

The steps labeled *Derive Optimal Caching Strategy* in Fig. 10 presents the manual optimal solution derivation effort incorporated into this result set. First, developers must enumerate and check the correctness according to the domain constraints, or each potential caching architecture for both the ProductDAO and ItemDAO. Developers must then enumerate and check the correctness of the overall caching architectures produced from each unique combination of ProductDAO and ItemDAO caching architectures. After determining the set of valid caching architectures, developers must use the Pet Store's modeled request distribution, memory constraints, and response time goals to derive the optimal cache sizes and best possible response time of each caching architecture. Finally, developers select the optimal overall architecture and implements it using C-SAW and AspectJ.

As shown in Fig. 11, refactoring the weaving solution to accomodate the solution model change in request type distributions forces developers to repeat the entire process. First, they must go back and perform the optimal solution derivation process again. After a new result is obtained, the existing solution implementations in C-SAW and AspectJ must be refactored to mirror the new caching structure.

7.5 Deriving and Implementing an Optimal Caching Solution Using AspectScatter

Figure 12 contains the steps required to accomplish both the initial implementation of the Pet Store caching solution and the refactoring cost when the request distribution changes. In steps 1 and 2, developers use AspectScatter's DSL to specify the caches, joinpoints, and constraints for the weaving problem. Developers then define the weaving goal, the response time of the application in terms of the properties of the joinpoints, and advice elements woven into a solution. The goal is later used by AspectScatter to ensure that the derived weaving solution is optimal.

The next two steps (3 and 4) require the developer to create a model transformation using AspectScatter's transformation templates, as described in Sect. 6, to specify how to transform the platform-independent weaving solution into a C-SAW implementation. The approach thus represents a higher-order transformation where C-SAW transformations are generated from more abstract transformation rules. The subsequent three steps define a model transformation to produce the AspectJ implementation. Finally, AspectScatter is invoked to deduce the optimal solution and generate the C-SAW and AspectJ implementations.

The bottom of Fig. 12 presents the steps required to refactor the solution to accomodate the change in request distributions. Once the aspect weaving problem is defined using AspectScatter's DSL, the change in request distributions requires updating one or both of the request distribution properties of the two joinpoints (*i.e.* the ProductDAO and ItemDAO) in the AspectScatter DSL instance. After the properties are updated, AspectScatter is invoked to recalculate the optimal caching architecture and regenerate the C-SAW and AspectJ implementations using the previously defined model transformations.

	Aspect Scatter				
	Initial Implementation				
Activity	**Step**	**Min Lines of Code**	**Max Lines of Code**	**Min Steps**	**Max Steps**
Create Aspects		12	12	6	6
Identify/Define Joinpoints		12	12	2	2
Derive Optimal Caching Strategy	Define Weaving Goal	1	1	1	1
Implement Weaving Specification for C-SAW	Create AddCache Model Transformation	8	8	1	1
Implement Weaving Specification for C-SAW	Create Root AddCaches Model Transformation	6	6	1	1
Implement Weaving Specification for AspectJ	Create ProductDAO / ItemDAO Proxy Model Transformation	22	22	2	2
Implement Weaving Specification for AspectJ	Create Cache Beans Model Transformation	18	18	6	6
Implement Weaving Specification for AspectJ	Create Cache Beans to ProductDAO/ItemDAO Methods Model Transformation	1	1	1	1
Implement Weaving Specification	Invoke AspectScatter	1	1	1	1
Totals		81	81	21	21
	Refactoring for Request Distribution Change				
Identify/Define Joinpoints	Update Request Distribution Properties	1	2	1	2
Implement Weaving Specification	Invoke AspectScatter	1	1	1	1
Totals		2	3	2	3

Fig. 12. Manual Effort Required for Using AspectScatter With Caching Optimization

7.6 Results Analysis and Comparison of Techniques

By comparing the initial number of lines of code (shown in Figs. 9–12) required to implement the caching solution using each of the three techniques, the initial cost of defining an AspectScatter problem and solution model transformations can be derived. AspectScatter initially requires 81 lines of code versus between 24 and 100 for the approach based on existing techniques. The number of lines of code required to implement the initial weaving specification grows at a rate of $O(n)$, where n is the number of advice and joinpoint specifications for both AspectScatter and existing approaches. The more the advice and joinpoint specifications, the larger is each weaving specification.

The benefit of AspectScatter's use of model transformations becomes most apparent by comparing the refactoring results. AspectScatter only requires the developer to change between 1–2 lines of code before invoking AspectScatter to regenerate the C-SAW and AspectJ implementations. Using the existing weaving approaches, the developer must change between 24–200 lines of code. Moreover, this manual effort required by the existing approaches is incurred *per solution model change*. Thus, AspectScatter requires a constant or $O(1)$ number of changes per refactoring while existing approaches require $O(n)$ changes per refactoring.

For a single aspect weaving problem without optimization that is implemented and solved exactly once, both AspectScatter and the manual weaving approach exhibit roughly $O(n)$ growth in lines of code with respect to the size of the weaving problem. The more caches that need to be woven, the larger the weaving specifications have to be for both processes. For a single weaving in this scenario, we cannot directly show that AspectScatter provides an improvement since it has an equivalent big O bound.

If we calculate the weaving cost over K refactorings, however, we see that AspectScatter exhibits a bound of $O(2K + n) = O(K + n)$ lines of code. ApsectScatter requires an initial setup cost of $O(n)$ lines of code and then each of the K refactorings requires manually changing 1–2 lines of code. The manual approach requires $O(n)$ lines of code changes for each of the K refactorings because the developer may have to completely rewrite all of the joinpoint specifications. Over K refactorings, the manual process requires $O(Kn + n) = O(Kn)$ lines of code changes. Thus, AspectScatter provides a better bound, $O(K + n) < O(Kn)$, on the rate of growth of the lines of code changed over multiple refactorings.

When optimization is added to the scenarios, AspectScatter's reduction in manual complexity becomes much more pronounced. With existing approaches, each time the weaving solution is implemented, the developer must calculate the optimal cache weaving architecture. Let γ be the number of manual steps required to calculate the optimal cache weaving architecture; then the cost of implementing the initial weaving solution with an existing approach is $O(n + \gamma)$. The developer must implement the $O(n)$ lines of code for the weaving specification and derive the optimal architecture.

Since we are doing a big O analysis, we will ignore any coefficients or differences in difficulty between a step to implement a line of code and a step in the derivation of the optimal caching architecture. We will say that n lines of code require n manual steps to implement. The next question is how the number of steps γ grow as a function of the size of the weaving problem. The caching optimization problem with constraints is an instance of a mixed integer optimization problem, which is in NP, and thus has roughly exponential complexity. Thus, $\gamma = \theta^n$, where θ is a constant.

The overall complexity of the existing approach for the optimization scenario is $O(n + \theta^n)$. Note that this complexity bound is for solving a single instance of the weaving problem. Over K refactorings, the complexity bound is even worse at $O(n + K(n + \theta^n))$. With AspectScatter, the solver performs the optimization step on the developer's behalf and the θ^n manual steps are eliminated. When optimization is included and K refactorings are performed, AspectScatter shows a significantly better bound on manual complexity than existing approaches:

$$O(n + K) < O(n + K(n + \theta^n))$$

One might argue that a developer wouldn't manually derive the optimal caching architecture by hand but would instead use some automated tool. We note, however, that this is essentially arguing for our approach, since we are using an external tool to derive the caching architecture and then using code generation to automatically implement the solution. Thus, even using an external tool would still require a developer to rewrite the weaving specification after each refactoring and would also add setup cost for specifying the weaving problem for the external tool and translating the results back into a weaving solution. Our approach automates all of these steps on behalf of the developer.

A final analysis worth looking at is the effect of the number of weaving platforms on the complexity of the weaving process. For both processes, the overhead of the initial setup of the weaving solution is linearly dependent on the number of weaving platforms used. In the experiments, AspectJ and C-SAW are used as the weaving platforms. Given P weaving platforms, both processes exhibit an initial setup complexity of $O(Pn)$.

With existing processes, when K refactorings are performed, the number of weaving platforms impacts the complexity of each refactoring. Rather than simply incurring $O(n)$ complexity for each refactoring, developers incur $O(Pn)$ per refactoring. This leads to an overall complexity bound of $O(Pn + KPn)$ for existing processes versus a bound of $O(Pn + K)$ for AspectScatter. As we showed in the previous analyses, even for a single weaving platform, such as just AspectJ, AspectScatter reduces complexity. However, when numerous weaving platforms are used AspectScatter shows an even further reduction in complexity.

7.7 Weaving Performance

There is no definitive rule to predict the time required to solve an arbitrary CSP. The solution time is dependent on the types of constraints, the number of variables, the degree of optimality required, and the initial variable values provided to the solver. Furthermore, internally, the algorithms used by the solver and solver's implementation language can also significantly affect performance.

Our experience with AspectScatter indicated that the weaving process usually takes 10 ms to a few seconds. For example, to solve a weaving problem involving the optimal weaving of 6 caches that can be woven into any of 10 different components with fairly tight memory constraints requires approximately 120 ms on an Intel Core 2 Duo processor with 2 GB of memory. If a correct—but not necessarily optimal solution is needed—the solving time is roughly 22 ms. Doubling the available cache memory budget essentially halves the optimal solution derivation time to 64 ms. The same problem expanded to 12 caches and 10 components requires a range from 94 ms to 2,302 ms depending on the tightness (i.e. amount of slack memory) of the resource constraints.

In practice, we found that AspectScatter quickly solves most weaving problems. It is easy to produce synthetic modeling problems with poor performance, but realistic model weaving examples usually have relatively limited variability in the weaving process. For example, although a caching aspect could theoretically be applied to any component in an application, this behavior is rarely desired. Instead, developers normally have numerous functional and other constraints that bound the solution space significantly. In the Pet Store, for example, we restrict caching to the four key DAOs that form the core of the middle-tier.

In cases where developers do encounter a poorly performing problem instance, there are a number of potential courses of action to remedy the situation. One approach is to relax the constraints, *e.g.* allow the caches to use more memory. Developers can also improve solving speed by accepting less optimal solutions, *e.g.* solving for a cache architecture that produces an average response time below a certain threshold rather than an optimal response time. Finally, developers can try algorithmic changes, such as using different solution space search algorithms, *e.g.* simulated annealing [39], greedy randomized adaptive search [39] and genetic algorithms [39].

8 Related Work

This section compares our research on AspectScatter to related work. Section 8.1 compares and constrasts AspectScatter to other model weavers. Section 8.2 compares the CSP-based model weaving approach to other aspect-oriented modeling techniques. Finally, Sect. 8.3 compares AspectScatter to other approaches for incorporating application requirements into aspect-oriented modeling.

8.1   Model Weaving

Reddy et al. [38] propose a technique that uses model element signatures and composition directives to perform model weaving. Reddy's approach focuses on different challenges of model weaving and is complementary to the constraint-based weaving approach used by AspectScatter. AspectScatter focuses on incorporating and automating the solution and optimization of global weaving constraints. Reddy's approach, however, is targeted toward the difficulties of identifying joinpoints and correctly modifying the structure of a model to perform a merger. First, model element signatures can be incorporated as a CSP filtering step, as described in Sect. 4.6. Second, the composition directives developed by Reddy can be used to implement the platform-specific weaving model produced by AspectScatter. In contrast, AspectScatter, can derive and optimize the global weaving solution, which Reddy's techniques are not designed to do.

Cottenier et al. [14] have developed a model weaver called the Motorola WEAVR. The WEAVR provides complex weaving and aspect visualization capabilities for models. Although WEAVR has numerous capabilities, it is designed for a different part of the model weaving process than AspectScatter. AspectScatter sits above multiple weaving platforms to manage the overall global weaving solution. Motorola WEAVR, in contrast, is a specific weaving platform used to merge models and visualize model weaving results. The two tools are synergistic. Motoroal WEAVR is a weaving platform that provides numerous analytic and modeling capabilities. AspectScatter is a high-level weaver that can be used to produce weaving specifications for WEAVR. Furthermore, WEAVR is not designed to model and solve complex global constraints that AspectScatter is built for.

8.2   Aspect-Oriented Modeling

Lahire et al. [29] motivate the need for and describe a potential solution for incorporating variability into AOM. Their work motivates some of the challenges addressed in this paper, namely the challenge of managing variability in how advice can be applied to joinpoints. AspectScatter offers an implementation of a solver designed to: (1) handle the solution variability presented by Lahire et al., (2) incorporate global constraints to ensure that individual variable solution weaving decisions produce an overall correct solution, and (3) optimally choose values for points of variability when multiple solutions are possible. Lahire et al. initially explore and describe a potential solution for capturing and handling AOM variability. AspectScatter provides a concrete approach to handling numerous facets described by Lahire et al.

Morin et al. [36] have also developed a generic model of aspect-oriented modeling. Their technique generalizes joinpoints to model snippets and pointcuts to model templates. AspectScatter also adopts a generalized view of pointcuts and joinpoints. AspectScatter provides global weaving constraints and optimization, whereas the techniques developed by Morin et al. are for situations where there is no ambiguity in which potential joinpoints a template should be matched against. AspectScatter automates part of the weaving design process, the derivation of the global weaving solution, whereas Morin et al. propose techniques to generically model how a weaving solution is applied. Each technique is geared toward a different phase of the weaving process. AspectScatter solves the weaving solution derivation challenges, and Morin et al. techniques address the platform-specific weaving solution implementation.

8.3 Models and Constraints

Lengyel and Levendovszky [33] present a technique for validating the correctness of model transformations by tying constraints to transformation rules. Lengyel's technique provides a method for identifying cross-cutting constraints and refactoring them into aspects. These techniques for capturing transformation constraints as aspects is complementary to AspectScatter. While Lengyel's techniques are designed to help maintain the correctness of model transformations, AspectScatter is designed to automatically maintain the correctness of model weaving. Moreover, AspectScatter is designed to derive solutions to constraints but Lengyel's techniques are for checking constraints and identifying aspects. Lengyel's techniques could be used to help guarantee the correctness of the transformations that AspectScatter uses to produce the platform-specific weaving implementations.

Baniassad and Clarke [7] have developed an approach to help identify aspects in designs and trace the relationship between aspects and requirements. Their approach is related to AspectScatter's incorporation of global system requirements and goals into the aspect weaving specification. Baniassad and Clarke techniques help identify and trace the aspects and their relationship with requirements whereas AspectScatter is designed to capture and *solve* requirements guiding the placement of aspects into a system. Thus, although the approaches are both related to understanding and managing how requirements affect aspects, the challenges that Baniassad and Clarke address (*i.e.* identification and tracing of aspects) are different than AspectScatter's (*i.e.* capture and solving of weaving requirements and goals).

9   Concluding Remarks

A significant amount of manual effort is incurred by the inability to encode the global application requirements into the model weaving specification and honor them during the weaving process. This gap in existing model weavers encourages developers to manually derive and maintain solutions to the global weaving constraints as the underlying solution models evolve. Moreover, developers may need to implement the global weaving solution in the pointcut languages of multiple model weavers.

This paper describes how providing a model weaver with knowledge of the entire set of joinpoints used during the weaving process ahead of time makes it possible to map model weaving to a CSP and use a constraint solver to derive a weaving that can incorporate global, dependency, and expression-based constraints. From our experience using AspectScatter's approach of mapping model weaving to a CSP, we have learned that CSP-based model weaving reduces manual effort by:

1. Capturing and allowing the weaver to solve the global application constraints required to produce a weaving solution,
2. Informing the weaver of the overall solution goals so that the weaver can derive the best overall weaving solution with respect to a cost function, and

3. Encoding using model transformations to automatically generate implementations of the global weaving solution for each required weaving platform.

By capturing and leveraging this critical set of domain knowledge, AspectScatter can automate the complex process of deriving weaving solutions and maintaining them as solution models change. By applying Aspect Scatter to the Java Pet Store case study, we showed that the CSP-based weaving approach scaled significantly better than existing approaches in terms of the number of manual weaving steps. Although this paper has focused on cache weaving, the same techniques could be applied to other domains, such as optimally configuring applications for mobile devices.

AspectScatter is an open-source tool available from http://www.eclipse.org/gmt/gems

Acknowledgment

This work was supported in part by the National Science Foundation under NSF CAREER CCF-0643725.

References

1. Apache Foundation's JMeter, http://jmeter.apache.org
2. AspectJ, http://www.eclipse.org/aspectj/
3. HyperJ, http://www.alphaworks.ibm.com/tech/hyperj
4. .NET Pet Store, http://msdn2.microsoft.com/en-us/library/ms978487.aspx
5. Sun Microsystem's Java Pet Store Sample Application, http://java.sun.com/developer/releases/petstore/
6. The Spring Framework, http://www.springframework.org/about
7. Baniassad, E., Clarke, S.: Theme: an Approach to Aspect-oriented Analysis and Design. In: Proceedings of the 26th International Conference on Software Engineering, Scotland, UK, May 2004, pp. 158–167 (2004)
8. Bézivin, J.: From Object Composition to Model Transformation with the MDA. In: Proceedings of TOOLS, Santa Barbara, CA, USA, August 2001, pp. 350–354 (2001)
9. Bézivin, J., Jouault, F., Valduriez, P.: First Experiments with a ModelWeaver. In: Proceedings of the OOPSLA/GPCE: Best Practices for Model-Driven Software Development Workshop, 19th Annual ACM Conference on Object-Oriented Programming, Systems, Languages, and Applications, Vancouver, Canada (March 2004)
10. Bistarelli, S., Fargier, H., Montanari, U., Rossi, F., Schiex, T., Verfaillie, G.: Semiring-based CSPs and Valued CSPs: Basic Properties and Comparison. In: Jampel, M., Maher, M.J., Freuder, E.C. (eds.) CP-WS 1995, vol. 1106, pp. 111–150. Springer, Heidelberg (1996)
11. Bistarelli, S., Montanari, U., Rossi, F.: Semiring-Based Constraint Satisfaction and Optimization. Journal of the ACM 44(2), 201–236 (1997)
12. Budinsky, F.: Eclipse Modeling Framework. Addison-Wesley Professional, New York (2003)
13. Cohen, J.: Constraint logic programming languages. Communications of the ACM 33(7), 52–68 (1990)
14. Cottenier, T., van den Berg, A., Elrad, T.: The Motorola WEAVR: Model Weaving in a Large Industrial Context. In: Proceedings of the International Conference on Aspect-Oriented Software Development, Industry Track, Vancouver, Canada (March 2006)

15. Czarnecki, K., Helsen, S.: Feature-based Survey of Model Transformation Approaches. IBM Systems Journal 45(3), 621–646 (2006)
16. Del Fabro, M., Bézivin, J., Valduriez, P.: Weaving Models with the Eclipse AMW plugin. In: Eclipse Modeling Symposium, Eclipse Summit Europe, Esslingen, Germany (October 2006)
17. Elrad, T., Aldawud, O., Bader, A.: Aspect-Oriented Modeling: Bridging the Gap between Implementation and Design. In: Batory, D., Consel, C., Taha, W. (eds.) GPCE 2002. LNCS, vol. 2487, pp. 189–201. Springer, Heidelberg (2002)
18. Fletcher, R.: Practical methods of optimization. Wiley-Interscience, New York (1987)
19. France, R., Ray, I., Georg, G., Ghosh, S.: An Aspect-Oriented Approach to Early Design Modeling. IEE Proceedings-Software 151(4), 173–185 (2004)
20. Gomaa, H.: Designing Concurrent, Distributed, and Real-time Applications with UML. Addison-Wesley, Reading (2000)
21. Gray, J., Bapty, T., Neema, S., Tuck, J.: Handling crosscutting constraints in domain-specific modeling. Communications of the ACM 44(10), 87–93 (2001)
22. Hannemann, J., Murphy, G., Kiczales, G.: Role-based Refactoring of Crosscutting Concerns. In: Proceedings of the 4th International Conference on Aspect-oriented Software Development, Chicago, Illinois, USA, March 2005, pp. 135–146 (2005)
23. Hilsdale, E., Hugunin, J.: Advice Weaving in AspectJ. In: Proceedings of the 3rd International Conference on Aspect-oriented Software Development, Lancaster, UK, March 2004, pp. 26–35 (2004)
24. Holzner, S.: Ant: The Definitive Guide. O'Reilly, Sebastopol (2005)
25. Jampel, M., Freuder, E., Maher, M.: Over-Constrained Systems. Springer, London (1996)
26. König, D., Glover, A., King, P., Laforge, G., Skeet, J.: Groovy in Action. Manning Publications (2007)
27. Kumar, V.: Algorithms for Constraint-Satisfaction Problems: A Survey. AI Magazine 13(1), 32–44 (1992)
28. Kurtev, I., van den Berg, K., Jouault, F.: Rule-based Modularization in Model Transformation Languages Illustrated with ATL. In: Proceedings of the 2006 ACM Symposium on Applied Computing, Dijon, France, April 2006, pp. 1202–1209 (2006)
29. Lahire, P., Morin, B., Vanwormhoudt, G., Gaignard, A., Barais, O., Jézéquel, J.-M.: Introducing variability into Aspect-Oriented Modeling Approaches. In: Engels, G., Opdyke, B., Schmidt, D.C., Weil, F. (eds.) MODELS 2007. LNCS, vol. 4735, pp. 498–513. Springer, Heidelberg (2007)
30. Ledeczi, A., Bakay, A., Maroti, M., Volgyesi, P., Nordstrom, G., Sprinkle, J., Karsai, G.: Composing domain-specific design environments. Computer 34(11), 44–51 (2001)
31. Li, W., Hsiung, W., Kalshnikov, D., Sion, R., Po, O., Agrawal, D., Candan, K.: Issues and Evaluations of Caching Solutions for Web Application Acceleration. In: Proceedings of the 28th International Conference on Very Large Data Bases, Hong Kong, China (August 2002)
32. Luo, Q., Krishnamurthy, S., Mohan, C., Pirahesh, H., Woo, H., Lindsay, B., Naughton, J.: Middle-tier Database Caching for E-business. In: Proceedings of the ACM SIGMOD International Conference on Management of Data, Madison, Wisconsin, June 2002, pp. 600–611 (2002)
33. László Lengyel, H.C., Levendovszky, T.: Identification of Crosscutting Concerns in Constraint-Driven Validated Model Transformations. In: Proceedings of the Third Workshop on Models and Aspects at ECOOP 2007, Berlin, Germany (July 2007)
34. Michel, L., Hentenryck, P.V.: Comet in context. In: PCK50: Proceedings of the Paris C. Kanellakis Memorial Workshop on Principles of Computing & Knowledge, San Diego, CA, USA, pp. 95–107 (2003)
35. Mohan, C.: Caching Technologies for Web Applications. In: Proceedings of the 27th International Conference on Very Large Data Bases, Rome, Italy, September 2001, p. 726 (2001)

36. Morin, B., Barais, O., Jézéquel, J.-M., Ramos, R.: Towards a Generic Aspect-Oriented Modeling Framework. In: Models and Aspects Workshop, at ECOOP 2007, Berlin, Germany (July 2007)
37. Nelder, J., Mead, R.: A Simplex Method for Function Minimization. Computer Journal 7(4), 308–313 (1965)
38. Reddy, Y., Ghosh, S., France, R., Straw, G., Bieman, J., McEachen, N., Song, E., Georg, G.: Directives for Composing Aspect-Oriented Design Class Models. In: Rashid, A., Aksit, M. (eds.) Transactions on Aspect-Oriented Software Development I. LNCS, vol. 3880, pp. 75–105. Springer, Heidelberg (2006)
39. Reeves, C.: Modern Heuristic Techniques for Combinatorial Problems. John Wiley & Sons, Inc., New York (1993)
40. Schiex, T.: Possibilistic Constraint Satisfaction Problems or How to Handle Soft Constraints. In: Proceedings of the Eighth Conference on Uncertainty in Artificial Intelligence, San Mateo, CA, USA, pp. 268–275 (1992)
41. Shavor, S., D'Anjou, J., McCarthy, P., Kellerman, J., Fairbrother, S.: The Java Developer's Guide to Eclipse. Pearson Education, Upper Saddle River (2003)
42. Software Composition and Modeling (Softcom) Laboratory. Constraint-Specification Aspect Weaver (C-SAW). University of Alabama at Birmingham, Birmingham, AL, http://www.cis.uab.edu/gray/research/C-SAW
43. Valesky, T.: Enterprise JavaBeans. Addison-Wesley, Reading (1999)
44. Van Hentenryck, P.: Constraint Satisfaction in Logic Programming. MIT Press, Cambridge (1989)
45. Voelter, M., Groher, I., Heidenheim, G.: Product Line Implementation using Aspect-Oriented and Model-Driven Software Development. In: Proceedings of the 11th International Software Product Line Conference, Kyoto, Japan, September 2007, pp. 233–242 (2007)
46. Wallace, R., Freuder, E.: Heuristic Methods for Over-constrained Constraint Satisfaction Problems. In: Jampel, M., Maher, M.J., Freuder, E.C. (eds.) CP-WS 1995. LNCS, vol. 1106, pp. 207–216. Springer, Heidelberg (1996)
47. Warmer, J., Kleppe, A.: The Object Constraint Language. Addison-Wesley, Reading (2003)
48. White, J., Schmidt, D.C., Mulligan, S.: The generic eclipse modeling system. In: Proceedings of the Model-Driven Development Tool Implementors Forum at TOOLS 2007, Zurich, Switzerland (June 2007)
49. Zhang, J., Cottenier, T., van den Berg, A., Gray, J.: Aspect Composition in the Motorola Aspect-Oriented Modeling Weaver. Journal of Object Technology 6(7)

MATA: A Unified Approach for Composing UML Aspect Models Based on Graph Transformation[*]

Jon Whittle[1], Praveen Jayaraman[2], Ahmed Elkhodary[2], Ana Moreira[3],
and João Araújo[3]

[1] Dept. of Computing, Lancaster University, Bailrigg, Lancaster LA1 4YW
[2] Dept. of Information and Software Engineering, George Mason University, Fairfax, VA 22030
[3] Dept. of Informatics, FCT, Universidade Nova de Lisboa, 2829-516, Caparica, Portugal
whittle@comp.lancs.ac.uk, praveenjayaraman@yahoo.com,
aelkhoda@gmu.edu, {amm,ja}@di.fct.unl.pt

Abstract. This paper describes MATA (Modeling Aspects Using a Transformation Approach), a UML aspect-oriented modeling (AOM) technique that uses graph transformations to specify and compose aspects. Graph transformations provide a unified approach for aspect modeling in that the methods presented here can be applied to any modeling language with a well-defined metamodel. This paper, however, focuses on UML class diagrams, sequence diagrams and state diagrams. MATA takes a different approach to AOM since there are no explicit joinpoints. Rather, any model element can be a joinpoint, and composition is a special case of model transformation. The graph transformation execution engine, AGG, is used in MATA to execute model compositions, and critical pair analysis is used to automatically detect structural interactions between different aspect models. MATA has been applied to a number of realistic case studies and is supported by a tool built on top of IBM Rational Software Modeler.

1 Introduction

Aspect model composition is the process of combining two models, M_B and M_A, where an aspect model M_A is said to crosscut a base model M_B. As such, aspect model composition is a special case of the more general problem of model fusion. A number of techniques and languages have been developed to specify how M_A crosscuts M_B, and, in particular, how M_A and M_B should be composed.

Broadly speaking, there have been, to date, two approaches for specifying aspect model composition. In the first approach, M_A and M_B are composed by defining matching criteria that identify common elements in M_A and M_B and then applying a generic merge algorithm that equates the common elements. Typically, matching criteria are based on easily identifiable properties of model elements. For example,

---

[*] This paper is an extended version of a paper previously published at the 2007 International MODELS conference [1]. There was also a workshop paper on the MATA tool [2]. The main new contributions are the section on code generation and the evaluation and discussion section. The section on aspect interactions is also new.

S. Katz et al. (Eds.): Transactions on AOSD VI, LNCS 5560, pp. 191–237, 2009.
© Springer-Verlag Berlin Heidelberg 2009

two class diagram models can be merged by equating classes with the same name. Examples of this approach include Theme/UML [3] as well as work by France et al. [4]. In the second approach, mechanisms for specifying and weaving aspects from aspect-oriented programming (AOP) are reused at the modeling level. There has been a significant amount of research, for example, that identifies a joinpoint model for a modeling language and then uses the AspectJ advices of before, after, and around for weaving. Examples of this type include [5, 6].

These two kinds of approaches are not always sufficient. A merge algorithm in the first approach based on general matching criteria will never be expressive enough to handle all model compositions. Matching by name, for example, may not work for state diagrams. Given two states with the same name, the states may need to be merged in one of a variety of ways depending on the application being modeled: (1) the two states represent the same thing, which implies making the states equal; (2) the two states represent orthogonal behaviors of the same object, which implies enclosing the states by a new orthogonal region; (3) one state is really a submodel of the other, which implies making one state a substate of the other; and (4) the behaviors of the two states must be interleaved in a complex way, which implies weaving the actions and transitions in a very application-specific way to achieve the desired result. Only the first of these can be accomplished based on merge-by-name. Furthermore, these are only four of the many possible options, and so it is not generally sufficient to provide a number of pre-defined merge strategies. In practice, to overcome this problem, the modeler may additionally specify what Reddy et al. [7] call composition directives—that is, operators that override the default merge algorithm. However, understanding the interactions between the default algorithm and the composition directives is a difficult task, and, in particular, does not work easily for behavioral models (cf. [8]).

In the second approach, specific elements in a model are allowed to be defined as joinpoints and others are not. For example, in state diagrams, some approaches [5] define actions as joinpoints. Others, however, define states as joinpoints [9]. One could even imagine more complex joinpoints, such as the pointcut of all orthogonal regions. (This pointcut might be used, for example, by an aspect that sequentializes parallel behaviors.) Defining only a subset of a model's elements as joinpoints seems to be overly restrictive. In addition, limiting advices to before, after, and around (as is done, for example, by both [5] and [9]) is also rather restrictive since it may be desired to weave behavior in parallel or as a sub-behavior of a behavior in the base.

This paper takes a step back to reassess the requirements for aspect modeling languages. The result is the technique and tool MATA (Modeling Aspects Using a Transformation Approach), which tackles the above limitations by viewing aspect composition as a special case of model transformation. In MATA, composition of a base and aspect model is specified by a graph rule. Given a base model, M_B, crosscut by an aspect model, M_A, a MATA composition rule merges M_A and M_B to produce a composed model M_{AB}. The graph rule r: LHS $\rightarrow$ RHS defines a pattern on the left-hand side (LHS). This pattern captures the set of joinpoints, i.e. the points in M_B where new model elements should be added. The right-hand side (RHS) defines the new elements to be added and specifies how they should be added to M_B. MATA graph rules are defined over the concrete syntax of the modeling language. This is in contrast to almost all known approaches to model transformation, which typically define transformations at the meta-level, that is, over the abstract syntax of the modeling language. The restriction to concrete syntax is important for aspect modeling because a modeler is unlikely to have enough detailed knowledge of the UML metamodel to specify transformations over abstract syntax.

MATA currently supports composition for UML class, sequence, and state diagrams. In principle, however, it is easy to extend MATA to other UML models (or, indeed, other modeling languages as long as a metamodel for the language exists) because the idea of using graph rules is broadly applicable. MATA makes no decisions on joinpoint models, for example, which would limit the approach to specific diagram types.

One advantage of using graph transformations for aspect model composition is that graph transformations are a well-understood, formal technique with formal analysis tools available. In particular, critical pair analysis can be used to automatically detect dependencies and conflicts between graph rules. MATA applies critical pair analysis to detect interactions between aspects. This can be done because each aspect is represented as a graph rule and so the problem of aspect interaction can be stated in terms of dependencies between graph rules. Not all kinds of interactions can be detected–the technique is limited to structural rather than semantic interactions–but critical pair analysis offers a fully automatic, lightweight method for finding these structural interactions between aspect models.

This paper gives a full description of the MATA language for aspect model composition, its underlying graph transformation representation, and the use of critical pair analysis for detecting aspect interactions. It also describes the tool support for MATA, which is implemented on top of IBM Rational Software Modeler. The contributions of this paper can be divided into three categories as follows:

1. A unified, expressive approach for aspect model composition:

   - MATA is agnostic with respect to the modeling language to be composed as long as there is a well-defined metamodel for this language.
   - MATA is more expressive than previous approaches because it views aspect model composition as simply a special case of model transformation.
   - MATA handles both structural and behavioral models in the same way.

2. A usable graph transformation language for aspect model composition:

   - Graph rules in MATA are written in the concrete syntax of the modeling language, not in the abstract syntax. This allows them to be specified graphically in a way that is very similar to defining models for the underlying modeling language.
   - Graph rules in MATA provide support for *sequence pointcuts*, where a pointcut is a *sequence* of elements, which allows rich specification methods available in graph transformations to be available for aspect model composition, but in a way that is accessible to model developers.

3. An automatic technique for detecting structural interactions between aspect models:

   - Critical pair analysis has been applied to detect interactions between models given as UML class diagrams, sequence diagrams, and state diagrams.

The paper is organized as follows. Section 2 motivates why a new, unified, and expressive approach to aspect model composition is needed. Section 3 provides background on graph transformations necessary to describe the MATA approach. Section 4 describes the MATA language and Sect. 5 explains the application of critical pair analysis for detecting aspect interactions. Section 6 presents an extended example illustrating MATA and is followed, in Sect. 7, by a description of MATA tool support and, in Sect. 8, by a discussion of how MATA has been applied in practice. Conclusions follow in Sect. 9.

2 Motivation

This section motivates why existing approaches to aspect model composition are not expressive enough. The goal here is to show either that existing approaches cannot specify compositions in certain cases or that they cannot do it in an intuitive way. To illustrate this, we use a simple but non-trivial, example of an aspect model composition and argue that previous approaches are non-optimal.

Note that this paper takes a rather general definition of the term aspect such that any view of the system can be called an aspect. This means that many existing decomposition techniques (e.g. use cases and features) can be seen as aspects. This interpretation is consistent with that of many authors [6, 10, 11]. The examples in the paper will reflect this definition. This general view in particular means that our technique for handling aspect models works just as well for crosscutting and non-crosscutting concerns. In other words, we handle aspectual and non-aspectual concerns in a uniform way.

Figure 1 is an example of using UML use cases to maintain separation of concerns in a distributed application. The idea here (following [6]) is that the use case models are maintained separately throughout system development and that they can be composed at any time using aspect composition. The LHS is a use case for calling a remote service and consists of a state dependent class ServiceController and a state diagram that defines its behavior. The RHS is a use case for handling a network failure, which contains the same class ServiceController, but with a different set of attributes and a different state diagram. This second use case describes a limited number of attempts to retry a service.

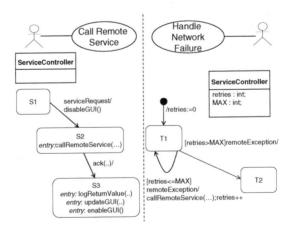

Fig. 1. Maintaining Use Case Separation of UML Models

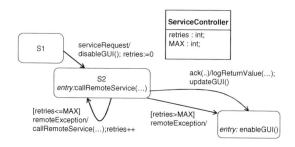

Fig. 2. Desired Composition of State Diagrams from Figure 1

The RHS crosscuts the LHS in the sense that whenever *callRemoteService* appears on the LHS, the RHS behavior should be used to handle a failure. This turns out to be a non-trivial example of crosscutting behavior. Prior to calling the remote service on the LHS, a GUI is disabled (via the action *disableGUI*). The GUI is only re-enabled (via the action *enableGUI*) once the remote service has been called **successfully**—the service call succeeds, a log is taken, and the GUI is updated before the GUI is re-enabled.

Now, consider the desired result from composing the RHS with the LHS—this is shown in Fig. 2. Note that when failure-handling is incorporated, what is now needed is that the GUI should be re-enabled whether the calling of the remote service succeeds or not. That is, even if the maximum number of retries is exceeded, *enableGUI* must still occur. Furthermore, logging and updating must only occur if the service call succeeds.

Capturing this composition is quite difficult if a composition model based on that of AspectJ is used. Existing work on (AOM) might, for example, define a joinpoint as the occurrence of the action *callRemoteService*. One might then insert behavior after or around this joinpoint in such a way that *enableGUI* is called whether or not the service call succeeds, and that logging/updating is not called in the failure scenario. This is possible but would really require the definition of two separate aspects, each with separate joinpoints—one joinpoint being the state containing action *callRemote-Service()* to which the *[retries<=MAX]* transition would be added, and the other being the transition with event *ack/* to which *logReturnValue()* and *updateGUI()* would be added as actions. In addition, one would need to use an around advice to ignore the first two entry actions in state *S3*. The effect is that the failure handling model on the RHS gets broken into pieces, thus becoming harder to understand the failure handling aspect in its own right. This effect goes against many of the ideas of modeling in that models ought to be easily readable.

Capturing this composition using some kind of default merge algorithm is also difficult. For example, one could proceed by defining a correspondence between states and then merging those states. The obvious thing to try would be to equate *T1* and *S2*, but the merge based on this correspondence would fail to re-enable the GUI if the maximum number of retries is reached. If one tries to solve this, in addition, by equating *T2* and *S3*, then the GUI will be re-enabled, but the logging and updating will occur even if the remote service call fails, which is contrary to the requirements given above. Therefore, composition directives would be needed to refactor the result of equating states. The problem with such composition directives is that it is hard to know exactly which directives to use because one has to first visualize the result of the merging. For large state diagrams, it becomes very complex to be able to predict where composition directives will need to be applied after the merge is complete.

As it turns out, one neat way to handle this example is by defining a so-called *sequence pointcut* [12]. A sequence pointcut should be used when it is not enough to consider a single element as a joinpoint, but instead, the joinpoint should be a *sequence* of elements. In this example, the key sequence starts with disabling the GUI and ends with re-enabling the GUI. This is because the GUI must be both disabled and re-enabled whatever the outcome of the remote service call. If one could specify that the pointcut is the sequence of actions/events between *disableGUI* and *enableGUI*, then one can easily capture the fact that the aspect should only apply to sequences where the GUI is first disabled and then later re-enabled. This allows one to specify, *on the same diagram*, that the failure handling (i.e. the aspect) behavior begins after *disableGUI* and ends with *enableGUI*. Further details on how sequence pointcuts can be defined in MATA are given in Sect. 4. Sequence pointcuts are not currently possible with most AOM approaches[1], although some AOP languages do support them [12].

More generally, when composing crosscutting state diagrams, it may be desirable to use advices that are more expressive than before, after or around. For example, an aspect state diagram may need to be composed *in parallel* with a base state diagram, or an aspect state diagram may need to be inserted *inside* a state in the base diagram (i.e. the base state becomes a composite state). In fact, composition should allow two diagrams to be composed using any of the syntactic constructs of the modeling language. In the case of state diagrams, for example, composition could be achieved using orthogonal regions, composite states, or even history states.

In other words, aspect-oriented model composition may require models to be composed in complex ways rather than just before or after each other. Previous approaches to AOM do not support such complex compositions. It is for this reason that we propose a new model composition language in this paper.

3   Background

Before going on to explain the details of the MATA language, this section first presents necessary background material. MATA is based on the technique of graph transformations and so a brief introduction to graph transformations is given in this section. We also briefly describe critical pair analysis, which will be used to detect interactions between aspects.

3.1   Graph Transformations

A graph consists of a set of nodes and a set of edges. A graph transformation is a graph rule $r: L \rightarrow R$ from a LHS graph L to a RHS graph R. The process of applying r

---

[1] The only known approach that does allow this is joinpoint designation diagrams (JPDDs) [13] but JPDDs do not support expressive advices.

to a graph *G* involves finding a graph monomorphism *h* from *L* to *G* and replacing *h(L)* in *G* with *h(R)*. Graph transformations may also be defined over attributed typed graphs. A typed graph is a graph in which each node and edge belongs to a type. Types are defined in a type graph. An attributed graph is a graph in which each node and edge may be labeled with attributes where each label is a (value, type) pair giving the value of the attribute and its type. In a graph rule, variables may be used to capture a set of possible values and/or a set of possible types.

Graph rules have previously been used for transforming UML models (e.g. UML refactorings [14]). Such work requires that UML models be represented as graphs. The usual approach is to define node types as the metaclasses in the UML metamodel. Graph rules can then be shown graphically using object diagrams.

As an example, Fig. 3 shows a (simplified) fragment of the UML state machine metamodel. A state machine contains 1 or more (orthogonal) regions, each of which contains states. Each transition is from a source to a target state and has a trigger and actions. States may also have actions. A state may contain 0 or more regions. A state is composite if it contains 1 or more regions. If it contains 2 or more regions, then the regions in this state are orthogonal. The *State* metaclass has an attribute *isComposite* indicating whether or not the state is composite. Finally, states, triggers, and actions have names (as represented by a generalization relationship to *namedElement*).

Figure 4 is an example graph transformation which moves all outgoing transitions from a composite state to its substates. The notation used to define this graph transformation is that of [14]. (We defer to [14] for the subtleties of this notation.) Nodes in the graph are given as rectangles. Nodes are attributed and typed and so the UML object diagram notation can be used to represent them. There are two additional notations. First, a set of nodes of a certain type is shown by a stacked rectangle. For example, *regions* is a set of Regions associated with a composite state. Secondly, the cross in the figure is a negative application condition and says that any match against the LHS graph cannot have a substate with a transition trigger called *triggerName*.

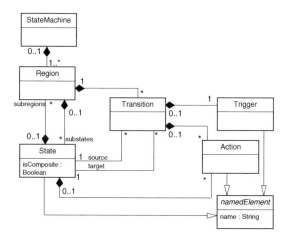

Fig. 3. UML State Machine Metamodel

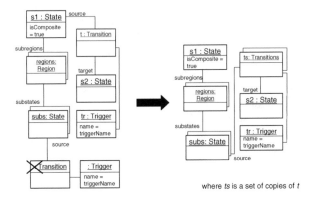

Fig. 4. Graph Rule to Move Down Transitions

The LHS in Fig. 4 matches any graph with at least one composite state with an outgoing transition. Furthermore, there should not be a transition on any of the substates with the same trigger. The RHS redirects the matched transition to all substates (by creating copies) thus moving the transition down in the state hierarchy.

3.2 Critical Pair Analysis

Critical pair analysis is a technique invented for term rewriting systems to check whether a set of rewrite rules is confluent. A set of rewrite rules is confluent if for all x,u,w with $x \gg u$ and $x \gg w$, there exists a z such that $u \gg z$ and $w \gg z$. Here, $\gg$ denotes the application of zero or more rewrite steps–i.e. $x \gg u$ means x rewrites to u in any number of rewrite steps. If a set of rewrite rules is finitely terminating, that is, there are no infinite rewriting sequences, then, confluence implies that all terms have unique normal forms. This in turn implies that, for a given term, the set of rules can be applied in any order and the result will be the same. This is an important property because it allows rules to be applied exhaustively without any concern about interactions or dependencies between rules.

As a simple example, consider a rewrite system consisting of two rules, p_1 and p_2 with p_1: $f(X,X) \to X$ and p_2: $g(f(X,Y),X) \to h(X)$, where X and Y are variables. This is not a confluent rewrite system. This can easily be shown by choosing the term $g(f(a,a),a)$ for a constant a, which rewrites under p_1 to $g(a,a)$ and under p_2 to $h(a)$. Since there is now no way to rewrite $g(a,a)$ and $h(a)$ to the same term, the rule set is not confluent.

Critical pair analysis examines potential overlaps between rules. For instance, if X is unified with Y, p_1 and p_2 overlap at $f(X,X)$. This leads to two possible rewriting results for the term $g(f(a,a),a)$ because either of the two rules can be applied. $(g(a,a),h(a))$ is called a critical pair and corresponds to the two possible ways of rewriting $g(f(a,a),a)$. By analyzing all possible critical pairs, all potential overlaps are examined, i.e. all ways that might lead to divergent results are analyzed. In essence, therefore, critical pair analysis is a way of detecting structural interactions between rules.

Formally, critical pairs can be defined as follows. If $x \rightarrow y$ and $u \rightarrow v$ are two rewrite rules with no variables in common (rename them if there are), and if x_1 is a non-variable subterm of x unifiable with u via most general unifier θ, then the pair $y\theta$ and the result of replacing $x_1\theta$ in $x\theta$ by $v\theta$ is called a critical pair.

Critical pair analysis has been adapted to graph rules—see, for example, [15]. In the context of MATA, since an aspect is a graph rule, critical pair analysis can be applied to detect overlaps, i.e. interactions, between aspects. When applied exhaustively, critical pair analysis will find all aspects (i.e. graph rules) that are in conflict or are dependent, where conflict and dependency are defined as follows:

- Aspect A conflicts with aspect B if the application of aspect A prevents aspect B from being applied.
- Aspect B is dependent on aspect A if the application of aspect A is necessary for aspect B to be applied.

Examples of conflicts and dependencies for UML aspect models are given in Sect. 5.

4   Specifying and Composing Aspect Models with MATA

This section describes how to specify and compose aspect models with MATA. MATA considers aspect composition as a special case of graph transformation. The key difference with existing graph transformation approaches such as FUJABA [16] and VIATRA2 [17] is that these approaches define transformations using the abstract syntax of the modeling language. For example, the transformation in Fig. 4 refers to metaclasses such as *Region* and *State*. Even for a simple transformation such as the one in Fig. 4, the use of abstract syntax soon becomes complicated and it becomes very difficult to specify such rules correctly. This is particularly true for UML sequence diagrams because the metamodel for interactions in UML is quite complicated. Since MATA is targeted toward model developers, not metamodeling experts, its aspect models must be specified in a way that is intuitive for users unfamiliar with the intricacies of the UML metamodel. This means that aspect rules should be specified using the concrete syntax of UML rather than UML metaclasses.

For the most part, specifying a graph rule over UML using concrete syntax is straightforward. As long as a metaclass has a concrete visualization, users can draw diagrams using this visualization and it can be translated automatically to the relevant metaclass. Abstract metaclasses, which do not have a concrete syntax realization, cannot be drawn using concrete syntax. Such abstract metaclasses cannot be used in MATA and so MATA should not be viewed as a general purpose transformation language, but rather a transformation language specialized toward aspect model composition. For aspect model composition, abstract metaclasses do not need to be used.

MATA aspect models, therefore, are graph rules written in concrete syntax that are translated into equivalent abstract syntax for the purposes of executing the transformation. MATA does include some extensions to UML's concrete syntax that are necessary to support its notion of sequence pointcuts. Recall from Sect. 1 that sequence pointcuts are used to match against a sequence of model elements in the base. In MATA, this can be a sequence of transitions in state diagrams, or it can be a sequence of messages in sequence diagrams. Sequence pointcuts turn out to be a very powerful mechanism for specifying aspects in a way where the aspect is as ignorant as possible of elements in the base.

The remainder of this section explains the MATA language in detail. First, an overview of how to specify aspects in MATA is presented. This is followed by details on specifying joinpoints and advices in MATA.

4.1 An Overview of Using Aspects in MATA

Figure 5 provides an overview of how aspect models are specified in MATA. A *model slice* is defined as a collection of structural and behavioral models (UML class diagrams, state diagrams, and sequence diagrams) that capture a particular view of the system. The base model slice captures the core system model with crosscutting concerns removed. An aspect model slice captures the models for a particular cross-cutting concern.

The base model slice is composed of a set of base models. Similarly, an aspect model slice is composed of a set of aspect models. Base models are written in standard UML. Aspect models are written in the MATA language and are defined as increments of the base models or other aspect models. Each aspect model describes the set of model elements affected by the aspect (i.e. the joinpoints) and how the base model elements are affected (i.e. the advices). Note that an aspect model can only be defined as an increment of a model of the same type; for example, sequence diagram aspects can extend base sequence diagrams but not base state diagrams.

The following process can be used to develop and compose aspect models. The modeler first develops the base model slice and a set of aspect model slices. Each aspect model slice is written as an increment over the base model slice or as an increment over other aspect model slices. The user then invokes the MATA composition engine to compose the base slice with a selected subset of the aspect slices.

Before performing the composition, MATA applies critical pair analysis to detect interactions within the set of chosen aspect slices. Interactions can be detected

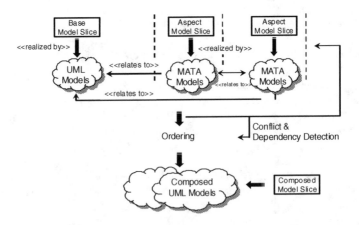

Fig. 5. An Overview of MATA

between models of the same type. The results of this analysis are provided to the user and result in one of the following three conclusions:

1. There are no interactions.
2. There are interactions that mean that the aspects must be applied in a particular order. The user then specifies this order.
3. There are interactions that cannot be resolved by applying the aspects in a particular order. Instead, either the base or aspect models must be modified to remove these unwanted interactions.

Once all interactions have been resolved either by (2) or (3), the modeler instructs MATA to compose the chosen aspects with the base. The result is a new model slice that can be inspected, analyzed, or from which code can be generated. Note that there is no necessity to actually compose the models. The key point is that the MATA specification contains a precise description of the aspect and base relationships. This description can either be used in composition or can be used to generate aspect-oriented code by generating the code for each model slice and generating the AOP code that specifies how to weave the aspect code into the base. In fact, MATA comes with a code generator that does exactly this, resulting in AspectWerkz [18] code (see Sect. 7).

Note that MATA does not address how to partition a problem into an appropriate set of aspect slices, i.e. how to decide on the right set of aspects. This is a more general problem, which is out of the scope of this paper, but existing techniques for identifying aspects during requirements engineering, such as [19], could be applied to identify requirements-level aspects and then model these aspects during the analysis and design phases using MATA.

4.2 Joinpoints, Advices and Aspects in MATA

There are no explicit joinpoints in MATA. Any model element can be a joinpoint and pointcuts are defined as patterns over these model elements. Similarly, there are no restrictions on the advices in MATA. In particular, MATA is not limited to before, after, and around advices. Instead, any model element of the underlying model language can be used. For example, composition in parallel is allowed in state diagrams using orthogonal regions.

Hence, an aspect model in MATA consists of two parts, a *pattern* and a *composition specification*. Application of an aspect model to an existing base model is done in two stages:

1. Find a match for the pattern in the base model.
2. Modify the base model at the matched locations according to the composition specification.

This is just a standard application of graph transformation techniques.

4.2.1 MATA's Pattern Language

A pattern in MATA can be either a simple pattern or a complex pattern. (This distinction is made purely for presentational purposes.) A simple pattern is just a UML model with some elements marked as *pattern variables*. Pattern variables are typed over UML metaclasses and are regular expressions prefixed with a vertical bar "|" to denote that they are variables. For a simple pattern, matching the pattern against a UML base model consists of finding an instantiation of the pattern variables in the aspect model such that the structure of the aspect model is preserved. Standard efficient algorithms for matching in graph transformations can be used for this [20].

Complex patterns include patterns that define sequence pointcuts. Sequence pointcuts are currently provided for state diagrams and sequence diagrams, and are described next.

Sequence pointcuts in state diagrams

Sequence pointcuts in state diagrams are a general way of matching against multiple elements at once. This is particularly useful, for example, when one wants to match against a sequence of transitions beginning and ending with a particular event, but where the events on intermediate transitions are unimportant. Sequence pointcuts introduce new concrete syntax into patterns because multiple model elements must be matched against. However, the concrete syntax is extended in as minimal a way as possible.

A state diagram sequence pointcut, therefore, is an abstract representation of a family of state diagrams and contains pattern variables. In complex patterns representing sequence pointcuts, pattern variables have multiplicities. A pattern variable |X has a multiplicity of one. A pattern variable $|X^+$ has a multiplicity of one or more. A complex state diagram pattern matches a state diagram if all the pattern variables can be instantiated to elements of the state diagram in a way that preserves the variable's metaclass and multiplicity.

State Diagram Sequence Pointcut Syntax. We denote the type of a pattern variable by (|X : T). Only the metaclasses in the list below are allowed to have pattern variable multiplicities. We assume the metamodel of Fig. 3 in the remainder of this paper.

1. (|X : State) matches against a single state. ($|X^+$: State) matches against one or more states and also matches the transitions between these states. More precisely, $|X^+$ will match a fully connected substate machine–that is, each state included in the match must be connected by at least one transition to another state included in the match.
2. (|X : StateMachine) matches a single state machine. ($|X^+$: StateMachine) is not allowed (because it is unnecessary).
3. (|X : Action) matches a single action. ($|X^+$: Action) matches a sequence of one or more actions.
4. (|X : Trigger) matches a single event. ($|X^+$: Trigger) matches a sequence of one or more events.
5. (|X : Region) matches a single orthogonal region. ($|X^+$: Region) matches one or more regions within the same composite state.

Whenever possible, the concrete syntax of a pattern variable is the same as the UML concrete syntax of its type. See Fig. 6 for examples.

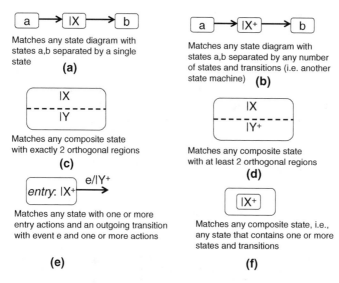

Fig. 6. State Diagram Pattern Examples

Figure 6(a), for example, matches any sequence of states starting with a state named *a*, ending with a state named *b*, and with another state in between (different from *a* and *b*). In contrast, the variable |X⁺ in Fig. 6(b) matches one or more states in between *a* and *b* as well as any transitions between those states. This means that |X⁺ represents any number of states and transitions with at least one of those states connected to the incoming transition shown, and at least one state connected to the outgoing state shown. In a similar way, Fig. 6(c) and 6(d) show how to match against a specific number of regions and one or more regions, respectively. Figure 6(e) is self-explanatory. Figure 6(f) matches a state which contains a state machine, i.e. there must be at least one substate, but the composite state may contain any number of substates and transitions.

Note that, for any simple pattern, the name of the pattern variable may be omitted–so, Fig. 6(a) would be equivalent if |X was removed.

State Diagram Sequence Pointcut Semantics. The pattern-matching semantics for state diagram sequence pointcuts is given by mapping each pattern to a typed graph consisting of instances of the appropriate metaclasses. If a pattern element has a multiplicity of one, it maps to a single instance of its metaclass. If it has multiplicity of one or more, it maps to a set of instances. To illustrate, Fig. 7 shows the mapping to metaclass instances for the patterns given in Fig. 6(c) and (d). The first pattern will match any composite state with exactly two orthogonal regions. The second pattern will match any state with at least 2 regions.

A slight complication is introduced by the use of |X⁺ to match against a set of states and transitions in Fig. 6(b) and (f). In Fig. 6(f), for example, instead of mapping |X⁺ to a set of instances of State, it must be mapped to an instance of Region containing any number of instances of State and Transition. This issue arises because of the peculiarities of the UML metamodel.

State Diagram Pattern Example. Figure 8 shows the state diagram pattern required in the example of Sect. 2. Recall that a sequence pointcut was deemed to be useful. The figure illustrates how to specify a sequence from *callRemoteService* to *enableGUI*. The pattern variable IX⁺ matches against any number of actions in the target state of the transition but will not match against *enableGUI()*. The effect is that the state diagram pattern matches any sequence starting with the *callRemoteService()* action, followed by a transition, and by one or more entry actions, and ending with the action *enableGUI()*.

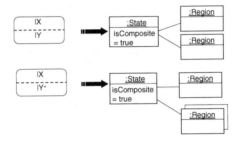

Fig. 7. Metaclass Instance Representation of Patterns

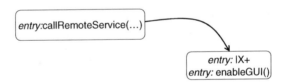

Fig. 8. State Diagram Sequence Pointcut for Figure 1

Sequence pointcuts in sequence diagrams

Sequence pointcuts are also supported in sequence diagrams, but are somewhat simpler. A sequence pointcut here corresponds to any sequence of ordered model elements, including messages and combined fragments. To match the concrete syntax closely, a new interaction fragment is introduced, with interaction operator **any**. An **any** fragment is a variable that will match against any sequence of messages and/or combined fragments. In Fig. 9, the *Call Remote Service* use case from the LHS of Fig. 1 is instead modeled as a sequence diagram. This is shown on the top half of Fig. 9. The bottom half of Fig. 9 gives a sequence pointcut equivalent to that shown in Fig. 8, but for sequence diagrams. Note how this sequence pointcut is agnostic about the messages occurring in between *callRemoteService* and *enableGUI*.

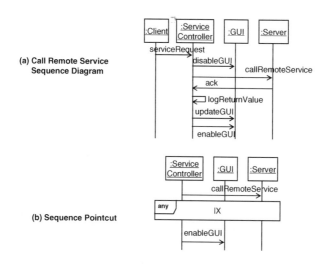

(a) Call Remote Service
Sequence Diagram

(b) Sequence Pointcut

Fig. 9. Sequence pointcuts for sequence diagrams

4.2.2 MATA's Composition Specification Language

MATA's pattern language identifies model elements in the base models that are crosscut by the aspect models. MATA also gives a way to define how model elements from the aspect should be composed with model elements from the base. MATA represents an aspect as a graph rule $r: L \rightarrow R$, where L and R are UML models, as a single UML model in which model elements may be annotated with one of three stereotypes— <<create>>, <<delete>> or <<context>>.

Given a pointcut definition as a MATA pattern, model elements from the aspect that should be added to the pattern are marked with the <<create>> stereotype. Similarly, elements may be removed using the <<delete>> stereotype. Simple examples are shown in Fig. 10 for state diagrams. In (a), the pointcut is any state (where an explicit pattern variable |X has been omitted) and the aspect elements added are a state a and a transition to a. In (b), the pointcut is any pair of states with a transition between them, and the aspect element is a superstate that is added so that it contains these (and only these) two states. In general, <<create>> and <<delete>> can be used to add (or remove) any kind of aspectual model element. For example, an aspect could be added as an orthogonal region to an existing base model that matches a state pattern—see Fig. 10(c).

The use of <<create>> is "optimized" in the sense that if a state is stereotyped as <<create>>, then any of its substates or transitions are also created. Hence, in Fig. 10(a), the transition is created but does not need to explicitly be given a <<create>> stereotype. This optimization reduces the number of stereotypes a user must specify. However, in Figs. 10(b) and 10(c), the user wants to wrap a composite state around existing states. To stop these substates from being created, they are stereotyped as <<context>>. <<context>> therefore overrides the "optimization". In particular, in Fig. 10(b), although the outer state is marked with <<create>>, the use of <<context>> means that the two inner states are matched against rather than created.

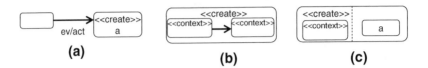

Fig. 10. Examples of Composition Specifications

MATA's composition stereotypes can also be applied to class diagrams and sequence diagrams. We illustrate with some examples of sequence diagram composition specifications.

Figure 11 gives an example MATA aspect rule to add parallel behavior in a sequence diagram. Figure 11(a) is the MATA rule itself and (c) shows the application of the rule to a particular example. (In (a), the lifelines are pattern variables—as before, the pattern variables do not need to be explicitly named.) Figure 11(a) has two parts to it—the pattern to match against and elements to add. As with state diagrams, <<create>> in MATA sequence diagrams is "optimized" so that if <<create>> is applied to a combined fragment, it will also be applied to everything inside the fragment unless it is marked with <<context>>. Similarly, if <<create>> is applied to a lifeline, it is also applied to any messages that are sent to or are received by this lifeline. <<delete>> works in the same way.

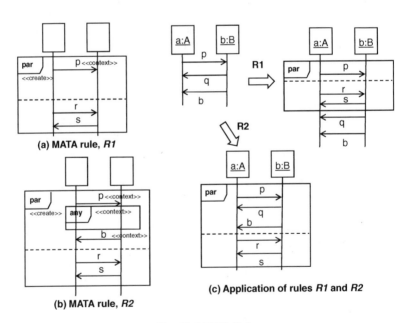

Fig. 11. MATA Rules

Hence, for the **par** fragment in Fig. 11(a), <<create>> also applies to messages r and s. To avoid <<create>> being applied to p, it is marked with <<context>>. Therefore, the match defined in Fig. 11(a) is any pair of lifelines with a message p from one lifeline to the other. The effect of applying the rule in Fig. 11(a) is to introduce a new **par** fragment around all instances of message p, and this new fragment will have messages r and s occur in parallel with p. This is shown in Fig. 11(c).

Figure 11 also shows an example of how sequence pointcuts and composition specifications can be used together in MATA. The rule R2 in Fig. 11(b) will match any two lifelines with messages p and b with any number of messages between p and b. (Note that the messages matched by the **any** fragment need not have the same sender and receiver lifelines as p and q–that is, the lifelines across which **any** is drawn are irrelevant.) The result of applying the rule is shown in Fig. 11(c). Note how the result is different than if rule R1 is applied. For R2, the pointcut is the sequence of messages p, q, b, and so these messages all appear in the first operand of the **par** fragment.

Semantics of MATA's composition language

As already indicated, the use of the <<create>> and <<delete>> stereotypes are "optimized" to reduce the burden on the modeler of applying these stereotypes. This "optimization" is governed by the rules of neighborhood; for example, if <<create>> is applied to a model element, it is also applied to all of its neighbors. Similarly, it holds true for <<delete>> and <<context>>. Since this optimization process can get quite involved for complex examples, we define here precisely how the optimization works.

The semantics is defined by transforming an aspect into the equivalent graph rule in the form LHS $\rightarrow$ RHS. This is done in two steps. First, the stereotypes <<create>>, <<delete>> and <<context>> are propagated throughout the aspect model. Second, the stereotypes are eliminated by transforming the aspect into a graph rule.

In the first step, each stereotype is propagated to its neighbors. A neighbor may be an immediate neighbor or a remote neighbor. For a given model element, its immediate neighbors are all those related model elements that are considered strongly related to it. For example, the trigger events on a transition are strongly related to the transition itself because they cannot exist without the transition. States are strongly related to their transitions because if a state is deleted, then its transitions must be deleted lest a hanging transition remains. Container states are considered to be strongly related to the elements they contain. For example, composite states are strongly related to the contained states. On the other hand, a transition is not strongly related to its target or source state because the transition can be deleted without deleting the states and the result will still be a well-formed model.

Table 1 gives the immediate neighbors for the model elements considered in this paper.

A remote neighbor of a model element is any neighbor of an immediate neighbor of the model element. The immediate neighbors are designed both to ensure termination of the propagation process and, as much as possible, to avoid aspects introducing ill-formed models.

There are two precedence rules that must be taken into account during the propagation process. This is because a model element may end up with more than one MATA stereotype either because different stereotypes were propagated from different directions or because the user has specifically assigned a stereotype. In the former case, <<context>> always takes precedence over <<delete>> or <<create>> and so <<delete>> and <<create>> are removed in this case. In the latter case, the user-defined stereotype always takes precedence. For example, if a model element is marked as <<delete>> by the user but <<context>> is propagated to it, then <<context>> is removed. If the propagation process ends up with <<create>> *and* <<delete>> both applied to the same element, then there is an inherent inconsistency in the aspect rule and the rule should not be applied. This can happen, for instance, if the user specifies that a state should be deleted but an incoming transition to that state should be created. Obviously, one cannot create a new transition to a state that is marked for deletion.

The following summarizes the propagation process.

for each MATA-stereotyped model element, m, in the aspect model:
    let N be the set of immediate neighbors of m;
    propagate the MATA stereotypes of m to all elements of N;
    for each n in N,
        apply the propagation process
    end foreach
end foreach

for each model element, m, in the aspect model:
    eliminate MATA stereotypes according to the precedence rules
    if m is stereotyped with both <<create>> and <<delete>>, STOP
end foreach

The second step of the semantics definition is to construct the equivalent graph rule. This is done easily. <<create>> and <<delete>> are simply a way of representing both the LHS and RHS of a graph rule on the same diagram. The familiar LHS→ RHS notation can be obtained by considering the LHS as all elements either with no stereotype or with <<context>> or <<delete>>. The RHS is the LHS but with the <<create>> elements added and the <<delete>> elements removed. The Appendix discusses how we do the conversion from UML models in concrete syntax to typed graphs.

Although the propagation algorithm is designed as much as possible to ensure the result of applying an aspect is a well-formed model, there are still situations where this cannot be guaranteed. For example, if state X has a transition to Y and both Y and the transition are marked as <<context>>, whereas X is marked as <<create>>, then this rule looks for an existing transition with some undefined source state and creates a new source state for the transition. However, a transition cannot have two source states. We leave as future work to define constraints over how rules are defined that would either avoid such rules or alert the user. Experience has shown that such rules rarely occur in practice.

Table 1. Immediate Neighbors for Some Common Model Elements

The table should be read as follows. The second column lists model elements. For each of these elements, if a MATA stereotype is applied to it, then all elements from the third column are also given the stereotype. So, for example, if a class has a <<delete>> stereotype, all associations connected to this class will also be deleted.

Diagram	Model element	Immediate Neighbors
Class diagram	Class	Connected Association, Contained Attribute, Contained Operation
	Aggregation or Composition Association	Aggregate or Composite Classes
	Generalization	Child Classes
	Other Association	None
State diagram	State	Incoming or Outgoing transition, Substates, Entry or Exit Actions
	Transition	Event on the transition, Action on the transition, Guard on the transition
	Event	None
	Action	None
Sequence diagram	Combined fragment	Model elements contained in the fragment
	Lifeline	Incoming or outgoing message
	Message	None

4.3 MATA Example

Finally, in this section, we return to the remote service call example introduced in Fig. 1. We now consider how to specify this aspect composition in MATA. The base model slice consists of the models on the LHS of Fig. 1. The aspect model slice is an adaptation of the models on the RHS of Fig. 1. The aspect models must be put into MATA syntax so that they define the failure handling behavior as an increment over the base model slice. Figure 12 therefore shows the state-dependent part of the aspect model slice for failure handling. To make it easier to read, elements that are created or deleted are in bold italics. Note that a MATA rule contains the pattern to match against, the aspect model elements, and the composition operators that detail how those aspect elements are merged with the base. The effect of applying this rule is that: (1) a match is found in the base model with the state diagram sequence pointcut, and (2) the matched submodel of the base is modified by creating and deleting elements according to the <<create>> and <<delete>> composition operators. Note that a combination of <<create>> and <<delete>> is used to move the actions that match against |X$^+$.

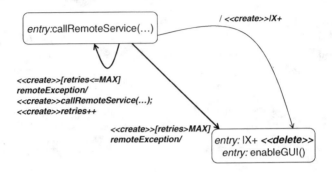

Fig. 12. MATA Specification of the Example in Figure 1

5   Detecting Aspect Interactions

Since aspect models are represented as graph rules in MATA, critical pair analysis can be applied, as explained in Sect. 3, to detect interactions between aspects. In this section, we introduce a small example to illustrate how this works. The example is for class diagrams, but the same principles apply to sequence and state diagrams.

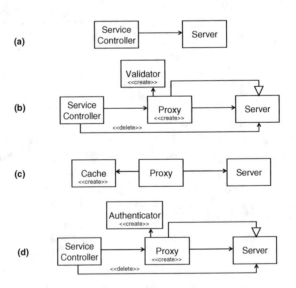

Fig. 13. Simple Example of Aspect Model Interaction

(Note how the concept of immediate neighbor is used so that, for example, <<create>> does not need to be applied to the association from Proxy to Cache.)

Recall the ongoing example, which involves the call of a remote service from a *ServiceController* to a *Server*. Figure 13(a) gives a simple class diagram illustrating the relationship between *ServiceController* and *Server*. Figure 13 (b)-(d) shows three aspects that might be specified to add functionality to the network communication. Figure 13(b) introduces a basic proxy server that simply validates a request before forwarding it. Figure 13(c) is an aspect introducing caching to an existing proxy, and Fig. 13(d) adds an access control proxy. The intention is that all three of these aspects will be added to the base so that all communication between the *ServiceController* and *Server* goes through a caching, validating, access control proxy.

Following the process to use MATA outlined in Sect. 4.1, the modeler would instruct MATA to apply all three aspects and, before actually composing the models, it would apply critical pair analysis to detect dependencies and conflicts between the aspects. Because of the simplicity of the example, it is easy to see in this case that there are indeed serious aspect interactions and that a random order of application of the aspects may result in an incorrect result. For example, if aspect 13(d) is applied to the base first, then aspect 13(b) can no longer be applied because it cannot match the result obtained after applying aspect 13(d)–aspect 13(d) removes the association between *ServiceController* and *Server*, which is needed to match and apply aspect 13(b). Aspect 13(c) will still apply but the result of applying the aspects in this order means that, since 13(b) cannot be invoked, the proxy validity check will not occur. For large examples, such details could easily be overlooked, resulting in incorrect models as a result of applying aspects.

Table 2 summarizes the results of critical pair analysis applied to this example. The table tells us that there is conflict from aspect 13(d) to aspect 13(b). In particular, this means that if aspect 13(d) is applied, then aspect 13(b) cannot be. This matches the intuition in the previous paragraph. Conflicts are generally more serious than dependencies. Dependencies can be dealt with by applying the aspects in a particular order (and this can be specified in the MATA tool). Conflicts, on the other hand, can sometimes be resolved by enforcing an application order, but, in the worst case, imply a fundamental inconsistency in the specification that should be fixed.

Table 2. Dependencies and Conflicts in Figure 13. An entry for row X and column Y implies a dependency or conflict from X to Y.

row→column	Aspect (b)	Aspect (c)	Aspect (d)
Aspect (b)		Dependency	Conflict
Aspect (c)			
Aspect (d)	Conflict	Dependency	

Table 3. Revised Dependencies and Conflicts

row→column	Aspect (b)	Aspect (c)	Aspect (d)
Aspect (b)		Dependency	Dependency
Aspect (c)			
Aspect (d)			

For this example, the modeler might realize, based on the results in Table 2, that a better model would allow aspect 13(b) to introduce the basic validating proxy and then other aspects should add functionality layers on top of this proxy. This would result in modifying aspect 13(d) to only introduce the *Authenticator*. (It would look identical to Fig. 13(c) except *Authenticator* would replace *Cache*.) Once this is done, and critical pair analysis is re-run, the results in Table 3 are obtained. Table 3 shows us that aspects 13(c) and 13(d) are now orthogonal since there are neither dependencies nor conflicts between them. This implies that the application order of 13(c) and 13(d) is irrelevant. However, there are still dependencies from aspect 13(b) to the other rules and so aspect 13(b) must be applied before those. The modeler should therefore specify to apply 13(b) first followed by either 13(c) or 13(d).

6   Extended Example

The preceding sections have introduced the major concepts in MATA. To bring everything together, this section provides an extended example of MATA that includes both static and dynamic models. A cell phone application is used to illustrate the concepts that have been introduced so far.

We will model three use cases for a simple cell phone—*Receive a Call*, *Take a Message*, and *Notify Call Waiting*. The goal here is to compose models for the three use cases. To do this, we will consider *Receive a Call* to be the base use case, and the other two use cases to be aspects. The base use case is modeled in UML, whereas the aspect use cases are modeled as MATA models, that is, as increments of the base models. Note that the models for the aspect use cases refer only to those elements in the base that are needed for the modifications to take place.

Figure 14 shows (simplified) static and dynamic models for the base use case, *Receive a Call*. The phone contains a ringer, a phone component, a display unit, and a keypad. Upon receiving an incoming call, the phone notifies the user by displaying the caller information on the display unit and sending a ring message to the ringer. The user is allowed to either accept the call (then hang up later) or not accept (i.e. disconnect) the call.

Figure 15 gives the behavior models for the two aspects: *Take a Message* and *Notify Call Waiting*. Figure 15(a) is a sequence diagram for *Take a Message*. If the phone rings for a specified amount of time (i.e. there is a timeout), the call goes to a messaging system. In MATA, this is specified by creating a new **alt** fragment since forwarding to voice mail is an alternative scenario to the case where the callee accepts the call. Note that an **any** fragment is used to match against all messages coming after *Ring* in the base. This is needed since once a message is taken, the user should not be able to pick up the call or disconnect it. Hence, the **alt** fragment must be wrapped around all messages in the base concerned with call pick up or disconnect.

In Fig. 15(b), the aspect rule matches any two states that have a transition between them with an event named *Incoming call*. The effect of the aspect is to add an additional transition capturing the voicemail behavior. When this rule is applied, the two states will match against *Idle* and *Waiting* in Fig. 14(c). The effect is to add a transition from *Waiting* back to *Idle*.

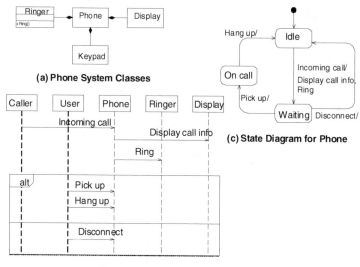

(a) Phone System Classes

(b) Receive a Call Scenario

(c) State Diagram for Phone

Fig. 14. Models for the Base Use Case

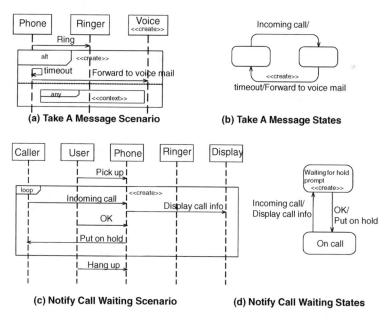

(a) Take A Message Scenario

(b) Take A Message States

(c) Notify Call Waiting Scenario

(d) Notify Call Waiting States

Fig. 15. Aspect Models for Take a Message and Notify Call Waiting

Figure 15(c) introduces messages for putting an incoming call on hold when a call is already underway. These new messages are only relevant when a call is taking place, that is, in between messages *Pick Up* and *Hang Up* in the base. Hence, the **loop** fragment is marked with a <<create>> stereotype and this fragment is inserted in between *Pick Up* and *Hang Up*. Note that, in this case, it would be sufficient to leave out the *Hang Up* message in 15(c), which, in effect, would insert the new behavior *after Pick Up*. However, we include *Hang Up* because there may eventually be other occurrences of *Pick Up,* which should not be affected by the aspect.

Figure 15(d) introduces a new state, *Waiting for hold prompt*, into the base to capture the new behavior for the call waiting use case. Note that the two transitions in 15(d) implicitly have <<create>> stereotypes because they are immediate neighbors of the newly created state.

6.1 Interactions between Aspects

We can see that there is a dependency between the two state diagram rules for *Take a Message* and *Notify Call Waiting*. This dependency arises because *Notify Call Waiting* creates a transition with event *Incoming Call* (Fig. 15(d)) whereas *Take a Message* matches against the event *Incoming Call* (Fig. 15(b)). Hence, if *Take a Message* is applied to the base before *Notify Call Waiting* then any incoming call that is received during an existing call cannot be sent to voicemail. Figure 16 gives the results of composing the two aspects with the base in either order. In 16(a), *Take a Message* is applied to the base before *Notify Call Waiting*. In 16(b), it is applied after. The difference is that there is an extra transition from *Waiting for hold prompt* to *On call* in 16(b) which captures the fact that an incoming call may be sent to voice mail even when there is currently an active call taking place. The difference in the composed state diagrams arises because the rule for *Notify Call Waiting* introduces a new transition with event *Incoming call*. Hence, when the *Take a Message* rule is applied in 16(b), there are two transitions with event *Incoming call* and so the rule applies twice.

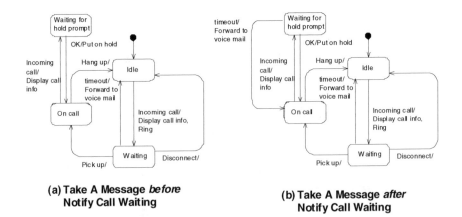

(a) Take A Message *before* Notify Call Waiting

(b) Take A Message *after* Notify Call Waiting

Fig. 16. Base and Aspect State Diagrams Composed

MATA detects these kinds of dependencies automatically. Ultimately, the modeler must decide which order is the correct one, but MATA can at least provide some assistance in flagging cases that must be considered more carefully. If there are no conflicts or dependencies, then the rules can be applied in any order. Critical pair analysis is particularly important when aspects are reused in a different context than originally intended since new conflicts and dependencies may then arise inadvertently.

7 Tool Support

7.1 Overview

This section describes the implementation of the MATA tool. MATA is designed as a vendor-independent tool but currently works on top of IBM's Rational Software Modeler (RSM). Each model slice is modeled as a package. Within this package, the class diagrams, sequence diagrams, and state diagrams for the slice are maintained. A simple UML profile is applied so that the base model slice is stereotyped as <<base>> and aspect model slices are stereotyped as <<aspect>>. Users may select a subset of the aspects and the tool generates the composed model for all of these aspects and the base. The user may also define an ordering of aspect composition in case one aspect needs to be composed before another. If an ordering is not specified, the tool selects an order non-deterministically. Critical pair analysis is always applied before composition and the results are presented to the user.

Since MATA uses graph transformations as the underlying theory, it relies on an existing graph rule execution tool to apply graph rules. The graph rule execution tool used is AGG [21]. MATA converts a UML base model slice, captured as an instance of the UML2 metamodel by RSM, into an instance of a type graph, where the type graph represents a simplified form of the UML2 metamodel. MATA composition rules are converted into AGG graph rules and are executed on the base graph automatically. The results are converted back into a UML2 compliant model and are displayed in RSM. Critical pair analysis is done by AGG and the results are converted into RSM so that detected dependencies and conflicts can be understood by the user.

The details of the conversion to type graphs are not given here. It suffices to say that for simple patterns, the mapping is a straightforward transformation from a UML metamodel instance to a type graph instance. Full details are given in [22]. For sequence pointcuts, the transformation is more complex because AGG does not directly support these. The effect is achieved by tagging model elements to keep track of their relative positioning and then using a sequence of graph rules to manipulate the sequence pointcut matches. This is an implementation detail that we do not go into here. So far, sequence pointcuts have been implemented for sequence diagrams but not for state diagrams.

In principle, MATA could use any existing graph rule execution tool (e.g. VIATRA2 or FUJABA) as its underlying engine, but AGG was chosen because of its support for critical pair analysis. Although built on top of an existing engine, MATA provides some unique features that make it very suitable for aspect modeling and composition, namely: (1) graph rules are defined graphically using the concrete syntax of UML rather than using metaclasses; (2) MATA supports sequence pointcuts, that is, an aspect may match against a sequence of messages or a sequence of transitions. This is supported directly in the MATA rule syntax; (3) the stereotype <<context>> is unique to MATA; and (4) dependencies and conflicts between aspects can be detected automatically using critical pair analysis.

7.2 Generating AspectWerkz Code from MATA Models

In general, the user has a choice whether to compose the aspect and base models during modeling or to compose them once code has been generated from them. In the former case, the composed models can be used to generate code using existing code generators. In the latter case, aspect-oriented code is generated automatically using MATA's built-in generator, which generates AspectWerkz [18] code. AspectWerkz was chosen for its dynamic weaving capabilities[2] since this research has been conducted within the context of a larger project on integrating model-driven development and runtime weaving. The code generator, however, aims to decouple the MATA representation from the particular AOP language used, and therefore, introduces an intermediate layer in the mapping. This layer defines a metamodel of common AOP language constructs and can be mapped to different AOP languages supporting those constructs.

The remainder of this section gives a brief introduction to AspectWerkz, a short description of the code generation facilities in MATA, and a short example.

7.2.1 AspectWerkz

AspectWerkz is a Java-based AOP language that does not add any new language constructs to Java, but instead supports declaration of aspects via Java annotations. AspectWerkz has now been merged with AspectJ. However, the full dynamic weaving capabilities of AspectWerkz are not available in AspectJ and so we continue to use AspectWerkz in this paper. AspectWerkz includes support for dynamic weaving of aspects, which makes it possible to redefine advices and introductions at runtime without any class reloading or new weaving phase as well as to declare new pointcuts at run time. AspectWerkz was chosen to be the target of MATA's code generator because of its ability to support research projects in adaptive systems. However, because of the merge of AspectWerkz and AspectJ, it would be straightforward to adapt the code generator to produce AspectJ code (albeit without the runtime weaving capabilities). An alternative AOP language with run time weaving facilities would be PROSE [23]. Partly because of the uncertainty of future runtime weaving languages, MATA's code generator has been implemented following MDA principles, that is, by mapping first to an intermediate platform-independent aspect metamodel before mapping to AspectWerkz.

In AspectWerkz, annotations can be used to define aspects (see Fig. 17). An aspect is just a class with the annotation *@Aspect*. The usual advices–before, after and around–can also be defined using annotations. For example, in Fig. 17(b), an around advice is defined to add new behavior to *method1* when *field1* is set to *1*. Introductions in AspectWerkz can be defined using mixins. Figure 17(c) shows a mixin for adding new fields and methods to *Class1*. Note how the mixin is just a class with an annotation.

---

[2] Although Aspectwerkz has now been integrated into AspectJ 5, the runtime weaving capabilities do not exist in AspectJ 5.

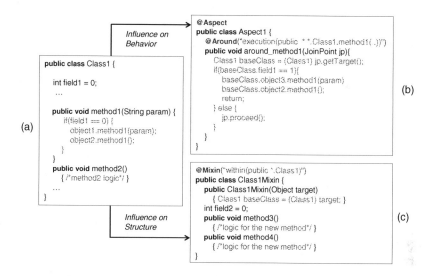

Fig. 17. Syntax of AspectWerkz

7.2.2 Code Generation in MATA

MATA currently generates AspectWerkz code from UML class diagrams and UML state diagrams. It takes a base model slice and a set of aspect model slices (selected by the user) and generates Java code for the base model slice and an AspectWerkz aspect for each of the aspect model slices. State diagrams are implemented using the State pattern.

To maintain independence from the target AOP language, code is generated in two phases. The first phase maps MATA models to an AOP metamodel that defines the concepts common to the most widely used AOP languages but does not commit to a particular AOP language. The second phase generates AspectWerkz code from this metamodel but could be adapted fairly easily to generate, for example, AspectJ code.

The intricacies of the code generator are outside the scope of this paper. Instead, we present a simple example. Recall the cell phone example from Sect. 6. Figure 14 shows the base state diagram, whereas Fig. 15 shows an aspect state diagram that introduced a new state and transitions for the Notify Call Waiting use case.

Figure 18 gives the code generated for these two state diagrams. The LHS of the figure is an implementation of the base state diagram using the State pattern. The RHS uses mixins to add new states and transitions to the base behavior. Note, in this example, that a single new state is created (*Waiting for Hold Prompt*). This is implemented as a new object that implements the *State* interface. In Fig. 15, a new transition, *Incoming Call*, is added to the *On Call* state. This is captured in the aspect code by a mixin applied to the *OnCall* class. There also needs to be a mixin applied to the *Phone* class to redirect the new transition *OK*. The upper portion of the RHS of Fig. 18 is a book-keeping code needed to ensure proper placement of the aspect code.

```
public class Caller
   { /* caller interfacing logic */ }
public class User
   { /* user interfacing logic */ }
public class Phone {
   public void incomingCall(String info)
      { curState.incomingCall(info); }
   public void pickUp() { curState.pickUp(); }
   public void hangUp() { curState.hangUp(); }
   public void disconnect() { curState.disconnect(); }

   //State Machine Implementation
   public interface State {
      void incomingCall(String info);
      void pickUp();
      void hangUp();
      void disconnect();
   }
   class Idle implements State {
      public void incomingCall(String info) {
         display.displayCallInfo(info);
         ringer.ring();
         curState = waiting;
      }
      void pickUp() { /*do nothing*/ }
      void hangUp() { /*do nothing*/ }
      void disconnect() { /*do nothing*/ }
   } //other states follow the same approach..
}
public class Ringer() {
   public void ring() { /*ringing logic*/ }
}
public class Display() {
   public void displayCallInfo(String info)
      { /*display logic*/ }
}
```

```
@Aspect
public class NotifyCallWaiting extends MAspect {
   @Around("execution(public * ReceiveACall.Caller.*(..))"
      +" || execution(public * ReceiveACall.Phone.*( .)}"
      + ... /*all base classes referenced by the aspect*/)
   public void crosscut(JoinPoint jp) {
      if(enabled == true)
         this.weave(jp);
      else
         jp.proceed();
   }/*. .
}
```

```
@Mixin("within(public * ReceiveACall.Phone)")
public class Phone extends PeerClass {
   //initialization code...
      public void incomingCall(String info) {
         curState.incomingCall(info); }
      public void oK() { curState.oK(); }

   //State Machine Implementation
   interface State
      { void incomingCall(String info); void OK(); }
   @Mixin("within(public ReceiveACall.Phone$OnCall)")
   class OnCall extends PeerState implements State {
      void incomingCall(String info){
         display.displayCallInfo(info);
         setCurState(waitingForHoldPrompt);
      }
      void OK() {/*do nothing*/}
   }
   class WaitingForHoldPrompt extends PeerState implements State {
      void OK(){
         caller.putOnHold();    //instance of NotifyCallWaiting.Caller
         setCurState(OnCall);
      }
      void incomingCall(String info) {/*do nothing*/}
} // other mixins follow the same approach..
```

Fig. 18. Code Generated for the Cell Phone Example

8   Evaluation and Discussion

This section presents a preliminary evaluation of MATA. In [24], the authors argue that an aspect composition language should satisfy a number of basic requirements. (The arguments made in [24] specifically address aspect-oriented requirements engineering but the discussion generalizes to modeling). We include five of these requirements here and assess whether MATA satisfies them. According to [24], an aspect composition language should aim to be:

1)   **Environment-friendly.** A composition language should allow an aspect to be defined without requiring changes to the base model. In particular, the base should not need to be structured or designed in a particular way to support the aspect. This is a special case of obliviousness. If a composition language is very limited in expressiveness, for example, it might require the base to be structured in a particular way. The base would still be oblivious to the aspect, in the sense that it does not expose any aspect-specific interfaces, but the composition could only take place under certain design restrictions applied to the base. In the same way, an aspect should not need to be written in a special way so that it can be composed with the base.

2) **Scalable.** A composition language should scale to large industrial models.
3) **Familiar.** In order to ease adoption of the composition language, it should already be familiar to model developers.
4) **Formal.** The composition technique should be as formal as possible without the formalism becoming a barrier in practice.
5) **Exhaustive.** Models may be composed in many different, complex, and un-expected ways. A composition technique must be exhaustive in that it should provide the means to express all desired compositions. For example, for composing sequence diagrams, composition rules should cover not just se-quences and alternatives (i.e. before/after/around) but also concurrency, loops, and interleaving.

We now assess how MATA performs against these criteria. We will focus in this pa-per on exhaustiveness and will present the results of a small empirical study that suggest that (1) MATA is more exhaustive than competing approaches and (2) that exhaustiveness is required in practical examples. First, however, we will briefly discuss the other requirements. Scientific studies have not yet been undertaken for these.

8.1 Environment-Friendliness

Regarding the first requirement, MATA clearly satisfies it because MATA allows any change to the base model. Hence, any design decisions in the base could ultimately be modified. This is in contrast to other approaches in which only a selection of prede-fined model elements are allowed to be joinpoints. Therefore, it might be difficult or impossible to modify base elements not in this predefined selection. In Sect. 2, we saw an example where approaches based on AspectJ might be able to define a compo-sition but would do so in a non-optimal way because either the aspect or the base model would have to be broken into fragments, that is, they would have to be written in a particular way to support the composition. The treatment of this example using MATA does not require such decomposition.

As noted above, this criterion is a special case of obliviousness. Recently, a num-ber of authors [25, 26] have argued that full obliviousness is not desirable and that programs should have well-defined interfaces for aspect composition (e.g. joinpoint interfaces). While this argument does not negate the points made in the previous paragraph, we broadly agree with this way of thinking and note that MATA could easily support such interfaces in the future. Currently, all model elements are accessi-ble as joinpoints, but these could potentially be limited by the user. The difference with previous approaches would be that the modeler, instead of the language designer, would have full control over which joinpoints to limit.

8.2 Scalability

This criterion is always difficult to provide evidence for. We have applied MATA in a variety of settings for reasonably large examples, which tends to suggest, at least ini-tially, that it is straightforward to specify aspects using MATA. The major application areas to which we have applied MATA are as follows:

1. *Modeling Software Product Lines.* Jayaraman et al. [27] report on how MATA was used to model features as aspects in software product line development. Each feature is represented as a model slice as an increment over other features. Critical pair analysis was applied to detect feature interactions. As part of this work, Jayaraman et al. took an existing product line–namely, the microwave oven product line from Gomaa's book [28]– and modeled it using MATA.

2. *Maintaining the Separation of Use Cases throughout the Modeling Process using the technique in [6].* We conducted an experiment to refactor a number of student design solutions into an aspect-oriented MATA design –see Sect. 8.5 for details.

3. *Modeling Security Requirements as Aspects.* We have applied MATA to the problem of modeling security concerns during requirements engineering. In particular, security use cases were modeled as MATA sequence diagrams and were composed with sequence diagrams for the base use cases. This approach has been conducted on a number of case studies including an electronic voting system [29] and requirements for a positive train control system [30] under consideration by the Federal Railroad Administration.

These case studies lend evidence that MATA can be used in practice. For larger industrial models, there is, of course, an efficiency question regarding both the graph transformation composition mechanism and critical pair analysis. For both of these, MATA relies on AGG's implementation. In our experience, we have found that composition is very efficient. Critical pair analysis, however, can take time. The efficiency depends on the complexity of the metamodel for the diagram being analyzed. For class diagrams, critical pair analysis generally takes only a few seconds. For state diagrams, it can take a few minutes on large examples. For sequence diagrams, it has taken up to one hour in our most complex case study. This is because the interaction metamodel for UML is very complex. In fact, we have made a number of simplifications to the metamodel to allow us to translate it into a type graph in AGG that allows relatively efficient analysis. This does mean that not all of the modeling elements in sequence diagrams are currently supported by MATA. We consider it a future research question to develop an efficient analyzer for large UML models. The work presented here provides evidence that the analysis would be useful but further work is required on a more efficient implementation. In particular, critical pair analysis in AGG is a very general implementation and it may be that it can be specialized for the specific tasks that MATA takes care of, meaning that the efficiency could be improved.

8.3 Familiarity

For MATA, familiarity means that the MATA language should be as close to UML as possible. Graph transformations are traditionally written over the abstract syntax of a modeling language because this is the most general approach. However, in MATA, aspects (which are graph rules) are written in concrete syntax with a small number of extensions to support sequence pointcuts. The use of UML's concrete syntax makes MATA broadly applicable because no experience with metamodeling is required.

8.4 Formality

Since MATA is based on graph transformations, it is founded on a strong formal foot-ing. The application of critical pair analysis is possible because of this foundation.

8.5 Exhaustiveness

This is the main criterion considered in this paper. As discussed in Sect. 1, there have been two types of approaches to AOM. The first is to use a generic merge algorithm (that can be tailored) to compose an aspect and a base model. The second is to reuse and adapt the joinpoint model and advices from AspectJ. Henceforth, we will refer to the first approach as GM (for generic merge) and the second as AJ.

MATA is more exhaustive than either GM or AJ because any model element can be a joinpoint and any model element can be an advice. However, the question remains whether the additional expressiveness is actually required in practice. To answer this question, we undertook an investigation of existing design solutions to see which kinds of compositions are needed in practice. Our experiment attempted to answer the follow-ing question: In practical examples, are model composition mechanisms like GM or AJ enough or is more expressiveness needed? The investigation was undertaken for the use case slice technique of Jacobson and Ng [6]. Use case slices are a way of maintaining a use case-based decomposition throughout the development lifecycle. As an example, for state diagrams, this means that each use case maintains its own state diagram and these state diagrams are composed during late design or implementation to obtain the overall design.

In [6], Jacobson and Ng do not adequately address how to compose use case slices during design. Their approach is to apply AspectJ-like composition operators. The hypothesis of this paper is that such operators are not expressive enough. To test this hypothesis, we examined existing UML designs, refactored those designs to reflect the use case slice technique of Jacobson and Ng, and then investigated the level of expres-siveness required to compose designs from different use case slices. Because of the availability of the models, we chose to study seven student team design solutions, each expressed in UML consisting of use cases, class diagrams, interaction diagrams, and state diagrams. Only the use cases and state diagrams were considered in the study, and we focused on compositions of state diagrams from different use case slices.

Projects were conducted by teams of three to four students. Each of the seven pro-jects tackled the same problem statement using the same set of use cases. The scale of the student solutions is clearly not industrial in size and the results offered here are meant to be just the first step.

Based on an analysis of the compositions required in the state-dependent use case slices, we identified four categories of composition that occurred.

C1: One-to-One State Matching. The first category includes model compositions that can be expressed using simple matching of states. In other words, for two state diagrams, $S1$ and $S2$, with state sets $\Sigma1$ and $\Sigma2$, the composed state diagram $S1 \bullet S2$, can be obtained by defining a one-to-one mapping $\theta: \Sigma1 \rightarrow \Sigma2$. Figure 19(a) gives an example. In the student solutions, this case occurred typically when two use cases defined state diagrams that were joined together into a loop.

C2: Many-to-many state matching. This category is an extension of the previous one whereby states in the two state diagrams have a many-to-many relationship, i.e. $\theta(\sigma)$ is a set for any state σ. This allows a much richer form of composition. In particular, it allows for the creation of composite states (see Fig. 19(b)).

C3: State diagram refactoring. In this category, one or more of the state diagrams must be refactored to enable composition to take place. In other words, one state diagram cannot be inserted in its entirety into the other. Rather, it must be broken up before being inserted in multiple places. This type cannot be handled by state matching because matching cannot refactor a state diagram. Figure 19(c) illustrates this.

C4: State diagram refinement. In this type of composition, additional behavior (i.e. states and transitions) must be added when composition takes place. Clearly, state matching does not apply because state matching cannot refine behavior. This type of composition is necessary in cases where two use case slices have been developed independently but where there are dependencies between the slices that must be resolved when the slices are composed. A typical example concerns access to data. If a single use case slice reads from a data object, then no data access synchronization is required. However, if another use case slice writes to this data object, when the two use case slices are composed, an access synchronization mechanism such as mutual exclusion must be added. Figure 19(d) gives an example.

Based on the student design solutions, we found that all four categories of composition occur for use case slice development. The relative frequency for the four categories was as follows: 13%, 39%, 46% and 2%.

The GM approach supports only category C1 although it can be easily extended to support C2 (as was done in [31]). It does not support categories C3 and C4.

The AJ approach does not support C2 since, for example, composite states cannot be wrapped around multiple base states simply using before/after/around. The AJ approach partially supports categories C3--C4. In some cases, a composition of these types requires container model elements to be wrapped around existing elements–see Fig. 19(d), for instance. AJ does not support this. In some cases, especially for

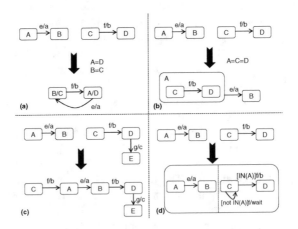

Fig. 19. Composition Categories

category C1, quite complex compositions occur that could be specified by AJ, but the aspect would have to be first refactored into multiple fragments, each of which is then inserted at a different place in the base. We view this as a non-optimal approach to composition because it involves representing fragments of an aspect model separately, which leads to problems in reusability and readability. Finally, in other cases, AJ cannot make a distinction between different kinds of composition. As an example, in Fig. 19(c), inserting the LHS state diagram **after** *f/b* could have two possible results: either stay in state *B* or go to state *D*. With AJ, it is not generally possible to make such a distinction.

MATA supports all categories because the entire state machine diagram syntax is available. For example, two use case slices can be merged in parallel using UML orthogonal regions. The results of the investigation reveal that, at least for use case slice composition, a greater degree of expressiveness is required in practice. Further investigation is required, of course, to see if these results are true for other aspect-oriented software development methods.

9 Related Work

There is a large body of work on AOM, although much of this has been restricted to structural models. Work of note that considers behavioral models is the Motorola WEAVR tool for state machines [5], Song et al.'s work on weaving security aspects into sequence diagrams [32], and Klein et al.'s work on semantic composition for interaction diagrams [33]. The WEAVR tool considers actions in state machines as joinpoints and uses "around" advices to weave in aspect state machines. WEAVR is the first commercially available aspect modeling tool but focuses only on state machines. In addition, it is tailored toward SDL state machines and concentrates on executable modeling and so is more suited to detailed design rather than earlier analysis and design phases.

There has been some work that composes aspect sequence diagrams. Song et al. work [32] has only a very limited set of composition operators and does not provide tool support. However, it does address how to verify the result of the composition by annotating models with OCL expressions, which could then be checked against the composed models. However, the work appears to be in its early stages. Reddy et al. [34] compose aspect sequence diagrams by using special tags that allow an aspect to be broken into pieces and then inserted at different points in the base–for example, at the beginning, in the middle, or at the end of the base messages. Whilst interesting, the MATA approach is more general and subsumes these operators. Indeed, earlier work by some of the authors of this paper considered composition of sequence diagrams using a limited set of composition operators [35]. This work has also been subsumed by MATA. Klein and Kienzle [36] describe a case study of composing aspect sequence diagrams. In this approach, one sequence diagram describes the pointcut and another describes the advice. The paper presents a case study using the semantic composition of scenarios described in [33]. The latter is important work that goes beyond syntactic mechanisms for defining pointcuts but instead relies on the semantics of the modeling language for matching an aspect. This reduces, to some extent, the fragile pointcut problem for aspect sequence diagrams but does incur a performance overhead. Such techniques could potentially be incorporated into MATA.

Other work on AOM includes, of course, Theme/UML [3]. Theme/UML is an example of the generic matching approach considered in Sect. 8 and suffers the limitations in expressiveness noted there. Katara and Katz [37] provide an approach for AOM of sequence and state diagrams based on superimposition. This is quite similar to MATA in that aspects are defined as increments over other models (either the base or other aspects). However, Katara and Katz [37] does not support a fully-fledged pattern language for defining pointcuts, which limits the quantification possible. Although Katara and Katz do give consideration to identifying dependencies between aspects, these dependencies must be found manually and documented on a so-called concern diagram. Indeed, MATA can be thought of as providing automated support for developing and/or validating such a concern diagram.

Generic aspects can be seen as a kind of design pattern. Hence, work on instantiating design patterns and applying aspect models is closely related. Indeed, there has been some work on automatically instantiating generic descriptions of design patterns [38, 39] and using such techniques in AOM [31, 40].

MATA views aspect composition simply as model transformation. This is a point of view that has also been noted by others. A general discussion of the similarities of model composition and model transformation is presented in [41]. One interesting point described there, and discussed elsewhere, is that aspect composition could either be specified by a generic model transformation language or by a dedicated aspect composition language, or indeed that there is a spectrum of possibilities lying in between. MATA tends toward the use of a generic model transformation language but tailors this to ensure familiarity of the language to modelers. In this sense, it is different than using a completely general transformation language, such as the one based on QVT, but retains the power and flexibility of a generic transformation language. Dedicated aspect composition languages risk sacrificing expressiveness because a limited number of composition operators would be provided. For example, France et al. [42] provide such a limited number of matching and composition operators but the user may override these if necessary, or indeed define new operators. However, this requires programming skills. MATA brings flexible composition without requiring any knowledge of programming or the need to understand the code in an existing composition framework. France et al. [42] is also limited to class diagrams. It is not clear how these techniques would extend to behavioral models.

MATA provides two key contributions to AOM. First, is the support for detecting aspect interactions. Second, it supports sequence pointcuts. To date, there has been limited support for detecting aspect interactions in AOM. Aspect interactions are a well-recognized problem but research has tended to focus on how to document interactions rather than uncover them automatically (cf. [37, 43--45]). The only known work is [46], which translates aspect UML models into Alloy so that they can be verified. This approach does not consider behavioral diagrams but requires pre/post-conditions to specify operations on class diagrams. Furthermore, it is more of a general verification approach not specifically geared toward interactions. This means that it could potentially uncover more semantic interactions (which MATA cannot) but at the cost of a more expensive analysis. At the programming level, there has been research on detecting interactions using static analysis [47, 48].

Although expressive pointcut mechanisms, such as sequence pointcuts, have been considered for AOP [12], to the authors' knowledge, this paper is the first work to bring expressive pointcuts to behavioral models. Related work that is closest to ours is joinpoint designation diagrams (JPDDs) [13]. JPDDs are similar to defining patterns using graph rules. Something similar to sequence pointcuts can be defined but the advices are limited to before/after/around. Furthermore, the advantage of using graph rules is the existence of formal analysis techniques. In addition, JPDDs focus on defining joinpoints and are not so much concerned with composition. MATA provides a full composition tool in which very expressive composition relationships can be specified. This is not possible with JPDDs.

This paper considers joinpoints to be static in the sense that the runtime semantics of behavioral diagrams is not taken into consideration. Dynamic joinpoints can also be defined for behavioral models, such as state diagrams [9]. However, since currently models are most commonly used for communication and documentation, and are not necessarily executed, static joinpoints are perhaps more useful in current modeling practices. It would be interesting to extend MATA to dynamic joinpoints, however.

More generally, model composition has been addressed outside of the AOSD community. In particular, [49] investigates how to merge state machines using composition relationships and category theory. This is similar in many respects to our work but has a different goal in that it addresses how to reconcile models produced by different development teams.

10   Conclusion and Further Work

This paper has presented a new approach for AOM wherein aspect composition is considered to be simply a special case of model transformation. A language and tool, MATA, has been presented, which allows modelers to maintain aspect models separately, detect structural interactions between aspects automatically, and compose a chosen set of aspects automatically with a set of base models. The approach goes beyond previous work in that:

- MATA provides a unified approach to aspect model composition. Any modeling language with a well-defined metamodel can be handled in the same way. Currently, UML class, sequence, and state diagrams are supported, but extensions to other modeling languages would be straightforward and would provide the same capabilities in detecting interactions and automating composition.
- MATA provides a richer aspect composition language. Joinpoints are defined by an expressive pattern language and any base model element (or combination of elements) can be a pointcut. In particular, MATA provides the first full support for sequence pointcuts at the aspect modeling level.

MATA is supported by a tool built on top of IBM's Rational Software Modeler. It has been applied in a range of application areas, including security modeling, software product lines, and modeling of use case slices.

There are a number of interesting avenues for further work that would build upon MATA. First, base models in MATA are currently completely open, in the sense that any base model elements can be accessed by aspect models. This has shown to be absolutely essential in some application areas. In particular, for the software product line method PLUS [28], which can be handled in MATA by modeling features as aspects, models of non-kernel features can be added to models of the kernel in many and varied different ways. It would not have been possible to restrict the joinpoint model and still allow the case studies from [28] to be modeled faithfully.

However, it may be desirable for other application areas to restrict the joinpoint model so that only certain base model elements can be affected by an aspect. This kind of approach would potentially support improved modular reasoning for aspects. MATA could support such a technique easily as interfaces could be designed on top of the existing language. In any case, we feel that the modeler should be in control of whether or not full access is required by the aspects and it is not up to the language designer to restrict the joinpoint model for him/her.

Another area where MATA could potentially be extended is to provide domain-specific composition operators, built on top of the existing language. A key contribution of this paper is that MATA allows all modeling languages to be handled in a uniform way. However, the current composition operators in MATA are quite low level because they are at the same level as the underlying modeling language. One could imagine defining more abstract operators, for example, in software architecture composition that would be then mapped down to MATA's operators. This would raise the level of discourse of aspect modelers but would retain the strong benefits of the MATA foundations. However, such a path should be taken with caution. A great deal of effort has already gone into language design for existing modeling languages and it is not completely clear that an additional layer of abstraction would be beneficial.

Along similar grounds, MATA's composition is purely syntactic currently. This means that aspect modelers define aspects based on the syntactic elements of the underlying modeling language. While this is in line with current practice in modeling, it would be interesting to investigate semantics-based composition techniques, similar to those developed for aspect-oriented requirements engineering languages [50]. This would allow modelers to specify aspects in terms of semantic concepts of the domain rather than syntactic modeling elements. For example, one might wish to define the pointcut of all model elements related to access control. The techniques in [50] rely on natural language processing techniques to extract semantic content from textual requirements documents and it is not clear how such an approach could be adapted to analysis and design models. However, it is certainly an open area of research that could provide fruitful solutions to the fragile pointcut problem in AOM.

The usability of the MATA composition language has not yet been fully tested. Although a number of realistic case studies have been undertaken, we have limited experience with real users. The intricacies of the propagation algorithm are such that it may be difficult to grasp for novices. However, use of propagation is always optional and the user may choose to explicitly provide stereotypes. So far, MATA provides no support for validating the composition of base and aspect. It is possible to get unexpected results if there are interactions between aspects that cannot be detected by critical pair analysis. A simple example is if two aspects each create an instance of the same class. Then the result will have two copies of this instance where only one may be desired. There may be lightweight techniques that can help with validating the composition. Another usability issue is in maintaining the generality of the aspects. Generic aspects should be designed where possible so that they can be reused. This is certainly easy to do in MATA because of the rich pattern-matching facilities. However, from a usability point of view, more research is required as to how to guide users to specify good (i.e. generically applicable) aspects.

One of the main points made in this paper is that aspect composition approaches based on generic match and merge algorithms–for example, those that merge model elements by name–are not very practical. This is a claim backed up by preliminary empirical evidence in Sect. 8.5. On the other hand, there may be some advantages in combining a MATA-like approach with these generic merge algorithms. Once again, this could provide a way of raising the level of composition abstraction in MATA. Care would need to be taken, however, to ensure that the problems of generic merge algorithms–that the results of composition are hard to predict and adapt–do not carry over to the MATA context.

Finally, we hope that the expressive composition mechanisms provided by MATA might have some consequences for AOP. Whilst modeling is different from programming, it seems that AOP could also benefit by more expressive pointcut languages or more expressive advices. We believe that the rich language available in MATA might offer some insights as to how such languages should be developed.

References

[1] Whittle, J., Moreira, A., Araújo, J., Rabbi, R., Jayaraman, P., Elkhodary, A.: An Expressive Aspect Composition Language for UML State Diagrams. In: Engels, G., Opdyke, B., Schmidt, D.C., Weil, F. (eds.) MODELS 2007. LNCS, vol. 4735, pp. 514–528. Springer, Heidelberg (2007)

[2] Whittle, J., Jayaraman, P.: MATA: A Tool for Aspect-Oriented Modeling based on Graph Transformation. In: Workshop on Aspect Oriented Modeling at the International MODELS Conference, Nashville, TN (2007)

[3] Clarke, S., Baniassad, E.: Aspect-Oriented Analysis and Design: The Theme Approach. Addison Wesley, Reading (2005)

[4] France, R., Ray, I., Georg, G., Ghosh, S.: Aspect-oriented approach to early design modeling. In: IEE Proceedings - Software, vol. 151, pp. 173–186 (2004)

[5] Cottenier, T., van den Berg, A., Elrad, T.: Motorola WEAVR: Model Weav-ing in a Large Industrial Context. In: Aspect-Oriented Software Development (AOSD), Vancouver, Canada (2007)

[6] Jacobson, I., Ng, P.-W.: Aspect Oriented Software Development with Use Cases. Addison-Wesley Professional, Reading (2004)

[7] Reddy, Y.R., Ghosh, S., France, R., Straw, G., Bieman, J., McEachen, N., Song, E., Georg, G.: Directives for Composing Aspect-Oriented Design Class Models. In: Rashid, A., Aksit, M. (eds.) Transactions on Aspect-Oriented Software Development I. LNCS, vol. 3880, pp. 75–105. Springer, Heidelberg (2006)

[8] Fleury, F., Baudry, B., France, R., Ghosh, S.: A Generic Approach for Automatic Model Composition. In: Workshop on Aspect Oriented Modeling at MODELS 2007 (2007)

[9] Zhang, G., Hölzl, M., Knapp, A.: Enhancing UML State Machines with Aspects. In: Engels, G., Opdyke, B., Schmidt, D.C., Weil, F. (eds.) MODELS 2007. LNCS, vol. 4735, pp. 529–543. Springer, Heidelberg (2007)

[10] Lopez-Herrejon, R., Batory, D.: Modeling Features in Aspect-Based Product Lines with Use Case Slices: An Exploratory Case Study. In: Kühne, T. (ed.) MoDELS 2006. LNCS, vol. 4364, pp. 6–16. Springer, Heidelberg (2007)

[11] Rashid, A.: Views, Aspects and Roles: Symphony or Random Noise? In: Panel Statement at Views, Aspects and Roles Workshop associated with ECOOP 2005 (2005)

[12] Douence, R., Fritz, T., Loriant, N., Menaud, J.-M., Segura-Devillechaise, M., Sudholt, M.: An Expressive Aspect Language for System Applications with Arachne. In: Aspect-Oriented Software Development (AOSD), Chicago, Illinois, pp. 27–38 (2005)

[13] Stein, D., Hanenberg, S., Unland, R.: Expressing Different Conceptual Models of Join Point Selections in Aspect-Oriented Design. In: Aspect-Oriented Software Development (AOSD), Bonn, Germany, pp. 15–26 (2006)

[14] Markovic, S., Baar, T.: Refactoring OCL Annotated UML Class Diagrams. In: Briand, L.C., Williams, C. (eds.) MoDELS 2005. LNCS, vol. 3713, pp. 280–294. Springer, Heidelberg (2005)

[15] de Micheaux, N.L., Rambaud, C.: Confluence for Graph Transformations. Theoretical Computer Science 154, 329–348 (1996)

[16] Wagner, R.: Developing Model Transformations with Fujaba. In: International Fujaba Days, Bayreuth, Germany, pp. 79–82 (2006)

[17] Balogh, A., Varro, D.: Advanced Model Transformation Language Constructs in the VIATRA2 Framework. In: ACM Symposium on Applied Computing (Model Transformation Track), Dijon, France, pp. 1280–1287 (2006)

[18] Boner, J., Vasseur, A.: Tutorial on AspectWerkz for Dynamic Aspect-Oriented Programming. In: Aspect Oriented Software Development (2004)

[19] Moreira, A., Rashid, A., Araújo, J.: A Multi-Dimensional Separation of Concerns in Requirements Engineering. In: International Conference on Requirements Engineering (RE), Paris, France, pp. 285–296 (2005)

[20] Rudolf, M.: Utilizing Constraint Satisfaction Techniques for Efficient Graph Pattern Matching. In: Ehrig, H., Engels, G., Kreowski, H.-J., Rozenberg, G. (eds.) TAGT 1998. LNCS, vol. 1764, pp. 238–251. Springer, Heidelberg (2000)

[21] Taentzer, G.: AGG: A Graph Transformation Environment for Modeling and Validation of Software. In: Pfaltz, J.L., Nagl, M., Böhlen, B. (eds.) AGTIVE 2003. LNCS, vol. 3062, pp. 446–453. Springer, Heidelberg (2004)

[22] Jayaraman, P.: Interaction Verification and Model Composition in Product Lines Using MATA in Dept. of Information and Software Engineering. MS Thesis Fairfax, VA. George Mason University, USA (2007)

[23] Nicoara, A., Alonso, G.: Dynamic AOP with PROSE. In: International Workshop on Adaptive and Self-Managing Enterprise Applications at CAiSE, Porto, Portugal (2005)

[24] Mussbacher, G., Amyot, D., Whittle, J., Weiss, M.: Flexible and Expressive Composition Rules with Aspect-Oriented Use Case Maps (AoUCM). In: Moreira, A., Grundy, J. (eds.) Early Aspects Workshop 2007 and EACSL 2007. LNCS, vol. 4765, pp. 19–38. Springer, Heidelberg (2007)

[25] Griswold, W., Sullivan, K., Song, Y., Shonle, M., Tewari, N., Cai, Y., Rajan, H.: Modular Software Design with Crosscutting Interfaces. IEEE Software 23, 51–60 (2006)

[26] Aldrich, J.: Open Modules: Modular Reasoning about Advice. In: Black, A.P. (ed.) ECOOP 2005. LNCS, vol. 3586, pp. 144–168. Springer, Heidelberg (2005)

[27] Jayaraman, P., Whittle, J., Elkhodary, A., Gomaa, H.: Model Composition in Product Lines and Feature Interaction Detection using Critical Pair Analysis. In: Engels, G., Opdyke, B., Schmidt, D.C., Weil, F. (eds.) MODELS 2007. LNCS, vol. 4735, pp. 151–165. Springer, Heidelberg (2007)

[28] Gomaa, H.: Designing Software Product Lines with UML: From Use Cases to Pattern-based Software Architectures. Addison-Wesley Object Technology Series (2005)

[29] Kohno, T., Stubblefield, A., Rubin, A., Wallach, D.: Analysis of an Electronic Voting System. In: IEEE Symposium on Security and Privacy, pp. 27–40. IEEE Computer Society Press, Los Alamitos (2004)

[30] Hartong, M., Goel, R., Wijesekera, D.: Use Misuse Case Driven Forensic Analysis of Positive Train Control: A Preliminary Study. In: 2nd IFIP WG 11.9 International Conference on Digital Forensics, Orlando, FL

[31] Araújo, J., Whittle, J., Kim, D.-K.: Modeling and Composing Scenario-Based Requirements with Aspects. In: International Conference on Requirements Engineering, Kyoto, Japan, pp. 58–67 (2004)

[32] Song, E., Reddy, R., France, R.B., Ray, I., Georg, G., Alexander, R.: Verifiable Composition of Access Control and Application Features. In: ACM Symposium on Access Control Models and Technologies (SACMAT), Stockholm, Sweden, pp. 120–129 (2005)

[33] Klein, J., Helouet, L., Jézéquel, J.-M.: Semantic-Based Weaving of Scenarios. In: Aspect-Oriented Software Development (AOSD), Vancouver, Canada, pp. 27–38 (2006)

[34] Reddy, R., Solberg, A., France, R., Ghosh, S.: Composing Sequence Models Using Tags. In: Aspect Oriented Modeling Workshop at MODELS 2006 (2006)

[35] Whittle, J., Araújo, J.: Scenario Modelling with Aspects. In: IEE Proceedings - Software, August 2004, vol. 151, pp. 157–172 (2004)

[36] Klein, J., Kienzle, J.: Reusable Aspect Models. In: Aspect Oriented Modeling Workshop at MODELS 2007 (2007)

[37] Katara, M., Katz, S.: Architectural Views of Aspects. In: Aspect-Oriented Software Development (AOSD), Boston, Massachusetts, pp. 1–10 (2003)

[38] Kim, D.-K.: Evaluating Conformance of UML Models to Design Patterns. In: International Conference on the Engineering of Complex Computer Systems (ICECCS), Shanghai, China, pp. 30–31 (2005)

[39] Kim, D.-K., Whittle, J.: Generating UML Models from Domain Patterns. In: Software Engineering Research, Management and Applications, pp. 166–173 (2005)

[40] Kim, D.K.: A Pattern-Based Technique for Developing UML Models of Access Control Systems. In: 30th Annual International Computer Software and Applications Conference (COMPSAC), Chicago, IL, pp. 317–324 (2006)

[41] Baudry, B., Fleurey, F., France, R., Reddy, R.: Exploring the Relationship between Model Composition and Model Transformation. In: Aspect Oriented Modeling Workshop at MODELS 2005 (2005)

[42] France, R., Fleurey, F., Reddy, R., Baudry, B., Ghosh, S.: Providing Support for Model Composition in Metamodels. In: IEEE International EDOC Conference, Annapolis, Maryland (2007)

[43] Zhang, J., Cottenier, T., van den Berg, A., Gray, J.: Aspect Interference and Composition in the Motorola Aspect-Oriented Modeling Weaver. In: Aspect Oriented Modeling Workshop at MODELS 2006 (2006)

[44] Sanen, F., Loughran, N., Rashid, A., Nedos, A., Jackson, A., Clarke, S., Truyen, E., Joosen, W.: Classifying and Documenting Aspect Interactions. In: Workshop on Aspects, Components and Patterns for Infrastructure Software at AOSD, Bonn, Germany (2006)

[45] Bakre, S., Elrad, T.: Scenario-based Resolution of Aspect Interactions with Aspect Interaction Charts. In: Aspect-Oriented Software Development, Vancouver, Canada, pp. 1–6 (2007)

[46] Mostefaoui, F., Vachon, J.: Design-level Detection of Interactions in Aspect-UML Models using Alloy. Journal of Object Technology 6, 137–165 (2007)

[47] Douence, R., Fradet, P., Südholt, M.: A Framework for the Detection and Resolution of Aspect Interactions. In: Generative Programming and Component Engineering, Pittsburgh, PA, pp. 173–188 (2002)

[48] Douence, R., Fradet, P., Südholt, M.: Composition, reuse and interaction analysis of stateful aspects. In: Aspect Oriented Software Development, pp. 141–150 (2004)

[49] Nejati, S., Sabetzadeh, M., Chechik, M., Easterbrook, S., Zave, P.: Matching and Merging of Statecharts Specifications. In: International Conference on Software Engineering, pp. 54–64 (2007)

[50] Chitchyan, R., Rashid, A., Rayson, P., Waters, R.: Semantics-Based Com-position for Aspect-Oriented Requirements Engineering. In: Aspect-Oriented Software Development (AOSD), Vancouver, Canada, pp. 36–48 (2007)

Appendix

This appendix describes how MATA performs the conversion from a model in concrete syntax to a type graph in AGG. This conversion process is performed automatically.

MATA considers a subset of the UML metamodel (we do not yet consider the full UML2 metamodel) and maps it to a corresponding type graph. The type graph represents the metamodel in the AGG syntax. In the current scope, the chosen UML metamodel subset contains commonly used modeling elements of class diagrams, sequence diagrams, and state machines. MATA converts a base model into an AGG graph and converts an aspect model into an AGG graph rule.

To illustrate, we present a simple example for a family of printers. A printer will be modeled as the base and an optional feature, a sheet rotator (which allows printing on both sides of a sheet), will be modeled as an aspect.

Class Diagrams

The base model contains an assembly of an abstract controller object called Printer. The Printer aggregates PrintRoller and PrintNozzle objects. Figure 20 shows the class diagram of the Printer base model in concrete UML syntax. The graph metamodel used to represent the class diagram is shown in Fig. 21. The corresponding host graph of the Printer base model is shown in Fig. 22. The class diagram concepts supported by MATA are:

1. Class/Interface–A class or an interface is represented by a node of type Classifier. The Type attribute indicates whether the node is a class or an interface. Additional attributes such as Name and Visibility indicate the name and visibility of the element. The attribute isAbstract is used to represent an abstract class.

    a. Property–A graph node of type Attribute represents properties of classes and interfaces. These nodes are connected to the owning Classifier nodes via an edge of type Owns. The attributes Name,

Visibility, isStatic, Lower and Upper indicate the name, visibility, static nature, lower and upper bound of the attribute, respectively.

b. Operation–A graph node of type Operation represents operations supported by classes and interfaces. An operation node is connected to the owning classifier node via an edge of type Owns. The attributes Name, Visibility, isAbstract, and isStatic indicate the name, visibility, abstract, and static nature of the operation, respectively.

2. Generalization–An edge of type Extends represents the generalization relationship between two classes or interfaces. The edge connects the corresponding nodes of type classifier.

3. Realization–An edge of type Implements represents the realization of an interface by a class. In the graph metamodel, this edge connects a classifier of type interface to a classifier of type class.

4. Association/Composition/Aggregation–An edge of type Association represents a relationship between two classifiers. Table 4 explains the representation of different kinds of relationships such as associations, compositions, and aggregations as well as other association-related attributes.

Fig. 20. Class diagram for Printer Kernel feature

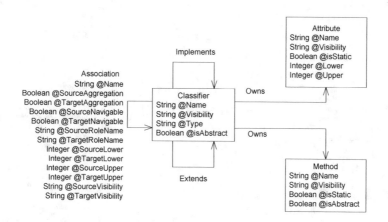

Fig. 21. Graph metamodel for class diagram (in AGG syntax: e.g. String @Name means Name is of type String)

Table 4. Graph metamodel attributes of an Association

Attribute	Description
SourceAggregation	Represents the aggregation kind of the source classifier of the association.
TargetAggregation	Represents the aggregation kind of the target classifier of the association.
SourceRoleName	Represents the name of the source role of the association.
TargetRoleName	Represents the name of the target role of the association.
SourceLower	Represents the lower bound of the source of the association.
TargetLower	Represents the lower bound of the target of the association.
SourceUpper	Represents the upper bound of the source of the association.
TargetUpper	Represents the upper bound of the target of the association.
SourceVisibility	Represents the visibility of the source of the association.
TargetVisibility	Represents the visibility of the target of the association.

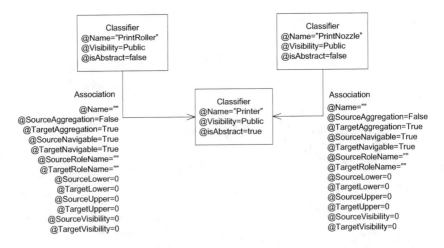

Fig. 22. Host graph for Printer Kernel class diagram

Sequence Diagram

The Printer object receives a print command from an external user and sends a message to the PrintRoller to lift a sheet from an external paper tray. Then, it sends a message to the PrintNozzle to start printing on the sheet and when the sheet is printed, the PrintRoller ejects the sheet. The process repeats if the print job requires more sheets.

Figure 23 shows the sequence diagram of the Printer Kernel in concrete UML syntax. The graph metamodel used to represent the sequence diagram is shown in Fig. 24. The corresponding host graph of the Printer Kernel feature is shown in Fig. 25. The sequence diagram related concepts supported by MATA are

1. Interaction–An interaction of type sequence diagram is represented by a node of type Sequence Diagram.

2. OccurrenceSpecification/GeneralOrdering–An OccurrenceSpecification is represented by a node of type Sequencer. The after association of GeneralOrdering is represented by an edge of type Next between two Sequencer nodes. These nodes are also used to indicate the start and end of interaction diagrams, interaction fragments and interaction operands. For example, the start and end of an interaction are represented individually by two sequencer nodes that are connected to the Sequence Diagram node by edges of start and end type, respectively.

3. Lifeline–The lifeline of a participant in a sequence diagram is represented by a node of type Class. The name of the lifeline is preserved by the Name attribute of the node. MATA does not support explicit creation or destruction of a lifeline and assumes a lifeline to exist throughout the interaction diagram.

4. CombinedFragment–A fragment is represented by a node of type Fragment.

    a. InteractionOperator–The interaction operator of a fragment is preserved by the Operator attribute of the node representing the fragment.

    b. InteractionConstraint–A constraint applied on a fragment is preserved by the Guard attribute of the node representing the fragment.

    c. Interaction operand–Each operand of a fragment is represented by a node of type Operand.

5. Complete Asynchronous Message–Complete asynchronous messages are represented using nodes of type Message. The name of the asynchronous message is preserved by the Name attribute of the Message node. The sending and receiving lifelines of a message are indicated by edges of type Receiver and Sender from the Message node to the class nodes, respectively.

6. EventOccurrence (Send/Receive)–The receive and send events of a message are represented individually by sequencer nodes connected by an edge of type Next.

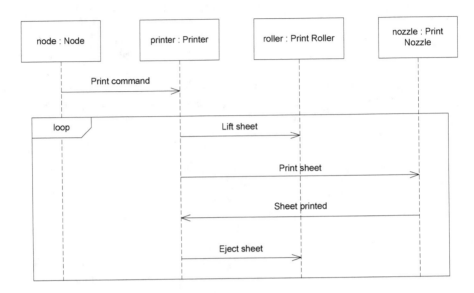

Fig. 23. Sequence diagram for Printer Kernel feature

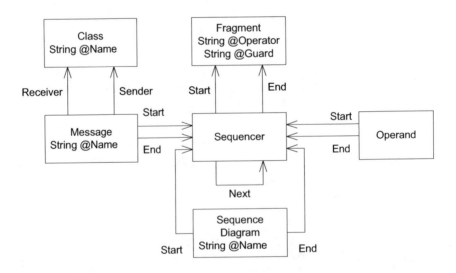

Fig. 24. Graph metamodel for sequence diagram

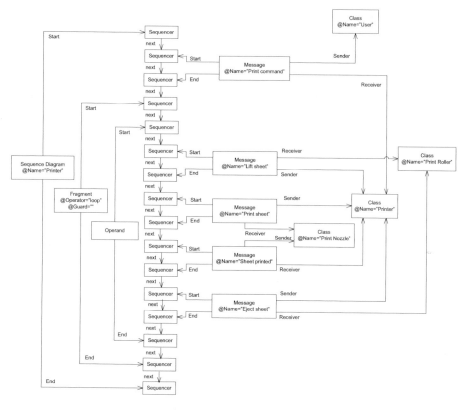

Fig. 25. Host graph of Printer Kernel sequence diagram

MATA Syntax

MATA translates a UML model annotated with the MATA stereotypes to a graph rule. The procedure for generating the graph rules is as follows:

1. Instantiate a graph rule with a left and a right graph.
2. For each element in the source model:
   2.1. If the element is stereotyped with <<create>>, create a graph node and add the node to the right graph.
   2.2. If the element is stereotyped with <<delete>>, create a graph node and add the node to the left graph.
   2.3. If the element is stereotyped with <context>>, create two graph nodes and add one to the left graph and the other to the right graph. Add mapping information between the nodes.
   2.4. If the element is not associated with any stereotype:

2.4.1.   If the element is a nearest neighbor of another element in the model then apply the stereotype of the neighbor to the element and repeat step 2. For example, if a class element is stereotyped with <<create>> or <<delete>> then the same stereotype is implicitly applied to all attributes and methods that are owned by the class.

2.4.2.   Else, create two graph nodes and add one to the left graph and the other to the right graph. Add mapping information between the nodes.

Sheet rotator Aspect

The sheet rotator aspect adds flip sheet functionality to the PrintRoller object. The static view transformation for this rule, called AddFlipMethod, is shown using concrete syntax and graph syntax in Figs. 26 and 27, respectively.

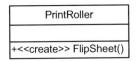

Fig. 26. Concrete syntax for rule AddFlipMethod

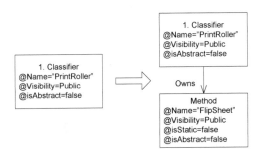

Fig. 27. Graph syntax for rule AddFlipMethod

This functionality is invoked only if one side of the sheet has been printed and the print job requires more sheets. The Printer object adds an alternate flip sheet message to an existing eject sheet message. The printer sends the lift sheet message only if the sheet has been ejected or if the first sheet is being printed. Two separate transformations are used to execute these changes. The first rule to add an alternate flip sheet message is called AddFlipMessage and is shown using UML concrete syntax and graph syntax in Figs. 28 and 29, respectively. The second rule to make the lift sheet message optional is called MakeLiftOptional and is not shown here.

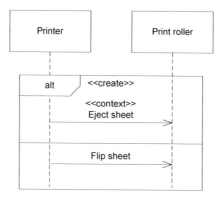

Fig. 28. Concrete syntax for rule AddFlipMessage

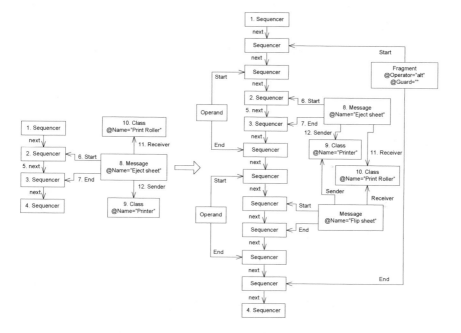

Fig. 29. Graph syntax for rule AddFlipMessage

Model-Driven Theme/UML

Andrew Carton, Cormac Driver, Andrew Jackson, and Siobhán Clarke

Distributed Systems Group,
Department of Computer Science and Statistics,
Trinity College Dublin, Ireland
{firstname.lastname}@cs.tcd.ie

Abstract. Theme/UML is an existing approach to aspect-oriented modelling that supports the modularisation and composition of concerns, including crosscutting ones, in design. To date, its lack of integration with model-driven engineering (MDE) techniques has limited its benefits across the development lifecycle. Here, we describe our work on facilitating the use of Theme/UML as part of an MDE process. We have developed a transformation tool that adopts model-driven architecture (MDA) standards. It defines a concern composition mechanism, implemented as a model transformation, to support the enhanced modularisation features of Theme/UML. We evaluate our approach by applying it to the development of mobile, context-aware applications-an application area characterised by many non-functional requirements that manifest themselves as crosscutting concerns.

1 Introduction

Aspect-oriented software development (AOSD) extends the decomposition and composition mechanisms of existing software development paradigms in order to more effectively modularise interdependent concerns [5]. Theme/UML is part of the broader Theme approach to aspect-oriented analysis and design [1], extending standard UML to explicitly support both the modularisation and composition of concerns in design.

We recently conducted an investigation into the application of Theme/UML to the design of mobile, context-aware applications, which motivated much of the work described in this paper. Mobile, context-aware computing is a computing paradigm in which applications can discover and take advantage of contextual information such as user location, time of day, nearby people/computing devices and user activity [26]. Such applications can run on a range of diverse computing platforms and in multiple deployment environments, from personal digital assistants and mobile phones running Java, to small embedded wearable devices supporting C. In specifying applications of this nature, software developers must consider non-functional mobility and context-awareness concerns that negatively impact software complexity and therefore make the use of Theme/UML appropriate. It emerged from our investigation that although Theme/UML can aid the modularisation of mobility and context-awareness concerns, the prevalence

S. Katz et al. (Eds.): Transactions on AOSD VI, LNCS 5560, pp. 238–266, 2009.
© Springer-Verlag Berlin Heidelberg 2009

of multiple target environments and the lack of support for automated model-to-code transformations restricted the contribution our designs made towards producing widely deployable solutions. This finding motivated extensions (with supporting tools) to the Theme/UML approach that reduce the effort required to progress from a single system model to multiple deployable applications derived from this model. A model-driven software engineering process was adopted to support the automatic generation of platform-specific models and code from a generic model, thereby addressing platform heterogeneity.

Model-driven engineering (MDE) is an approach to software development that emphasises the use of models as primary engineering artefacts. It addresses platform heterogeneity by abstracting platform-independent models and providing means to automatically transform these models to one or more specific target platforms. The model-driven approach, through architectural separation of concerns, promotes portability, interoperability and reusability [21].

In this paper, we present our work on integrating Theme/UML with an MDE process. We have developed a tool that supports the specification of platform-independent models with Theme/UML and subsequent automatic transformations to platform-specific models and code. This tool is compliant with the model-driven architecture (MDA) standards defined by the Object Management Group (OMG) [10], while retaining the general purpose and intention of the original Theme/UML semantics. We have defined an MDA process with a composition phase implemented as a model transformation, allowing developers to avail of the enhanced modularisation features in Theme/UML. Aspect-oriented platform-independent models, specified in Theme/UML, are automatically transformed to object-oriented platform-specific models and code, giving the developer powerful decomposition and composition capabilities at design time without tying them to an aspect-oriented platform. To demonstrate our approach, we implemented transformations to two mobile environments, J2ME and .NET CF. We conducted a case study-based evaluation by applying the tool to the implementation of a mobile, context-aware application with a number of non-functional requirements that manifest themselves as crosscutting concerns.

The remainder of this paper is as follows. Section 2 describes the model-driven Theme/UML tool from an implementation perspective, while Sect. 3 discusses the application development process it facilitates. Section 4 presents a case study of our approach as applied to the development of a mobile, context-aware application with crosscutting requirements. Section 5 discusses related work while Sect. 6 provides a summary of this paper and a brief overview of our continuation of this work.

2   Model-Driven Theme/UML: Implementation

In this section, we present the implementation of the model-driven Theme/UML tool. We first outline our initial design decisions and then describe the implementation phase. The section concludes with a discussion of the challenges and difficulties encountered.

2.1   Initial Design Decisions

Our initial design decisions concerned how best to integrate and implement Theme/UML with current MDA guidelines, technologies and tools. Theme/UML is defined as a meta-object facility (MOF)-based extension of the UML 1.3 beta R7 metamodel [11]. This version of the UML originated before the OMG updated their standards to conform to the MDA vision [22], currently at version 2.1.1. As such, this definition was not compatible with the current standards and conventions, and consequently hindered our objective to offer Theme/UML as an MDA solution. In order to achieve this objective, we investigated three strategies.

The first strategy involves extending the UML 2.1 metamodel. This is a heavy-weight solution that requires augmentation of the appropriate metaclasses and metarelationships [17] to support the Theme/UML extensions. However, porting Theme/UML to UML 2.1 proved prohibitively challenging, primarily because of the significant dissimilarity between the two versions of the UML metamodels. Furthermore, invasive metamodel changes to the UML preclude the use of standard UML tool support.

Next, we investigated the use of a marking[1] UML profile to support the expression of a composition specification, while using UML Package Merge to realise Theme/UML's composition semantics. As a UML Profile is a lightweight extension mechanism supported both at the modelling level and by the UML compliance levels[2], any compliant UML graphical tool would be adequate. The UML Package Merge is part of the UML metamodel that allows one package to be merged with another, accommodating the interoperability of tools by allowing a higher level of compliance to be merged with a lower level one. In Theme/UML, a `theme` is defined as an extension of a `package`; therefore UML Package Merge could potentially have been used to define Theme/UML's composition semantics by redefining the UML Package Merge at the metamodel level [13]. However, heavyweight metamodel extensions had been ruled out as impractical due to lack of tool support. Investigating Package Merge as a foundation for defining Theme/UML's composition semantics proved to be unsuccessful at the modelling level also, as it lacks the ability to support additional types [30]. Further evidence suggested that the Package Merge is not suitable for meta-model builders and the definition of transformations [29].

The third strategy, similar to the second, involved the definition of a marking UML Profile. The process involves marking a model to indicate the composition specification and then mapping this specification to an instance of a new composition metamodel. A composition metamodel defined in MOF can be used to indicate the structure and behaviour of Theme/UML's composition semantics. We decided that this strategy was more favourable than the others for two

---

[1] Marking is a technique that allows a set of elements in a UML model to be identified for transformation in a non-invasive way [19].

[2] UML is stratified into a number of horizontal layers of increasing capabilities called compliance levels. These are points at which a tool can claim compliance to the standard.

reasons. The first advantage is gained from the distinct separation of the graphical extensions in the UML and the definition of the composition semantics. The composition semantics can evolve independently from the graphical extensions by extending the composition metamodel. Likewise, if more expression is needed in the marking, only the marking profile and the mapping to the composition metamodel need to change. The second advantage relates to the difficulties of using UML Package Merge in defining the composition semantics, in which their structure and behaviour are expressed entirely in textual form in the UML standard. The use of a composition metamodel, in our opinion, better captures and illustrates these semantics in a more formal manner.

Apart from deciding how best to integrate Theme/UML with the MDA process, we had to decide on which, if any, third party tools to use. Given that we were working with a standard modelling language, we adopted a standard UML editor called MagicDraw[3]. This tool exports models in Eclipse Modelling Framework XMI format, a format commonly supported by MDA tools. For code generation, we adopted the openArchitectureWare (oAW)[4] model-driven generator framework, which aids the production of source code from XMI. The decision to adopt only standard tools and formats means that developers are free to use one of the many UML editors or source code generators that support XMI.

2.2   Implementation

The design process is separated into three distinct phases that relate to the activity of the designer during that phase-the modelling phase, the composition phase and the transformation phase. Figure 1 illustrates the mapping specifications and definitions that enclose each phase with a description of their implementing technologies parenthesised beneath each.

Modelling Phase. Designers use Theme/UML (see Appendix A for more details) during the modelling phase to modularise application concerns. Two requirements had to be met in order to accomplish the implementation of our MDA strategy at this phase.

1. Theme/UML's composition semantics must be defined in the form of a marking profile.
2. A graphical UML tool is required that supports both the definition of a UML profile and the standard UML features that Theme/UML requires (i.e. Class and Interaction Diagrams).

The first requirement motivated the definition of a Theme/UML Marking Profile, illustrated in Fig. 2, that extends UML 2.1 and supports the designer in creating a composition specification. In this case, the marks guide the designer in creating a composition specification by decorating the UML elements

---

[3] MagicDraw 12.5, http://www.magicdraw.com

[4] openArchitectureWare, http://www.openarchitectureware.org

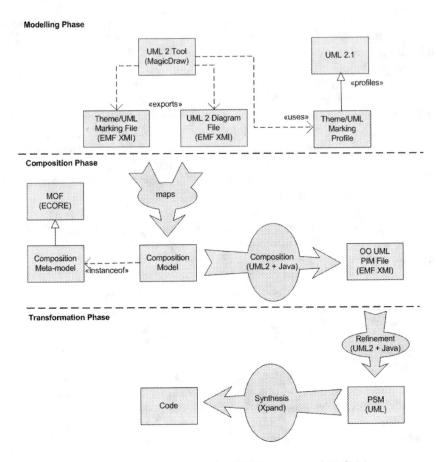

Fig. 1. Model-Driven Theme/UML Mappings and Definitions

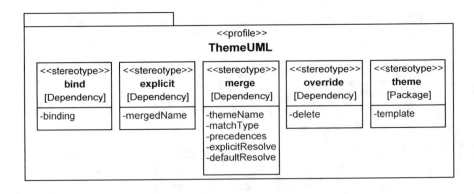

Fig. 2. Theme/UML Marking Profile

with stereotypes and tagged values from the Theme/UML Marking Profile. We use this lightweight extension mechanism to support extension of Theme/UML without requiring invasive changes at the UML metamodel level. There are five stereotypes indicated in the Theme/UML Marking Profile. A theme stereotype allows a UML Package to be marked to indicate that it may be used in a composition relationship. If the theme is to be designed as an aspect, then the tagged definition template indicates the string that represents the template parameters that trigger crosscutting behaviour. A merge stereotype is placed on a Dependency to indicate the themes involved in a merge composition relationship. The tagged definitions of this stereotype (themeName, matchType, precedences, explicitResolve and defaultResolve) can be applied on the stereotype to indicate the properties of the merge. The override stereotype can be placed on a Dependency and indicates an override composition relationship, while the tagged definition delete represents the elements to be deleted. A bind stereotype is applied to a Dependency and is constrained as a binary dependency between an aspect and base theme. The tagged definition binding represents the elements that instantiate the templates of the aspect theme. Finally, an explicit stereotype allows explicit matching of concepts in a composition relationship and the tagged definition mergedName indicates the composed value.

Magicdraw was chosen to meet our second requirement for three reasons. First, it supports UML 2.1 modelling and therefore supports the implementation of a UML Profile definition. Second, it exports to the Eclipse Modelling Framework[5] (EMF) XML Metadata Interchange (XMI), which is compatible with transformations at the later stages of the MDA process. Third, it supports both class and sequence UML diagrams, which is a necessity for Theme/UML.

After completing a design in Theme/UML, the tool exports two files-the Theme/UML Marking Profile File and the UML 2 Diagram File. Both files are serialised with the EMF XMI.

Composition Phase. The composition phase allows the designer to automatically compose the model according to the composition specification that was created during the modelling phase. This phase is implemented using two transformations. The first transformation takes the two files from the output of the Modelling Phase and maps them to create a composition model that is an instance of the composition metamodel. The second transformation takes this composition model and executes it to produce an EMF XMI file that holds the object-oriented PIM. This horizontal transformation, as illustrated in the middle of Fig. 1, is termed a composition.

Mapping. The first transformation is defined as a mapping from the Theme/UML Marking Profile (c.f. Fig. 2) to the Composition Metamodel (c.f. Fig. 3), as illustrated in Fig. 1. The mapping specification uses the UML elements decorated with marks to transform them into a composition model. This is achieved in two steps. In the first step, an associated element in the ComposableElement hierarchy (c.f. Fig. 3) is created that corresponds to the

---

[5] http://www.eclipse.org/modeling/emf/

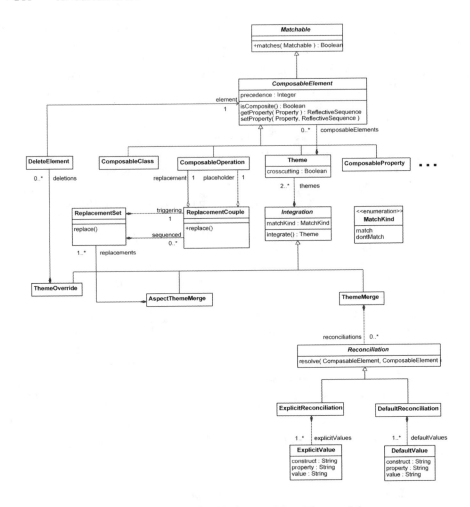

Fig. 3. Theme/UML Composition Metamodel

UML element being mapped. For example, a UML `Package` with a `theme` stereotype applied in the UML Design Model specifies the creation of a `Theme` element
in the composition model. In the second step, a detailed composition specification is created in the composition model that maps each composition relationship
and its properties in the UML Design Model to their equivalent in the composition metamodel. For example, a UML `Dependency` with a `bind` stereotype in
the UML Design Model specifies the creation of an `AspectThemeMerge` in the
composition model, with a `binding` tagged value on that stereotype, resulting
in the creation of its respective `ReplacementSet` and `ReplacementCouples` as
containing properties for that integration type.

As a result of using strings as tagged values, the mapping implementation heavily relies on parsing techniques and the use of the Object Constraint Language
(OCL) as a means to extract and query elements in the UML model, respectively.

In particular, OCL proved especially useful in supporting Theme/UML's pointcut selection mechanism.

Composition. Figure 3 illustrates the metamodel used to describe the structure and behaviour of Theme/UML's composition semantics[6]. Each element that can be involved in a composition is defined by a `ComposableElement`. A `ComposableElement` implements a `Matchable` element that abstracts the notion of a matching criterion. This matching criterion is specific to each element and is implemented in a manner appropriate to the element being matched. For example, a UML Operation is matched to the name of the operation, the types of the parameters and the type of the return value. An `Integration` is an abstract metaclass that describes the way in which themes are to be integrated. The three integration strategies that Theme/UML defines are `ThemeMerge`, `ThemeOverride` and `AspectThemeMerge`. Each have their additional metaclasses and metarelationships that define how the integration is supported and behaves.

A `ThemeMerge` integration describes how base themes are to be composed. This necessitates a definition of how overlapping specifications are resolved through the `Reconciliation` hierarchy. An `ExplicitReconciliation` allows a designer to indicate an explicit preference in the composed theme if elements in a merge match, using one or more `ExplicitValues`. An `ExplicitValue` indicates the specification of a single matching element, referencing the `construct` property of the element and the `value` of that element upon composition. Likewise, a `DefaultReconciliation` allows a designer to specify the default value for elements of a particular type if a conflict arises between elements of that type in the composition. The reconciliation can have one or more `DefaultValues`. A `DefaultValue` indicates the specification of a single matching element of a particular type and the `value` of that type upon reconciliation. The final reconciliation strategy defined by Theme/UML is precedence. A precedence reconciliation specifies precedence on a composable element when a match occurs in a merge. A precedence strategy is integrated into an attribute of a `ComposableElement` rather than having its own metaclass.

The second integration strategy defined by Theme/UML, `ThemeOverride`, describes how one theme's specification is overridden by that of another theme. This metaclass can contain a set of `DeleteElements` which indicate the elements that get deleted upon the override.

The third integration strategy, `AspectThemeMerge`, specifies how an aspect theme is composed with base themes. Each `AspectThemeMerge` has a number of `ReplacementSets` equivalent to the number of sequence diagrams in each aspect theme that it represents. Each `ReplacementSet` must have one triggering `ReplacementCouple` and can have many sequenced `ReplacementCouples`. A `ReplacementCouple` references both a placeholder `ComposableOperation` and its replacement `ComposableOperation`.

The composition metamodel was realised in Ecore and implemented using EMF libraries. Ecore is the EMF's meta metamodel and is synonymous with

---

[6] Due to space limitations, Fig. 3 only illustrates a subset of the composable elements.

MOF, with some slight variations. The EMF implements both the UML 2 standard and the OCL standard with Ecore in Java and provides a supporting library called UML2. The EMF also defines its own XMI schema that allows libraries to read and write any EMF-based model.

While the composition metamodel defines the structure and behaviour of Theme/UML's composition semantics, a mapping specification defines how these semantics are executed. In our approach, we implemented a mapping specification that targets an object-oriented PIM. In this case, all the integration strategies are executed. However, if a transformation to an AO PIM is desired, the metamodel is extensible enough to support the definition of a mapping specification that only executes some of the integration strategies (e.g. targeting an asymmetric AOP platform would require only the overlapping specifications to be resolved).

Transformation Phase. The output from the composition phase is an object-oriented PIM that can be transformed into a platform-specific model. Rather than go straight from a PIM to code, we made the decision to go to an intermediate PSM. The reason for this is that the proposed approach is elaboration-oriented, meaning the PIM is not computationally complete and does not contain the full executable specification [18]. The PSM is open for re-factoring and elaboration of low-level details by the designer. There are two transformations implemented in this phase, refinement and synthesis, which support the developer in moving from a PIM-based design to a PSM-based design and finally to code respectively.

After choosing a target platform, a model-to-model transformation refines the object-oriented PIM into a PSM suitable to model the concepts for the chosen platform. This refinement requires a number of platform-specific extensions. For each PSM, a UML profile is created that extends the standard UML datatypes with those that are specific to the language and platform. The profile can also include the namespaces and datatypes needed to further elaborate the PSM. The transformation was implemented using Java and the UML2 library.

The second transformation, illustrated as synthesis, allows a PSM to be transformed into code. This transformation is implemented using a template-based code-generation technology called XPand-part of the oAW framework. In general, there are two main approaches for model-to-text (M2T) transformation, visitor-based approaches and template-based approaches [3]. Template-based tools such as XPand use a text-based declarative language as a means for selection of model nodes and iterative expansion. We decided to use Xpand to transform the UML class diagrams to code. For the generation of behavioural code with sequence diagrams, we used a visitor-based approach implemented in Java. Sequence diagrams are written in the UML in-order, and so a visitor-based approach is more desirable than a template-based approach as the visitor can step through the full trace in order and generate code on the fly. As XPand supports Java extensions, the two approaches could be integrated, producing both compilable structural and behavioural code from the class diagrams and sequence diagrams respectively. The code generation capabilities could be extended by implementing support for standard UML behavioural diagrams.

2.3   Discussion

This section discusses the difficulties and challenges we encountered while implementing our approach to the integration of Theme/UML with current MDA standards, guidelines and technologies.

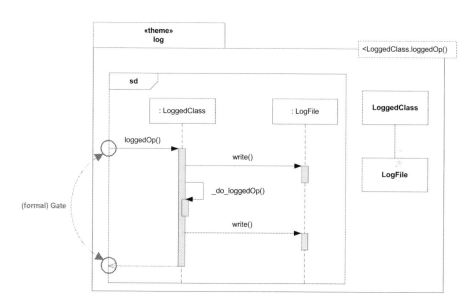

Fig. 4. UML 2.1 sequence diagram

Modelling Triggering and Returning Messages. In Theme/UML, UML sequence diagrams are used to indicate how and when the crosscutting occurs in relation to the abstract templates of an aspect theme. The UML metamodel in which Theme/UML was defined had no support for indicating a message in the case where the sender or receiver was unknown. Consequently, this resulted in these messages being drawn without a sender or receiver, violating a number of constraints of the metamodel. This would be especially problematic in the creation of a mapping specification, where it is assumed all UML models are compliant to the constraints and are well-formed. However, the UML 2.1 metamodel has improved the definition of sequence diagrams. A `Gate` is a connection point for relating a `Message` outside an `InteractionFragment` with a `Message` inside the `InteractionFragment`. With Gate support, the sender and receiver of the initial triggering message can now be unspecified while conforming to the constraints of the metamodel. Figure 4 shows the updated Theme/UML semantics and notation for indicating triggering and returning operations, explicitly indicating where the gates are.

Modelling Composition Relationships. Theme/UML defines an n-ary composition relationship for elements that are to be composed by its merge. As a profile extension can only mark existing UML metaclasses, profile extensions for n-ary relationships were required. `Association` is restricted as a relationship between certain types; therefore, `Dependency` is the next best option, allowing n-ary relationships between `NamedElements`. It emerged that MagicDraw only supported one-to-one relationships with a `Dependency`, and as such deviates from the standard. To work around this, the desired relationships were emulated by drawing an additional `Dependency` on the `Dependency` that was drawn between two model elements. This workaround could be successfully implemented since a `Dependency` itself is a `NamedElement`. However, the solution necessitated extra parsing logic to determine all the elements participating in a composition relationship.

Modelling Sequence Diagrams. When we began designing our tool, we surveyed a number of UML 2 modelling tools, including Topcased[7], Poseidon[8] and Rational Software Architect[9]. We decided to use Magicdraw as the community edition was free; it offered export to EMF XMI and had support for class and sequence diagrams. However, it emerged that the EMF XMI export implemented by MagicDraw was faulty for sequence diagrams. We based an alternate approach on the UML2 editor provided by the UML2 library of the EMF. This workaround involves using this tree-based graphical tool to create the sequence diagrams by hand. The graphical tool offers the designer a little more abstraction than working with the raw XMI directly (which requires detailed knowledge of the specification). Although this workaround is undesirable from a designer perspective, it was the only option available as no other free tool surveyed was capable of viewing or writing sequence diagrams to EMF XMI correctly. Once a tool that supports sequence diagrams becomes available, it can be used instead.

Code Generation for Sequence Diagrams. A visitor-based approach was adopted to generate code from sequence diagrams. However, we discovered that the sequence diagrams in the UML 2.1 specification are currently unsuitable for the purpose of code generation. The OMG Revision Task Force for UML[10] currently lists a number of pending revisions. One such revision describes that the arguments of a `Message` can only be `ValueSpecifications`, and the creation, referencing and assignment of variables in the underlying model remains ambiguous. To get around this restriction, a `LiteralString` is used to pass arguments in textual form. However, this solution is undesirable because it precludes complete validation of the model. We are currently awaiting publication of the next UML 2 standard to evaluate the fixes for these issues in order to provide better support for code generation from sequence diagrams.

---

[7] http://www.topcased.org
[8] http://www.gentleware.com
[9] http://www-306.ibm.com/software/awdtools/architect/swarchitect
[10] http://www.omg.org/issues

Selection of Transformation Tools. Prior to the design of our tool, we investigated a number of Model-to-Model (M2M) transformation languages such as ATL[11], Kermeta[12] and oAW Xtend[13]. The UML 2 is a large and complex metamodel, and writing valid transformations has been proven to be both challenging and intricate [8]. At that time, we found it easier to use the EMF and UML2 libraries in Java. One of the difficulties we observed with tools like ATL was that it was difficult to transform from a source UML model to a destination UML model when changes to only a small number of meta-model items were required. A tool such as ATL requires rules to copy every single element in the UML metamodel (which is very large) to a new model. Using the libraries, copying a full model requires only a few lines of code and is therefore more feasible. With the rapidly improving state of model-driven tools, however, modern M2M tool support can potentially achieve what we desired during our development phase. For example, ATL now supports superimposition, which allows new rules to be superimposed onto another set of rules, e.g. a full UML2 copy transformation. Redoing our transformations in this manner may be an interesting piece of future work as we believe that working with model-transformation tools is a good way of reducing the complexities of designing mapping specifications and increases extensibility and usability for both the developer and the user.

3 Model-Driven Theme/UML: Process

Tool support that integrates both aspect-orientation and MDA is inadequate without a complementary systematic process that clearly defines its use. Previous research on aspect-oriented design (AOD) has amalgamated work on best practises to produce a unified and refined AOD process [14]. Likewise, the MDA Guide [22] provides a flexible and extensive treatise on model-driven processes. Using both individual processes as a basis, we have devised an integrated process.

3.1 Process Phases

The requirements of the application should be analysed with a view to identifying concerns before design begins. Theme/Doc, a concern identification approach, supports aspect-oriented requirements analysis and provides explicit mappings from its output to Theme/UML [1]. Theme/Doc can be realised in the MDA process by taking the role of a computation-independent model, where a transformation realises the mappings to a PIM. Other aspect-oriented requirements analysis approaches can be used, provided a mapping exists to Theme/UML, such as that outlined by Sánchez et al. [25]. It is not pertinent to the outlined approach whether this mapping is realised as a manual transformation (indicated by completely elaborating the PIM) or by a semi-automatic transformation (where some artefacts are generated). Future work will investigate tool

---

[11] http://www.eclipse.org/m2m/atl

[12] http://www.kermeta.org

[13] http://www.openarchitectureware.org

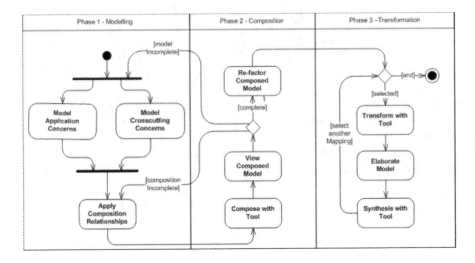

Fig. 5. The Model-Driven Theme/UML process

support for these mappings. If automation is provided, the designer would begin with a set of pre-generated UML artefacts that could be further elaborated. This process is illustrated in Fig. 5 as an activity diagram, with the three phases represented by swimlanes.

Modelling Phase. The modelling phase illustrates two activities-modelling base application concerns and modelling crosscutting concerns. As Theme/UML supports a symmetric decomposition, and its concern spaces are considered declaratively complete, both of these activities can be done concurrently and independently of each other. This is illustrated by the fork in Fig. 5, and allows themes to be designed in isolation–either by an individual or a team of designers. Each theme is modelled inside a UML Package and should not reference any element outside the package. This ensures that the concern is declaratively complete. The UML Package has the stereotype `theme` applied from the Theme/UML Profile. As aspect themes are modelled relative to their abstract templates, it is necessary for the designer to indicate this using the tagged value `template` from the Theme/UML Profile. Each theme has a sequence diagram for each sequence of templates. This sequence diagram illustrates the interaction of the templates with the behaviour of the theme itself.

When themes have been modelled, the designer applies the composition relationships, specifying how themes are to be composed. At the coarsest level of granularity, the individual themes themselves are marked for composition. Support is also available to indicate finer compositions that deviate from the composition specification of the composite container. Base themes use a `merge` stereotype applied to a `Dependency` from the Theme/UML marking profile. The `themeName` tagged definition indicates the name of the final composed theme. The `matchType` allows a matching strategy to be applied to the merge, with the `precedences` stereotypes indicating the ascending order of the merge. The `defaultResolve` and `explicitResolve` stereotypes are available as reconciliation options if a conflict arises. An `explicit` stereotype, applied to a `Dependency`, indicates a deviation from the default composition of a `merge`. The `bind` stereotype is used similarly to the merge, but indicates how aspect themes are composed with the base themes. The composition of the aspect theme is indicated using a `binding` tagged value to show how the templates are instantiated to the elements of the base themes. Once the composition relationships have been applied, the designer can then proceed to the composition phase as indicated in Fig. 5.

Composition Phase. Given a UML model with Theme/UML marks applied, the designer can use the tool to compose themes. As illustrated in Fig. 5, the designer can view the composed model and can then choose to take one of three actions. The designer may go back to the modelling phase in the case that the composition relationships need to be reapplied or adjusted due to the composed model being incorrect or incomplete. The second possibility involves going back to the start of the modelling phase to edit the model. Finally, the designer can decide that the composed model is complete.

The next step in the process is refactoring the composed model. We decided to make the composed model open for refactoring for two reasons. The first reason is the possibility of cycles in generalisations. This problem may occur as a result of merging different class hierarchies. The problem has been addressed theoretically through the use of subject-oriented flattening [28,23]. Tool support and process integration for this solution remain future work. Currently, if the problem arises in the composed model, the designer can correct it manually.

The second reason for making the composed model open for refactoring is the need to resolve ambiguities that may arise in the composed model. Conceivably, while designing themes, matching associations may get modelled at different points in each class hierarchy. After composition, these will get duplicated and consequently result in redundant associations. Theme/UML does not naturally cater for these conceptual ambiguities in the semantics of its integration strategies.

Transformation Phase. To begin the transformation process, the designer chooses the target platform. The tool takes the PIM, and using the mapping for the target environment, produces a PSM representing the domain-specific extensions of the PIM for that environment. In our approach, the object-oriented PIM that is produced from composition is refined to either a J2ME or .NET CF PSM. A PSM is a direct representation of the underlying platform, modelling precise library support and features of the specific environment. From a pragmatic point of view, it is usually not suitable to model the full specification in the PSM. For example, one could imagine that programming a complex algorithm would be much more effective through the use of code, rather than tediously modelling it with a UML activity diagram [12]. If the full structural and behavioural specification is not modelled in the PSM, it can be specified subsequently in the source code. After elaborating the design of the PSM, the designer can transform from model to code. This kind of transformation is known as synthesis or code generation [20].

4 Case Study

In this section, we present an overview of a case study that we conducted in order to assess the applicability of model-driven Theme/UML to an application development scenario. The case study demonstrates how our approach facilitates both the separation of concerns in a mobile, context-aware auction system and the subsequent automatic composition of these concerns to produce platform-specific models and source code. The auction system offers typical functionality such as placing and browsing bids, managing accounts and purchasing goods. It also offers context-awareness features such as notification of auctions that may be of interest to the user, and mobility features such as ensuring that the user is in a valid location before a transaction can proceed and adapting the user interface (UI) to changes in the environment.

Analysis of the requirements specification for the auction system with Theme/Doc identified six base themes and three aspect themes. The base themes cater for the following behaviour:

- Enrolling with the system.
- Browsing auctions.
- Joining auctions.
- Bidding on auctions.
- Transferring credit.
- Administration of auctions.

The aspect themes support the following crosscutting behaviour:

- Adapting the UI (specifically the backlight) based on system events.
- Determining and querying user location.
- Recommending auctions based on user profile and auction history.

Starting at the modelling phase, the analysis provided by Theme/Doc allowed us to create and elaborate a detailed design of each theme. In the interest of brevity, we do not include design of all themes, although we include the enroll (cf. Fig. 6) and join (cf. Fig. 7) base themes and the adapt-ui aspect theme (cf. Figs. 9 and 10) as examples of themes designed for the auction system application. We will refer to these themes throughout the remainder of the case study overview.

After completing the design, we applied the composition relationships to the themes and their elements to create a specification that would indicate the integration of all the themes. Figure 8 illustrates a merge between the two base themes, enroll and join. The merged theme is given a name, auctionSystem, through the use of the themeName tag definition. Examination of the base themes reveals that we generally used the same vocabulary to model the same concepts, and so a match[name] matching criterion is attached to match elements with

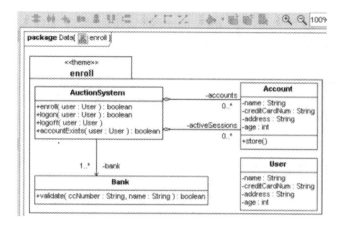

Fig. 6. MagicDraw screenshot of the `enroll` theme

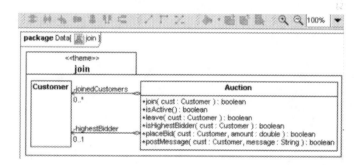

Fig. 7. MagicDraw screenshot of the `join` theme

the same name and type. During this process, the concept of User in the enroll
theme was found to be the same as that of Customer in the join theme. An
explicit composition relationship was applied to resolve this conflict. This relationship specifies that the two classes are the same and that they should be
merged under the unified Customer class.

Aspect themes can be integrated through the bind composition relationship.
A bind is defined as a specialisation of a merge integration and supports merging
of the structure and behaviour of an aspect theme with a base theme. Figures 9
and 10 illustrate the adapt-ui theme, along with its composition specification
to the base themes enroll and join. As illustrated in Fig. 10[14], the sequence
diagrams in aspect themes specify how (advice) and when (joinpoint) in relation to the abstract templates the crosscutting behaviour takes place. The

---

[14] The sequence diagram is not currently shown as part of the aspect theme due to
the error with MagicDraw's sequence diagram export behaviour (see Sect. 2.3). We
show a manually constructed sequence diagram as well as part of the UML2 tree
editor's view of the behaviour under discussion.

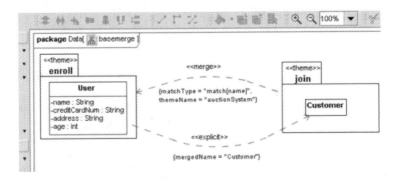

Fig. 8. MagicDraw screenshot of the base merge composition specification

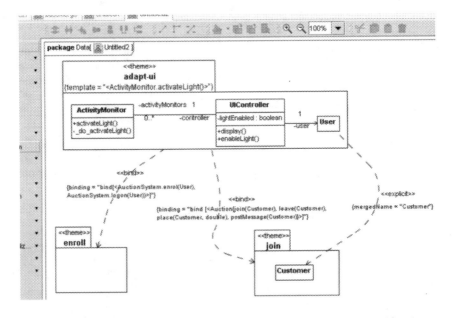

Fig. 9. MagicDraw screenshot of `adapt-ui` and its composition specification

activateLight() joinpoint in the adapt-ui theme acts as a placeholder to the operations identified in the bind statement. It is these operations that actually trigger activation of the UI backlight following the base-aspect merge.

At the composition phase, we used the tool to take the themes and related composition relationships and merged them. The result of this composition specification, applied in Fig. 8, is depicted in Fig. 11. For ease of illustration, we only show the result of the bases being merged. Figures 12 and 13 show the result of the full composition produced by the tool, i.e. the composition specification applied in Fig. 8 and Fig. 9. The classes that were shared among multiple themes

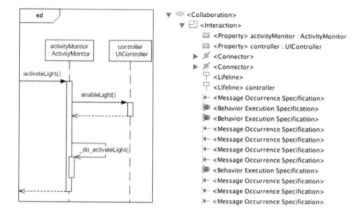

Fig. 10. Two views of the `adapt-ui` crosscutting behaviour

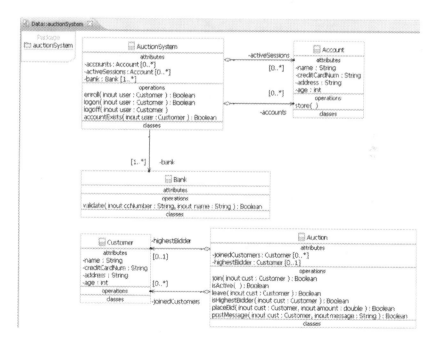

Fig. 11. Screenshot of the merged base

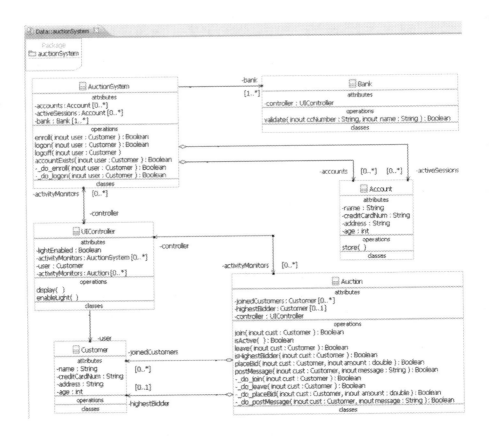

Fig. 12. Screenshot of merging `adapt-ui` with the `enroll` and `join` themes

have been unified, e.g. the resultant merge of the same class has all the operations belonging to separate versions of that class before the merge. Also, there is no `User` class as it has been merged with its new name, `Customer`.

The aspect theme was also composed with the base themes. For example, the `ActivityMonitor` behaviour in the `adapt-ui` theme gets merged with the `AuctionSystem` through the binding to the `enroll` theme. The `logon` and `enroll` operations are renamed to `_do_logon` and `_do_enrol`, respectively. The new `logon` and `enroll` operations now contain the crosscutting behaviour that they have been merged with. The case is similar for the `join` theme.

With the object-oriented composition of themes completed and no refactoring necessary, it was possible to produce a PSM. In the transformation phase, we choose both available target platforms, J2ME and .NET CF. The tool was used to transform the object-oriented design produced in the previous phase into the two target PSMs, adding in more concrete detail for each specific platform as appropriate. Figure 14 illustrates the J2ME PSM produced during the

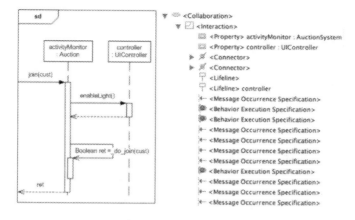

Fig. 13. Two views of the merged `adapt-ui` crosscutting behaviour

transformation process, depicting the modified datatypes for J2ME platform and the automatically generated accessors and mutators.

At this point, either the J2ME PSM or the .NET CF PSM could be inspected. As a PSM is refined from a computationally incomplete PIM (i.e. the approach is elaboration-oriented), it was necessary to further elaborate the model both structurally and behaviourally using platform-specific library extensions. Either PSM can be elaborated partially or to completion at the model level, with the remaining elaboration achieved through code. After elaboration, the PSM was ready for synthesis, i.e. transformation to source code. The J2ME and .NET CF source code that was automatically generated for the `join` method (which includes crosscutting `adapt-ui` behaviour) is illustrated in Fig. 15.

4.1   Discussion

We observed from this case study that Model-Driven Theme/UML has a positive impact on system modularity when applied to the development of an application with crosscutting mobility and context-awareness concerns. Theme/UML facilitated the separation of concerns at design time that would have otherwise resulted in scattering and tangling in core system behaviour. Through the specification of composition relationships between modularised concerns, it was possible to produce a design with which the tool could operate. Given a collection of modules and a description of their relationships, the tool automatically generated platform-specific models for J2ME and .NET CF platforms. The tool then used these PSMs to generate source code for the respective target platforms, saving time and reducing the risk of error introduction. The tool supports a solution-focused development approach that allows developers to concentrate on the design of the initial model and avail the benefits of automatic PSM and code generation.

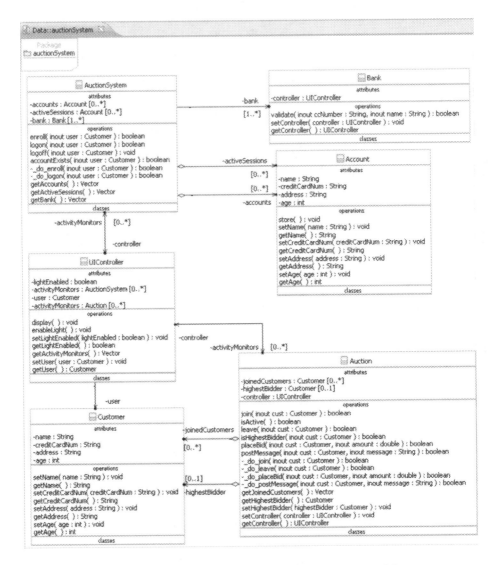

Fig. 14. Screenshot of the platform-specific J2ME model

```
//   @generated
     public bool join(Customer cust) {
         controller.enableLight();
         bool ret = _do_join(cust);
         return ret;
     }
```

```
//   @generated
     public boolean join(Customer cust) {
         controller.enableLight();
         boolean ret = _do_join(cust);
         return ret;
     }
```

Fig. 15. Source code generated from the .NET CF (left) and J2ME (right) PSMs

5 Related work

Composition Directives [24,27] is an approach implemented in Kermeta called Kompose [6,7] and supports the composition of both aspect and base UML models. This work takes a hybrid symmetry approach to merging, i.e. the composition procedure does not distinguish between an aspect and a base model, and was designed to deal with the inadequacies of a simple name-based matching strategy. For example, when merging two operations with the same name but different argument lists or return values, a simple name-based matching strategy would produce a merged result using just the names as matches. The Composition Directives approach supports different model elements having unique, sensible matching strategies, according to their syntactic properties. To accomplish this, a composition metamodel was devised. The idea of a composition metamodel in our work was originally inspired by this approach, but we subsequently focused on supporting the original definition of the Theme/UML semantics. The similarities include an abstraction of the matching criterion, as well as an enumeration of the composition elements. In terms of differences, contrasting composition algorithms are employed. Theme/UML defines an abstract integration type and therefore the composition algorithm is iterative. Alternatively, Composition Directives defines a single merge implemented as a recursive composition algorithm.

The Atlas Model Weaver (AMW)[15] is a tool that facilitates the creation of links between models [4]. It is based on the Eclipse Modelling Framework (EMF) and is part of the ATLAS Model Management Architecture (AMMA). The links are stored in a weaving model that conforms to a weaving metamodel. AMW can be used to support aspect weaving[16], although it is not centred specifically around the notion of aspect-orientation. While our approach specifies a metamodel that defines how models get composed, AMW defines a metamodel for weaving links between models. It allows models to be visualised in a tree-like manner and supports the association of links between two metamodels or models using the weaving metamodel. It also defines the notion of a weaving session in which the weaving metamodel, the models and their metamodels are loaded and links are defined and woven. Contrary to this approach, our approach uses a UML profile to define the weaving/composition relationships at modelling time. The AMW weaving process does not distinguish between primary and aspect models, making it purely symmetric.

The Motorola WEAVR [2] is a commercial add-in to the Telelogic TAU tool[17] and is designed for use in telecoms systems engineering. WEAVR is a translation-oriented approach that includes a joinpoint model for state machines. It uses the Specification and Description Languages (SDL) and UML standards to fully model reactive discrete systems and produce executable code. Unlike our approach, which is elaboration-based, WEAVR is a translation-based approach that uses state machines and an action language to fully specify the application

---

[15] http://www.eclipse.org/gmt/amw
[16] http://www.eclipse.org/gmt/amw/usecases/AOM
[17] http://www.telelogic.com

logic at the model level. Similar to our approach, it uses a UML Profile to specify aspect-oriented extensions. For example, to illustrate an aspect, a class is extended with the `aspect` stereotype, allowing tagged definitions in the form of attributes, operations, signal definitions and ports, which are treated like intertype declarations. Furthermore, it allows precedence of connectors to be applied to the same pointcut, aiding the management of aspect interference. This feature is not catered for in Theme/UML.

XWeave is a model weaver that supports composition of different architectural viewpoints. The weaver facilitates software product-line engineering, allowing for variable parts of architectural models to be woven according to a specific product configuration [9]. Xweave adopts a form of asymmetric aspect-orientation, unlike Theme/UML, which defines both symmetric and asymmetric forms. Aspect models are woven into a base model using two strategies, name matching and explicit pointcut expressions. Name matching supports weaving through equivalence of elements in the base and aspect models if both elements have the same name and type. This is similar to the matching criterion defined in our composition metamodel. Pointcut expression weaving is based on the oAW expression language, which is itself similar to OCL. This approach is more powerful than the wildcard-based string selection mechanism used by Theme/UML. One drawback of the XWeave approach is the limited support for advice. Base model elements cannot be removed, changed or overriden by aspect models and hence they only support additive weaving. Theme/UML supports these features through the semantics of its integration strategies.

Modelling Aspects Using a Transformation Approach (MATA) [15] is a UML aspect-oriented modelling tool. Unlike our approach, which is based on model composition, MATA uses graph transformations to specify and compose aspects. Using the UML metamodel as a type graph, any UML model can therefore be represented as an instance of this type graph and a transformation based on graph theory applied on it. The tool currently supports class, sequence and state diagrams. The aspect model consists of a set of graph rules that can be applied as a graph transformation to the base model using a pattern. MATA is built on top of IBM's Rational Software Modeler and uses the graph rule execution tool AGG as a back-end for graph transformations.

Klein et al. [16] suggest an approach for weaving multiple behavioural aspects using sequence diagrams. In their approach, a base scenario describes the behaviour of the system using a sequence diagram, and a behavioural aspect describes a concern that crosscuts this base scenario. They propose various types of pointcut, allowing joinpoints to be matched even when extra messages occur in between and also demonstrate how these can be statically woven. This approach formally defines a more concise custom metamodel and addresses the semantic difficulty of explicitly composing one sequence diagram with another. Although this approach differs from Theme/UML in that it supports asymmetric separation, it is considered a complimentary approach that could be integrated to enhance Theme/UML's support for behavioural modelling.

6 Summary and Future Work

In this paper we have presented our efforts to integrate AOSD techniques with the MDE process. We have described new tool support for model-driven Theme/UML from both an implementation and a methodological perspective, and illustrated the capabilities of the tool by means of a case study.

We are currently investigating revisions and extensions to the tool to support both the modularisation of distributed, real-time embedded (DRE) concerns at the model level and transformations to embedded platforms. In addition to this work, we are developing an aspect-oriented MDE tool suite. The tool suite combines the work described in this paper with similar work that was conducted in tandem. This related work provides similar capabilities in terms of modularisation of concerns at the model-level, but differs from the approach described here in terms of the types of transformations supported.

Acknowledgments

We would like to acknowledge the support of AOSD-Europe and of Lero: The Irish Software Engineering Research Centre, funded by Science Foundation Ireland. Thanks also to Jorge Fox for his comments on earlier drafts of this paper.

References

1. Clarke, S., Baniassad, E.: Aspect-Oriented Analysis and Design. The Theme Approach. Object Technology Series. Addison-Wesley, Boston (2005)
2. Cottenier, T., van den Berg, A., Elrad, T.: The Motorola WEAVR: Model Weaving in a Large Industrial Context (2007)
3. Czarnecki, K., Helsen, S.: Classification of Model Transformation Approaches. In: OOPSLA 2003 Workshop on Generative Techniques in the context of Model Driven Architecture (October 2003)
4. Didonet Del Fabro, M., Bézivin, J., Jouault, F., Breton, E., Gueltas, G.: AMW: a generic model weaver. In: Journées sur l'Ingénierie Dirigée par les Modèles (IDM 2005), pp. 105–114 (2005)
5. Filman, R.E., Elrad, T., Clarke, S., Akşit, M. (eds.): Aspect-Oriented Software Development. Addison-Wesley, Boston (2005)
6. Fleurey, F., Baudry, B., France, R., Ghosh, S.: A generic approach for automatic model composition. In: Aspect Oriented Modeling (AOM) Workshop, Nashville, USA (October 2007)
7. France, R., Fleurey, F., Reddy, R., Baudry, B., Ghosh, S.: Providing support for model composition in metamodels. In: EDOC 2007: Proceedings of the 11th IEEE International Enterprise Distributed Object Computing Conference, Washington, DC, USA, p. 253. IEEE Computer Society, Los Alamitos (2007)
8. France, R.B., Ghosh, S., Dinh-Trong, T., Solberg, A.: Model-Driven Development Using UML 2.0: Promises and Pitfalls. Computer 39(2), 59 (2006)
9. Groher, I., Voelter, M.: XWeave: models and aspects in concert. In: AOM 2007: Proceedings of the 10th international workshop on Aspect-Oriented Modeling, pp. 35–40. ACM Press, New York (2007)

10. Object Management Group. Model-Driven Architecture, http://www.omg.org/mda (accessed October 22, 2007)

11. Object Management Group. OMG UML Specification Version 1.3., ftp://ftp.omg.org/pub/docs/ad/99-06-03.pdf (accessed October 25, 2007)

12. Hailpern, B., Tarr, P.: Model-driven development: the good, the bad, and the ugly. IBM Systems Journal 45(3), 451–461 (2006)

13. Jackson, A., Barais, O., Jézéquel, J.-M., Clarke, S.: Toward A Generic And Extensible Merge. In: Models and Aspects workshop, at ECOOP 2006, Nantes, France (2006)

14. Jackson, A., Clarke, S.: Towards a Generic Aspect Oriented Design Process. In: Bruel, J.-M. (ed.) MoDELS 2005. LNCS, vol. 3844, pp. 110–119. Springer, Heidelberg (2006)

15. Jayaraman, P.K., Whittle, J., Elkhodary, A.M., Gomaa, H.: Model composition in product lines and feature interaction detection using critical pair analysis. In: Engels, G., Opdyke, B., Schmidt, D.C., Weil, F. (eds.) MODELS 2007. LNCS, vol. 4735, pp. 151–165. Springer, Heidelberg (2007)

16. Klein, J., Fleurey, F., Jézéquel, J.-M.: Weaving multiple aspects in sequence diagrams. In: Rashid, A., Aksit, M. (eds.) Transactions on AOSD III. LNCS, vol. 4620, pp. 167–199. Springer, Heidelberg (2007)

17. Object Management Group. UML 2.0 Infrastructure Specification, http://www.omg.org/docs/ptc/03-09-15.pdf (accessed October 25, 2007)

18. McNeile, A.: MDA: The Vision with the Hole, http://www.metamaxim.com/download/documents/MDAv1.pdf (accessed October 30, 2007)

19. Mellor, S.J., Balcer, M.: Executable UML: A Foundation for Model-Driven Architectures. Addison-Wesley Longman Publishing Co., Inc., Boston (2002); foreword By-Ivar Jacoboson

20. Mens, T., Czarnecki, K., Van Gorp, P.: Discussion – A Taxonomy of Model Transformations. In: Bezivin, J., Heckel, R. (eds.) Language Engineering for Model-Driven Software Development. Dagstuhl Seminar Proceedings, vol. 04101, Internationales Begegnungs- und Forschungszentrum fuer Informatik (IBFI), Schloss Dagstuhl, Germany (2005)

21. Miller, J., Mukerji, J.: MDA Guide Version 1.0.1. Technical report, Object Management Group (OMG) (2003)

22. OMG. MDA Guide Version 1.0.1, http://www.omg.org/docs/omg/03-06-01.pdf (accessed November 2, 2007)

23. Ossher, H., Kaplan, M., Katz, A., Harrison, W., Kruskal, V.: Specifying subject-oriented composition. Theory and Practice of Object Systems 2(3), 179–202 (1996)

24. Reddy, Y.R., Ghosh, S., France, R.B., Straw, G., Bieman, J.M., McEachen, N., Song, E., Georg, G.: Directives for Composing Aspect-Oriented Design Class Models, pp. 75–105 (2006)

25. Sánchez, P., Fuentes, L., Jackson, A., Clarke, S.: Aspects at the Right Time. In: Rashid, A., Aksit, M. (eds.) Transactions on Aspect-Oriented Software Development IV. LNCS, vol. 4640, pp. 54–113. Springer, Heidelberg (2007)

26. Schilit, B., Adams, N., Want, R.: Context-Aware Computing Applications. In: Proceedings of the Workshop on Mobile Computing Systems and Applications, Santa Cruz, CA, US, pp. 85–90. IEEE Computer Society, Los Alamitos (1994)

27. Straw, G., Georg, G., Song, E., Ghosh, S., France, R.B., Bieman, J.M.: Model composition directives. In: Baar, T., Strohmeier, A., Moreira, A., Mellor, S.J. (eds.) UML 2004. LNCS, vol. 3273, pp. 84–97. Springer, Heidelberg (2004)

28. Walker, R.J.: Eliminating cycles in composed class hierarchies. Technical Report TR-2000-07, University of British Columbia (2000)
29. Zito, A., Dingel, J.: Modeling UML 2 Package Merge With Alloy. In: 1st Alloy Workshop (Alloy 2006), Portland, OR, USA, pp. 86–95 (2006)
30. Zito, A., Diskin, Z., Dingel, J.: Package Merge in UML 2: Practice vs. Theory? In: Nierstrasz, O., Whittle, J., Harel, D., Reggio, G. (eds.) MoDELS 2006. LNCS, vol. 4199, pp. 185–199. Springer, Heidelberg (2006)

Appendix

A   Theme/UML Overview

The Theme Approach is an aspect-oriented methodology that encompasses the requirements analysis, design and mapping to implementation phases of the development lifecycle [1]. Theme/Doc provides a systematic means to analyse a text-based requirements specification in order to identify base and crosscutting concerns and the relationships between them. Theme/UML is an aspect-oriented modelling language that supports the design of concerns and maintains the relationships previously identified by Theme/Doc. The Theme Approach also details mapping specifications from Theme/UML to aspect-oriented programming languages such as AspectJ.

Theme/UML is aspect-oriented design language with an accompanying methodology. The Theme/UML design language is a Meta-Object Facility (MOF) extension of the UML 1.3 beta R7, enhancing standard UML with new modularisation and compositional constructs. The accompanying methodology provides guidelines on the use of these new constructs. The constructs include a new type of classifier called a *theme*, a composition relationship and three integration strategies-*merge, override* and *bind*.

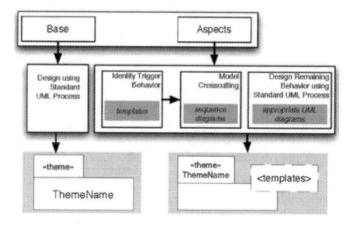

Fig. 16. Designing with Theme/UML

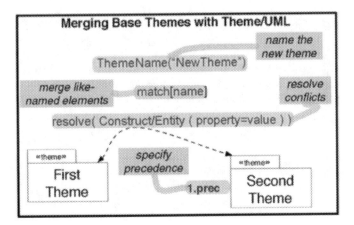

Fig. 17. Merge Integration Strategy

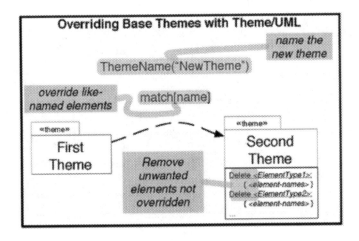

Fig. 18. Override Integration Strategy

A theme is a construct based on the existing definition of the standard UML *package* and encapsulates the design specification of a base or aspect concern. As illustrated in Fig. 16, a base theme is designed using the standard UML process and can include any of the standard diagram types. An aspect theme is one that encapsulates a crosscutting concern and is designed relative to the abstract templates, with sequence diagrams specifying when and how the templates interact with the base themes.

As Theme/UML aligns to a symmetric decomposition, themes are considered to be declaratively complete. This means that the design specification of a concern is self-contained and does not reference anything outside the theme in which it is defined. This property allows a more rigorous separation of individual themes from each other. Consequently, this property may result in overlapping

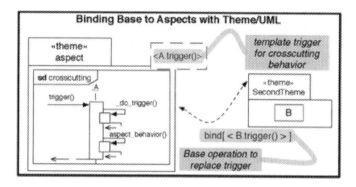

Fig. 19. Bind Integration Strategy

concepts being represented in multiple individual theme designs. Consequently, these concepts must be reconciled at composition time.

Theme/UML supports compositional constructs for both overlapping and crosscutting specifications. An overlapping or shared concept can arise because equivalent concepts can be considered in more than one theme. A *merge* integration strategy can exist between two or more themes and allows like-named elements to be matched, thereby resolving conflicts between themes. Figure 17 illustrates a merge between two themes. The *match[name]* property indicates that elements are to be matched and merged based on name and type. *Theme-Name("NewTheme")* indicates that the result of the merged themes will produce a new theme called *NewTheme*. To achieve resolution of conflicts, Theme/UML supports three reconciliation strategies. The first strategy, *prec*, indicates the precedence of each theme's design specification in the merge. Figure 17 illustrates that the second theme has a higher precedence than the first theme, and therefore, its design specification will get priority in the merge. The second reconciliation strategy is an *explicit* reconciliation that takes the form *resolve(Entity (property = value))* and allows any property of any specific *Entity* in a theme to be assigned a *value*. The third reconciliation strategy is a *default* reconciliation and has a similar form, with *Construct* replacing the *Entity* instead (c.f. Fig. 17). In this case, any property of a UML construct (e.g. operation visibility kind) can be given a value (e.g. private) and this reconciliation gets executed during the merge. The second kind of composition extension that Theme/UML supports for overlapping specifications is called an *override*. An *override*, as indicated in Fig. 18, is a relationship between two themes where one theme's design specification overrides the other. The semantics of the integration properties are similar to the merge. One difference is that elements can be explicitly indicated to be deleted in a theme prior to the merge.

For crosscutting specifications, an integration strategy called a *bind* facilitates the composition of an aspect theme with a base theme. Figure 19 depicts an aspect theme being bound to a base theme. The aspect theme is designed in relation to the abstract templates. In this example, the triggering template operation is called *A.trigger()*. The sequence diagram illustrates the behaviour of the aspect theme in relation to this triggering behaviour. The operation *_do_trigger()* encapsulates the existing behaviour of the operation in the base theme that is bound to the template method in the aspect theme. The sequence diagram is important in representing how and when the crosscutting behaviour is executed with respect to the base themes it is crosscutting. The bind specification represents the instantiation of the aspect theme. The operation *B.trigger()* is the operation being bound to, and the triggering template operation is replaced with this method upon the aspect's instantiation.

Author Index